☆

I Can't Believe
I Said That!

☆

KATHIE LEE GIFFORD

I Can't Believe
I Said That!

An Autobiography
with
Jim Jerome

POCKET BOOKS
New York   London   Toronto   Sydney   Tokyo   Singapore

"Listen to My Heart," © 1991 David Friedman
MIDDER Music. Words and music by David Friedman.

Special thanks to:

Neal Barr
"Carnival *(and other authorized trademarks)* and the patented ship
funnel design are the registered trademarks of Carnival Cruise
Lines, Inc."
Jim Goss
David Friedman
Home Furnishings Council
Yongestreet Productions
Dick Zimmerman

POCKET BOOKS, a division of Simon & Schuster Inc.
1230 Avenue of the Americas, New York, NY 10020

Library of Congress Catalog Card Number: 92-56723

ISBN: 0-671-74241-8

First Pocket Books hardcover printing November 1992

10 9 8 7 6 5 4 3 2 1

POCKET and colophon are registered trademarks of
Simon & Schuster Inc.

Printed in the U.S.A.

To my wonderful husband, Frank, who because he knows my heart, can forgive my mouth. And to my precious Cody, who just plain loves me because he doesn't know any better. They have brought me the greatest joy I've ever known.

Acknowledgments

When I began writing this book, I came up with The Two Commandments of memoir-writing to guide me. *Thou Shalt Be Honest* and *Thou Shalt Not Hurt Others*. Once Jim Jerome and I were in high gear, we faced The Third Commandment: *Thou Shalt Hit All Thy Deadlines*. Observing that one was merely a question of long hours and plenty of help from others. Living by the first two proved more challenging, since they tend to negate each other. There were more than a few tears shed in the retelling, but many more howls of laughter. I trust that friends and family know I've tried to be fair, even though there are rarely fewer than two sides to any story.

We owe a deep debt of gratitude to those who helped me tell mine by telling theirs. Thank you, most of all, Mom and Dad, Michie and Davy, for helping me find my way home again to a childhood every kid should be blessed enough to remember.

I have shared the best and worst of times with several people who have played important roles in my life. Their thoughtful and gracious help deserves much thanks: Regis Philbin, for his very warm, heartfelt—and very *funny*—Foreword; Paul Johnson, who shared his side of our unhappy marriage and who, I am glad to say, has gone on to a successful career and life; Marla Maples, for letting us all in on what *really* went on while Frank and I were away (with a generous, suite-talking assist at the Plaza courtesy of Donald Trump); my "LIVE!" producer Michael Gelman and program director Art Moore; dear friends Chris Tardio and Jantina Jurriaans Flessing; Howie Masters and Tory Baker Masters, and Susan Winston for the wake-up call from my "Good Morning America" days; Gary Bernstein for his wonderful photography; and Larry Gatlin, whose voice is always a thing of beauty, singing or speaking the truth.

ACKNOWLEDGMENTS

The beloved, trusted members of my extended family kept life as I know it going while we worked: My Nanny from Heaven, Christine Gardner; my faithful assistant, Mickey (the Warden) Kaufman; and my wonderful caretakers, Ted and Frances Kessler.

I need to say a special thank-you to my "road crew," who put up with my exhaustion, lack of humor, and frustration as I worked to finish this book with the clock ticking down: Paul Mann, my arranger and conductor; Joel Seidman, my drummer; and Michie and Denise Carley, my wonderful backup singers, who were so patient and comforting to me during our infamous "Summer Tour." I'm so grateful for all the years they've shared the stage with me.

Jim had indispensable help. If Reege and I ever do a segment on America's Speediest Tape Transcribers, Jean Brown will be our first guest. Robin Shallow never hesitated to go out of her way so Jim could find his way through all the host chats. Video whiz Mark Pines came through in a pinch, as did Cathy Rehl, at "Good Morning America." Amy Zimmerman and Peter Klein at *People* offered expert software support. Our literary agents kept the wheels rolling: Jim Stein of the William Morris Agency; my dear friend and lawyer, Ron Konecky, and, for Jim, ICM's Amanda Urban.

Thank you, Jim Jerome, for guiding me along as I shared my life all these months—through all the sesame noodle sessions!—and for patiently waiting out my emotional outbursts.

I owe this book's very existence to an awesome editor, Judith Regan, who first approached me with the idea. I can't imagine an editor who is more tirelessly, more fiercely committed to a vision of what makes a book work. She began this project as my editor and ends it as my friend. Thank you, Judith—as one mom to another— for helping me birth this baby.

And finally—thank you, Frank Newton Gifford. May there always be but one side to our story.

Foreword

Where Would You Be Without Me?

by REGIS PHILBIN

I have teased Kathie Lee many times on our show about this book, but the truth is, I'm very concerned: Why is she writing this book? What the heck is going on? She's thirty-nine years old. Where's the drama? What has she done? What could she *possibly* know about life? Today's best-sellers are usually filled with tragedy, misery, scandal. This is a woman who has never had *any* of that. If she's ever been abused, it's been by *me*.

Where's the ugly? I tell her I want *ugliness;* she tells me she has bunions. There are no *flaws,* no weaknesses. She tells me there are tragedies in her life, that we've been through a lot together. What, she broke up with a boyfriend once? You call *that* a tragedy? Is that what we're talking about? But look what happened from that: the next day she woke up and had lunch up the street with Frank Gifford and hasn't been seen alone since!

What has she been writing about all these months? There's no incest, no drunkenness, no . . . Look, I'm just trying to help her, to think of topics for the Sally Jessy Raphael Show. She couldn't even *get* on that show—and we're on the same station in New York.

Let me tell you something before you read this book: if you look carefully you'll see a light glowing over this woman's head. The first time I met Kathie Lee I was coming down Broadway on the West Side, having just taken a workout at Jack La Lanne. It was a Saturday morning and I was missing California very much.

I didn't know it was her right away. I thought she was just some California girl. California *person,* excuse me! I see her coming toward me, and this person looked mighty good.

And then as we got closer, I realized it was somebody I'd actually seen before, though not very often, on "Good Morning America." And then I got real close—and I had to *shield my eyes*. The halo was *that* bright over her head!

I'm not kidding you. This is one of God's favorite children. He has steered her in the right direction every time. He steered her *right to me*, right? So what is there to write about? There, I just finished her book for you. One paragraph, that's the story: *God's Favorite Child*—with *the* show-business break of all time.

Okay, let's just talk seriously for a second. Kathie Lee's led a terrific life. She's made things happen for herself. She has chutzpah, she has poise, she's so agile. And can she charm! I've seen her in everybody's company, from the President of the United States—who, incidentally, wouldn't leave me alone, who wanted to forget about everybody else and hang out with *me*—to Ravishing Rick Rude, the professional wrestler. And she overwhelms people. Really, she does.

I have seen this woman go through a remarkable transformation. When she came to me she was a homeless waif. Has she endured adversity? No question. She got herself a town house, then painted and decorated it so that it was the best-looking town house on West Seventieth Street.

You want tragedy? You want triumph? Her dressing room when she joined the show was a cell, a pit: it had to be fumigated. Look at it now. Beautiful. Laura Ashley wallpaper!

Struggle? Misery? She went to the Hamptons, bought herself a country house. Everybody's gotta have a house in the Hamptons, right? Bought it on her own—a remarkable story.

In all honesty, it has been a blessing for me to work with Kathie Lee, with someone who has my own wacky, sometimes naughty sense of humor. We both laugh at the same things. We laugh at each other. We laugh, most importantly, at ourselves.

People watch us and assume our opening "host chat" segment is easy to do. It's totally spontaneous, but it's not easy to keep it going for seventeen minutes. And it's gotten longer over the years as we've grown more popular. Sometimes we can't shut it down. But we have to or else we'd be cheating a guest. That's our favorite part of the show.

I think we're a pretty powerful team right now, and part of it is because we're not barbecuing and playing tennis together every night. That keeps the edge sharp. Keeps things unpredictable and spontaneous. And it keeps our *hostility* fresh and natural.

After Joy and I moved to within a mile of Kathie Lee and Frank, she accused me in host chat of never getting enough of her, of *following* her into the Connecticut woods just so we could be close all the time. "If you think you're driving in to work with me in the morning, FORGET ABOUT IT!" she squawked.

"Can I tell you, if I have to WALK, I will not drive with you," I answered. I was pumped. She had *attacked* me.

"I don't want you hanging around my house, all right?" she said back. Boy, this was getting ugly.

"You see me with my thumb out, you just pass me by," I said. "Keep on going."

She shook her head so hard I thought her *lip gloss* was going to fall off. "I can't believe it," she moaned.

"I can't believe it either," I told her. Then it hit me: "Here's the beautiful part of this show," I said. "This is the way this show works. Believe me. It's because we *don't* see each other. We don't say anything to each other off the show. Maybe once in a while on special occasions you get lucky, you catch me. We must *not* let anything happen—"

"—to this magic," she interrupted. She's always cutting me off, and she did it again when I was saying something important. "Let's not get too buddy-buddy," she warned.

"That's part of the whole thing. We're not too buddy-buddy. A little ambivalent strain here! Have you *noticed?*"

But by keeping some distance between us we keep our "chemistry" and "synergy" full of tension and energy. That's all we ever hear about. How do we make that chemistry work? If we knew every detail of each other's life, it wouldn't work. We'd seem rehearsed, stilted, predictable. We'd look like all the morning news shows. We can't have that. The foundation of our success has been those genuine real-life stories everyone can relate to and the way we share them with each other.

Critics have inferred that because we're joined at the hip on-camera we must be genuinely antagonistic. Forget it. Kathie and I truly love and respect each other as the best of friends, colleagues—and, yes, even *neighbors* now.

We also have an understanding, a confidence in each other that allows me to say damn near anything that will be accepted—and get it thrown back at me. We've become an acquired taste—my vinegar and Kathie Lee's honey—and that taste has been acquired, I'm happy to report, by more than two hundred stations around the country as of the fall of 1992. The tension of live TV is what drives us, and we've had the time of our lives learning to roll with it in front of the cameras and our wonderful audience.

The fact that our success is largely due to that live chemistry actually shocked me. When the show caught on, I was, frankly, certain it was because we were sex objects. I was appalled to learn from market research that it was not our sex appeal but the fact that fans respond to us as ordinary, everyday people caught in moments that sometimes become extraordinary or absurd.

We try to show the human, vulnerable side of life—and that life can be a great equalizer. And that's what we think is funny—poking holes where we're each so vulnerable. And because we're so different, we're easy targets for each other's zingers. Audiences love it when we're giving it to each other.

I remember when Kathie-the-gardener told in host chat of the time she suffered such bad allergies over the weekend she couldn't garden. I mean, it was the end of this woman's world! So naturally, it was Frank to the rescue. He straps on this huge backpack filled with water and a pump to hose down the whole place in fifteen minutes. "He was like Waterbuster," she said. "Scared Cody to death!"

I looked concerned and mimicked what Kathie might say to Frank: "'Okay, Waterbuster, could you put your apron on and go into the kitchen now?' I have to talk to Frank," I said. "And the sooner the better."

This was war. "Are you saying my husband's a wimp?" The audience roared.

"Uh-uh," I said.

"I say he's perfect," she bragged.

"I say he's a good guy . . . who's very susceptible to . . . manipulation," I answered.

"Don't think so. He only does what he wants. What about Joy?"

I smiled. "Joy does her *own* watering and her *own* cooking."

"And what do *you* do?" she asked.

"I take very good care of Joy."

That's the story of our lives, right there.

Can this woman ever dish it out and run with it when you give her an opening! We mentioned mother-child bonding to a trivia-question caller. Kathie had been home a few days with the flu. We somehow got on the subject of—you guessed it—Cody Cody Cody. "Every *day* we had Cody here," I said, rolling the eyes. "We all bonded together."

"Yeah," she told the caller. "He'll be warped for the rest of his life as a result of all this bonding with *him*."

I shrugged it off. "He doesn't know who I am. Co-host. Uncle. No idea." But she wasn't finished with me.

"This was the funniest thing," she said. "I'm home, right, so I see what my child watches in the morning. Cody's nanny, Christine, had us on. Cody took one look at you and you know what he said? I swear, he said, 'I don't yike dat show.'"

I made a fist. "That's war, Cody. WAR!"

We have a terrific time. There's nothing else like it on TV. All I hear and read in my mail is that we offer people an hour of relief from all the doom and gloom that everybody else is thriving on. We broke this show in when Geraldo had a chair smashed over his head and broke his nose on the air, Phil was wearing a dress, Sally was walking with hookers, Oprah was losing sixty-five pounds. Nobody noticed us because we weren't doing any of those things; we were just talking about simple everyday things. It's taken a while to get where we are. We didn't come in like gangbusters the way Oprah did or even Geraldo. That's not our style. People start competing with yesterday's show, and so they go for something even more outrageous; that sort of program can lose its ability to shock.

People flipped around the dial, stopped with us, and said "Hey, what's this all about? This is something *new.*" New? We're actually doing the oldest stuff on television—normal, human routines. When Lucy had that baby in the early fifties, that was a breakthrough. Her fans adored it. The women went crazy. Everybody could relate to it. When Kathie had *her* baby forty years later, that basic but very powerful connection took hold and was phenomenal.

Our audiences watched Kathie Lee get bigger, we all practiced Lamaze, and women everywhere went through all of the sensations and feelings she was experiencing. It was a graphic piece of television—and none of it, I have to tell you, any more memorable than the day *I* walked out of the studio with a thirty-five-pound empathy belly and waddled around town as the World's First Pregnant Man. Did Geraldo do that? You didn't see *that* on Oprah. I mean, come on. Me and my little Puddin'—we stole the show! The audience loved those moments. Every pregnant woman in the country was watching us to find out how Kathie and I were feeling. No one sent *me* handmade gifts, however, which, of course, hurt my feelings, but what can you do?

As our show has become a ratings winner in the nineties, Kathie has handled our success—and the pressures it brings—with extraordinary grace. She's got so much going on right now. She's a tireless and devoted mom to Cody and a loving wife to Frank, and she's a great businesswoman with super instincts.

But she's going through a phase where everybody wants her to do something, whether it's appearing or singing at a charity benefit, making a commercial, promoting her line of clothing—or writing a book with *absolutely no scandal* in it. I've never seen so many things converge on one person as they are for her now.

I've only seen her on the edge of exhaustion once in a while. But she's always up. I don't know *where* she gets her incredible energy. I can't even tell when she's down, because we both come to the show knowing that we've got to be up for each other. Frankly, I've never seen her distressed or sick. I've never seen her angry.

Which is why I want to know, How can you write a book today if it's not about violence, ripoffs, or recovery? I mean, what is Kathie recovering from? Making oatmeal for Frank this morning? Winning Maryland's Junior Miss pageant as a teenager? No, she's recovering from *allergies*. You don't get on Sally Jessy with allergies and a couple of bad moods, right?

Well, I have to confess that I know Kathie Lee well enough to know her life has had its share of drama, humor, struggle, heartache, love, and inspiration. I also know one thing about her not everyone knows: Kathie Lee is one of life's great fighters, a remarkable, resilient, very funny woman with a fascinating story to tell and a gift for touching people with the passion of her convictions.

Her life reads like a textbook on how to cope with everything life throws at you when you strive to be a successful career woman, wife, and mother—and of course, *most* importantly, the very fortunate person sitting in that chair every morning next to me!

We have a running gag on the show where I'll mention that Phil or Oprah or Sally Jessy has some controversial theme on the same day that our producer, Michael Gelman, has, say, "Amazing Fish Day."

I tease Gelman about this mostly during the sweeps, when all the daytime and prime-time shows throw their most sensational stuff at you. So, while the other guys are offering Transsexual Lesbian Life-styles or Fathers Who Sleep with Their Sons' Girlfriends, what does Gelman have? How to Bake the Perfect Blueberry Pie! God *forbid* we should ever have like *two minutes* of sexy stuff on our show.

"REEGE!" Kathie squealed when I complained about this on the air once. "We don't really *want* to be a part of that."

"*I* want to be a part of it," I shot back at her. The audience was *totally* on my side. They loved it. "I want SEX!" I shouted. "And I want SLEAZE! I want MUD! I want FILTH! And I want it NOW!"

Where would Kathie be without me? That's what I want to know—and where the heck was she *before* me? That's what I'm *dying* to know. It *must* be quite a story. I'm sure it's the greatest story ever told!

Listen to my heart, listen to it sing,
Listen to my voice, it wants to tell you everything.
There's so much to say, I don't know where to start,
But if you want to know the love I'm feeling, listen to my heart.

—from "Listen to My Heart,"
words and music by David Friedman

Introduction

What a Wonderful World

Writing your life story is a little like being asked to pick out what to wear at your own funeral. It has its advantages. You want to look great, so you find a dress that, as they say, is to die for. After all, you're going to be in it for a long time.

But you know you're bound to upset somebody no matter how great you look. My mother will think my skirts too short. My husband will think I have on too much makeup. Even worse, curious strangers will say, "Oh, look, she's so much *thinner* in person!"

These are the risks you take. So why bother? The answer's the same as with any other challenge I've faced: Why not?

If Reege thinks the virtue of writing this book is to find the drama, my husband frankly thinks it's to omit the drama. My wonderful, sexy, gentle husband would prefer that I write, "I was born in Paris, France, I brushed my teeth, went to college, got to New York, met Frank Gifford, fell in love, married the most wonderful man in the world, and lived happily ever after. Oh, and I had Cody."

I truly wish it had been that way, that we had met as virgins when we were both twenty and had the rest of our lives to grow old together. But he insists I wouldn't have liked him at twenty. He's probably right.

When you make a lifetime commitment to a partner, you've got the rest of your lives to build a shared future. It's the unshared *past* you don't necessarily want to know from. Frank's worse with this stuff than I am. I did live a very full, at times turbulent, life before Frank. But I would never want to hurt anyone by writing a book. My primary concern is to be absolutely honest with myself and fair to those I've loved.

I understand Frank. I sometimes find it hard to accept that Frank was married twice before, had children by another woman, and has probably enjoyed the company of a few other ladies in his time. Do I enjoy thinking of Frank sharing happiness with or making love to another woman? *Yeah, right!* Which is so childish, so stupid, so selfish, so jealous—and so ME!

The truth is, you don't have any idea what's going to be thrown at you in life. When you write a book you get to take a long look back. And then it really hits you: This isn't the way my life was supposed to be. I wasn't supposed to be married twice. I didn't know how many children—or stepchildren—I was meant to have. I never imagined that my own son would be so much younger than my step-grandchildren. I never planned on co-hosting a morning show. I was supposed to fall in love, get married (once!), remain faithful, have children, love our grandchildren—and die. And have a whole lot of July Fourth picnics in between. And I never figured I'd be waking up every day next to a man who looks so much prettier and smells so much sweeter than I do. It's *so* awful!

My life has thrown me some amazing curves, unfortunately not the kind that fit snugly inside a sexy size four. About the only head *these* curves have spun around is my own, leading me to basic lessons that have given me strength to survive the worst times and humility to ground me during the best times.

Most importantly, I've been lucky enough to discover that, while fame and money are all well and good, what truly enriches your life is loving, giving, and caring for others. Your overnight ratings can soar and sink, but love and compassion are the constants that make you a star every day in your own life. Remember that 1970s *Love Story* notion of love—"never having to say you're sorry"? Well, I'm sorry. It's a bunch of poop. Love in the real world means saying you're sorry ten times a day if that's what it takes to keep from hurting someone. Love is compromise, but compromise isn't always surrender; it can be a way to say "I love you, I care about you."

I've also learned there is no distance more vast and lonely in the world than the space between two unhappily married people in the same bed, and that there's no sweeter closeness than the intimacy between two happily married people in love.

Life seemed so simple and joyous when I was growing up. No one tells you life will become a battleground for your heart and soul. When I began my "walk with Jesus" at the age of twelve, His message was so clear: Make something beautiful of your life. Shine in the light of God's love. Be a blessing, not a burden. As kids, we were taught to "bloom where you're planted"—that is, to find joy in whoever you are, whatever you become, and spread it around generously.

That metaphor wasn't supposed to make me think of manure but it does: manure is stinky and smelly when piled up in a heap, but if you spread it around and let some rain fall, it will make things grow and become beautiful.

I was spreading it around all over the map for years, and some of what sprouted frankly wilted. It takes a few seasons of planting to figure out who you're supposed to be, and I'm getting there. I aworked my buns off shuttling between the worlds of Christian and secular show business. The spirit and the flesh. Between my Bible and my baby fat, let me tell you, I had plenty of both going for me back then.

As a teenager I sang with Anita Bryant in Southern Baptist churches and witnessed Christians being "slain by the spirit" at Oral Roberts's revivals. I la-la'd on "Name That Tune" in Hollywood, hee-hawed on Nashville's "Hee Haw Honeys," sang for Jim and Tammy Faye's PTL Club in Virginia, and opened in Vegas for Rich Little. In 1982 it was on to New York and "Good Morning America," where I was a correspondent and fill-in host for Joan Lunden— and where I met Frank, the Tight End of my dreams. By June 1985 I was teamed with the co-host of my dreams, the only man alive I can be as naughty with as I want without ruining a marriage. *Poor Reege!*

After much searching and confusion, I have finally found some measure of inner peace. My life has taken some dramatic, even bizarre, turns—some by default, some by the divine hand of God. But I got here. We all get there. I believe that. One of my favorite songs, "On My Way to You," by Marilyn and Alan Bergman and Michel Legrand, says it best: "If I could change a single day, what went amiss or went astray, I may have never found my way to you."

Actually I might just touch up a few little days back there when plenty went amiss on my way to Frank and Cody and Reege. But look what I have to show for my patience and faith: a life I share with a gorgeous partner who is also my confidant, my lover, my best friend in all the world, my shrink, and the father of our son; a wonderful home; and, after twenty-five years, a career burning on all jets, in the micro, and on the grill. It's so good it's scary. I'm *too* happy. When is it all just going to just hit the fan?

And it might. It took Reege and me five years to become so-called media darlings, for what it's worth, but I know it can all vanish in the blink of an eye—or, in my case, the slip of a tongue. People love me and hate me for the same reason: I make my living spilling my guts. I open my mouth and say whatever pops into my head. Taping live, we're unscripted, unrehearsed, on the edge, without a net. One wrong dumb offensive word and I'm history. Gone.

I don't think Lloyd's of London would insure this mouth. So I pray. Every morning, before my feet even hit the floor, I say this little prayer: "Dear God, please help me to not say anything to hurt anybody today," meaning, of course, with my mouth—my greatest asset and my worst liability.

They don't call me spontaneous and irreverent for nothing; but it would make me crazy if I went for a gag at someone else's expense. Scripture asks, What does it profit a man (or a woman) if she should gain the world—not to mention the top share in her time slot—and lose her very soul? That's also a great lesson; I've got more to lose than ever.

I wouldn't mind losing some of my more clueless critics, not that I waste much time thinking about them. But some folks just don't know *what* to make of me. It bugs them when they can't peg you. The politically correct ones must see me as some sort of women's movement mutant. I was P.C. (politically correct) by the age of seventeen—on my own, working and paying the bills. But, excuse me, I also have NO problem whatsoever admitting that I never felt complete, never felt truly treasured as a woman, until I married Frank.

And Frank's a living time warp, a child of the Depression who grew up with *nothing* around the oil fields of California and Texas. His idea of having it all would probably make some hard-core feminists retch, though he has always been my greatest supporter. It's to be home with Cody and me (ideally, I'd work a lot less, if at all), wake up, smooch, lounge a little, play with Cody, make him breakfast, play eighteen holes of golf, come home, throw some swordfish on the barbecue as the dogs bark at the deer (okay, so we named our two bichons frisés Chablis and Chardonnay after our favorite wines— Sonoma and Cutrer or Pouligny and Montrachet just seemed a bit much), open a fine bottle of wine with a few friends, shoot pool in Frank's game room to Patsy Cline or Barbra Streisand on the CD jukebox, make love, and go to sleep.

And I'm sorry: it's all sounding better and better to me every day. *My* toughest 1990s-woman conflict *isn't* having it all. It's finding the time to pencil it in.

No wonder the new women's buzzword is "backlash." We wanted freedom, equality, choice, but we didn't want ulcers, back pain, heart attacks, and guilt as neglectful wives and moms. And we wanted three orgasms each lovemaking session. It's not possible, unless *maybe* you go on vacation, unplug the phone, and concentrate *solely* on your lover. Which, by the way, I can't recommend *strongly* enough. Our little Codesville is living, loving proof of that!

Let's face it. I'm an anomaly. A thriving career woman who also stands up for traditional values. That's why women tell me I've inspired them—by being a role model, by quoting Scripture, or by unapologetically gushing my love for my family. Or simply by saying it's okay for a woman to succeed *and* remain totally feminine about her need to be needed and loved and emotionally taken care of by a man.

We liberated women have built ourselves up for major disappointment and disillusionment because we've set unattainable standards. That's another reason why our show works. I show my audiences that I'm still struggling like every other woman to come up with the right answers, the correct balance in my life. Behind the appearance of glitz and glamour, I know I am exactly who I am, spreading more stinky compost with Reege every morning and blooming where I was planted.

People tell me they identify with my frailties, my humanity, my inadequacies. My *complexion*. I love nothing more than to laugh at myself and to find humor in life's calamities.

Like the time I got to go to the White House and had a zit the size of Arkansas. Or like the time a pro wrestler disrobed and had my face painted over the crotch of his tights—and Reege's face on his butt.

Frank caught this class act on TV and was ready to rip this guy's face off. He would have settled for our producer Michael Gelman's eyeballs.

Or like the time a male guest hugged me on the set and then wouldn't unclinch. He fell in love on the spot, smooching and clutching me until he was just about fully *aroused*. Max was, I believe, the last chimpanzee we had on the show.

And I'm sorry. Why *not* talk about my fabulous not-ready-for-prime-time thighs? People say I'm crazy, I don't have thighs. I not only have them; I'll be at war with them for life. Even at my thinnest I had *wuggies*, which is what my mom calls those saddlebags. It wasn't bad enough she gave them to me; she even made up a name for them so I could identify the enemy. Thanks, Mom. When I weighed 104—we're talking skeletal—I still had two pounds of wuggie on each side.

And is there anything so immoral about talking about your bunions? Don't we already have enough reality programming starring society's perverts and killers? Zits, thighs, bunions, and breast pumps are *my* reality programming. They're facts of life. My grandmother was crippled by bunions; my mother's big toe crosses so far over, it lives in Delaware with the rest of her foot in Maryland. I'm not even forty and my big toe's already inching toward Jersey.

Thank God I have a man who loves me as I am!

I'm convinced our show has tapped into a need these days for normalcy, honesty, and good, clean, self-effacing nonsense. Much of our mail comes from patients in hospitals who watch us right before chemotherapy and from people in a lot of pain and suffering. "Thank you," they say, "for helping me through the hardest time in my life. At nine o'clock I knew I could take myself out of my own life for an hour and laugh a little."

Knowing we're doing some good is so rewarding to both Regis and me. We're not curing cancer or AIDS, but I'm all for the healing people derive through laughter.

I also know that for every fan who expresses gratitude, there's another who's unloading attitude. *Yes, I am fully aware that there are people out there who look at me and want to throw up.* The critics hated me for years. I was the Barry Manilow of television. A born-again Bette Midler. They were just dead set against me. Your skin's supposed to loosen and sag as you approach forty. Well, mine's just getting thicker.

I've been called "excitable," "sickeningly sweet," "ding-y," "the perfect TV cutie, except she's wacked." And let's not forget "boisterous." *So I sing loud!* God gave me small breasts and huge lungs. I can't help it. Just don't call me perky. Don't call me a cupcake. Tom Shales of the *Washington Post* called Frank and me a couple of marshmallows by the fire when we did the 1984 Olympics together. More recently Tom told a reporter doing a magazine piece on me that I was "a genius." Great quote. The reporter's editor took out the genius part. Story of my life.

I honestly don't know about *genius,* but a perkmeister I am not. Mary Hart is perky. She loves everybody. Never says a nasty thing about anybody. I'm no Little Goody Two-Shoes. Not with *this* edge I'm not.

Just ask the queen of England. On "Good Morning America," where everything was scripted and TelePrompTered, I couldn't always go by the questions writers scripted for guests. That would have been like being sentenced to an entire childhood having to color inside the lines. No way.

I was alongside David Hartman once and introduced a piece on England's royal family: "In this segment we'll examine the impact that Princess Diana has had on the British fashion industry." I paused, looked at David, then blurted out, "Maybe she can help the queen."

David almost slid off his chair. You could hear gasps throughout the studio. I just said what everybody was thinking: *How can you be the richest woman on the face of the earth—and be the dowdiest? Come on, Your Majesty, go out and buy yourself a hat that looks decent on you. And don't wear those frumpy frocks! You're the queen of England!* I looked around and thought, *I can't believe I said that!*

When Barbara Walters was on our show she asked Reege and me, "What's the biggest misconception people have about you?"

Reege answered first: "That people see me as a big loud jerk who just runs off at the mouth."

Misconception, Reege, not cold hard fact!

Just kidding! And then it was my turn to answer. I wasn't trying to be flip with her. "People think that because I'm happy I'm therefore shallow."

Okay, so miracles *do* happen. I was at a photo session for the Miss America pageant before Reege and I hosted it in 1991. One of the sponsors was a jeweler so they wanted me to wear something of theirs. I picked a pretty top-of-the-line bracelet.

But the bracelet had a bad catch on it.

I was dressed to the nines in a gorgeous gown and looked smashing. Then I had to go potty, but the ladies' room was about a mile and a half away. I had to practically get on a bus up Sixth Avenue to get there. So I go to the bathroom and come back—and the photographer or someone asks me, "Where's the bracelet?"

No bracelet. Gone. I freaked. My assistant, Mickey, and I race a mile and half back to the ladies' room. Mickey's a registered nurse and has worked on plenty of psychiatric wards. I call her the Warden. She's great under pressure—and under water.

We start peering down into the toilet and Mickey sees something in there glistening. I mean, the salvage teams checking out the *Titanic* had nothing on us. Thank goodness I'd only gone pee-pee. So Mickey reaches down and fishes the bracelet out. It was so heavy the water couldn't flush it.

We went back and never told the people because it was, like, "Hey, here's your bracelet—almost went to the Bronx, by the way." What can I say? A miracle.

Because I'm happy I'm a ditz? That's the rap. Just because I don't dwell on the negative things in life means I lack substance and depth? That's ludicrous. My life has been *neither* as relentlessly happy nor as excruciatingly frivolous as people might assume. There's drama. And joy. And anguish. In short, there's a real life. Trust me. Keep reading.

Success never comes without a price. Never having been a worrier, I now worry all the time. I wake up in the middle of the night contemplating everything that's happening to me. I worry about my career and its impact on my responsibilities as wife and mother; about the world Cody is growing up in; about the fact that I'm married to a man twenty-three years older than I who is at a very different stage of life.

Frank is a better husband to me than I am a wife to him—and he works harder at it. Frank understands the value of things better than I do, and I'm working on that. Frank, who was a star NFL rookie the year *before* I was born, had two unsuccessful marriages before ours.

I had one unsuccessful marriage and was almost thirty-five before I achieved any significant career success. I'm glad it took this long in a way, because now I appreciate it all the more.

Frank's had all the career glory a man could ask for. With two ex-wives, three children before Cody, and five grandchildren, he's come to see that what's important in life isn't awards and ratings points.

But I still haven't proven enough to myself. I'm still striving for the respect of my peers and new creative challenges. I'm looking for longevity. In my heart I know Frank's right. But I'm still caught up in it all. I'm on a roll. It's hard not to be thrilled by it—and impossible not to resent it when it robs me of time with him that becomes more precious every day.

But this is not stuff to cry over. Cry over an abused child, a child who feels unloved. Cry over a family of eight in one room who perish in a fire because they didn't have a smoke detector.

My success has only made me more aware of the millions of children who do not have the blessings I had, the millions of neglected children who go to bed hungry, unloved, and abused because of the breakdown of family values in America. And here I am being cheered for "having it all" when millions of decent, hard-working Americans are having it all taken away from them as they lose their jobs, their livelihoods, and worst of all, their self-esteem. I feel guilt over my blessings, and I'm outraged at other people's losses.

If some see me as shallow for wanting to feel joyful rather than jaded, that's sad. There is already so much pain in life, so much negativity and cynicism in our culture. Pain will find you sooner or later. Instead, I look to sources of comfort and joy. I cope with what hurts, learn my lessons, and move on.

If I am grateful, ultimately, for anything, it is that I was born to two parents who said, "This is our child of love, a baby we planned and will love and watch over for the rest of our lives." To know my parents' love is to define commitment and conviction. Their unconditional love—and the values they instilled in me—have been the most important guideposts and inspirations for my life. And that is a gigantic plus in the kind of world we live in. I always felt my parents accepted me as I was and expected me to try to make a difference, to leave the world a better place.

Not that I was qualified to do that. I grew up doubting I'd ever be great at anything. To this day I do not believe I'm great at anything. Except decorating. I'm a *great* decorator. But I knew I could go out and fail and still receive their love. Family was the center of my parents' universe. Neither had grown up in a stable home. My father made no secret of placing family above career and was passed over several times for advancement. He didn't care. How can a child get more from a parent than that?

Their love kept me rooted during an adolescence that often had me wondering what planet I was living on. My family instilled in me an unwavering faith in Jesus Christ through the 1960s while my friends rocked to "Sympathy for the Devil." At almost any other time in our nation's history I might have been applauded for upholding my values—go to church, love family and God, save yourself for your husband—but this was the sexual revolution and all of a sudden I was the weirdo, the antithesis of the norm. Other kids did drugs; I did *crafts*. I never knew where I fit in.

But I grew up feeling unique; I believed that God made me the way I am for a purpose. It's taken me a while to understand that purpose, but it's finally coming into focus.

As a child, my idols weren't movie star sexpots (you couldn't tell, right?) but strong, independent, utterly feminine TV comediennes—Lucille Ball, Carol Burnett, Mary Tyler Moore. And Barbra Streisand, the ultimate class act. What amazing talents!

Me, I wasn't born a technically great anything, but I did feel from day one that I was a born performer. I was part Jewish but a total ham. I wasn't beautiful, and my younger sister, Michie, sang much better. I was theatrical but not destined for greatness as an actress. I was a born clown and should probably have cut my losses and run off to join the circus. Actually, I have—with Reege.

My childhood wasn't all laughs, though. Mom, when really mad, would come at Davy, my older brother, Michie, and me with the filthiest thing in the house—a disgusting flyswatter. And this was a devoutly Christian woman who believed passionately in oral and every other kind of hygiene! If cleanliness was next to Godliness, this was a flyswatter from hell.

And Daddy took pride in living up to his nickname, "the Ogre," whenever boys dared to come calling. But my parents were my anchor when I followed Mom's lead and accepted Jesus Christ. They were my anchor at twenty-one when I tried to make something beautiful of my life in Hollywood—which turned out to be a contradiction in terms. I didn't go into show business filled with angst, craving approval from anyone. I already had approval. That was the greatest career break I ever had.

Still, in Hollywood I was far from home—in every way. They may call it the City of Angels but I had one devil of a time there for six years. I took my share of hits. I was the callback queen, never anyone's all-out first choice for anything, never quite right for this commercial or that network pilot. But I never stopped believing in myself, never stopped feeling nurtured and cherished

10

by my family, never turned to bottles, pills, or drugs. I refused to let rejections affect my abilities or my sense of worth as a person.

My personal life was another story. When my career was just taking off in 1978, I watched my sister lapse into a coma and very nearly die after surgery to remove her colon. A grotesque and humiliating sexual harassment incident shattered my naïveté about the "glamorous world of show business." And for six years I lived in a painful marriage that became a brutal test of my faith in myself and, more importantly, in the Lord. When it ended, I was shattered and disillusioned.

If I came out of it all with any hope of moving toward a new life—on my way to becoming me—it was because people who loved me never stopped caring passionately for my well-being and happiness.

Not long ago I received an award from the Police Athletic League of New York for charity work I'd done on behalf of inner-city children. In my brief speech I wanted to get across the point that life isn't about getting what you want; it's about giving back what others need. "If you've been blessed in life," I remember saying, "you feel you've never done enough—and I might be the most blessed woman before you."

I know I can never do enough. Children get to me more than anything because I had the very rare good fortune of receiving the love of two parents. The inequity and injustice of a lonely, suffering child makes me crazy. This is why the charity work I do means so much to me. I do it out of a mixture of guilt, outrage, and an ever-deepening sense of duty. I wasn't raised to feel the world exists for me, but that I exist for the world. We were born to laugh and bring joy into each other's lives.

Besides, I'd rather feed a hungry child than write a check to Uncle Sam and then read about some senator using my tax money to fly off on a junket to the Bahamas, keep a mistress in a Georgetown apartment, or ponder military cutbacks while sitting on a $1,000 toilet at the Pentagon. That stuff makes me furious.

What holds me together in this often maddening, terrifying world is the solid foundation of love and acceptance my parents built for me. I received that blessing the easy way. It was handed to me.

But there was another way I came to understand the importance of feeling loved and treasured. It was during a time when the devotion and security I naïvely assumed would be a constant in my life as an adult woman and wife were desperately missing. I still remember the first time it hit me that I would now have to learn about love the hard way—and this moment marked the beginning of the loneliest, most painful period of my life.

The beginning of my first marriage.

How Do You Keep the
Music Playing?

At around midnight on April 23, 1976, barely a year after striking out from my parents' nurturing, loving home to seek fame and fortune in Hollywood, I found myself in an old beat-up taxi at the airport in Acapulco, Mexico. Moments later I was being driven to the exotic Las Brisas resort. The driver was a maniac who must have thought he was in a Grand Prix qualifying heat.

If *anyone* knew about qualifying heat that night, it was me. At twenty-two I was a virgin. I'd been a teenager during the 1960s sexual revolution but the only thing I ever did "all the way" was cling to the belief that saving myself for my husband on our wedding night was the most romantic, beautiful thing a girl could do.

Now all I could think was: I'm going to die a virgin, going to die a virgin. All this time I wait and this lunatic's DRIVING ME OFF A CLIFF!

At least I wasn't going to die alone. The bride and groom—the last virgins left in the continental United States—were sharing this midnight ride on the verge of doom.

The groom was a tall, handsome gospel music composer and arranger named Paul Johnson. Paul had waited seven years longer than I had; he was twenty-nine. This trip was the climax of our wedding day. We'd said, "Till death do us part." I just hadn't figured the "do us part" part could come a mere twelve hours later with one dumb hairpin curve to oblivion.

The maniac somehow made it to the resort, barely negotiating a series of hazardous turns as Paul and I hung on for dear life. That ride seemed to last as long as the flight from L.A. But we survived. As we pulled up to exquisite Las Brisas, I kept muttering, "It's a miracle, it's a miracle."

The rest of my wedding night, however, was not. We were driven up a winding road in a pink Jeep to our private little bungalow—our *casita*—overlooking the ocean. It had its own private pool and gorgeous, flowing bougainvillea. Luscious tropical scents filled the warm night air. It was so incredibly, perfectly romantic and seductive. My heart was pounding.

We dumped our luggage in our room, popped some champagne from the bar, and walked out to the veranda to gaze out over Acapulco in the distance and the immense, shimmering Pacific— and to toast our marriage. It was a breathtaking view—the twinkling lights below, the starry sky, the moonlit coastline.

But you can only watch lights glisten for so long, you know what I mean? We stayed out there for a half hour or so. I had waited all my life so my husband could gaze at a beautiful body on our wedding night, not a beautiful body *of water!* I said to Paul, "Let's go in."

Poor Paul. He was so nervous he had closed the door behind him and locked us out of the adorable *casita*. We were absolutely exhausted, emotionally wrung out, the champagne was kicking in. Who could blame him? Still—pardon the pun—this mishap put a slight pall on the proceedings. Paul had to climb down off the balcony and chase the pink Jeep all the way to the main office for another key. Then he got a ride back.

And I started thinking: This isn't meant to be.

Paul was as scared as I was. We both wanted everything to be perfect. It was so weird. I was terrified. I was like THE most virginal virgin anyone's ever known. Even Frank can't believe there was a time in my life when I was like that—not because I'm such an animal or anything, but I've just become so comfortable with my sexuality. I'm sorry, but anyone who's instantly relaxed with being naked in front of somebody for the first time and having someone explore intimate parts of the body is either lying about being relaxed—or lying about it being the first time. Believe me, I was neither lying NOR relaxed. I just don't think that kind of thing comes naturally to most people. Not in the world I came out of. In fact, I believe the only male sex organ I had actually seen by the age of twenty-two was the one that was attached to Zorro, the family dog. As far as I knew, they were ALL like that.

Paul came in and we had some laughs about what had happened. I went to run a bath and get ready to slip into my little negligee. We're not talking Frederick's of Hollywood, by the way. This was all very sweet, very innocent, very poignant, and just a wee bit pitiful.

Sweet in that there were so many dreams wrapped up in this moment for each of us.

Pitiful in that it was all so hopelessly, so heartbreakingly doomed.

Here was this wonderfully gentle twenty-nine-year-old man who had never once "tried anything" on me or pressured me. One of the nicest things about him. A complete gentleman.

But now I've got some raging hormones going. *I mean* I was ready! My lifelong self-consciousness about my body seemed, miraculously, to fade right away. I was not an ugly woman, by the way, back then. These days I work too hard. You should have seen me then. I was divine. Gorgeous! Seriously, I'd always had this attitude about my body—not a positive one, either—and was always trying to hide it. But the minute that ring went on, and God said to me it was right to enjoy my body, let me tell you, I really did look *divine*. Relaxed? Forget it! It was, like, YABBA-DABBA-DOO! I lost every inhibition I'd ever had. It was time for candles and romance, time to *boogie* and swing from the chandeliers.

And yet we just couldn't seem to get relaxed with each other. It saddens me to think about it now. We were so uncomfortable with each other, and I felt responsible and disappointed for both of us. I spent the first night of my married life sobbing my eyes out, feeling we had just made the *biggest mistake* of our lives.

My mind struggled to find hope that we could turn it around. I wanted to believe that it was the nervousness, the newness of things between two inexperienced people. This would be a growing process. Paul and I truly loved each other, loved God. I thought ahead to the next day, when we'd go swimming, relax with each other. It would get better. Things would work out, I told myself. There was plenty of Pollyanna in me.

We both came to the marriage with so many expectations because we had both waited so long. We placed unrealistic burdens on each other.

This wasn't the way I had dreamed it would be, the way my parents and the Bible had promised it would be if I was a good Christian girl and lived the Lord's excellent way. They said there should be a devouring of two people—sexy, wonderful, intimate—when they marry in God's eyes and truly love each other. I was looking for a guarantee. . . . I thought because we had "done it by the book" it would be the way I'd always imagined.

The scary part was that you don't take an oath before God and then break it—not in my family or in Paul's. Marriage was a done deal. Where I come from, you make your bed, you lie in it. You don't run home to Mama. Mama herself had briefly left Daddy when she was pregnant with their first child, but she came to her senses. They had made it work for more than forty years and counting. And that's where I came from.

I lay there in this strange bed, lost and heartsick. Still, I *wanted* to run home. Home was where I could always go, no matter how bad things got, to find in my roots the love, security, and forgiveness that had made everything else possible.

But in the darkness, I knew I was a long way from home now.

People Who Need People Are the Luckiest People in the World

☆

Mom and Dad had always told me I was their true "love child"—the only one of three they planned, the one born during what they call the happiest, sweetest, most romantic time of their young married life together. It was easy to see why that time was so magical for them. In the early 1950s, the navy shipped my father to Paris for a two-year tour at SHAPE (Supreme Headquarters Allied Powers Europe). The Allies were rebuilding postwar Europe. My parents were building postwar family life in a small apartment in a renovated barn on the outskirts of Paris. Davy was already toddling when they arrived in France. Like any other young American couple, they instantly fell under the spell of April in Paris. Actually, November must not have been too shabby, either; I was born the following August, conceived in a small upstairs bedroom with a fireplace and rough, unfinished wooden walls.

About thirty years later in August 1983, the most wonderful gift I received was the one I gave my parents: a trip to France and back to the place of my birth. I gave it to them in a collection of five gift-wrapped boxes within boxes, the smallest one bearing the note that said, "You're going to France." But my parents, knowing my French was adequate for the job of translator, twisted my arm until I said, *Ça suffit!*—and we were off to Paris.

We stayed in a beautiful hotel right off the Place de la Concorde. But the highlight of the trip wasn't the Eiffel Tower, the Musée Picasso, or even dinner at Régine's—although you can bet we squeezed in a side trip or two there. We knew exactly what we wanted to see, though there are no guidebooks or Sunday travel-section articles about this place. It was a day trip, less than an hour's drive, off the beaten tourist path to the now chic suburb of Orgeval on the western outskirts of Paris.

We were nervous as we neared the town—afraid that an *autoroute* was running through what used to be there or that the picturesque countryside had been destroyed by *le shopping mall*.

We were wrong. Amazingly everything was as it should have been. The old converted barn was still standing. We approached silently, in awe. When Mom and I noticed that one side had been boarded up, both of us began to weep. But then we walked around to the other side. Suddenly a woman popped up in the window and, after a few seconds of stunned silence, all heck broke loose.

C'était extraordinaire! It was Micheline, all grown up, and, seconds later, Madame Goupy rushed to the window. She was alive! They were having dinner! *Incroyable!* Our former neighbors and friends were still in the same place. They raced from the window, we raced around front, and Madame threw the front door open to a burst of recognition and an eruption of joyous *Mon Dieu*'s with weeping, bouncing embraces and an outpouring of emotion I will never forget.

I had finally come home to see the room where I was conceived and where I spent the first four months of my life.

It was an exquisite homecoming for all of us. The affection between the families had survived undiminished by time. There was so much catching up to do that we had to come back two more times. It was fascinating. Madame Goupy was now in her seventies, still a robust, vigorous *bonne femme*. Monsieur Goupy was ailing in the hospital. Micheline, who was a schoolgirl in the early fifties, was now approaching midlife. (My younger sister was named after her.) Pierre, the Goupys' son, was living in central France, and we visited him, too. Being there finally brought all those old stories—and the great abiding warmth between the families—to life for me.

One reason those bonds had survived so long was that Madame had been for my young mother the mother she never knew. And what was not to love about Paris for Mommy and Daddy? They were young; Paris was a time of adventure and commitment, where they discovered romance all over again after a rough start. Most importantly, Paris was where they had realized that their home and their children would be the most important sources of love and joy and fulfillment in their lives.

It's impossible to comprehend my parents' fierce attachment to family without understanding the pain each of them often felt in childhood. My father came from a broken home, hardly knowing his father. My mother lost her mom when she was two and came from no home at all; she spent her entire youth in a lonely, sometimes desperate search for roots and a sense of belonging.

We heard those stories from such an early time they became part of us. I was aware my whole life how hard life had been for my parents. It tenderized me toward them, made me aware of their pain as children and teenagers. It's funny. When Daddy told us all his old stories, he never talked with sadness about his past. But Mom can really tell a story, and she liked to lay it on real thick. She can be very dramatic. She knew how to wring us dry—and she had the goods. We'd sit around her and listen, and then we would start to sob and sniffle and say, "Mommy, you had the worst life. We'll be good to you, we will, we will." Sometimes I thought maybe she did that to control us, to make us be a little sweeter. But I don't think so. She's not that devious. But it had that effect anyhow.

Mom has been hauling around the Louis Vuitton of emotional baggage all her life. She still gets absorbed in—and at times obsessed with—her past. I find it astonishing that this incredible woman who brought me into the world and who taught me so much about how to love had everything she ever loved taken from her so young. I don't know how she got through it without turning goony on us. But she never gave up. I don't have to look far to figure out where my own capacity to roll with it comes from. She's a woman who, had she had the financial opportunity, could really have benefited from a therapist. And vice versa, by the way. Hers is an incredible story to sit and listen to, especially if you're collecting a hundred bucks for fifty minutes of listening. But instead of a shrink, Mom found some healing through telling *us* her extraordinary tales for free, for love.

My mother's ancestors came from Yorkshire, England, in the mid-1800s and settled around Toronto. The family business, small-town newspapers and printshops, prospered. Sometime in the early 1900s, her grandfather and her father, Alfred Cuttell, who was born in Canada, came to Brooklyn, New York, to carry on the printing trade. They did quite well for years.

Alfred was a handsome, refined young man with a gift for classical violin and good taste in women. He married a young German woman named Florence Edlich who, from the one photograph I've seen of her, was a slender, exquisite beauty with delicate features and a great mane of hair. (I know: The resemblance is striking!) They got down to business in a hurry: Florence gave birth to son Alfred in 1926, daughter Marilyn in 1928, and another baby girl in 1930—my mother, Joan Nancy Cuttell.

If their joys came in threes, so did their tragedies. First the family business was wiped out shortly after the stock market crash of 1929. Then, in 1932, Alfred lost not only his six-year-old son but also his beautiful young wife. Little Alfred died from complications after an acute appendicitis. Florence died of tuberculosis while she was still in her twenties.

Alfred was absolutely mad for his stunning young wife and little boy and totally went off the deep end. My mother was barely talking. Her father had no inner resources, no spiritual faith, to get him through his pain, and he fell apart. He never played the violin again. He became a hopeless alcoholic. Unable to raise his daughters, he took them to Washington, D.C., where they were raised mostly by his parents. Mama Cuttell was in her seventies, and her body was gnarled and crippled by arthritis. Mom and I trace our bunions back to her, too. She could barely walk. Still, she was stoic and resourceful, giving the young girls all the love and attention she could. Though my mom never stopped loving her dad, she has always said that Mama Cuttell was the most influential force in her early life.

But young Joan still witnessed domestic strife as an impressionable six-year-old. Alfred took up with and married a woman who was an alcoholic. They would drink and get nasty at dinner. This terrible woman would get into screaming brawls with Mama. Things once got so out of hand a neighbor had to call the police, and a scary black paddy wagon rolled up and hauled the whole family off to the station house.

In 1941 Alfred died, leaving Mama and Papa Cuttell to raise the girls, who were now thirteen and eleven. Mama gave to her granddaughters a sense of order and self-esteem. She got them to pray with her in church, instilling faith in them as a refuge from life's unrelenting sorrows.

After teaching the girls to pray, Mama had them learn to type. She selflessly pawned all of her antique treasures, including cut-crystal bowls, to pay for the sisters' summer typing classes. Mama was determined that, after she was gone, the girls would be able to find work and make their way in the world.

She must have sensed the end was near. In 1943 Papa passed away; dear old Mama died two years later, just as World War II was drawing to a close.

Joanie's battles were just beginning. At this point Mom would tell us through her tears: "I was very unhappy. But I was feisty. I knew I was going to survive. And I had a sense of dignity. I held my head up high. I was going to win this battle. I didn't know how, but I was."

Marilyn sent my mom back to Toronto with Mama's body to be buried in the Cuttell family plot. Mom then stayed with an aunt and an uncle, a furrier who promised to put her in school there. Instead, he put her to work in his sweatshop, ripping out linings so that old coats could be remodeled. He paid her only twelve dollars a week—and then took back half of that for her keep.

Still—and this is the part that rips me up—she was so desperate for love and a secure home that she would go out and spend her money on little gifts for her aunt and uncle. She'd leave them on their pillow. "It was as if," she'd say, "I was trying to buy their love."

Not even that worked. A couple of months later the uncle showed up at the factory with my mother's one suitcase. "This isn't working out," he said coldly. "You're going back to your sister in Washington." My mom was fifteen years old.

Mom's sister, Marilyn, was now seventeen and had quit school to work as an all-night cashier at the old Statler Hotel. She wasn't looking for more responsibilities. After a gloomy eighteen-hour train ride from Toronto, with a long layover in Buffalo, Mom walked up to her sister's brownstone apartment at 6:00 A.M., lugging a suitcase with all her worldy possessions crammed inside, hoping and praying that her sister would welcome her. Marilyn saw Joan approach as she sat in the window smoking a cigarette, having just come off her shift.

"Son of a bitch!" Marilyn muttered. She was facing her own crises and didn't know how to handle another one.

To this day all these images are incredibly vivid to me, none more powerful than this one: my mother at fifteen coming down the street with that little suitcase in her hand after being shipped off to Canada and coming back now, lost and unloved with no place else in the world to go, no one else in the world to care for her. The painful truth is that both sisters were equally in need of love and direction.

It's a moment I have never, thank God, had to face. That's killer stuff; it's devastating to me even now. They had both been through so much, but Mom and her sister ultimately triumphed. They had suffered the same losses and hurts and found family in each other. Mom never told us these tales with woe-is-me self-pity. But her stories made me, I feel, a basically sympathetic person. I do believe it comes from the natural process of a daughter identifying with a mother and, more specifically, from our primal connection to her pain. Even today there are times in my busy schedule when she visits and I have to remind myself that Mom has very special needs, that I should try extra hard to put a lid on self-involvement. I usually say a special prayer when she comes that the Lord will help me to be sensitive toward her.

The sisters shared a bedroom in the apartment of Mama Cuttell's next-door neighbor, a woman who took railroad workers in as boarders to support herself. They had pullout sofas. One Saturday, Mom rode a streetcar out to Mount Pleasant, where her best friend Babsy lived. They had been friends since the days when Mom had lived with Mama Cuttell. Babsy's mother, Dottie, urged Mom to go back to school and move in with them, if she agreed to work after school and on weekends and vacations to pay her room and board. Some deal. She'd been down that road before, but she agreed. So she moved in and went to work typing envelopes in a brokerage firm.

This arrangement made Mom miserable. Then it got worse. When she was in the eleventh grade, Dottie wanted to buy the house but couldn't afford it unless Mom *quit* school and went to work full time. Incredibly, Mom once again gave in.

Small wonder that the church had become my mother's main source of strength and comfort. Then, at the age of eighteen, she came across what would eventually become the source of security and love in her life. His name was Aaron Leon Epstein.

What Joanie and Eppie most had in common was the uncommon harshness of their pasts. Daddy hadn't had an easy time of it himself. His ancestors were Russian Jews who came here in the 1870s. They took the German-Jewish name of their Stateside sponsor and settled among the Jewish communities of north Baltimore. Actually his grandmother definitely didn't come over on a boat. She was already here, a full-blooded Native American from North Carolina. That's the legend, anyway. But we've never nailed down exactly what tribe she was from. I was told all my life I was part Cherokee. Then it was Crow. The latest is Blackfoot.

The Epstein tribe, however, thrived in the tobacco trade as wholesale jobbers, rolling and packing cigars, shipping and selling retail. They had their own factory and made lots of money. My father's father, Meyer Epstein, had a reputation as something of a wildman. My father always said I got my showmanship genes from him. I'm not sure if I should be flattered, since Daddy said he wasn't very handsome and was a great snake charmer and carnival barker.

At least they say he sang quite well. The story goes that my father's mother, Evelyn, whose family came from Annapolis, traveled by boat to a carnival along the Chesapeake Bay and first set eyes on Meyer when he was in the snake pit charming snakes.

What I may have gotten from Meyer and Daddy was the need to be into a bunch of different things at once. Meyer also was a bootlegger during Prohibition, he made quite a bit of money in the family's wholesale cigar business, and he ran a successful neighborhood grocery store.

My father was born in 1924. He was the youngest of three sons; there were five children in all. Some of his earliest memories are of licking and sticking labels on liquor bottles to help with the bootlegging business. By the time my father was a young boy, his father's troubles had already started. If Meyer wasn't filling those liquor bottles, he was emptying them down his throat and developed a drinking problem. Meyer was called Sam, which was weird, since a younger brother was already named Sam, and they called him "Little Sammy." Uncle Sam, Meyer's brother, went on to become—and still is—a wealthy tobacco and candy merchant in Baltimore.

There was always plenty of money to go around, but Sam began to give a lot of it away. Frankly, I'd prefer to think I got Sam Epstein's heart of gold rather than his art of snake charming.

People still talk about Sam's legendary generosity. It is said that some of the synagogues around Baltimore were built with his money. My mom got an earful about this one day when she worked as a volunteer in a Christian bookstore in Annapolis. One day a very cultured and sweet elderly lady got to talking, and she said, "What's your name?" Mom told her. The woman gave her a long, curious look, then asked, "Are you married to one of the Epsteins of West Annapolis?" "I'm married to Leon Epstein," Mom said. And the woman nodded slowly with recognition. "Oh, my dear," she said, "that father of Leon, Sam Epstein, had a heart of gold, a heart like our Savior. You know," she went on, "we used to have a poorhouse down on West Street and sometimes those poor black folk wouldn't have any turkeys for Thanksgiving or presents under the tree at Christmastime. We always knew who to get in touch with—Sam Epstein. And he'd come in there with turkeys and new flannel pajamas for everybody. Man absolutely had a heart of gold."

Unfortunately Sam wasn't nearly as magnanimous when it came to his own children. He and Evelyn split up when Daddy was six or seven. Though he sent support money for the kids, this big-hearted man mostly neglected them. Like my mother's father, he became a heavy drinker. If Mom's family was nonexistent, Daddy's was, by today's standards, dysfunctional.

Sam and Evelyn tried to reconcile as Daddy entered high school in the fall of 1936. By then Daddy wanted to get out of Baltimore. He always likened his childhood to that of Huck Finn—clamming, crabbing, and paddling along the Chesapeake Bay. Daddy literally was out of his water and hated city life. The school looked and felt like a prison. He didn't have any fun and by Christmas he begged to go home to his creek and live with his aunt and uncle in Annapolis. His mother gave in and let him go. Three or four months later Baltimore apparently wasn't any fun for Evelyn either; she left Sam for good and came back home to Annapolis. It's sad. I hardly remember him. Gram didn't think much of old Sam, but Dad always spoke of him with respect.

Daddy saw his father only a few more times in his life. Sam abandoned his family and later took up with another woman but never married her. He drifted in and out of his children's lives. He died when I was seven or eight. As he lay on his deathbed, Gram said to Daddy, "Your father is dying. He's calling for you kids and wants to say his final good-byes." Only Daddy went.

"Forgive me, son," was all Sam could say.

Daddy clasped his frail hand. "I forgive you, Pop," was all my father could answer. In his heart, Daddy could forgive this scoundrel of a father in his final moments of life. My father was just a kid himself then, with kids of his own.

As a child I rarely saw my father's side of the family. Strangely, one day after the show a woman came out of the audience and said, "Hi, I'm your cousin Ellen." She was actually Daddy's first cousin—Little Sammy and Aunt Sarah's daughter. The name wasn't even familiar. My grandmother didn't stay close to that side after the split. Back then the twenty-mile ride from Annapolis to Baltimore on the old roads took forever, and the city seemed a long distance away. Once a month, though, my parents would drive into town to Lombard Street and buy bagels, challah, sweet butter, and candy from Uncle Sam. It was funny. Cousin Ellen got upset when I referred to my grandfather as a carnival barker. She said it wasn't true. These were things I'd been told all my life. I like the stuff I learned growing up, and I don't want to find out it isn't true. But was Meyer *really* charming snakes when he met Gram? My daddy said he was and that's always been good enough for me.

Now, my grandmother—Gram—is another story altogether. She

became a formidable presence in all our lives, just as Mama Cuttell had been for my mother. Having held her large family together despite an absent, hard-drinking husband, Gram, even after she remarried, was stern, tough as a rock, and suffered no nonsense from anyone. If I missed out on anything in life it was having grandparents who just adored me and let me do just anything. She didn't even keep any condiments in her house. You were lucky if you got salt and pepper on your food. It was like, "It's chicken, it's good for you, so just shut up and eat it."

Gram had what we called a "jeweled vase" on the second-floor landing. It was probably cheesy and encrusted with fake stones, but Michie and I were fascinated by this hideous thing and would spend hours staring at it. And this bugged Gram. "It's a damned pot," she'd yell in her crabby voice. "Doesn't require all that attention. Why don't you kids go out and play like real kids." So we'd leave—and I'd sneak back in for another look.

It's amazing we never broke it. Or stole it. I only stole once in my childhood and that was from my father's sister who was also named Evelyn; we all called her Aunt Sissaboo. She lived right behind Gram in Annapolis. It was summer. Her house was empty. Everyone was outside. I went into the bathroom and for no reason just swiped one of these tiny perfume samplers she had lined up in a tray. I felt like the world's worst felon. I suffered so. I told my parents three days later, and they were appalled. They ordered me to march right over there, apologize to Aunt Sis, and return the perfume sample. When I carried it in, it felt like a three-ton sample. Guilt has a way of weighing heavy. That perfume was probably My Sin.

To be honest, it was a lot easier to respect Gram than to love her. I always had a negative feeling about her when I was little. She was what I didn't want to become. I saw her as hard, cold, and hairy. That's where my serious prejudice against female facial hair comes from. I just have this problem with it: Tweeze it, pluck it, or Nair it, but don't make me look at it. If I ever saw one hair coming in on my chin or something I'd be after it with a butcher knife before it had a chance to express itself, because I will *not* be like my grandmother.

In her later years, though, Gram was fun to be around, even though she may have been a little senile back then. Some of the funniest things I remember in my life are with Gram. She'd wear these old housedresses and roll down her stockings and sit there on Easter Sunday with the Easter basket right between her legs and kind of stare out around the room with this wild look in her eye. When my brother Davy graduated from Washington Bible College, one of the strictest, staunchest, most conservative schools you can find—the cheerleaders' dresses go down to their ankles—Gram was there and it was a stifling hot June day. She was always a firm believer in drinking water. So she had her brown bag and ice cubes and water, though no one figured it was water. So during this one very still moment in the outdoor ceremony, there's Gram knocking back her water, yelling into the silence, "Hot as HELL in here." We all just wanted to sink down in our chairs and die.

My first Christmas married to Paul, we came east and had a party, and Gram came over. She was the only family member besides Michie that Paul truly enjoyed. She was just so fascinating, so unpredictable. He went over to her and said, "So, Gram, have you missed me?"

She looked at him and said, "Missed you? I don't even know who the hell you ARE!"

One thing you can say about Gram: she was an equal opportunity *destroyer*. When I flew in from L.A. for Davy's wedding, Daddy assigned me the task of looking after her, which was no small job. I sat down next to her in the front pew as we were waiting for the procession to start. Gram was getting itchy, looking all over the place, not quite sure what was happening. Suddenly she looked right at me and said, "And what's YOUR name?" That was when I knew she was really slipping. Then the organ music started and as Davy marched down to wait for his bride, Sandy, Gram said, "Who's THAT?"

"Grandma," I said, "that's Dave. He's your grandson."

Finally a nod of vague, fleeting recognition. "Oh, yeah, oh, yeah," she mumbled. Then she snapped her head back to me and said, "So what's he DOING up there anyway?"

"It's a wedding, Gram, he's getting married." At the end of the ceremony, they handed a rose to each of the three grandmothers, and Gram just tossed hers to the floor. "Gram, your rose," I said and she answered, "Oh, forget it, I got a million of 'em at home."

Daddy was always so patient and loving with Gram, who called her son Leon. She would ask him, "Now, Leon, tell me, what was the name of that man?" And Daddy would say, "Who, Mama?" And she'd say, "That man, you remember, what was his name?" And Daddy would say, "Now, Mama, which man do you mean?" And she'd say, "You know, Leon, that man I met and later married, your *father*. What was his *name*?" My sister would just drop to the floor, we'd be laughing so hard. We got to the point where Michie and I made a pact before we went to her house that we wouldn't even *look* at each other because if we did it was all over. If we were talking, say, about Lawrence Welk, Gram would suddenly blurt out things like "Oh, I like Lawrence Welk. He's the one who sits on my porch with me. Eats watermelon. Nice man."

Old Gram. Maybe *that's* where it comes from—the shooting-off-my-mouth gene, that extra saying-whatever-pops-into-my-head chromosome or whatever it is. Got that from Gram. Only without the hardening of the arteries—yet.

Because she was Protestant, Grandma's five children were raised halfheartedly in the eighteenth century Episcopal church in Annapolis's Church Circle. It wasn't always easy for my dad to grow up with a mixed heritage. One day when he was ten, he was on his way to church when a gang of young boys started throwing rocks and yelling, "Christ-killer! Christ-killer!" This was in the mid-1930s when fascism and anti-Semitism were on the rise, and it was an experience my half-Jewish, half-Gentile father would never forget. That story for my dad is like the tale Mom tells about coming off the train with her suitcase. It's the one I remember most vividly. In fact, Frank always said to me, "You have no idea what your father went through as a Jew in the navy during the war. You can't imagine the hell he endured." Daddy never talks about it. I wish he would. The world is full of extraordinary people—and we knew two of them as Mommy and Daddy.

Then there was the story of how Mom saved Gram's soul. We'll never forget the ride they took over the Chesapeake Bay Bridge very near the end of Gram's life. Mom had been concerned about her getting so old and not knowing the Lord. But she didn't like to preach around Gram because it never did any good. One Sunday my parents picked her up for lunch. They were driving over the bridge when Mom started telling Gram about what happens after you die and about eternal life and all that. "Grandma," she asked, "have you ever accepted Jesus into your heart?"

And Grandma, this unbelievably stern woman who would normally have just said, "That's none of your business and we're not discussing it," calmly said, "No, I don't believe I have," which left more than enough room for my mother to make her move. And when my mother makes a move for the Lord, it's pretty much a done deal.

"Well, Grandma, would you like to do that now?"

"Well," she said, "yes, Joan, I believe I would."

So on the Bay Bridge my parents said the Sinner's Prayer with Gram. This is the prayer to repent all your past sins and accept Jesus, which Gram did that day on the Bay Bridge.

Gram died just a short time later. She was close to ninety years old. Mama, Gram, and Mom—three incredible women.

After Daddy graduated from high school he went to work as a clerk at the Naval Academy Officers' Club, earning $12.50 for a seven-day week. He was there when he heard about the Japanese attack on Pearl Harbor. He felt such allegiance to the men he got to know there that he immediately quit his job and joined the navy, lying about his age. Only a muscle weakness in Daddy's eye kept him from becoming a navy pilot.

Daddy eventually signed up for Officer Candidates School. Then the horror of war struck home: Daddy's stepfather was killed in the Pacific; his brother Paul was killed in Saint-Lô during the Normandy invasion; and his brother Carol (pronounced Carl) was seriously wounded at Remagen Bridge. Daddy asked to be sent to the front but his request was denied. He got so upset he briefly went over the hill—AWOL. Before he could ship out again, the war ended.

As a member of the navy in peacetime, Daddy went all over the place—to Europe for one stint, then to the Pacific, where he worked as an assistant to the civilian director of A-bomb testing. At Bikini and Eniwetok he witnessed half a dozen blasts and then participated in tests to study the bombs' impact on metals, marine life, humans, and climate.

When it came to ladies, Daddy felt some real heat and impact up close back in Washington when, in August of 1948, he went to work in the Naval Research Laboratories. Her name was Joanie Cuttell.

My mother was a secretary there with piercing blue eyes, a massive mane of strawberry-blond hair so thick it would stay on top of her head with one pin, a voluptuous figure, and a face that was movie star glamorous, very Marilyn Monroe-ish. Daddy has always said Mommy was more beautiful than any of her children—thank you, Dad—and we were all pretty babies. But my mom, we're talking drop-dead gorgeous. And—thank you, Mom—I didn't get her perfect skin, or her luxuriant, wonderful hair, or her dazzling blue eyes, or her rather ample bosom; I got her thighs, her wuggies.

This bombshell also had a proud, haughty facade designed to keep the boys in uniform about six miles away. She had learned from Mama that no matter how bad you had it in life, you were a lady and you held your head up high. She wasn't really haughty; she was shy, extremely insecure, and frightened. But she was beautiful and that, plus her facade, intimidated other women. They preferred to see her as stuck-up. She was proud, but never stuck-up.

Daddy, meanwhile, had learned to whistle, whoop, and holler

from a convertible with his buddies whenever he spotted Joanie standing on a corner. Most people would not have blamed him, but she did. She found such behavior disgusting and humiliating and didn't want *anything* to do with my dad.

Mom admits he was cute but cocky, a terrible flirt with a sense of humor who'd tilt his navy hat to one side when he strode past her desk. That made her sick. He kept asking her for a date, and she kept turning him down.

At least that's what she always said. Daddy remembered it just a bit differently. He said she'd go around asking people if they needed cigarettes just so she would have another excuse to cruise by his office and check him out.

Bottom line: He was crazy about her.

And no way this was ever going *anywhere*.

Daddy probably fell in love with her the minute he spotted her. He's never told me that, but that's my fantasy about them. He wanted to be Mommy's knight in shining armor and save her. He felt sorry for her. And he did rescue her. But I know Mommy was not in love with him in the beginning.

We're not talking about two veterans of the dating game, either. Mom had hardly gone out at all; Daddy had been traveling all over the world since he was seventeen; but at twenty-four, he still had never had a serious relationship with a woman. He was not a cad, a user. He had seen his own mom suffer so much; he was very protective of his sisters and always had great respect for women.

So, while mom played it cool, she couldn't help but notice that Eppie was no beer-guzzling womanizer like so many other officers and cadets. He was funny, but he also seemed grown up, mature, responsible, working full time as a navy court stenographer and then driving fifty miles to Beverly Beach at night and on weekends to play sax in a jazz combo, the Five Moods.

Nothing Daddy did could get *her* in the mood. He finally wore her down for a date. She says she accepted only because she didn't want to crush the poor guy. So they went out to hear jazz great Charlie Barnet with some of Dad's pals, including a Five Mood band member named Jim and his date, Tootie. Mom drank Cokes all night and really had an attitude. She didn't want to be there and made that clear. On the dance floor, when Daddy's hand slipped down to Mom's backside, her hand lashed out across his face and before you could name that tune, she was in a taxi heading home. She admits she was a dud—and believe me, she gets no argument from Daddy on that.

She was such a dud, in fact, that Tootie leaned over and asked Daddy, "Ep, what could you possibly see in her? She is so conceited, so stuck-up."

Undaunted, Daddy said, "Well, I'll just have to knock her down a few pegs, and then I'm going to marry her."

But he didn't exactly start hammering at those pegs like a maniac or anything. "Cautious" doesn't quite describe the way Daddy pursued Mom: three dates in about a year's time. But they worked closely together and actually got to know each other through all the teasing.

Then Daddy made a bold move: he invited her to meet Gram out in Annapolis because Gram had started thinking this relationship was getting up a head of steam. Momentum? With a date every four months?

Gram must've known her son pretty well. That weekend date has gone on now for over four decades. When Daddy went to pick Mom up on Saturday morning, Dottie—the woman she lived with—made a threat: if Mom went to Annapolis, she wouldn't be welcome back. Daddy felt it was more about money than morals. Dottie saw Mom—and Mom's income—slipping away. Mom was, she herself says, "an emotional cripple" at that time. She needed someone strong who could take care of her. She always said, "I just went with whoever pulled the hardest."

And you better believe that was Daddy. He not only pulled the hardest—he was suddenly pulling the fastest. Talk about a guy snapping out of it!

"She doesn't need to come back," Daddy angrily told Dottie. "I can take care of her." He was really steamed. He saw it as an abusive situation. He felt Dottie was using Mom as a wage earner and didn't give a hoot about her. And besides, Babsy—Dottie's daughter—was quite promiscuous and my mom was real uncomfortable with that. Daddy didn't want her in that environment any longer, and he intended to make sure she left it for good.

He told Mom right there to pack everything she owned because she wasn't coming back. Once he got to Annapolis, Daddy drove straight to the chaplain at the naval academy and got a marriage license. On Monday, August 29, 1949, they were married in the academy's basement chapel. Monday was the only night he and Jim, his best man, had off from the Five Moods. The wedding was put together so quickly that only a few close friends showed up, and they didn't even get it together to have a photo taken. Babsy and Dottie never bothered to show.

Mom gave birth to David Paul Epstein nine months to the day after the marriage and finally had a place to call her own—a small apartment just beyond the navy base in a wooded development. But she and Dad paid a price for being impulsive: Mom wasn't ready for pregnancy or child-rearing. And she certainly wasn't ready for the nausea.

Or for the Epstein family's reaction. Gram, who had known nothing but heartache and hard work all her life, thought she was too young and didn't make Mom feel accepted. She feels the family treated her horribly. Mom came into a very tight family; they felt that *nobody* was good enough for Leon, although that attitude mellowed over time.

And, sure, my parents would be the first to tell you they've had their ups and downs, but they've made their marriage work. Sometimes I think my daddy's been a lot happier with Mom than she has with him. She frustrates him, but he adores her. He loves her in a very possessive way. My daddy is still learning—and having trouble learning—to say "I love you." And to let her be a person. He's a very strong human being and my mom struggles against that.

I would be shocked to discover my daddy had been unfaithful. Strangely enough, I'd be less shocked if my mom had been because she's such a romantic. She has an earthier sense of humor, too, which is ironic. If you tell a slightly off-color joke with sex in it, Daddy will get embarrassed; Mom will howl.

Daddy's the kind of man who would give Mommy *the money* to buy Chanel No. 5 every Christmas. Which is hardly the romantic way to go. And my mom longs for romance. A lot of women do. I know I do. As a young girl Mom escaped the misery of her own life by reading Hollywood fan magazines; she swooned over Tyrone Power, dreamed he could fall in love with her if only their paths would cross. "If only he knew me, he'd love me," she'd say breathlessly. She was a dreamer.

I'm lucky that Frank is, by nature, very romantic. So many times—when Frank gives me a little card or does some sweet little thing—I'll think, Gee, I hope Daddy does this for Mom. But Dad didn't grow up in a home that showed him or rewarded that behavior. Not that Frank did, either, but he got it somewhere. I hate to think about *how* and *with whom* he learned it, but even though it bugs me, my life now is a lot happier with him because he's *learned.* If Daddy's still got some learning to do when it comes to romance, he never shortchanged Mommy when it came to that other classic obstacle to making love last: commitment. My parents were ecstatic when Davy was born, and there was no better way to rededicate themselves to their marriage and family life than to live in the City of Lights. They first lived in a Paris hotel right in the romantic heart of Paris, where they discovered tree-lined boulevards, sidewalk cafés, walks along the Seine.

Then they decided to get a place in Orgeval. They rented one of two apartments in the converted barn and became fast friends with their neighbors, the Goupys, who lived in the adjoining apartment. Language was a major challenge. But my mother makes friends everywhere. The first thing she says when she meets someone is "Tell us about *you*." The first week, she tapped on Madame Goupy's door with her foot—bearing a fresh-baked chocolate pie on one upturned palm and a French dictionary on the other.

"Bonjour, madame," Mom said to the astonished Madame Goupy. She offered up the pie, announcing, *"Pour vous."* Which pretty much exhausted her vocabulary. Her neighbor stared with widening eyes. *"Pourquoi?"* Why—she asked. Blank stares. Poor Mom had to go to her pocket dictionary for that one; then she looked up her answer.

Slapping her chest, she said, *"Amie, amie."* Yes, she was a friend. The Epstein-Goupy language lab was now open for business. Thus began a great *amitié* anchored in very little language and much miming, signing, pointing and, above all, feeling.

The Goupys had hated the pompous "Ugly American" colonel who lived there before. So Mom and Dad were welcomed into traditional French family life with unusual warmth and hospitality. Monsieur Goupy was a cabinetmaker who rode his bicycle to his shop every morning. Madame Goupy cared for their four children, sewed their clothing, prepared every meal from scratch, cleaned, laundered— the works, the old-fashioned way. Monsieur Trébois, another neighbor, had a horse and delivered hay. He'd ride by the open kitchen window, and Mom would happily pass little Davy right through the window and onto the horse. It was a sense of community my mother had never known. It was one of the most blissful times of my parents' lives.

One Monday morning my mother looked out her window and marveled at the sight of Madame Goupy stooped over a huge black cast-iron caldron on a wooden stove in her backyard. She watched as the woman virtually boiled her dirty laundry, extracted the steaming mass, and began working the material back and forth incessantly against a large, crude scrub board. My mother's heart ached for this woman who endured her backbreaking chores with such *courage*.

My father had purchased an old wringer-washer, which they kept in the bathroom so it could drain into the tub. My mother had a brainstorm. She made herself understood well enough to lead Madame Goupy into the upstairs bathroom. There, to Madame's astonishment, my mother demonstrated this awesome, futuristic gizmo that immediately swept Madame Goupy's homemaking techniques out of the Dark Ages and into the twentieth century. *"Mon Dieu!"* she cried in disbelief.

From that point on, Mondays became wringer-washer day *chez* Epstein for both women. Madame would haul over a giant bundle of clothes, and she and Mom would spend all day laundering, laughing, taking tea breaks—bonding through bleaching. My mother never did learn much French, but she did learn to love this hardworking, big-hearted matriarch as the mother she never had.

Paris was a sweet time for my parents, who were finally becoming comfortable together as a young couple. It was into this world that I was born on the sweltering night of August 16, 1953, in the American Hospital at Neuilly. Madame Goupy had made elaborate preparations to serve as midwife, assisted by her neighbors, had Daddy not been able to get back home from the base in time.

My mom had wanted a baby girl after Davy, and from the start she knew she was carrying a girl. Just knew it.

I wonder how they got any of the female staff at the hospital to pay attention—Gary Cooper was in the room directly above Mom. (That was about as close to Tyrone Power as Mommy ever got.) Though visitors were not allowed on the maternity ward, my father sneaked a grinning Madame Goupy in to see my mother.

"Très bien, madame, très bien!" she cried. Then she broke out her smuggled booty: champagne and cookies to toast the arrival of Kathryn Lee Epstein. For my mom, after forty hours of labor, a little celebrating was in order.

And just four months later it was time to leave Gay Paree for the less exotic southern Maryland and the much less romantic Naval Air Test Center. My parents couldn't take everything home and agonized over what to leave behind. They would miss the adventure, the love, and the friendships of Paris.

Our much-loved Labrador, Blackie, went with the Trébois family.

The wringer-washer, of course, stayed with the Goupys.

And for all those years in between, the Goupys—and Paris, my birthplace—stayed with them.

You've Got to Learn
to Make Your Own Music

I remember my childhood as an incredibly sweet dream, so perfect, so insulated that I figured life was wonderful like that for everyone. I lived in a warm, fuzzy bubble that somehow didn't burst for years. In this bubble with me were my loving parents, older brother Davy, and baby sister Michele Suzanne, born twenty months after me on April 15, 1955.

Early on, this bubble was quite the mobile unit. From Paris we went to the Chesapeake Bay; then in December 1955, eight months after Michie was born, we sailed from New York to Bremerhaven, Germany, on the SS *United States* and rode a train down into Wiesbaden. My dad served with the navy's Rhine River Patrol, based at Wiesbaden in support of the Seventh Army—making sure the Russians weren't coming.

But this was Germany, and the Goupys weren't coming, either. I don't know how Mom did it. She found herself with three kids under five years of age in a foreign country, and Daddy was at the base all day long. No fun neighbors and no one was *sprechen*-ing *Sie Deutsch*, either. The first months were a real nightmare. Europe had its worst freeze in a century. Gas lines for heat snapped. Daddy says we walked across the Rhine River, which was frozen solid from Switzerland all the way to Holland. We stayed in one room for weeks, trying to keep warm. Our stuff was stuck en route. We eventually settled into more conventional base life, taking an apartment with long dark halls. I remember listening with Davy to "Zorro" and "The Shadow" over the Armed Forces Radio. I didn't grieve over our departure from Germany; in fact, I would learn years later just how miserable my parents were and why.

In December 1957 we ran and raced all over the decks of the SS *United States* as we sailed home (my cruise life started early) and by Christmas had settled on Monterey Avenue in West Annapolis. Daddy was now on his last station with the navy in Washington. We lived just a few blocks from Gram. Dad took up his jazz performances again. I had a backyard with a perfect apple tree for climbing and my own field of dreams nearby for inventing games and building forts. After boring base life, this was paradise.

A big part of paradise was caring for my baby sister. My parents, fearing I just might be jealous, had prepared me for her arrival by telling me, "Our baby's coming." I remember bathing, feeding, diapering, rocking, and hauling Michie all over the place until my little arms would just give out. She'd waddle across the gravel driveway of our neighbors, the Bowens, and I'd run after her to lift her so she wouldn't hurt her tiny feet. It was as if I were her mommy and she was my own little doll—except that this doll would grow up *taller, thinner, blond,* and with a *better singing voice!* But from day one, Michie's been more than a sister to me. She is one of my life's absolute treasures.

Brother "Day-Day" was more than a brother. He was a coach. Davy wanted a brother and, lacking one, turned us into tomboys. He brought us into the manly world of marbles and he taught us to throw, kick, hike, catch, and hit balls. I don't understand kids today living in front of TVs and Nintendo. Kids are supposed to be outside. I let Cody watch "Sesame Street" and his Disney movies like *Bambi, The Lady and the Tramp,* and *The Little Mermaid.* But to just give a child a remote control and total power over that box is crazy. Too many kids today are so fat. They're getting soft on software. They can't do monkey bars. Can't climb ropes. We're raising a generation of fat little TV and computer-game junkies.

In our make-believe world, Davy divided the world between Cowboys and Indians, Orioles and Yankees, Colts and Giants. Just as I was Michie's protector, Day-Day was mine; and while all my girlfriends were madly in love with him, he beat up many a jerk for me. Now, of course, he's praying for people's souls as a loving, healing pastor in Ottawa.

I got the show-biz bug early—with just a little encouragement from my parents.

When we were real little, Daddy, the weekend jazz musician,

would try to get his three kids to sing on tape. The first time Daddy recorded my voice on his old reel-to-reel tape recorder I was five years old. Michie was three. While we were singing "Jesus Loves Me" I stopped and looked at my father and said, "Daddy, where's da moosik?" I assumed that the background music would automatically start playing the second I started singing. Where was my band?

Poor Daddy had to break the news.

"Sweetheart," he said, "you have to make your own music."

And it's so true. You can't wait for the band to play or for the violins to come in. And you can't wait for other people to make you happy. You are responsible for making your own music in life.

As a first grader I debuted on stage as a squirrel in a school production of *Snow White*. It was my first cattle call—only it was a squirrel call. My chubby cheeks made me a lock for the part. My mom and I made this squirrel costume, and believe me, I've been in uglier costumes since! Of course, in my mind, I was King of the Forest out there. And, please, the *ecstasy* of those bows. I was hooked.

My nightmares started shortly thereafter when I wrote, directed, and starred in a one-kid performance of *Little Black Sambo*. Maybe it had something to do with standing alone at the head of the class with all my classmates staring up and laughing at me. And the quite distinct absence of deafening applause. In the nightmare I'm in front of an audience with no script, no rehearsal, and I'm faking it. Every second I wing it I'm *stricken with panic*, sure that they're going to find out I'm a fraud. An impostor. But then I always wake up just in time. I had that dream when I was six. I still have it. Story of my life.

I also wrote Disney that year in the hope of breaking into films. I wanted to be Hayley Mills or Annette Funicello so bad. I *loved* those 1950s Disney movies. I even wanted a new stage name—something more melodic than Epstein. Not that I was ashamed of my Jewish heritage; I was always proud of being Jewish. But I had something more romantic in mind, like Kathryn Lee Willowbrook, or Hepburn, when I visualized the marquee.

Disney's form letter urged me to pursue drama study, grow up, and get in touch someday. Sure, thanks.

When school was out, we were never allowed to be bored or to zone out with TV. If we did watch TV, it was usually our favorite comedienne, Lucille Ball. She was just the funniest thing going. Michie and I loved Lucy so much we were always trying to create our own versions of Lucy-and-Ethel sketches.

Mom and Dad encouraged us to be resourceful and active. If I was bored I raided the pantry and set up a corner store. We went sledding in winter, crabbing in summer. And year-round we'd spend every afternoon along nearby Weems Creek. There was a highway overpass with steep and jagged banks of rock under the roadway. We were always hiking up those rocks, which drove my parents crazy. They were terrified that we'd slip into Weems Creek and get washed down the Severn River and drown in Chesapeake Bay. No way! We learned to swim when we were tiny.

Summers were idyllic. We had feasts that went on for two days. We'd go through a dozen or more bushels of crabs. We'd spread newspapers over this long picnic table and eat, rest, wash our hands, play some ball, and come back for another mountain of crabs. We wanted those summer evenings to last forever and hated going to sleep at eight-thirty when it was still light out and we could still hear the other kids screaming and playing outside.

I never became a joiner. I squirmed on school committees, in church, in any group activities. I got so restless in Brownies that I formed a renegade faction that met at my house after troop meetings. The Brownie moms learned of this subversive movement and canned me—and made me *turn in my beanie*. So much for joining.

When I was eight my father left the navy after twenty years and we moved about twelve miles down the road to the new development of Belair-at-Bowie, built on the 3,200-acre Woodward estate. We were about the thirtieth family to move in. Bowie, one of the largest cities in the state, was a grazing pasture then. There was no store, no movie theater, and we had to be bused twenty miles to the nearest elementary school.

Home was a yellow three-bedroom Colonial with black shutters, but it felt like a mansion—immense, luxurious, and surrounded by mud. It was perfect. A clump of skinny young trees on a dumb molehill was our mountain where wars were fought and championships won. Mom always had to fetch us for dinner and measured our fun by how thick the mud was caked on our clothes.

Mom and Dad did show us the importance of hard work and the value of money. Daddy was always an extremely frugal man. He's had shoes for *thirty years* and he prides himself on being almost a country bumpkin in his indifference to trends. It's not that he's miserly. But if last year's shoes still fit, don't tell him what's *in* this year. If you told Daddy to buy something because everybody else had it, he'd only say, "All the more reason not to have it."

There was no way we'd ever get spoiled. Daddy made sure to instill in us a work ethic. He was our driver when we collected the zillions of empty bottles workers left at all the construction sites as Bowie was built. We washed them at home and carted them off to the supermarket. I opened a checking account with a fifty-dollar deposit and gloried in my hard-earned independence.

After he left the navy, Daddy got into the newspaper distribution business for the *Washington Post*. He went from door to door drumming up work with his new neighbors. He also began course work to become an insurance underwriter. Mom would also go from door to door selling eggs if we needed extra cash. Later on, she worked as a hostess showing model homes in a development five miles away. She was always my role model and she set impossibly high standards as a homemaker. Both my parents worked hard to build a home filled with love and affection and lots of cuddling. Never did a day go by that I wasn't told I was loved by both of them. Strangely, as hard as it was sometimes for Daddy to tell and show Mommy that he loved her, he always showered us with love. My daddy lived for his family. He loved me, cared for me, read me books, hugged me. I remember him driving up in his Volkswagen Beetle after his day in Washington and we would rush out of the house to greet him. We loved our Daddy. He always smelled so good. He always wore Old Spice, and to this day when I smell Old Spice, I remember hugging Daddy.

I was so secure in his and mom's love that I grew up assuming all kids were loved as we were. I was stunned to discover they weren't.

I had a girlfriend named Robin in grade school whom I loved very much. She was a championship diver. I will never forget seeing the enormous welts all over her body when we changed into our swimsuits. Her father used to take a belt to her and whip her and her brothers to shreds. She was so ashamed she could never talk about it. Children always think they're to blame. I remember asking my parents if she could come and live with us so her father wouldn't hurt her anymore.

I had another close girlfriend down the street. Her house was the only place my mom and dad would let me go for a sleepover—until her daddy insisted on bathing us together. I was maybe five or six. I was confused. I had a bad feeling each time this happened but I didn't want to be rude, so I went along. I wasn't fondled but I told my parents I never wanted to go over there again for the night.

Looking back, it makes me think how incredibly common this kind of thing is—and that most of it is far worse than what happened to me. Still, it had an impact. I became incredibly self-conscious and modest about my body. I remember being in a tight, stretchy little bathing suit when I was about that age and not liking it because it clung to me and outlined every part of my body.

My daddy, as affectionate as he was, was never sleazy and always so decent and moral and so darn healthy. Even when we tried—my sister and I—to be a little naughty, he foiled us. Some nights we would stir up some sort of commotion just to get Daddy to come and look in on us. And the reason we did this was so Michie and I could look in on him—knowing that Daddy wore only T-shirts with no underwear to bed at night. We'd try to get a peek in order to see what a "wing-wang" looked like. We had no idea. In our family that's how boys and girls were basically different. Boys had "wing-wangs"; girls had "pinkies." We thought we were so clever and had the situation covered—but so did Daddy. He'd come in, discreetly tugging his T-shirt down to his knees, and believe me, we never got a peek in twenty years. For almost twenty-three years I'd just look at dogs and say, "Is THAT what it is?" And then I got married.

Michie and I shared a bedroom—and a deep attachment. Most nights we had this little ritual where we'd stand in the doorway of the room, ready to turn out the lights and hit the sack. Then we had to say, "Jumbug!" and jump into bed because there were alligators under the beds, and we'd say, "Good night, good night, good night, you dirty bite." It was gibberish, but we had to do it or we couldn't go to sleep. If one of us was angry, we'd refuse to do it so the other one couldn't fall asleep.

Michie had another way of keeping me awake. She was a bed wetter. She was afraid to get up at night because of snakes and animals and things in the dark that could hurt her. So two or three times a week she would pee her brains out, get absolutely soaked and cold, and cry out to me. She was brave enough to hop into bed with me and lie beside me, which I let her do. And then she'd pee in *my* bed. Now *that's* close!

We were always busy with our projects. We had the Cucaracha Club with three friends and our pooches down by a nearby pond. We had some backyard carnivals and plays. And Michie, Davy, and I put out a handwritten newspaper called the *Children's Post,* using the shed Dad used for his *Post* distributorship.

As I neared my teens, there were other claims on my time. And on my heart. Like the Beatles—Paul, to be more specific. I had an insane crush on him and locked myself in my room for hours with that first LP, which Daddy made me buy with my bottle money. Mom knew exactly what I was going through. Paul, she told me, was my Tyrone Power.

A year or so later we had our own backyard carnival to raise money for Jerry Lewis's muscular dystrophy telethon. We baked cookies, performed magic tricks, dressed up our mutt Zorro in a top hat and tuxedo. We offered Kool-Aid, puppet shows, the works. Everyone came. Daddy got a brainstorm: he said I should raffle off my prized Beatles LP. That *killed* me. I couldn't believe he was making me do that. But he was teaching me a lesson about material attachments and the value of sacrifice and charity. That raffle brought in $58.52, which seemed like a fortune, and got us on TV. Michie and I went down to WTTV in Washington to present the check and I got to sit on the lap of Bozo the Clown. He was actually a jovial young guy named Willard Scott, who's gone on to bigger and better things. He and I still laugh about that day.

As I moved, ever so warily, from my secure, sweet childhood toward all the imponderables of puberty, I was surrounded by all sorts of Bozos: unwashed, wild-haired kids whose values were so different from mine, schoolmates who thought I was the weirdo, and were clueless as to what I was all about.

As the song said, it was "the dawning of the Age of Aquarius." The counterculture. The New Age. The sexual revolution. Everyone was doing his and her own thing, and let me tell you, there was good reason to believe they were also doing *each other's* thing.

My thing included doing needlepoint and making paper-and-wire flowers, being a folksinger and a cheerleader, becoming an upbeat but competitive grind with a three-nine GPA and being a National Honor Society scholar. I had school spirit, religious spirit, activities up the gazoo, a sense of humor, and a commitment to positive family values. And of course I had my virtue, my virginity.

In short, I was doomed to be misunderstood, out of touch. I was not your basic 1960s package. Ten years earlier or later a girl like me would've blended right in—as either a traditional, innocent "child of the fifties" or a performance-driven 1970s yuppie-in-the-making. But I was trapped in the sixties.

It was a confusing time of searching around and within for inspiration, for *meaning*. I wasn't looking for it where everybody else seemed to be looking—in the back seats of cars. It was Mom who helped to point the way.

It was probably the single most significant event in our family's life—and it happened with no warning. I will never forget that night.

I was nearing twelve years of age. I had gone out in the evening with some friends. When I came home I opened the door and found Michie and my mother in the living room. They were sitting together, sobbing, their eyes reddened and their faces glistening with tears. But instinctively I sensed they were not sad but relieved. And they were not on the same plane of reality they'd been on when I left. I thought: Whoa, what is going ON here?

It was astonishing. Mom had switched TV channels and tuned in to a Billy Graham crusade. Daddy was out of the house, probably at one of his insurance underwriting classes. Mom usually nixed the Graham TV crusades with some flippant comment, like "Oh, come on. I can get to heaven without Billy Graham. I'm a good girl, I'm virtuous, I've suffered." Mom's cynicism was matched only by her searching. She had listened to proselytizers who'd show up at the front door; she read *The Book of Mormon*, attended different churches. But as a family, we had never been especially religious. My mother would self-mockingly say she was "winging it." Though we respected my father's heritage, we were not practicing Jews, either. Because he and his father had been estranged, he had not been raised as an observant Jew but rather in his mother's Christian faith.

I felt a mixture of awe and apprehension. Mom had been watching television alone and had spontaneously knelt down in front of the TV set, asking Jesus to be the Lord and Savior of her life. She had had a classic born-again conversion: Christ promises he'll never forsake us, and when we receive him, we believe the Holy Spirit takes up residence in our hearts. "Nothing," she would say, "satisfied my heart like the Gospel of Jesus Christ."

Michie, having heard Mom weeping, was now kneeling and asking the Lord to come into her heart. The Christian faith was now a family affair. An enormous weight had been lifted. After Mom had spent years seeking the truth, Billy Graham had just smacked her with it. She now felt that Jesus knew she was capable of being saved. My dad, when he came home, heard the whole story from the three of us. Our minds were blown; we were about to be reborn.

My mother's almost Job-like series of trials and losses throughout her painful childhood had led her to seek comfort in prayer. But that was about it. While we were in Germany in 1957, though, she had experienced an agonizing spiritual crisis that was at the root of her conversion.

She learned she was pregnant with what would have been her and Daddy's fourth baby. The news crushed her. She simply could not face another pregnancy. But the alternative was equally devastating.

Suddenly her previously glib approach to God made her feel she had been, in her words, "completely nullifying the cross."

My mother suffered over her decision. She had never forgiven a friend for having had an abortion in Paris. But Mom and Dad came to see they had no realistic choice and traveled off to Switzerland to terminate the pregnancy. But afterward, the guilt and the psychological scars endured. My mother tried to bury this incident in her subconscious. Neither she nor Daddy ever said a word about it. But Mom was haunted by images of the baby she never bore. Though she gave everything she had to the three young children she did bring into this world, she still felt she had sinned against God and therefore needed His forgiveness.

And so for eight years she drifted through a sort of spiritual torment, listening, reading, watching TV evangelists as she sought some inner peace. She found it that night. "I heard the Gospel in all its purity," she would say, "and I knew that I was a sinner deserving of the cross. But Jesus died in my place."

When I heard the tale, I didn't blame her nearly as much as she blamed herself for her decision in Germany. My mom can be brutal on herself. A fourth child under seven years old might well have sent her off to the loony bin. She was still in her mid-twenties, had no help, was surrounded by a foreign culture, and she felt unsophisticated with no high school diploma. Worse, she had mourned virtually every single person she had ever loved and still feared that anyone she loved would abandon her or die. If Daddy was ever five minutes late, he'd pull off the road and phone home to reassure her he was on his way. Daddy's concern then for her emotional stability was quite legitimate.

Though Daddy didn't experience what he called Mom's "overpowering fireworks display," he did rededicate himself to the Lord on his next birthday, going forward and accepting Christ into his life. As Michie says, "We were all doomed, one by one—doomed to be saved. It was as if we had found a diamond, this wonderful gift we wanted to pass along to the people we love."

I began to feel a deeper, sweeter compassion for my mother. God sees into the heart. He knows what causes us to act in certain ways. He can then forgive us. And now that I am a mother myself, I can well understand her agony. I know she did what she did to preserve her sanity and protect her children. But to her, abortion is murder. Like my mother, I believe life begins at the moment of conception. But abortion is a complex moral and personal issue and I don't believe I have the right to impose my beliefs on another person, which is why I have declined requests from both pro-choice and pro-life groups to take a public stand. I hate abortion. I'm saddened every time I learn of a woman's need to make that decision. But I also hate the thought of back-alley abortions at the hands of butchers. I wish the funds spent to terminate unwanted pregnancies could be spent instead on preventing them.

There simply is no one blanket solution that can cover all the horrible scenarios that surround and complicate the abortion issue —rape, incest, birth defects, and so on. What bothers me most is that we've made the very concept—and the act of abortion—so convenient and so casual. I believe the precious value of human life has been betrayed and diminished. To many people leading the charge for choice, it's no more complex than removing a hangnail.

But let's not pretend that it isn't the terminating of a life. And many women live with the repercussions of their decision, believe me. Years later many women are haunted by the loss of that unborn child, even if they felt at the time that the procedure was justified. Though that difficult decision may have made sense for my mom in some ways, she suffered great guilt and desperately longed for forgiveness.

It was Billy Graham who introduced her to the Light that could finally lead her from her darkness.

And then that Light came shining my way.

And They Call It Puppy Love

My teenage years were ushered in with my first walk with Jesus and faded out with my last chance with Yancy—Yancy Bailey Spencer III, that is. The first experience joyously awakened my soul; the second joyously awakened my heart to an obsessive first love— and led to a crushing first rejection.

If there was a battle within me between the spirit and the flesh—Yancy's bronzed, surfer-Adonis flesh, to be exact—the spirit won the day. Actually, the spirit also won the night. But it got close there for a couple hours at the end.

When I was almost thirteen I was ripe for religion. I was actually just plain ripe. But I was not thrilled with the idea of puberty. You'd think in a wonderful, loving home a girl would say, "Hey, fine, I've got pubic hair, no big deal." Not me. I approached puberty not as an adventure but as an ordeal. Why would I want change? I had always had so much love, joy, and comfort. It was like seeing my brother in the backyard the day before he went off to college. Life would never be the same.

I watched in horror as my body transformed itself into woman-hood. Or some of it did, anyway. I got stuck with my mom's thighs but my father's chest, so where's the justice in *that?* Mom's got a much larger bosom than my sister and I have. Maybe if I'd inherited Mom's gorgeous hair, creamy perfect skin, and curvy figure I might have felt a little more gung-ho about growing up.

I saw changes in my friends—their bodies, clothes, values, voices —and they frightened me. One very dear girlfriend became a serious anorexic. She was terrified that if she grew breasts and became a woman, her father would stop loving her Mom and love her instead. That would destroy her parents' marriage and their entire family would break apart. This freaked me out. But my attitude wasn't as sick; it was just a longing to hang on to what had been good in my life. My mother, sister, and father had been going forward and finding Jesus; suddenly everything around me was in flux. I needed constancy.

I "found it" at the movies. Life was just one big Lost and Found back there in adolescence between the virginity and the spirituality. *The Restless Ones* was playing, ironically, at the old Capitol Theater in downtown west Annapolis where my Jewish grandfather had performed. It was a Christian film starring Kim Darby that showed the tragic consequences of a young girl having sex and doing drugs with her boyfriend. It worked for me—literally scared the heck out of me. The 1960s decade was a momentous and trying time for kids and parents. (Frank's older children were in their teens then and going through their own rebellions.)

After the film a local pastor asked people to come forward and receive Christ. If this was my religious epiphany it was subtle and simple. For many people religion can be so easy they stumble right over it. I felt like a child standing there, protected and loved, with God reaching out to me, saying, "Kathie, you can make choices in this life. Choose my way and I will help you make something beautiful of your life." Well, all I can say is, God knows I've given it my best shot.

We attended church on Sunday. We did youth activities. Davy was our last holdout. He was brilliant, inquisitive, skeptical. He read the great philosophers and novelists. He challenged the spiritual path of my parents, yet he'd fling newspapers from his bike, gaze up at the heavens, and compose poetry. As a teenager, he sought the Ultimate Authority in his life: reason or faith, the seductive darkness of Dostoyevski or the joyful enlightenment of Christ. Despite his skepticism, my parents always said Davy was the one in our family who was "destined to feel the hand of God."

If *I* ever felt the hand of God on me in church, it was probably to wake me up. The joining thing again. I can't sit still for very long. My mind wanders. If host chat went on for much more than fifteen minutes I'd probably pace around Reege. We never got anything done in school meetings and committees because we spent all our time figuring out *Robert's Rules of Order*. Who was Robert to tell me how to communicate? Those rules drove me crazy. It was like Mr.

45

Blackwell and the Best- and Worst-dressed lists. Show me the man's credentials.

Epstein's Rules of Order at home were more than sufficient to keep the peace, especially with a divine as well as parental chain of command. Our parliamentary process was Mom coming at us flailing her disgusting flyswatter and Dad coming at us with a raised hand or a dangling belt.

Dad was mostly a loving, hands-on father but sometimes we felt those hands on our sore buns when we were bad. Or the belt. Dad the disciplinarian could not be conned and suffered no nonsense. He always reminded us that he was our daddy, not our buddy. I got the fewest spankings, since Michie and Davy were more inclined to push Dad's buttons. We were just smart-aleck, back-talking kids in the devout, orderly Christian home of a military career officer. Oh, no, discipline was no big deal. I never rebelled in my life until I was twenty-nine. Then I became Attila the Hun.

Mom's style was to yell, *"Wait till your dad comes home!"* That put the fear of the Lord in us. But she was no slouch in her own right. Mom can be passionate, volatile, and really blow her stack. Or break down and cry, get moody, and flip out in anger. Or flip something *at us* in anger. Daddy was and is more even-keeled, but his fury made us listen; Mom's fury just made us either duck or laugh; we weren't the least bit afraid of her. Which, of course, made her more furious.

If Michie and I ever so much as *looked* bored or if the room looked a mess, she'd march in, empty the contents of our drawers on the bed and say, "Pick it up. PICK IT UP!" And we'd just scream with laughter.

"Oh, so you think that's funny?" she'd roar, eyes glaring, hands on her hips. Then she'd storm off. Mom was probably the most hygienically obsessed person on earth when it came to germs and grooming and brushing your teeth. We knew she was mad when she stomped back waving that gross flyswatter. And we'd scream, "She's *crazy*, the woman's *crazy!* There are *dead flies* on that thing!"

If it wasn't dead flies, it was flying chickens. She'd dump a platter full of chicken wings on the floor or she'd hurl the whole dang *bird* right past Daddy's or Davy's head. She slammed doors and stormed off, only to come back an hour later all chilled out. Mom was amazingly emotional and expressive. It drove me crazy when she watched her TV movies. In any love scene or dramatic moment she'd be on the couch, muttering, "Mmmph, oh, my," or "Uh-oh, uh-oh!" Mom's face hides nothing, ever.

Love was something they never hid. My parents were Ward and June Cleaver crossed with Billy and Ruth Graham. Their world revolved around their kids and church. They didn't just raise us; they *celebrated* us. They never missed a dance or singing recital, baseball game, school show—whatever. We always had a warm bed, clean clothes and—chucking chickens aside—the vast majority of Mom's tasty dinners ended up on our plates and in our bellies.

We weren't wealthy enough to belong to a country club, and they weren't the type anyway. They took maybe one vacation without us as I was growing up. We laughed all the time. Mom has a great sense of humor, which has kept her from being bitter about all her losses. And it's amazing to me that Dad's the man he is—strong and nurturing—because he had no strong father figure.

At fifteen, the normal time for adolescent rebellion, I was still very much committed to their fiercely protected milieu. I got so much love, humor, spiritual and emotional sustenance—and discipline— at home that I didn't feel an urgent need to defy or test my parents. But that year I did discover there was life beyond Bowie. Michie and I had begun singing in a folk group called Pennsylvania Next Right with five guys, and I fell madly in love with a surfer boy in Rehoboth Beach, Delaware, where my father had bought a summer place a year or so before.

Long-limbed at five feet seven, Michie was blessed with one of those golden-silky God-given voices that just drops out of the heavens. I had an ear for harmony, a natural sense of rhythm, and not much else. I was a ham with a Sarah Heartburn flair for drama. With Daddy's jazz background we had grown up listening to swing, to the Dorsey Brothers, Duke Ellington, Glenn Miller, and Ella Fitzgerald. As a little girl I'd lock myself in the bathroom, grab a hairbrush for a microphone, and wail into the mirror. Michie just used to walk around the house effortlessly mimicking the operatic voice of Jeanette MacDonald.

We sang to the Beatles, Peter, Paul, & Mary, Joan Baez, Judy Collins, and Bob Dylan, so folk was a natural outlet for us. Our first paid job was Gram's seventy-fifth birthday party. Dad gave us each five dollars. By then my new hero was Barbra Streisand. Her voice was untouchable. It just stopped me dead in my tracks as I walked through the kitchen once as she was singing "People." There was such powerful emotion in her voice. I was paralyzed. Tears were streaming down my face. It was my musical epiphany, the moment when I understood a song's power to change people's lives. I was so intent on improving that I once visited Michie's voice coach, Selma

Gottleib, for an evaluation. "Stick with the harmony," she said kindly. My pride was crushed. I cried the whole way home. But then my dejection shifted to anger and, finally, to determination.

I would show everyone. I could sing. That was always a difference between Michie and me: rejection ruined her and it motivated me.

We often played in D.C.-area hospitals like Bethesda Naval and Walter Reed. They were filled with young wounded Vietnam vets. We also played cool coffeehouses with candles and incense burning, "in" folk clubs, and schools and churches. We wore bell-bottom hip-huggers and our hair was long and straight. Michie and I, the two serious Christians in the group, wanted the music to heal, not harangue—to serve the Lord.

We sang for young Vets whose faces and bodies had been blown apart serving their country. I didn't buy the hip nonconformist countertculture slogans of other suburban kids, who looked and dressed exactly alike with their faded jeans, tie-dyed shirts, bandannas, love beads, peace signs, and wild hair. It struck me as hypocritical. Be your own person. Don't mouth the same slogans as everyone else.

My parents reinforced our humanistic approach. "You have a choice in life," Mom said once, "to issue messages of life or messages of death. While you are under this roof, you will not issue death messages. You will be part of the solution, not part of the problem, or you won't be a part of it at all."

One problem we tried not to be a part of was Bowie's brutally humid summers. Michie's asthma and my allergies made us both miserable in summer. The solution was ocean air. We'd loved Rehoboth Beach when we visited family friends. The year-round population of 2,000 exploded to 50,000 at high season. We talked about getting our own place. During the winter of 1966 we went looking for a quaint cottage, but Daddy had his eye on this weather-ravaged godforsaken old inn at the corner of Brooklyn and First in the heart of town on the coveted beach block. Mom hated it.

You could see her point. The elderly lady who owned it had not maintained it and it had become little more than a run-down crash pad for hippies. If it was an eyesore in summer, in winter, when Rehoboth was desolate and bone-chilling damp, the house looked scary and depressing. A For Sale sign rattled in the wind. Inside were dead birds, cracking plaster, crumbling stairs, lewd graffiti, and the dense musty odor of a grave.

I loved it. But as we walked behind the realtor, Mom kept tugging at Daddy's arm. "Ep, do we really *need* thirty rooms and seven baths?

If you let this guy talk you into buying this thing," she threatened in a whisper, "I'm divorcing you."

Maybe that was all the encouragement he needed. Back at the guy's office, Mom was ready to scream. Daddy placated her by pulling a reverse-*Godfather* routine. "Honey," he assured her, "we'll make 'em an offer they'll have to refuse."

It wasn't as if Daddy didn't have enough going on already. He still had thirty-five kids working on the newspaper distribution, and since 1963 he had been working in an insurance agency near the academy, developing insurance and financial programs for cadets. He was also taking insurance courses at night. Now he had a new brainstorm: innkeeper.

Mom was understandably torn. As a "true Christian on God's team," she knew God wanted her to encourage and support Daddy. But the cleaning! This was a thirty-room flophouse.

Daddy made a ridiculous low-ball offer of $23,000. No way they would take it, he figured. Mom committed the deal to the Great Realtor in the Sky and prayed all the way home: If God does not want us to have that place, they'll refuse the offer.

But He did, and they didn't—and Daddy got his thirty-room haunted house for twenty-three grand, paying cash from their savings. Considering it's probably worth fifty times that on a good real estate day now, it was an outrageously successful investment. But Rehoboth's never been about money. It's much more than that. It's become my parents' ministry, a true blessing in our lives.

In March we started to clean the place and it was so damp and cold we carried space heaters from room to room. But this was the coolest adventure we'd had in years. We aired the place out, scrubbed the walls and floors, and did some painting. Dad hired a handyman to rip up linoleum, install paneling, put in new wood floors, and rewire.

While renovating, Michie and I discovered a creaky old secret staircase with steps missing. It had been boarded up, but we tore down the boards and found that it led to a gabled loft with a small window. The plan was for us to live in the worst portion of the house and make the rest nice for guests. That loft became my bedroom. We called it the artist's room. I fixed it up, had my incense going, and listened to my albums. By Memorial Day weekend, 1967, Eppie's Rehoboth Inn was open for business.

The town derives its name from the biblical city on the Euphrates River. It was settled in the late 1800s as a Methodist Bible camp and seaside revival site. Mom and Dad truly believed the Lord had given them this inn to work for the Lord—by offering low group rates for church organizations. What they earned they poured back into upkeep and renovations.

Rehoboth was a 1960s melting pot of straight arrows who found God through faith and strung-outs who sought God through drugs and rock. I always seemed to be in life's none-of-the-above group. I remember one Friday night after we had done some cleaning, Mom was pooped and wanted to go get some ice cream and stroll along the boardwalk. "Sure, just let me get cleaned up," I said. Now, the boardwalk on Friday nights was all denim and long hair for both sexes. My mom could never tell the boys and girls apart—from behind, anyway. So I put on this little sundress with ruffles at the top and bottom, pulled my long silky straight hair back in a ponytail and went walking.

Minutes later two blue-jeaned cuties sashayed by, snapping their gum and sneering at me with a vicious "Get a load a Miss Priss over here" look. Mom was so furious I was sure she was going to head back to the inn and go after them with her flyswatter. She hurt so bad for me. "Forget it, Mom. I don't care." I shrugged. "I'm going to be me no matter what anybody says." And I meant it.

Rehoboth drew another group every summer that had neither pot nor piety on their minds—only water: wave-worshipping surfers a few miles down the coastline. Yancy's people.

My parents couldn't fail to notice the surfers with their beat-up old cars, smooth tanned bodies, baggy jams, platinum locks, and surfboards. They had one word for them: "dangerous."

Michie and I saw the same guys and had our own word for them: "perfect."

Each seemed more dangerous—more perfect—than the last one. But none was more perfect than Yancy.

Every summer, sun-bleached, sleek, and sinewy surfers from the Florida panhandle city of Pensacola drifted north to Rehoboth to escape the Gulf's killer heat and dead surf. The inlet boasted the best summer waves in the East—and the best-looking boys we'd ever seen. Michie and I risked sunstroke and skin cancer just to watch them on their boards. We'd awake before sunrise and get picked up at the inn to ride down to the inlet ten miles away and watch them surf until 10:00 A.M., when the lifeguards would come and ban the boards. If the surf was flat we'd hang out with them at the surf shop and talk, try to impress them, flip our hair all around—anything to make them never want to live without us.

When the day was done, Michie and I were done up and ready, waiting at a particular spot on the rickety old boardwalk until we saw white hair coming toward us. Then we'd cruise the bright, teeming boardwalk and Funland Amusement Park or sit and eat lemon ice and watch the parade of people go by.

I had been hanging out with a guy named Brad English. Brad was from Pensacola and he kept talking about the imminent arrival of Yancy, one of the top Gulf surfers. Yancy was their guru.

On July 4, 1969, I met him: "Hello, Kathryn. I'm Yancy." I almost fainted. There was this tall, gorgeous angel with the most mellow sea-blue eyes and a halo of blond ringlets framing his bronzed face. I smelled the salt water on his skin. This was *it!* I fell desperately, instantly in love. He was nineteen. I was fifteen, going on sixteen. *And they call it puppy lo-o-o-ove.* . . .

Yancy came from a different world. His parents had divorced when he was little. It was clear his main priority in life was surf, not school. I could forgive him that. In fact, I could have forgiven Yancy anything. But, like a mirage off the water, Yancy blew out of town the next day. Then he came back, twice. I was crazy for him. My heart never stopped pounding when we were together that first summer.

I spent my junior year daydreaming. I pictured Pensacola in winter, marking time till Memorial Day. Phone calls were too costly for us so we stayed in touch with swooning, romantic letters—sweet, innocent, nakedly poetic, nakedly ungrammatical. I had to hide the letters from my father. He said, "I'm not going to allow you to be with illiterates." I didn't care.

It was a miracle that I kept my average up. I had won the Superintendent's Award for scholarship and citizenship the year before, but I dreaded those awards assemblies. When I won I was way up in the balcony. I had on a really cute dress and it was the hottest day of the year. That trip from the balcony to the stage was the longest trip of my life. Not because of the heat. Because of the *pits!* The *stains!* I had armpit stains so large that dress should have been sent to hang in the Museum of Natural History. Those armpit rings could have fit around Saturn!

Worse, the guy who was handing out the award was an incredibly cute and perfect-looking senior. I was really attracted to him. He was one of the school's most popular leaders and a great-looking guy. This was right before the summer when things really got going with Yancy. Of course, that senior wouldn't give me the time of day—but he had to give me this award, with my sticky pits. And then he asked me out on a dinner date in Annapolis—and my parents let me go! I was fifteen. I couldn't believe my parents did that. I couldn't believe how much serious underarm protection I walked out with.

And what I *really* needed was a boxer's mouthguard. He dared to kiss me—and it was the worst kiss imaginable. Teeth against teeth and a sound track of growls and grunts. He had perfect teeth—and all of them were gnashing and grinding against mine. This was shocking. We're talking Enamel Hell here. Two automobile grilles mangled in a head-on. I figured he'd know all the right moves, be smooth and tender and seductive. Poor guy.

In my competitiveness and activities at Bowie High I was much more like Davy than Michie. He was Mr. Everything: great baseball player, top student, real popular. And always my great protector. We never bickered. He was my big brother in the sweetest sense, which is what Frank was to me when I first met him. Maybe that's why I loved the relationship so much. I had already had it, in a sense, with Davy. If somebody gave me a hard time at school, my brother would find him and beat him up.

But when it came to schoolwork, Michie just didn't care as much as I did, and as a result I always felt my parents had stiffer standards for me. I was a goody-goody; she was more defiant. I was on advanced placement tracks, but she knocked people out when she sang in school musicals. If I had the star temperament, Michie was happy to hide in the background. I was an extrovert with a flair for mimickry; Michie kept things much more to herself—a trait, we realized, that contributed to the medical crisis that would nearly kill her a decade later. But despite our differences and petty rivalries— and apart from a period in my senior year when we grew estranged —we were always the best of friends. If Michie privately resented going through the school system behind Mr. Everything and Little Goody Two-Shoes, I understood why.

Mom and Dad didn't ask for perfection, only our best. Daddy always said, "We love you too much to deny you the privilege of making mistakes."

Still, we weren't likely to usurp that privilege. Only Davy really made a whopper, and that was after he graduated from high school in late 1968. For three days life stood still for us because we didn't know if he was dead or alive.

Davy had enrolled in a Navy ROTC program at Miami University in Ohio. But he just didn't go for the uniform and the regulations so he bailed out. He took his newspaper route savings of $500 and flew to San Francisco, where he was to meet a high school friend who was working on a merchant ship. "Shipping out" was a cool, hippie-ish way to see the world and discover the Ultimate Truth. My parents thought he was nuts.

Davy could be combative and argumentative. But now all of a sudden he had become rude and uncommunicative. It was a total transformation. Now I know it was a normal rebellion, but at the time it was devastating to all of us as a family.

Poor Davy found that the ultimate truth was traveler's checks. He was promptly rolled and ripped off at the San Francisco airport. He was so embarrassed he couldn't bring himself to call home. He tried hitchhiking down the West Coast—and we learned all this long afterward—but the Santa Cruz police picked him up because a local law banned hitchhiking. They let him go, but Davy put his stuff in a bus depot locker and took off again—for San Diego.

For several dark days, we assumed he was dead. All I remember was the round-the-clock vigil by the phone, staring at each other, crying, and praying. Neighbors came and went. When Mom can't cook, you know she's in bad shape. We fasted and prayed.

My parents labeled that period of my brother's life "Davy's lost years." They were totally traumatized by the change in their baby who was now a young man searching for answers.

Almost a week later a postcard addressed to Dave arrived from the Santa Cruz police. It seemed to confirm our worst fears: "We have your suitcase. Please come and identify it or send someone to identify it and we will see that you get it."

But then we got a bizarre call from a ham radio operator in Bethesda. He'd received a ham message from Dave, who asked him to relay it: "I'm fine. Camp Pendleton, San Diego. Can't call."

Davy was in Marine Corps boot camp! Had he lost his mind?

"Oh, God, here we go," Daddy said. He knew that if Dave had had trouble with ROTC, Marine Corps grunt material he wasn't.

Davy put himself through boot camp. They insulted him, called him slime, gave him bayonet lessons. My brother, the cold trained killer! He got into disciplinary trouble and wound up in the brig; briefly, like Dad, went AWOL; and was sent for psychological evaluation. Then they tried to retrain him.

But at home we had no clue. It was a nightmare.

Mom's church friends held special prayer meetings. Retired CPO Epstein snapped into action, phoning Camp Pendleton every day at noon, demanding updates, warning them not to screw this kid up. "He's just green as grass," Mom said, sighing, resigned to the Lord's will and having visions of a firing squad at dawn. "If they send that boy to Vietnam," Daddy'd say, "he's gonna get somebody killed." Daddy's real fear was that Davy would be killed in the brig.

The Marine Corps discharged Davy in April 1969. Something *did* happen to him in the brig that transformed his life. Terror-stricken and sleepless, he began reading the New Testament for comfort, for hope. This became a turning point. He kicked around a few colleges in Maryland for a year and a half and ultimately, in the fall of 1970, enrolled at Washington Bible College in Lanham, Maryland. Mom had been right all along. Davy was the one who became a pastor. He was truly touched by the hand of God.

By Memorial Day I was thinking more in terms of being touched by the hand of Yancy. Right on schedule, he rolled up from the Gulf, searching for the Endless Wave; I blew in from Bowie, coping with the Endless Want. He and the guys usually crashed on the floor of a surf shop. He rarely came up to town on his own. Michie and I marveled at their migrant way of life. We had never seen or known guys like this. They had no money and lived from hand to mouth. A paycheck seemed out of the question. Some got high. All of them were living mellow and perfectly free.

I was already about as straight as I could be; I didn't smoke or drink. These guys had bodies to die for; I was so self-conscious about my own that I refused to go to the beach without a cover-up. I'd inch *backwards* into the water before I'd let anyone watch me in a bathing suit.

At night Yancy would drive us back up to Rehoboth Beach and we'd hang out on the boardwalk eating lemon ice. That was about it. Even with thirty-odd rooms there was no sneaking around the inn. The innkeepers didn't like the idea that Yancy was four years older. Plus, I knew I could probably never make love with Yancy until we got married. No, not probably. Definitely.

The truth was, the love I felt for Yancy was never about sex and lust. Yancy had "been with" only one other girl, someone he had broken up with. I already felt married in my heart. He never pressured me sexually. And while there was a strong physical attraction, the real bond was a union of the spirit without being "religious." We just clicked. Sex changes everything between two people and there is something special—a sense of lingering mystery and innocence—about the love between two people when sex remains at the "what if" stage.

"Mystery" may be too mild a word. When it came to my understanding of my own sexuality, we're not exactly talking Masters and Johnson. I knew every boy had a "wing-wang" and every girl had a "pinky," but I didn't know from lust. I knew from romance. From walking in the sun together by the sea.

I didn't feel sexual until college—and I went to Oral Roberts University, where I assure you we did not sit around the dorm talking about sex. I'd wake up from an exquisitely romantic (but never physical) dream with a throbbing, tingling, orgasmic sensation—and figure, Hmmm, so *that's* what it's like. It was all so foreign to me. Not only was I out of the loop of lust; I was dutifully observing all the classic taboos about touching oneself. I just figured that the dreams were God's way of satisfying me until the real thing came along. But the sensation sure felt good.

Mom, of course, never told us sex was dirty. (We always had these talks with Mom, not Dad, around the bathtub, where we talked about everything.) Sex, she said, was pure and beautiful *if* (1) you were married and (2) you loved each other. I was raised to be a gift to my husband, plain and simple. There were no gray areas allowed, such as (3) pure and beautiful sex with someone to whom you were not married, (4) being married but having *boring* sex or *no* sex at all, or (5) married people having pure and beautiful sex when they're married not to each other but to two *other* people. Those possibilities were simply not a consideration.

Mom and Dad made it easy to grasp: the Bible says the marital bed shall be undefiled.

Even Yancy could not lower those biblical criteria. The closest I ever got to feeling the earth move with him was riding the bumper cars in Rehoboth at Funland. I had an almost total hands-off policy on petting. It was mostly deep kissing and easy listening. We even had our own love song, James Taylor's "Fire and Rain." But most importantly, Yancy respected my walk with the Lord and made me feel he truly treasured me for who I was.

By the time Labor Day arrived I was filled with dread. The sun, sand, and palm trees of Pensacola seemed a lifetime removed from the cold, clammy suburban Maryland winter. I wrote gushing letters and came alive only when a letter came back. I kept all his letters, scores of them, in a box. Every fairy tale, every cornball Broadway show tune, every James Taylor or Carole King lyric got rolled up into my insanely obsessive love for Yancy. All I saw was Yancy, me, and the sea.

Pullleeze! Throw-up time!

My parents suffered as their once laughing, smiling carefree little girl would sullenly hibernate for hours in her room with her stereo going. I turned to sweets for comfort, gaining weight and losing countless wonderful high school moments because of my sulky isolation. I *must have* been a drag because Mom actually *urged* me to go on dates just to crack my apathy. These dates were so immature, so boring and shallow—*so pale* next to my Golden Boy.

Then I got a letter that destroyed me, shattered my dream world. The one girl he had slept with was back in his life. I wallowed in bogus self-centered drama and self-pity. As a Christian I felt like a complete fraud. I had gone forward to Jesus but couldn't accept any discomfort or sacrifice. I was a self-righteous Penelope Purity. I wanted instant happiness.

I grew cynical. "If this is Christianity," I moaned to Mom, "you can have it!" My mother was furious: I was a fair-weather Christian. She ordered me to my knees to praise Jesus. "Thank You, God, for all the lousy things You let happen to me," I said. "I'm so grateful for being miserable."

Sarcasm was a mistake. Mom was now glowering over me—and I came around. "Please forgive me, Jesus, for not trusting You. I need Your help, and I cannot make it without Your strength." And I believed that.

Winter faded into spring as my junior year ended, but I couldn't wait for Memorial Day. Yancy, who has gone on to become a major surfing promoter and entrepreneur, had come up for some surfing business. For once I wanted something so badly I broke the rules to have it. I played *hooky!* SHOCKING, right, Reege?

I left school in the morning, claiming I was sick with a cold. At lunchtime a senior named Mike decided to stop by the house and see if I was okay. Mike was a wrestler whom I had dated now and then and who was interested in me. Suddenly Mike was also interested in my health. I was fine, thank you very much, Mike; by then I was in Rehoboth. I had ridden there with friends in a convertible. I wanted to look gorgeous for Yancy. But it was a cold, rainy spring day and I looked like a ratty dishrag with wet, stringy, windblown hair in a schmatte tied around my head. And my lips were chapped.

"Is Kath okay?" Mike asked Mom.

"Sure," she said, concerned. "But she's in school."

"No, she isn't," Mike said. "She went home sick."

One day in my life I play hooky, and some guy I'm not even interested in blows my cover! It took them about ten seconds to find me by phoning the surf shop. I just thought, Oh, boy, my butt is baked now. I caught hell. That's the kind of teenager I was.

Rebel Without a Cold.

Life is so funny. Mike always seemed angry to me, but he was cute.

My mom really liked him a lot and always hoped Mike and I'd be a serious little item. After my Yancy dramas she wanted me to find a nice boy to go out with at my own school.

Years later Mike got a five-year sentence for conspiring to blow up an abortion clinic.

I was turning into a regular *problem child*. I once sneaked out a window at night with a girlfriend—after persuading my freaked-out sister to cover for me—to hang out with Yancy and the other surfers at the surf shop. Every creak in the place made Michie sweat bullets. And I did it only to prove I was cool, not hot. I proved it. I lay on the floor with the surfers, legs and arms pressed in, staring straight up at the ceiling, scared to death. Every time car headlights shone in the darkness I froze in panic. Miraculously my parents slept hard that night and we were out of there and home by dawn.

My brother and father did once nail Yancy and me as we walked the boardwalk. I had blown the 11:00 P.M. martial-law curfew when they caught up to us. Maybe it was close to midnight. My heart jumped into my throat when I noticed two shadowy figures behind us. "Oh, my goodness, Yancy, walk fast!" But they caught up and Daddy tore into us like I'd never seen. I was destroyed. He told Yancy he was no longer welcome in our house. He screamed and screamed. It was irrational. I thought for a second they would beat Yancy to a pulp.

Compared to that kind of romance and drama, school was a bore. I had no idea what lay ahead. By my senior year I felt a bit lost at school. I was full of contradictions: I was the captain of the cheerleaders, but I didn't sleep with the starting backfield; an Honor Society student who was rarely inspired by teachers and schoolwork; a high achiever who had no desire to go to a top university. If I had any career notions it was to get a degree in French and teach—in Florida—*avec* Yancy.

The truth was, I *was* sort of weird. My straight hair at one point fell nine inches below my waist. And it wasn't exactly hip that my mother taught me to sew all my own clothes. When everyone else was doing drugs to Hendrix, I did needlepoint, tons of it, to Streisand. I also made paper roses with wire and tissue paper. They were gorgeous works of art and we sold them to boutiques. My sister and I always had to leave parties early, when other people were still arriving. My parents never trusted boys who asked me out. Not that they were beating down the door, but if they tried, they'd only run into the Ogre.

And while my parents spoke of unconditional love—"the Excellent Way"—I felt repressed. The four-letter word I hated most was "mold," as in, "We've got to *mold* you." That drove me crazy. I'd say, "How dare you try to mold me? I am my own person. God made us all different." They weren't control freaks, but they made no apologies for our strict upbringing. It was "yes, ma'am," and "no sir." We couldn't be "sloppy" in our attitudes.

I sure wasn't sloppy when it came to boys. They knew where I stood. They could *read* my lips, but that was about all they could do with them. One kid tried to French-kiss me when I was in ninth grade and it was about the most disgusting thing imaginable. This was before Yancy, of course. When I told my girlfriends they all said, "Oh, yuck, he did *that? How awful!* Poor girl!" And then I walked away and they probably trashed the Big Prude behind her back. I sometimes suspected they just saw me as a big joke.

Then my mother would say: "Well, Kath, the boys respect you."

Yeah, great! And I was thinking: *A little less respect and a little more action, all right?* Can I tell you how tired of respect I was getting?

The Ogre had no problem dressing down any guys who came calling if they didn't pass muster. Pity the poor date who'd honk from the curb. If one of us started flying downstairs, Daddy would block us and say, "Whoooaaa, young lady. Back upstairs. If that's your boy out there tooting his horn for you, he's come to the wrong house." Any gentleman, according to Dad, would walk to the door and ring the bell. We were mortified by the Ogre who, to this day, loves to boast, "I volunteered for the job, and I was the best Ogre I knew how to be."

I clung proudly to my virginity when most other girls were in a race to lose theirs. I went to two baby showers before I went to my senior prom. I was religious when "Lord" was a four-letter word to many young people. I valued excellence in classes when most of my peers were figuring out ways to cut them. I cared deeply about my family when it was hip to denounce your parents as Establishment turkeys. I tried to heal Vietnam vets when my friends were calling them killers. I didn't feel that people understood me or my way of life. I felt set apart.

Winning the Bowie Junior Miss Pageant didn't exactly help. At the beginning of senior year my English teacher recommended I enter the contest. Yeah, right. When she half jokingly said she'd fail me if I didn't enter, I asked her where to sign up.

I won. I was shocked. Didn't I have enough problems already? You couldn't get any uncooler than winning a local pageant.

Actually, you could. You could win the state. Which I did, but not before visiting Yancy in Pensacola.

One night in the fall Yancy called with the welcome news that his efforts to patch things up with that other girl somewhere in the Midwest had failed. When he was driving back to Florida after a heavy rainstorm, he told me, the sky opened up, sunlight streamed down out of the dark skies and "Fire and Rain" magically came on the radio. This was the miracle I had prayed for.

We discussed getting engaged over the holidays in Pensacola, with plans to marry after graduation. I was in heaven. My parents smelled heartache. They trusted me—though Mom called Yancy's mom five times to check on all the room arrangements and then offered a classic send-off. "Don't give it away," she said. "A boy, if he gets what he wants, will just move on to the next thing. The Lord has so much in store for you if only you'll wait on Him."

"I've been strong before, Mom," I assured her, "and I'll be strong at Christmas."

Not! Yancy met me at the airport on December 27, 1970, with a meek smile and kiss on the cheek. I felt awkward and we weren't even out of baggage claim yet. Where was that Pensacola sun? It was pouring and dreary. We got in his beat-up VW convertible and drove to a secluded spot near a bridge over the gray, choppy Gulf. Where was James Taylor when I needed him? I saw rain; I didn't see fire. Instead, the station was playing Stephen Stills's "Love the One You're With" as rain slashed across the windshield and waves pounded the shoreline.

"Kathryn," he said so sweetly, "I'm so glad you're here." I started to echo his sentiments, but before I could say anything he interrupted me. "Because having you down here has made me realize how much I love Pam."

Pam? *Pam?* She wasn't even the one he'd visited in Wichita. *Who was Pam?*

I was in shock. And Stephen Stills was singing "If you can't be with the one you love, love the one you're with." Perfect. My stomach felt hammered and my lungs went airless. She was someone he had met weeks earlier, he told me. He didn't know exactly *how* he felt anymore, but seeing me had "clarified things." *Clarified?* I'll say. How about "nullified"?

I was so stunned by the unreality of this turnaround that I stayed the whole week. He wasn't malicious and I wasn't angry. I thought he was being duped by sex, that he was in torment now and that my love was being tested. I was just going to keep on loving him. The spirit versus the flesh.

"Yancy, I can't believe I'm losing you," I sobbed.

"You can't lose something you never had," he answered. That *really* helped.

"Okay, Yance. You're right. One can't own another human being. I wish you happiness. That's all I ever wanted for you."

Yeah, right. He'll be back, I bet privately.

So Yancy spent time with Pam and I spent time with Yancy's mom, who had remarried. I adored her. I learned that my bitter rival was a pretty fifteen-year-old blonde with lots of personal problems. She was much more "worldly" than I was—in so many ways!

How was a Bowie Junior Miss supposed to compete with *that?*

His mom wanted us to work it out. Yance, she explained, was intimidated by me, felt he could never measure up to my standards. The way he was going, I must say she had a point there. But even I was getting sick of my saintliness by now and I felt more inclined to lose my virginity to get the man I loved. I was confused and afraid.

On New Year's Eve Yancy's mom gave a little party in my honor. It was now or never for me. We all enjoyed a little Purple Passion punch, but I wanted to be in control to make my move. By midnight I was toasting the New Year on Yancy's lap.

Soon we were talking alone in the bedroom he shared with his brother, John, who is now a minister. We got about as far as prone on his bed as I felt myself filling up with heart-pounding anticipation.

And then, with no warning, something happened. His mother burst into the room without knocking: "Yancy," she screamed, "don't you do anything you'll be sorry for." I sat up and rearranged my clothing. This family was just *full* of surprises.

I was in shock—and somewhat offended. "Doesn't your mom know the kind of girl I am?" I asked Yancy.

He laughed. "Yes, and she wants you to *stay* that way!"

"Good night, Kathryn," he said as he directed me toward my sofa bed in the den.

Manhandled in the Panhandle, I finally had to cut my losses and get on home.

As I prepared for Maryland's Junior Miss pageant, I fasted and prayed in the dark. I waited for word from Yancy that he was mine all over again. Then the letter came. My prayers were *answered!*

WRONG. It was from his sister, with the devastating news that Yancy was marrying Pam in the spring. For once I felt life just might not be worth living. I felt abandoned not so much by Yancy as by

God. I had trusted God, waited for a miracle. I pounded my head against the wailing wall of my bedroom.

Somehow I won Maryland Junior Miss, sweeping the poise and appearance, physical fitness, judges' interview, and talent categories. As I was crowned, I thought: This is bizarre. Are there no other talented, intelligent people on this earth? As I walked the victory runway my crown of laurel leaves slipped down over my forehead and rested on my nose. Perfect!

Unfortunately, it was Michie who was slightly off-balance through all the Yancy and pageant stuff. Not surprisingly, by the time she was in high school she was, as she says, "marked." The baby sister act was wearing thin. She was tired of being protected by me, though my approval was always very important to her. So she started pushing my parents' buttons. And mine. She rebelled. She smoked. She needed to blaze her own trail and seek her own identity. Once, in an attempt to hide her smoking from my parents, she chewed on pine needles before coming home from a party. She was a terrible liar and always got caught when she defied my parents. She got bumped from cheerleading when she pulled a D in some class. She tried modeling at the urging of friends but was crushed by turndowns. I bounced back from that kind of rejection; she caved in.

Michie was eventually voted Bowie's Homecoming Queen, most popular, most talented—all of it. She did great work in musicals like *Carousel* and *The Music Man*, and she was a tremendous athlete, especially in tennis, with her long legs and arms. But she didn't work as hard on her schoolwork, and her grades showed it. After Davy, once the Belair Boys Club Boy of the Year, and "Little Miss Everything," as she'd sometimes sniff, she now had to deal with my self-absorbed obsession with Yancy and the Junior Miss application, making the gown, honing the talent act. Michie just began to feel lost in the shuffle at home. She internalized a lot of her anger and resentment and never opened up to Mom and Dad as Davy and I did.

I was so immersed in the national Junior Miss pageant by then that I didn't notice. On the questionnaire I was asked "What women do you most respect and emulate?" I answered Indira Gandhi, Golda Meir, and Anita Bryant—two prime ministers and an orange juice pitchwoman. I did admire Anita. She was a gifted Christian entertainer. She had a great image. She loved singing; she loved her husband, loved her kids, loved Jesus, and loved o.j. And, I later discovered, she was co-hosting the America Junior Miss show with Ed McMahon for NBC.

I got to Mobile in late April of 1971 for the ten-day pageant. There was great camaraderie and none of the cutthroat insecurity of a real beauty pageant where boobs and buns count for everything. Half of the fifty girls were born-again Christians.

If the battle between spirit and flesh needed the perfect metaphor, the pageant provided it. In a bizarre twist of fate—and the knife—Yancy and Pam were getting married on April 30 in Pensacola, forty miles away on the day of my all-important judges' interview.

I tried hard to focus. Anita introduced herself to all the girls and signed copies of her new book, *Mine Eyes Have Seen the Glory*. I worked hard on my talent act: a dramatic a cappella rendition of the old Negro spiritual "Go Down, Moses." And if that didn't go down well, reading a poem about slavery that I wrote myself would have to get them. Anita later told me she had heard me in rehearsal from outside the hall and turned to her husband and manager, Bob Green. "Oh, listen," she said. "They finally got a black girl in the pageant." Right. The one from Bowie.

I wore a blue peasant-style gown with a giant cross around my neck. I belted out the spiritual with gut-busting drama. I knew somewhere out in the audience my mother was pressing her palms over her ears at the big finish: "Tell old Pharaoh, Let my people go."

Then, on the night of April 30, it was time to let my Yancy go. I also let the pageant go. I totally blew the interview, made a fool of myself, broke down and cried before the judges, including Celeste Holm and Mary Ann Mobley. Case closed. I blathered on about what was happening. These were judges, not shrinks. But how could I sit there knowing Yancy was getting married to Pam less than forty miles away?

It gets worse. I later found out that at the time of the interview, while I was losing in love, I was leading in overall points. I had already won the Kraft Hostess competition, by planning a "Hang Ten Luau" theme party. My invitations had "hang ten" toes; I made a casserole decorated with ili ili lava rocks.

But I got so excited I ran up to spread the news to a young kid I had met who was there to sing on the show. I later found out that I had been spotted violating a pageant rule—talking to a boy!—and *had been officially disqualified*. Pulll-eeeze!

So Pam walked off with Yancy, Miss New Jersey walked off with the crown, and I walked off with $1,500 in scholarship prize money from Kraft—and a *fabulous* recipe for a dream that was now receding, along with Yancy, forever.

Out Here on My Own

I was asked all kinds of personal questions throughout the three Junior Miss pageants by judges, sponsors, competitors, and friends. Bob Green was making polite, almost trivial, conversation with me just before airtime in Mobile. He asked what I planned to do after high school. I had no idea my casual answer would determine the course of my life over the next three years.

I would travel to the Holy Land with my mom in June, I told him—Dad's graduation present. Then maybe I'd work at Disney World. Finessing the answer seemed better than admitting that I had applied to two Florida schools and planned my life around a surfer boy named Yancy who, as luck would have it, was *getting married* in a couple of days to somebody named Pam!

"Perfect!" Bob said. He grabbed my hand and hurried me backstage to his wife's dressing room. "Anita," he said, "the Lord has answered our prayers. We've got our baby-sitter for Israel!"

It turned out that Bob and Anita and my mother and I were by sheer coincidence going to attend the same ten-day Jerusalem Conference on Biblical Prophecy. Over the years my mom has become a self-taught biblical scholar. She devoured two or three books a week on the Holy Land and its history, archaeology, and anthropology. Her own Bible has handwritten notes on just about every page. So she was in her glory traipsing over the astonishing ruins of Jericho and Caesarea in 110-degree heat, kneeling and weeping beside me in the dank and sacred Garden Tomb where, it is believed, Jesus was resurrected.

I was also Anita and Bob's Holy Land nanny for their two older children, Gloria and Bobby. I had a blast when I was on my own with the kids, and Bob and Anita honored me generously with a sterling silver Crusader's Cross.

When I returned to Rehoboth that summer I ran into Yancy. I started to tell him about my trip to Israel, but he stopped me. "I know, Kathryn, I believe now." He and Pam had gone forward at Rock Church in Virginia Beach and accepted the Lord. The summer became a deeply spiritual time for us, as we spent many days and evenings together singing hymns and reading Scripture.

Toward the end of the summer Anita called out of the blue. "Bob and I haven't been able to get this off our minds," she said. "We want you to live and work with us. The Lord just hasn't given us a minute's peace over this."

My new home, Villa Verde, was a magnificent Spanish-style mansion in Key Biscayne, with tiled roofs, tropical gardens and palms, a boat docked on the bay, a pool, a sun-drenched terrace, and a dazzling view of Miami over Biscayne Bay. I lived in a little guest apartment over the office, which was a converted garage. Bob and Anita made me part of their family and wanted to groom me for a career in Christian entertainment. I adored their twins, Barbara and Billy, who were two and a half.

I did get plenty of warmth from their family. But I also underestimated how homesick I'd feel—and how brutal my office routine would be. I did everything, from making complex travel arrangements to organizing press clippings, from baby-sitting to grocery shopping and car-pooling. If Anita needed me on the road with her, I jumped. When she shot spots for the Florida Citrus Commission I was sometimes her stand-in for blocking shots and lighting. I'd be out there for hours in a citrus grove in killer heat with wilting, stringy hair and the bugs while she was being pampered in the air-conditioned trailer, practicing her big o.j. pitch: "It's not just for breakfast anymore."

Eventually I was singing gospel hymns on weekends and taking college courses at night. It was overwhelming, until then the hardest year of my life. I was used to running outside to buy ice cream when I heard the Good Humor man. I was used to having people in the house all the time. I went from a free-spirited loving home to a very controlled environment with all sorts of keys around my neck. A lot of my friends were at college having normal fun lives, and I was taking care of four kids and helping to run a major business.

I smiled through the day and called home at night, sobbing about how lonely and heartsick I was. But my parents were hard-liners: I had made a commitment for a year, and that was that.

I came to feel there was a strange sadness behind the sunny facade, some trouble lurking in Paradise. Anita and Bob seemed sealed off by their opulence, their electronic alarms and stone gates. Anita wrote books, sang "The Battle Hymn of the Republic" at the funerals of famous Americans like Lyndon Johnson, and performed in Vietnam with Bob Hope. But she had never heard of Elton John. Compounding their naïveté and isolation was an arrogance in Bob Green I sometimes found shocking. They still clung to the notion that Anita Bryant was not only the greatest singer in the world but just maybe the *only* singer in the world. Not Ella Fitzgerald. Not Mary Travers. Not Carole King. Everyone else was just faking it. I was appalled when they told me they didn't think Barbra Streisand could sing. To me she was pure genius. I'd just say, "Are you kidding me?"

I was there to learn the ropes, but these ropes felt more like a noose. I ended up learning more about what not to do with my life. I was helped in ways I never anticipated.

My adjustment to show "business" wasn't smooth. Bob could be discourteous to people and that broke my heart. I was raised to be polite and truthful to everyone. It was difficult when Bob urged me to yell at ticket agents or hotel clerks on the phone; winning through intimidation was never my game. I was asked to make up stories to people he wanted to avoid and to sign Anita's autograph on fan mail and photos. He shielded her from bad news, told her only the good. Maybe he felt that was necessary to her survival, but it only made me want to escape.

Sometimes you could cut the tension between them with a knife. I believed that Bob, who had quit his career as a Miami DJ to run Anita's recording career, resented his wife's fame and her role as the breadwinner. True, he loved the perks that came with the success he clearly helped engineer. But society tells us the man is in control, the man pays the bills. Perhaps he saw it as emasculating to be the force behind the scenes. I wasn't sure.

But Bob also had another, sweeter side, too. He was without a doubt a devoted and loving father and son; he took excellent care of his own mom and dad, who lived nearby. And he openly professed his love for Anita. But I saw more tension than tenderness—and almost none of the lusty teasing I witnessed at home. I never saw displays of warmth—no kissing, no calling each other "darling." In my home, Dad would playfully pat Mom's bottom or even fondle her breasts when he thought no one was looking. Mom would giggle or feign disapproval by growling, "Oh, Ep!" But we knew she loved every minute of it. The Greens' home was a business. Bob was Anita's manager. I felt sad for their children because they would never have a wide-open Grand Central Station home like mine.

Anita needed plenty of attention from men. Her father had married and divorced her mom twice before Anita was a teenager. If she had an ingrained distrust of men, she also longed for their affection. Yet she saw most men as takers, I felt, as weak. I had the feeling she did not have a lot of respect for her husband, and that was a big conflict for her.

She was a gorgeous, sexy woman, a former Miss Oklahoma and second runner-up in the 1959 Miss America pageant. She still had one of the greatest bodies going. She was years older than I was and hers was a lot better than mine. Men went nuts when she sang "Tumblin' Tumbleweed" in her adorable little cowgirl outfit, and yet she was saddled with this public image as a righteous prude. She was the antithesis of a '90s star like Madonna, but in person her mix of wholesomeness and sexiness did the trick. Men found that look devastating. Anita was also a tremendous flirt with an earthy, almost risqué sense of humor and a hearty laugh.

I always thought if Anita had been more comfortable with her own vibrant, humanness she'd have been a happier woman.

Anita cared enormously about being the best Christian mother and wife she could be. There was never a hint of infidelity on her part. I saw her as a very sexual, sensual woman in her prime. I was never there in the bedroom, but you *know* when you see a woman who is sexually satisfied. There's a relaxation about knowing you're loved. But I didn't sense that connection was there for her with a husband who often put her down so badly at home. It would break my heart because she really longed for love.

Anita would get a little jealous because Bob paid me generous compliments and plenty of attention even though I was nowhere near as attractive or sexy as she was. I was eighteen and fun to be around. I wasn't threatening; Anita was a big star. Her career went from crisis to crisis. So there were times when Bob and I would just be screaming over some joke or craziness in the office. And Anita would walk in and feel she wasn't in on it. Also, the kids loved me, I doted on them, and, because of the gospel shows, people were referring to me as the new Anita Bryant. The Greens were, in my view, living a lie for the sake of Anita's career, for their position in the Southern Baptist community—and, perhaps understandably, for the children they unquestionably loved and wanted to protect.

If I saw more of their lives than I bargained for, it was probably because I had no life of my own. I signed up for night courses in music and drama at Miami Dade Community College just to get out of the house. I went on three dates that whole year. And they were with my handsome grillework kisser from high school, who was in college down there, but there were no more head-on wrecks for *me*. Despite this unhappiness, Anita did inspire and guide me. She helped me with my breathing and singing and she was generous and unfailingly thoughtful. At Christmas she and Bob overwhelmed me with gifts, from clothes to souvenirs from their road trips. That side of Anita was wonderful and nurturing.

And she lived up to her mentor role. Bob ran a gospel booking agency called Fishers of Men Opportunities. If Anita wasn't available for a particular date, Bob recommended me in her place. My first job was in Tampa. I was hired to "testify" and sing before several thousand Baptists in an auditorium. From the way my knees shook before taking the stage, you'd have thought this was the Kingdome or Carnegie Hall. I got it together, though, and earned a gracious standing ovation—as tears streamed down my face.

Bob booked me into Southern Baptist churches all over the Southeast and I started getting paid. And known. Once, before a church performance, I was in the ladies' room with two women who thought they were alone. One said, "I'm really anxious to hear this gal sing. She's the new Anita Bryant, you know."

Anita, who might have seen herself getting a little older, wasn't always thrilled by such comments. Nor was I. I was flattered, but I also thought: I don't want to be the new Anita Bryant, or the new *anybody*. I just want to be me.

And, more and more, I just wanted to be home. The months dragged on. My culture shock never wore off. I was exposed to all sorts of novel experiences. There was, for instance, the pulpit-pounding, fire-and-brimstone style of the Greens' Southern Baptist preacher, Brother Bill Chapman. I came to dread those two hours on Sunday morning and afterward I always asked Anita for two extra-strength Tylenols. Brother Bill was an incredible orator, but through all his fiery, hypnotic exhortations I saw how a charismatic leader could use the pulpit more to instill a fear of God's wrath than to nurture God's love. So every Sunday members of his terrified flock would seek redemption for their sins. They really wore out that carpet walking up to the altar.

I wanted to grow in my walk with Jesus and I didn't feel I could grow there. I eventually saw many of those fire-breathing "brothers" who got off on how many souls they could save each week, how high attendance was in Sunday school, how much money they raised for the building fund, how many missionaries they had in the field. It was quantity over quality. And they seemed more intent on keeping people submissive by getting them saved and in a state of remorse and repentance every week than in teaching them how to live successful Christian lives in an un-Christian world. That's what church should be about: becoming a better, evolving, maturing Christian, not just keeping you a vulnerable, needy baby in Christ. These power-tripping preachers thrive on that. They have no stake in you growing up and becoming confident and secure because that would weaken their influence.

One friend of theirs who *did* have a very specific self-help program was Marabel Morgan. She and her lawyer husband, Charlie, lived nearby and were close friends. Marabel, a stunning and very feminine woman, became, of course, the "Total Woman" woman. She held seminars back then that formed the basis for her controversial best-seller a few years later. A Total Woman would greet her husband at the door at day's end (a career would only interfere with a TW's housekeeping and mothering chores) wrapped in Saran Wrap and offer him a martini. TW was a backlash against the 1970s feminist cry for sexual equality. Marabel unapologetically espoused marriage and old-fashioned values: "Find joy and fulfillment in serving others, particularly your husband."

And I listened. I became something of a TW myself (but without the Saran Wrap) when I first married.

But I felt happiest and most secure in the children's world. The highlight of my year was when Michie flew down to help me with Anita's Bible camp for girls in Boca Raton. Some of these kids were dropped off in Rolls-Royces. We housed them in an old motel with bunk beds. It was not your average camp. We had swimming, tennis, and accepting Jesus Christ as the Messiah.

Michie taught the girls everything she knew how to do—tennis, cheerleading, diving, swimming. There was also a Total Girl class on hair and grooming. Some of the kids' families belonged to exclusive clubs and worked with the top tennis pros in America, but at Bibletown the girls learned from my nationally unranked—but very game—sister. Poor Michie just wilted in the 100-degree Miami heat. But with their families gone and the pressure off them, the kids had a ball. We were always coming up with new stuff. I'd run past Michie, who'd ask me where I was off to. "I'm on my way to tumbling."

"*Tumbling?* Now we're tumbling?"

At night the kids would march in and say, "Come draw my bath and turn down my bed." Yeah, right. Was it *that* hard for them to grasp the difference between a camp counselor and a maid?

On the last night we put on a variety show and dinner for the parents. We created costumes and skits, and we let the kids roll around, get dirty, and make fools of themselves. They absolutely loved it.

But not even the buoyant Christian facade could fully protect me from the strains I felt at Villa Verde. I was anxious to leave and get on with my life. My parents knew I was part of the lie—what I see now as a dysfunctional lack of love and communication—and didn't want me there any longer.

One Sunday just days before my nineteenth birthday in August, I was typing in the office and Anita walked in. She was crying. "The kids and I don't want you to leave," she said. "But I know you want to go to school."

"What are you talking about?" I said.

"I just spoke to Oral," she said.

"Oral? Oral who?"

"Oral Roberts." Anita and Bob had made some half joking references to his flamboyant Charismatic faith-healing tent revivals. They, like me, were Fundamentalists. I didn't know what to say. "And," she went on, "he says you can study at his university. They'll make the arrangements."

"He has a university?"

"In Tulsa. You start in two weeks."

I had been praying for something or someone to come in and intervene in my life, but *Tulsa* wasn't exactly what I had in mind. I should probably have resented Anita for laying this on me as a *fait accompli.* But she knew I was drifting and unhappy, and she had acted out of love. And frankly I was so glad to be rescued from Key Biscayne that I jumped at the idea of Tulsa.

Anita apparently had helped swing a full music scholarship for me if I was accepted as one of Oral's World Action Singers. The twelve-member group appeared in Oral's NBC specials and weekly Sunday programs, which were taped in L.A., and traveled to his revivals. Because there weren't any openings in the group so close to registration, I had to enroll and wait, using my $1,500 Kraft prize money to pay my own way until then. My parents were delighted: a college where you could actually study Christ for credit in courses like Holy Spirit I and II.

When I landed in Tulsa I thought I'd gotten off on the wrong planet. This was Zululand. Everyone was scurrying around the airport with Bibles tucked under their arms going "Praise the Lord, brother!" and "Hallelujah, sister!" And I was going: "How long do I have to stay here, Lord?"

The 500-acre campus of Oral Roberts University rose out of the flat Oklahoma plains like some futuristic biblical Disneyland. I didn't think I was going to last very long. The bus ride from the airport to school was, in a word, dismal. I was the straight one surrounded by grinning buck-toothed nerds with thick glasses, shiny suits, and skinny ties. It wasn't any better on campus. You heard "Hallelujah" and "Love ya, brother" in coffee shops, classrooms, the library and bookstore. Some of these girls looked like real ice princesses with their mid-calf skirts, thick glasses, sensible shoes, and hallelujahs. The place was Orwellian, with geeks, Bible thumpers, sexy studs, gays, preachers' kids, and farmers' daughters. I'd see a nerd with twenty little pencils who'd breathe hello on me with the world's worst halitosis and I'd want to say, "Praise the Lord, brother—now go floss and brush!"

Anita had sung on Oral's show, but she took strong issue with his faith-healing ministry. She was a staunch Fundamentalist while Oral was a fervent, hard-core Charismatic Christian. She just thought the World Action Singers could offer me a wonderful career opportunity.

I felt utterly lost, as if I'd gotten stuck in some rigid, repressive cult. I signed up for drama, but Chekhov and Ibsen were banned; their plays were considered dirty. In music class I had to sing Streisand's "People" with my hands clasped to my breast like Beverly Sills doing an aria. Drinking on campus was not just illegal; it was considered sinful. In my home we drank wine and beer, and my parents were two of the finest Christians on earth. So in protest I kept an unopened bottle of brandy in my closet.

Men were not allowed in the women's dorm rooms. Many of these students had come from strict born-again homes where "sex" was a dirty word. But it soon became clear to me that some of these horny kids were thumping a lot more than just Bibles at night.

The Holy Spirit courses were required and Oral taught them himself in a big auditorium. What could not be taught was speaking in tongues. One major difference, to oversimplify, between Fundamentalists and Charismatics is that Charismatics go beyond a literal interpretation of Scripture. They believe in certain "gifts of the Spirit" such as healing, being "slain by the Spirit," and receiving the gift of tongues. Though I was surrounded by veritable chatterboxes of the Spirit, that never happened for me. Nor was I ever "slain by the Spirit" at ORU. I never even got *mugged* by the Spirit. Once, in the presence of Kathryn Kuhlman in L.A., I was knocked back and felt myself falling without fear. Maybe I was being slain by the Spirit; maybe I tripped over Kathryn's chiffon gown. I don't know.

My roommate was fluent in "tongues." She was a sweet-tempered girl named Karen DeBartolo who came from a Charismatic Ohio family. Karen was a brilliant musician and played classical piano. We had some important common ground. Gifts of the Spirit weren't part of it. Karen was the most meticulous, regimented individual I'd ever seen. Her fanatical discipline only exaggerated my more emotional, spontaneous side. She called her boyfriend and parents at the same time every Sunday. Next to her I was a worldly, slothful sinner.

We roomed together for two years and remained good friends, but we will never agree on gifts of the Spirit. Karen and I once spent a weekend sharing the Lord through song at a church retreat for a large Charismatic fellowship of businessmen. There was much speaking in tongues, healing, and being slain by the Spirit. We testified and many people were touched and came to know the Lord. It was incredible. We could feel God's presence. The Holy Spirit was really moving. I was exhausted afterward. Some people gave up drugs; others were reunited with estranged spouses.

Getting into bed Sunday night, Karen looked at me and said, "Kathie, the Lord used you so much this weekend. Imagine what you could have accomplished if only you'd had the Holy Spirit!"

I thought I'd done all right as it was. I was shocked. I felt I already *had* the Holy Spirit in me. That wedge between us—between any Fundamentalist and any Charismatic—will never vanish.

In December I finally auditioned for, and got, an alto spot with the World Action Singers. A new transfer student from a small college in Iowa got the only available soprano spot. Her name was Jantina Jurriaans, and we became best friends. A stunning blonde of Dutch lineage with the wholesomeness of a USC Homecoming Queen, Jantina had traveled the world for a year with another Christian singing group. We probably clicked because I could say and spell her last name. Also, she was a knockout and she had style. We spoke the same language and it wasn't tongues. It was mostly just giving each other goony looks and going, "How did we end up here?" I had found ORU's only other "sinner" and a soul mate.

Once I became one of the Singers my life improved immediately. We were rarely on campus. The group spent seven weeks each semester on the road, most of it in L.A. (It was during one of our fall 1974 recording sessions in Hollywood that I met the good-looking gospel music composer and producer, Paul Johnson.) Jantina and I roomed together when we were on the road, and, as she was the sex symbol of the group, I babied this woman. She was the world's heaviest sleeper, so I'd get her up and serve her tea in bed every morning. Jantina lives for food and so we always went out for sun in the daytime and for dinner at night—and we did very little else.

The Singers also traveled with Oral to many of his revivals throughout the Bible Belt. I saw some pretty amazing—and disturbing—things out there as part of the faith-healing line. People would come through and we would touch them and pray for them after Oral ministered to them and asked for their financial contributions. They came past us on crutches and canes and in wheelchairs; the blind tapped white canes, and many were bald from chemotherapy. It was overwhelming to see so much suffering and need. I never felt anything but compassion for those hurting, hopeful, precious people who came looking for a miracle. I'd watch in amazement as Oral would place his palm on each person's forehead and praise God with great oratorical flair and spiritual intensity. The person would sink back, slain by the Spirit, and I'd hear the gibberish of speaking in tongues. I felt like an outcast.

I now know that it is in my nature to trust, to have faith. But I never liked anything taking control of me. I never thought the Charismatic way was bogus per se because it derives from the Bible. But I did sense manipulation. For every truth in this world there is a falsehood; for every reality, an illusion. I began examining my own walk with the Lord and concluded that I could speak in tongues up the wazoo or raise a million dollars on TV every day, but if I didn't treat my fellow human being with love in my heart, if I walked by a beggar and felt no compassion, if I cheated on my taxes, then I wasn't a Christian. First Corinthians 13 puts it far more eloquently: "If I speak with the voice of angels but have no charity, or love, then I am but a clanging cymbal." In that time of the new TV evangelists and the rise of the Moral Majority, I saw so many students and Christians slapping on their "I Found It" bumper stickers like trophies. But my feeling was if they didn't truly nurture love in their hearts for others then they hadn't taken a genuine walk with the Lord. The emphasis wasn't on being a godly person and having the true gifts of the Spirit such as forgiveness and tenderness and patience.

Instead, too many people seemed content with advertising the glory of Jesus on their bumpers and going for quick hits of Christian faith. You can't just say, "Well, I've got this one gift, so I'm covered." It's the gift of trusting and living out your faith that truly makes you a believer.

I am not saying I am a better Christian than anyone else, but that was a cynical phase in my life. I had seen the illusion of Anita's "Christian marriage." The Greens' faith was genuine, but there was an element of hypocrisy to it as well. Anita is the first to admit this today. But I began to see it again around Oral's Charismatic culture. I saw it in the marriage, which eventually ended in divorce, between Oral's son, Richard, and his wife, Patty. They were a gospel duo who often sang with us. They projected one image in public and yet didn't seem to want to be together in private. I would later see how that could happen in my own very public Christian show-biz marriage.

But my qualms went beyond people's personal lives. We heard stories about fakery and decoys at revivals, used to create the impression of a potent Holy Spirit present to kindle a fire that would spread among the susceptible. I never personally saw any trickery, but the stories were always there.

What I did see—not necessarily with Oral—was the "revival team" counting money afterward. They functioned like gymnastics spotters for those slain by the Spirit. They'd break your fall—and then rack up your dollars afterward. That made me sick. I had contracts to sing in churches and never got paid. There was a lot of "We'll pick up your air fare," and then I'd fly in for a service and never get reimbursed. And while I came across many wonderfully dedicated spirit-filled Christians, the few who got all the notoriety were—and remain—the con artists.

Oral had a great message for the masses but he could barely talk to anybody one on one. He couldn't meet your eye and have a conversation. That disturbed me. Oral lived in a mansion. His son Richard lived in a mansion. I didn't see people whose lives emulated the humble life of Christ. It's not that no one lives up to my perfect standards. I just didn't feel that I was in the presence of people who were committed in their hearts. I sensed—then and later on throughout the Christian movement of the 1970s—an unmistakable worship of money and power. With Oral, it was, Let's build an empire. Let's get people to give every dollar they can so we can buy that City of Faith and this prayer tower—all these monuments to the electronic egos of the new evangelists.

Billy Graham is different. He doesn't bombard people every five seconds for money; he devotes only one percent of his time to fund-raising.

But Oral would say, "Sow out of your need," meaning the more strapped you were financially, the more you should give—to prove your faith. You've got $500 in the bank? Prove your faith in God by giving $499. He raised millions each year—and the average donation was something like thirty-four cents. So he was appealing to millions of very needy people to balance out the ones who gave $100,000 and $1 million.

With travel and all the eye-opening revivals, it got tougher for me to sustain my interest in the school. There wasn't much time for a social life at ORU. Then again, I didn't exactly *need* time for one. I wasn't pursued. I hated my body. I was still pining for Yancy.

I did date a few ORU guys, but I didn't fall in love. One guy I liked a lot was a preacher's son and the wildest guy on campus. But even he didn't try anything, which was amazing. I stopped the stud dead in his tracks without a move. I think they were all terrified of me. If they'd taken me home, their dads would've taken one look and warned them: "You do anything to this sweet young child, I'll kill you." I was *such* a prude then. I don't know how anybody stood me, frankly. *No one* was going to knock me down a few pegs.

Nobody even took a shot. Nobody. I don't think I was an ice princess. I didn't think of myself as frigid. I was just non-negotiable. Absolutely non-negotiable.

But my future *was* up for grabs. I saw the need to make some major changes. Why go on and get a degree that would mean nothing to me? The biggest change would be to quit ORU and pursue a singing career. I felt my life was fast approaching a turning point. I was seized by a profound need to take stock of where I'd been and what I'd come through. If I hadn't spoken in tongues, I soon found that the Holy Spirit could indeed move through me by way of a pen.

I took what remained of my World Action Singers scholarship money, rented an apartment in Tulsa, and spent the next three weeks scribbling down every spiritual thought I had about coming of age through the 1960s. The apartment had a nice fireplace and some of the ugliest secondhand furniture my parents could find to send me from back home. Michie, who was at ORU by then, moved in with me and kept me going as I wrote nonstop to create this inspirational diary.

Back then I was "spiritualizing" everything. I prayed and read Scripture; I heard God's answers spoken directly to me; I explained every occurrence as a manifestation of God's will. Now, I was committing it all to paper. I had no plans whatsoever to get it published, but, Lord, was I inspired! I simply wanted an intimate and honest record of what was in my heart and my soul. I thought it would be wonderful to lock it away until a daughter of my own hit adolescence and wondered about her mom—and, of course, accused her of not understanding anything. Of not understanding what it's like to be on the outside looking in. Of not being able to *relate*, of not *feeling* what it's like to be in love for the first time and to be crushed. I wanted this future daughter of mine to read these pages and know that her mom had indeed been there. I also wrote about how difficult but rewarding it was to hold on to my own set of values and come through that turbulent period with my faith—and virginity—intact.

A friend read the pages and wept. "That bad." I winced.

"No," she said. "I just wish I had had something this personal and inspirational to read when I was seventeen. There's nothing out there like this for kids. You've got to get this published."

"Yeah, right." It read like a combination of *Bowie, Maryland 20715* and *The Gospel According to Epstein*. "Get a grip," I said.

And then, of course, I got a publisher. The only one I knew was a Christian house in New Jersey, Fleming H. Revell. I knew about Revell because of the year I had spent with Anita Bryant, who had written for them. So I sent the manuscript out, promptly forgot about it, and headed west.

Months later, as I was about to get married, I would learn the shocking news that Revell was indeed *accepting* my manuscript with the working title *The Quiet Riot*. I was stunned. I was also paid—$10,000. I saw the book as being about the revolution from within—twenty years before Gloria Steinem's book on that very topic. You don't change culture, I felt. You change people. I believed that what went on in a person's heart was truly the most revolutionary thing in life.

But back on March 19, 1975, Daddy's birthday, as I landed in Los Angeles, I had no idea just how true that belief was about to become.

When I got to Hollywood, I knew that finding a cheap apartment and a good agent would be hard enough and that whatever and whoever I found wouldn't be good enough. Not for Joanie and Aaron

Leon Epstein, anyway. My parents, bless their hearts, also insisted I find Christian fellowship in the City of Angels. So I struck a deal with them. In return for some financial support and a few CARE packages, I agreed to live with a Christian roommate, find a solid church affiliation, and join a Bible study group.

Seek and ye shall find! My parents ask me to seek fellowship and I find holy matrimony with a devout Seventh-Day Adventist who has his own Bible group. Was I the perfect daughter or what?

By the time I left baggage claim at LAX that day, I had the Christian roommate, Judy Baxter, a friend from Oral Roberts University in Tulsa. Judy was generous enough to let me crash in her Glendale apartment while her roommate was away.

I had spent plenty of time in L.A. with Oral's World Action Singers, but my work had insulated me from the Hollywood scene and I had usually roomed with Jantina. Now I was on my own, which was why I needed the spiritual lifeline to my parents' values—not that I ever gave Mom and Dad a whole lot to worry about.

I even went to the Easter service at the Hollywood Bowl to ask for some guidance from heaven above—but I got it from the seat next to me. I was with Judy and Tim Archer, one of the Archers, the popular pop-gospel group. Tim and I had had a few casual dates when I was at ORU. He heard about my plight—Judy's roommate was due back—and said, "You can stay at my place. We're going on the road. It'll be empty. It's perfect."

I was soon hooked up with an agent, Dorothy Day Otis. Then I found the phone number Anita had given me for this "adorable Christian guy" named Tom Netherton. Tom was a singer on "The Lawrence Welk Show," and he really *was* cute. But I was still seeing Tim. Frankly I hoped Tom might get me a singing job with Welk.

Instead, he got me the job with God that my parents had requested. We had a nice, helpful chat, and then he said: "I have this great roommate, an ordained minister who leads a wonderful Bible study group in our apartment. A lot of show-business people come. I know he won't mind if you stop by."

This, too, was perfect. I felt alone, a little lost, and here was a bond of Christian fellowship with entertainment people. Why not? I said. "Great," he said. "His name's Paul Johnson."

That name was definitely familiar. Paul was a brilliant gospel composer and arranger whose work I had discovered when a friend at ORU turned me on to the fabulous Sharalee Lucas, the greatest vocalist I'd heard since Streisand. Paul's vocal and orchestral arrangements were gorgeous. Then, back in October 1974, when I was in L.A. with the World Action Singers, I had seen this attractive guy in the control booth with Richard Roberts, Oral's son. I recognized Paul's face from album covers. Paul also had his own thriving Christian music publishing company and label, Petra Records. I considered him a genius in the pop-gospel business.

I decided to be direct. I went over and introduced myself and told him how much I loved his music. Paul was mellow and gracious. The next day he was back at the studio and this time I ran across the stage and threw my arms around him to say hi. I think he was taken aback by my exuberance. I made more of a first impression that second time. Paul always liked to say that from day one I was "in his face," overpowering him, as he liked to put it, on 220 volts while he hummed along at 110.

Now, a half-year later, Paul turned up in my life again as the Bible group's scriptural guru and Tom's roommate. I was taken with Paul's laid-back but authoritative discipling skills. That's a position that I have seen exploited many times for ego, money, and power. But Paul's mastery of the Word came across, along with an aura of accomplishment and earnestness; he didn't seem to be power-tripping on Jesus.

It became clear as I got to know him better that he was a true Christian brother. I learned that even before he reached his teens in Seattle, he had seemed destined for the path to gospel. He'd been trained on classical piano, and he ran the local Pat Boone fan club; he later became Debby Boone's musical director. As a teenager Paul didn't run after girls or become a jock, though he was an excellent water and snow skier. Instead, he heard chords and movements in his head and could sit down and create symphonies.

Paul studied theology at Walla Walla College, a strict Seventh-Day Adventist school, and combined the best of his musical and religious training by producing gospel albums. His dedication was impressive. In L.A., Paul worked with the Campus Crusade for Christ. He did religious radio broadcasts and newspaper columns. By then, gospel was moving toward a pop crossover sound from hymns and barber-shop quartets. It was also a time of national healing after Watergate and Vietnam, and so the born-again cable, radio, book, and record industries all thrived while televangelists like Pat Robertson, Jimmy Lee Swaggart, and Jim Bakker built huge followings and financial empires. It was not ambition but artistry and faith that came through Paul's music as he created his niche in the new gospel scene. That was where I began to see my own career going.

My life was more the old gospel. I found a two-bedroom place in

Woodland Hills, near Paul's, which I shared with Judy, then Jantina, and my sister Michie after she left ORU. Tim was in and out of my life and I had some dates with Tom. Tom left Paul's place and had some dates with Jantina.

None of these relationships led anywhere, but then, I clearly wasn't trying to get anywhere. Casual sex was out. Driving around in mid-1970s Hollywood—the land of drugged teenyboppers in glittery raccoon-style mascara, platform shoes, and velvet hotpants—I felt as I had often felt as a teenager in my own high school—as if I'd landed on another planet. *I was the Last Hollywood Virgin.*

I focused on my career, got my head shots and composites together, and marched into my first commercial audition, for Ultra Brite toothpaste. I was so excited. An enormous woman was sitting at the reception desk. "Hi, I'm Kathie Epstein from the Dorothy Day Otis agency," I said, "and I've got—"

"Just smile, honey," she sneered—this perspiring hulk of a woman. So I grinned and up went her thumb with the "outta here" sign as she grunted, "Uh-uh."

Maybe it was those crooked little eyeteeth, like Cher used to have. I went running out the door. So I wasn't right for toothpaste. What was I thinking, with those fangs of mine?

Laughing hysterically, I ran out to my sister, who was waiting in the getaway car. Maybe that's when it first dawned on me: if I can laugh at myself, I'll be just fine.

Eventually I got a nighttime "day job" to pay the bills. I was the hostess in a Mexican restaurant in Encino. I led people to their tables and handed them their menus. Major challenge! But at least it was brief. I got a call from Paul, who told me a producer friend was in a bind in Las Vegas. A three-girl group was opening a country-music revue at the Landmark the next night and one of the singers had just dropped out. He needed someone who could hit the Strip running. I dropped the hostessing job like a hot tamale, though I figured my boss would warn me: *You'll Never Serve Lunch in This Town Again.*

A day later I was singing in Vegas. I learned the entire show in one day, then bought my Windsong Trio cowgirl outfit—a red and white ginghamlike apron dress that made me look like a "Hee Haw" reject.

Vegas was a grueling sentence: twenty-eight straight nights, two shows a night. I found the Strip incredibly depressing and lonely. Worse, I was rooming with my singing partners. One was just about the wildest woman I'd ever met; the other was a wild-woman wannabe. The first was a gorgeous former Miss World with a magnificent body and a taste for musicians. I couldn't believe it—next to *my* cheerleader thighs and wuggies! The other, the chubby daughter of a Southern Baptist preacher, was finally out from under Daddy's steeple.

It was amazing. Every morning when I got up, these two would be coming in. I'd pull the curtains open; they'd pull them closed. So I'd clear out and go for my $1.98 breakfast and read the papers with my hotcakes, eggs, and coffee. It was a complete disaster. I had zero in common with them, the preacher's daughter included. These gals gave a whole new spin to the notion of World Action Singers. They hated me. And frankly, the music stunk.

When I got back "home" to L.A., I found Paul's Bible group a source of security in a place where everything seemed alien and unsure. I was turning into the best second choice in town. I'd get dozens of callbacks but never the job. I struggled just to pay the bills. I finally landed my first commercial in January of 1976. At the auditions there was a woman who looked like me but had more experience, and during the callbacks it always seemed to come down to her or me. And she was ahead, like ten to zip. Finally we ended up doing a Knott's Berry Farm spot together. Her name was Nancy Morgan and she was living with an adorable young actor named John Ritter, whom she married. It was hard not to like her.

I got an audition to sing on the faith-healer Kathryn Kuhlman's Sunday morning CBS show. Dorothy, my agent, told me to bring a long dress, just in case they asked me to stay. She introduced me to Kathryn, who, with her fierce, wide-eyed gaze, low, dramatic voice, and flowing chiffon gown, was about the most bizarre person I had ever set eyes on. She sat at her piano and told me to sing "He Touched Me." And after I sang, *she* touched me. She wrapped her long, expressive fingers around my face and, leaning toward me, she whispered, *"It's adooooorable! . . . It's adooooorable!"* It was *sooo bizarre.* But I got the job.

Ten minutes later my hair was rolled and styled on the spot, my makeup slapped together, and I was in my gown singing "Amazing Grace" before four TV cameras. I remained the featured soloist on "I Believe in Miracles" for eight months until Kathryn died.

I believed in soaps, too. I did bit parts on "Days of Our Lives" two or three days a week for nine months. I had the recurring, if minuscule, part of Nurse Callahan. I was also the voice-over who'd say, "Flight 303 leaving for Phoenix," or "Dr. Horton. Dr. Horton. Please report to emergency."

Paul and I were also teaming up on my first gospel album on his label. Paul was my conductor and arranger and we had a wonderful working relationship in the studio. So the minute I was wrapped from "Days of Our Lives" I went straight to the studio.

Paul and I decided to title the record album "The Quiet Riot" to match my book project. His perfectionistic signature was all over those tracks. The sessions were a dream come true for me. I'd always thrived on the intensity and immediacy of performing, but the studio offered a whole new medium for self-expression. Plus, you can screw up and still get it perfect on the album. The stage is far less forgiving. And there's the intimacy of the studio when everyone else is gone and it's just you, the producer, and the headphones as you strive for the hardest notes, the subtlest shadings. Paul's painstaking meticulousness coaxed me to new standards. To this day I am struck by the power, sincerity, and simple grace of the music we created together.

The LP was an important bond, with all the late-night hours and walks out into the soft balmy nights during breaks. I was fascinated to learn about recording from Paul; I soon found myself helping him out by running errands, taking care of his house, and feeding his black dachshund, Petula Sue. I even played hostess at his parties.

We had some movie and dinner dates—sometimes up in Malibu by the ocean—and we began to feel more "aligned," as Paul put it, in our values and goals. Then, during one of the sessions, he was playing a track back and said, "I make love through my music." No one had ever said anything remotely like that to me. I didn't know if this was seduction, artistic ego—or some unconscious warning about our potential for intimacy.

His work was indeed wondrous, and I *had* fallen in love with his talent. But having had no experience *whatsoever* with the opposite sex, I was confused. Was I in love with the man, or simply in awe of his musical soul? The Bible sessions added a dimension to our companionship. His bachelor pad was a 1970s classic: an ugly black and brown shag rug, fake fur pillows, and leather couches. Paul would pick some Scripture, and we would comment on its bearing in our lives. It was easy to be impressed by Paul, who had all those eager new Christians at his feet. We felt truly "blessed" to be in his presence.

But if Paul and I openly shared his ministry, we were two virgins awkwardly coping with chemistry. We were taking our time, lots of time. Paul, I believed, started to feel some conflict over commitment. Around Thanksgiving he came out and said: "I like you a lot. You're attractive, but this is not happening. I don't want you to get hurt.

The Way They Were

Mom and Dad in the 1950s.

Daddy as a scout at his childhood home.

Mom (left) with her dad and sister, Marilyn.

Dad as a young navy man.

Dad (left) on the saxophone with his group, The Five Moods.

Mom, who, unlike me, never needed a cover-up at the beach.

My mom's grandma, whom she called "Mama," 1941.

Gram, Dad's mom, 1956.

A Star(?) Is Born

WORLD PREMIERE

The Pride of the Epstein's

starring the glamorous

KATHRYN LEE

16 August 1953 ✦ 11:30 p.m.

at the American Hospital in Paris

Produced by Leon & Joan Epstein

How's this for a simple birth announcement!

photos courtesy of
Kathie Lee Gifford

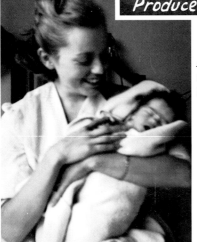

My gorgeous mom, moments after my birth.

At a few months old, I'm already having trouble keeping my mouth shut.

The Original Party Animals: the Epstein family, celebrating our return from Germany on the SS United States, 1957; I'm the cutie pie waving two American flags.

1955: This *was the last time my brother, David, dressed well. He's the least materialistic person I know.*

My first birthday, when life was a piece of cake.

1955: I looked a lot like Cody does today.

You better not pout, you better not cry, *Santa Claus is coming to Wiesbaden, Germany, Christmas 1956.*

1957: Just off the boat on U.S. soil, with my family. This one makes me cry.

One of my favorite pictures: David, six; me, three; and Michie, one. My brother took loving care of his younger sisters.

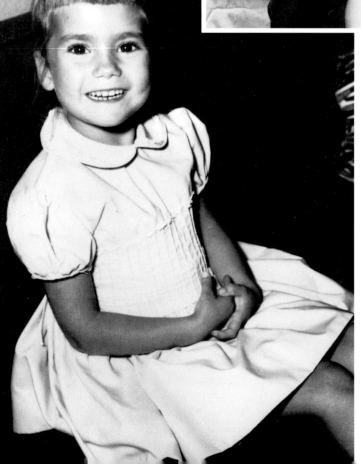

Four years old: my cutting-edge, ever-trendy 1950s hairstyle.

The Elementary Years

*First grade.
Annapolis,
Maryland.
Mrs. Heinz's
class.*

*Fourth grade.
A mother's dream.*

*Second grade. Mothers
should have to take a
course in cutting
straight bangs.*

photos courtesy of Kathie Lee Gifford

Bathing beauty . . .

majorette . . .

*and seven-year-old
Easter egghead. . . .
Do I look ready, or what?*

*The Enchanted Forest:
a typical family
vacation. My parents
never left us at home
. . . masochists that
they were.*

photos courtesy of
Kathie Lee Gifford

*A Real Class Act: I'm the raving beauty without the Brownie uniform, second
row from the bottom, far left. What a scandal I caused that year!*

WEST ANNAPOLIS
SCHOOL
GRADE 2
MRS MC WHITE
APRIL 1961

Pigtails, Buster Browns, and an unbearable hug.

1960s: The Inn at Rehoboth, ready to be condemned, scene of my first crush.

The home-sweet-home where I grew up.

The summer of '67: Double Trouble. My thighs, that is. My sister Michie's the one with the long, slender legs.

My earliest "activism" was singing to vets with the group Pennsylvania Next Right, during the Vietnam War. I'm the Michelle Phillips wannabe.

With Ed McMahon at the Junior Miss Pageant, 1971. My sweat shirt says CLEAN UP OR GIVE UP. Even then, I was an environmentalist. So ahead of my time.

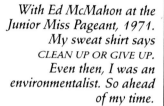

Singing "Go Down, Moses" for Maryland's Junior Miss with my customary flair for understatement.

*Crowned Maryland's Junior Miss.
I won in every category except
scholastic, the only one I thought
I'd win.*

photos courtesy of Kathie Lee Gifford

*Miss Priss Personified:
Off to Mobile, for the big Junior
Miss. Is this an outfit to die for,
or what?*

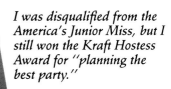

*I was disqualified from the
America's Junior Miss, but I
still won the Kraft Hostess
Award for "planning the
best party."*

With Anita Bryant in 1972.

"Oral Roberts Presents" . . .
Kathie Lee Epstein.

My blond-bombshell friend, Jantina, and me with the World Action Singers.

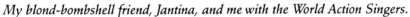

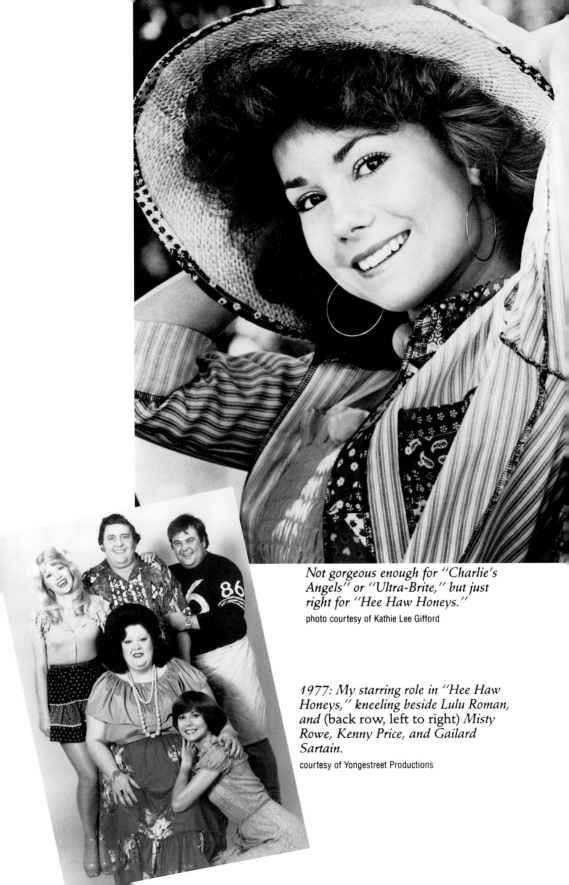

Not gorgeous enough for "Charlie's Angels" or "Ultra-Brite," but just right for "Hee Haw Honeys."
photo courtesy of Kathie Lee Gifford

1977: My starring role in "Hee Haw Honeys," kneeling beside Lulu Roman, and (back row, left to right) Misty Rowe, Kenny Price, and Gailard Sartain.
courtesy of Yongestreet Productions

April 23, 1976: Paul Johnson and me on our wedding day . . . sadly, one of our few truly happy days together.

photo courtesy of Kathie Lee Gifford

It's no small feet *to get to the top in show biz! My 1970s Dorothy Hamill hair . . . but my own bunions.*

© James M. Goss

My sister has always been with me . . . but now I go to her for advice.

Variety—the Children's Charity: the most rewarding part of my career.

1978: As a "Hee Haw Honey" I sang to my dad. My parents came to everything.

1989: Who knew that more than a decade later I'd be running away from Reege and Gordie Tapp on "Hee Haw"!

Backstage in Las Vegas with Paul Johnson, Frank Sinatra, Debby Boone, and Gabriel Ferrer.

You think it's easy being married to a man who is so much prettier than I am⸮!

Kathie Lee for Plaza South:
*I'm proud of the outfit,
but my feet are killing me!*

At home with Codesville—
as close to heaven as I know.
courtesy of The Home Furnishings Council

You're not the most important thing in my life. I need to be real honest about that."

Putting even the best spin on things, Paul let his work act as a buffer between us. Still, he was a giving friend and mentor. He took me with him when he had to perform his gospel music out of town. He saw the way I established a genuine ministry with young girls. There was real compatibility there.

Paul even wrote some heartfelt notes for the back of the album, saying that Kathie's "beautiful spirit and consistent walk with the Lord have won my respect as well as my affections."

His respect was fine; my parents were curious about his affections. My mother finally gave in and flew out in the late fall to check up on me. It had been a whole, what, six months? When the phone started ringing, it was, like, "So who's this guy named Paul who keeps calling? Are you serious about him?"

"Maybe. I'm not sure. He's not sure. We're not sure." I was teaching my mother, who had married Daddy at the age of eighteen in the late 1940s after about three dates, how to conjugate a new 1970s verb—to not be sure.

Paul came by and met Mom, and that went very well, though nothing she saw going on between us addressed her bottom-line question. No guy fools a mother—least of all the all-knowing, ever-inquisitive Joanie. But what was there not to like? Yes, he was older, but our age difference was almost exactly the same as the one between Mom and Dad. And he was good-looking, smart, gifted, and, without question, devout.

Then came Christmas. Paul and I flew east a day apart to appear on "The 700 Club" in Virginia. Then I took him home to Bowie. By this time Paul was beginning to feel a warming trend. I, too, had "mellowed," he said. He seemed more open to emotional intimacy and was beginning to evaluate me as a lifetime partner.

He had subtly "auditioned" me for the role. I saw the "unglamorous" side of his creative life—the crazed all-night ordeals to finish arrangements. I kept the pizzas coming and hung in there for him. For days on end he'd close himself off and not sleep, shower, shave, or change clothes. I didn't flinch.

And yet I was coming to see just how different Paul's upbringing in the Seventh-Day Adventist culture was from my own. In some ways that culture is close to Orthodox Judaism, with strict dietary laws, no drinking, no ornamentation or jewelry. One is expected to be very modest at all times. When I did a concert at a Seventh-Day Adventist church, my gospel album cover was tacked to a bulletin board to advertise the show. But they taped index cards over my ears to hide my earrings. I remember thinking, *If I open this mouth here, I'm dead meat because I am bound to offend somebody.* And this was a Christmas concert, too.

I figured I'd introduce each Christmas song by telling the story directly from the Bible. How could I go wrong, right?

I talked about the angel and the Holy Spirit coming upon Mary and her conceiving Jesus and how she and her "espoused husband" Joseph went on to Bethlehem on a donkey. I thought, *Great, I'm covered.* I did fine. I was getting all set to heave a sigh of relief that I had not offended anybody when a woman stormed toward me up the aisle, carrying a big Bible under her arm. This woman immediately ripped into me for saying that Mary and Joseph were "espoused" instead of married.

"I read it exactly from the Bible," I said in my own defense, to which she responded, "Yes, but it wasn't the King James Version!" That's when I gave up trying to please everybody.

If Paul's religious orientation was more disciplined than mine, so was his approach to music. Paul liked having total control. I went out onstage and let it rip. Paul didn't want anything to be heard until it was absolutely perfect; I put it out there and let it go. Paul was 90 percent technical finesse and 10 percent guts; I was 10 percent natural talent and 90 percent guts. Paul was Mr. Behind-the-Scenes; I was the born performer.

No problem. Some friends were confident that, beyond the shared values and interests, opposites attract. It could work. But others wondered—aloud. Paul, too, got mixed messages about me from his friends: I was too driven and high-energy for Paul—the 220 versus 110 thing. But at the same time we both recognized the potential in a life of ministry together.

Paul's father, Paul Johnson, Sr., came to visit once. He and Paul's mom, Genevieve, stayed at a Howard Johnson's on Ventura Boulevard a few miles from Paul's house. We all had lunch together and I knew they liked me. Dr. Johnson—Daddy Paul, we called him, one of the kindest, sweetest men in this world—took a long early-morning walk to Paul's the next day. He must have picked up on Paul's ambivalence, since, as I always heard it, Daddy Paul asked, "Are you crazy? How can you let this girl slip away? You're not going to find another one like this."

After Christmas it was my turn to defend him. My parents saw that I was crazy about Paul and they liked him very much. But they picked up his undemonstrativeness. Mom saw me nuzzle and cuddle with Paul in front of the fireplace. She was surprised he seemed so passive. My mother, this amazing woman who sees all and knows all, also *says* all. There is no withholding her mother's intuition. "How could he not want to hold your hand, put his arms around you—a handsome man and a beautiful young woman?" she later asked. "Two people in love can hardly stay away from each other. It makes me uncomfortable. You're not serious about this young man, are you?" I hedged, now more defiantly.

What I did not tell her was that when Paul left for New York, he spent some time away from me trying to work through his uncertainty about our relationship. Paul simply told me he was going to see if we could be together and be married. He said he needed to ask some questions about his own life, and I saw that as a positive step. I encouraged him because I knew Paul was a cerebral, introspective, and sensitive man who really wanted to do the right thing.

Whatever happened in New York helped. We moved closer to a commitment in the early spring. Mom still felt he wasn't right for me, but circumstances conspired to give us a reason to take the plunge. We were asked to appear on a Christian TV show in Holland. Paul was then scheduled to go on to London to score a documentary on Masada, the ancient Jewish fortress near the Dead Sea. If nothing else, the timing seemed perfect. But too many eyebrows would be raised if we traveled together unmarried.

I consulted Jantina, but she had her doubts. It was always the same thing: I was frisky and affectionate; he was laid back. To others the chemistry seemed to be off.

Other people's doubts only made me more protective toward Paul. It was none of their business. I was getting sick of hearing this about Paul—who, by the way, never knew how much I stood up for him. "He's a wonderful, brilliant artist. He's profoundly creative," I'd say defensively. What was the message? I would ask. That I should instead marry some guy with a reputation for nailing every woman he could? *Then* they'd be happy for me? Why would I, a virgin at twenty-two, want some macho jerk who'd rape me in my own home every night? I wasn't looking for that. I was looking for tenderness and sensitivity and warmth—for a man of God with whom I could spend my life.

And that was how I saw Paul; that was what I loved about him. I felt safe around him. And frankly, I had not seen that quality in too many so-called Christian men. Many of them were just as likely as the next guy to lead you down a path of destruction. Maybe the attitude was more subtle, but it was there. They'd put their arm around you in prayer—a slightly too familiar kind of prayer. Trust me: there's brotherly love and then there's *otherly* love.

With Paul, my feeling was this: We're virgins, and we'll learn all about love together. I found that an extremely romantic notion. And to be a gift to your spouse, to save yourself for him or her on your wedding night, was exactly what my parents had told me was most precious about love between two lifelong partners.

I saw our union reaching far beyond domestic routine. Our powerful spiritual bond was key. I could clearly visualize the future with Paul as not so much a marriage as a ministry. We'd be the Marvin Hamlisch and Carole Bayer Sager of gospel—and with a powerful ministry at that. I envisioned Paul doing seminars and me talking to the young girls. I could see us testifying and performing in churches together.

Paul was, in effect, the ultimate Christian catch—and the marriage made absolute sense for my life then. I had not often dated a Christian who knew the Bible better than I did, could quote Scripture better than I could, and tried as hard as I did to live the Christian life. Paul was the first guy who was my superior in terms of talent, spirituality, and biblical knowledge.

But would it *work?* Jantina and I sat for three hours at a quiet back table in the Red Onion in the Valley. The more we talked, the more I cried and felt confused, but Jantina dug in. She thought we were being impulsive. "Forget about getting married before you go to Holland," she said. "Get everything resolved first, and in three months you'll feel a hundred percent better about getting married."

A few days later I called Jantina, who'd left town to sing in a musical road show, to thank her for her advice—and to ask her a question: "Can you make it back for a wedding on April twenty-third?"

Michie, who by now was living out West, helped me put the wedding together in a couple weeks. Paul flew in a preacher friend of his—onetime baseball star Albie Pearson—to marry us in Paul's house in Woodland Hills, about ten minutes from our apartment. I had never met this friend, so I asked my brother Davy, who by then was a minister back home in Bowie, to assist as well.

At one in the afternoon they married us before two dozen friends and family members. This was a huge, exhilarating move for both of us. I was in love and I felt scared, nervous, and thrilled all at once. And then we were off to Acapulco to begin our life together.

I've Looked at Love
from Both Sides Now

☆

When I got married, I figured I'd give up my career, stay home, and be a Total Woman.

I was a Total Failure.

I became an ambitious woman by default. In the fall of 1978, just when I was achieving an unusual and exciting balance in both my gospel work and my secular projects, God stepped in to show all of us how little it all means—how powerless we really are to guide our destiny—when someone precious to you falls gravely ill and lies near death.

I came so close to losing my baby sister Michie that I raged against the Lord for the first time in my life for the pain He was causing her. It was the most frightening moment we had ever endured as a family, and it turned into the first real test of my faith. Michie did survive. My faith and family survived—both stronger than ever. But God came close to taking our Michie away.

After my upsetting wedding night in Acapulco, Paul and I managed to relax and swim and amuse ourselves for a couple of days.

We knew both sets of parents were home waiting for us, wondering how the kids were doing—kind of like waiting in Saint Peter's Square to see if white or black smoke would rise from the Vatican smokestack. We mainly did what Paul wanted to do. I was not interested in hiking up mountains and looking at ruins. I wanted to see stuff that *hadn't* been ruined yet.

A few days later Paul and I flew to Europe. As working honeymoons go, this one wasn't working very well. Not for me, anyway.

Paul spent most of the flight reading up on how to score films in preparation for his important hour-long project, *Masada: Monument to Freedom*. For me it was heartbreaking. It was a time when I wanted to nuzzle, cuddle, sip champagne, slip my hand under the blanket, and all that stuff people do when they're in love. All the stuff I do now. Poor Frank! He can't drive down the road to buy milk without me next to him.

We did the Amsterdam show, but then Paul got a bad headache. He was always battling horrible migraines, and when they came on he was almost incapable of working. But he got it together and we flew to London where he went into a creative frenzy, locking himself in the basement of a theater with a rented video machine and a piano. He emerged three grueling days later with one of the most brilliant symphonic works I've ever heard. I was truly proud of him. This was what Paul lived for, had prayed for all his life: conducting the London Symphony Orchestra for four days as the musicians played his own charts. I didn't want to stand in his way and he clearly preferred to work unencumbered, so I left after a couple of days.

I flew back to Tulsa, where I had scheduled a gospel show, and stayed with my friends Howard and Julie Twilley, whom I had met in Miami when Howard played for the Miami Dolphins. Now here was a couple that had always had a terrific love life. This much I knew because I had often stayed with them on weekends when I was at ORU and I always seemed to be around when they wanted to be alone. There was never a convenient time to knock on their bedroom door. There was always something going on with those two, but it was never embarrassing because it seemed so right, so healthy and loving.

Once back home alone in Paul's place in Woodland Hills with his black miniature dachshund, Petula Sue, I thought, This is so strange. I've been married for two weeks and already I'm separated from my husband. And this dog hated me when I first came into Paul's life. She's the only dog I ever hated too. She loved hopping up onto our water bed and sleeping on Paul's side. I had invaded her turf. She was the exact color of Paul's black and brown carpet and her yelping had driven neighbors so crazy that Paul had her voice box silenced. So you not only couldn't see her; you couldn't *hear* her. This was not a dog you cradled and smooched.

I wondered what kind of wife I was now supposed to be. My role models ranged from Mary Tyler Moore to Marabel Morgan, with Mom somewhere in between. I had loved TV's great comediennes as a girl—Lucille Ball, Carol Burnett, Mary Tyler Moore. They were strong, funny, independent, brazen, feminine, vulnerable. They were uninhibited; they took risks. They were in control of their lives and yet comfortable being silly. But newlywed life with Paul and Petula wasn't exactly the stuff of madcap sitcoms.

The world I grew up in didn't encourage young women to be truly successful career people, but rather fine mothers, wives, and Christian women. I had expected to be an updated version of my real-life role model—Mom. But my life was already so different from hers. She was the supremely competent Christian homemaker who always had the brownies baked and the picnics packed, who went to PTA meetings and all the school shows even when she was exhausted, who had dinner ready for everyone, and who broke her back with housework. But because my parents had vigorously promoted my independence and creativity, I was already on to a career as an entertainer. Not to mention that it was the Ogre's worst nightmare that I'd grow lazy and dependent and fall into the pit of marrying the first jerk who came along just to be married, to have a roof over my head and food on my table. I didn't. Paul unequivocally encouraged me to pursue my dreams. But I still wondered: Is that the right way to go for a wife?

I was confused. Like millions of other young women in the seventies, I searched for a definition of "womanhood" that worked for my life. I'd been singing for ten years, but I was no bra-burner. (I barely needed to wear one.) The radical approach has always turned me off. I never had a problem with feminism per se or with women's rights, the concept of choice, and equal opportunity. But radical feminists came on too strong for me—and frankly, though this may sound contradictory, they were often just so unappealing, so *un*feminine. I didn't see anyone in the women's movement who inspired me to say, "Gee, I want to be one of *them.*"

Gloria Steinem, though, was one exception. I thought she was attractive. She had style. She had groomed fingernails. I could relate to her kind of feminism. I admired her. We didn't agree on every issue, but I admired her intelligence and her passionate stance . . . and she had great nails!

I had considered Anita the ultimate Christian woman until I saw the sham of her life. That left Marabel and Julie Twilley, two women who had had a tremendous impact on me in Miami. They were classy-looking, feminine, happily married, good mothers. They made the notion of serving your husband seem not only respectable but attractive and loving.

I had no regrets about cutting back my career. Both the "Quiet Riot" album and book had come out to very positive responses. I was occasionally a member of the Paul Johnson Singers, along with Michie, for some of Paul's album and live gospel projects. But the commercials and pilots were always hit-or-miss deals. I was doing hundreds of go-sees, and it sometimes was heartbreaking to get so close, come back two or three times, and not get something. If I was waiting for some signal from Paul as to what kind of wife he wanted, none was forthcoming. He was doing his own thing—and doing it well and rather prosperously.

I decided to sweep this conflict under the rug. Actually, what I did was sweep it up *off* the rug. I decided to give up my career. I stayed home and *vacuumed*. I vacuumed all the time. By the summer of 1976, as America celebrated the Bicentennial, I had the cleanest carpets in California. And I scrubbed. I mopped. Later on, in an interview for *Today's Christian Woman* magazine, I called this my "waxy-buildup phase" and admitted Marabel's impact. "I emulated her," I said. "So when I got married, I wanted to be just like her. I was just the picture of fluff, waiting for Paul at night. I had taken my bubble bath, I had the candlelight dinner ready at five, and I'd be waiting for him at the door."

Now, this formula for happiness might have worked in a home with twenty-eight rooms and six baths. But I got through cleaning in a morning—and that left me the rest of the week. Paul was either at his office, in the studio, or sitting at the piano at home like Beethoven for days at a time. And when that happens, bills don't get paid, pools don't get cleaned, sheets don't get changed, dishes don't get washed. Little things like that happen when you're married to a Beethoven.

It started to get on my nerves. You can only vacuum so much, decorate so much. Plus, vacuuming was a horror show with Petula. I was always stepping on her or vacuuming her. It was like some wildlife show on cable, the way that rug totally camouflaged her. I don't know how many times I almost killed her. One day I vacuumed for the longest time and then I realized I hadn't run over Petula. This was very, very bizarre.

I thought, Petula Sue Johnson, if you're in that bed I'm going to kill you. I went into the bedroom. Not only was she in the bedroom, she was in the bed, on Paul's side of the bed, tucked snugly under the covers with her head on his pillow and her paws poking out over the covers. I'd never seen anything like it in my life. I looked at her, she looked at me. I looked at her, she looked at me. I finally said to myself, Any dog that can do that deserves my respect. That's talent. From that moment on, we were the best of friends. I gave her baths, cradled her, took her in the car with me everywhere. She was like my baby after that.

When you can't vacuum without crying, you're in deep pooky. First, I cried only when vacuuming. Then I was crying and *dusting*. Crying and *mopping*. Weeping and *bleaching*. You could call this my Wailing Wall-to-wall phase. I was a basket case, trapped and stifled. Then one night at dinner with Paul at home, I just totally cracked up. I twirled up some spaghetti with my fork, but I was shaking and sobbing so hard my fork couldn't find my mouth. "I'm living out of balance," I cried to Paul. "I need to get a life."

Paul surprised me and totally understood, even though he still recalls those first six months as the happiest he's ever been in his life. *Why not? That house was spotless!* "This Total Woman thing is bull," he said. "This isn't the girl I married. You're trying to be something you expected me to expect, and I'm not expecting that of you. I don't want the pressure to be home for a home-cooked meal at five o'clock. You need to work—commercials, auditions, singing. I don't want to be responsible for all your happiness. I don't want that burden."

Also, in Marabel's terms, he didn't want me to greet him at the door done up in Saran Wrap. He would have laughed. My independence worked for both of us. In the Christian press Paul would say he "pushed me out the door," and it's true; he was always my biggest thousand-percent-behind-me cheerleader. And the more I thrived outside the house, the more it took the heat off him to deal with being my husband.

Things started happening fast. In May 1977 I auditioned at Ralph Edwards Productions in Hollywood. "Get three songs ready," my agent said. Ralph was looking for his first La La Girl in fifteen years for "$100,000 Name That Tune." I was auditioning for the Leslie Uggams spot, and I was incredibly nervous as Paul drove me over.

To me an audition is thirty crazed people in a room waiting to be axed. A cattle call can be a real slaughter when the casting director's got a black belt in the martial art of rejection. I will never forget the one a few years later when I got a call to audition for the Kate Jackson spot on "Charlie's Angels" after Kate left the series. I nervously walked in, smiling, holding my glossies and résumé, telling the casting director how nice it was to meet her and all that. Before I even *hit the chair,* I was history. "Well, let me tell you right now that you're not right for 'Charlie's Angels,'" she told me.

"Why is that?" I asked, bile rising from my stomach.

Without missing a beat she said, "We're looking for a *pretty* girl. I'm not trying to offend you," she continued, ". . . but we're looking for a drop-dead *gorgeous* Jackie Smith type."

As I staggered out the door, I couldn't help myself. I leaned back in and said, "When you're casting a *cartoon,* let me know."

But this audition for "$100,000 Name That Tune" was obviously different. The reception area was empty. "I think I'm in the wrong place at the wrong time," I told the receptionist.

"You're Kathie Epstein, right?" she said. "They're all waiting for you inside." What? She led me to a small room where I met Ralph Edwards, some producers, a music historian, a director, and a writer. They were all quite friendly but very professional, and the writer looked very familiar. His name was Gary Bloom and he'd turned me down for a children's project he was putting together months earlier. "Too sophisticated," he'd told my agent, which was an amusing variation on the themes that had become so numbingly familiar: "not quite right for us"; "not quite what we're looking for"; "the look isn't there." Gary promised he'd hold on to my résumé and composite and keep me in mind for something *right.*

And he did. I later heard that when Ralph put the word out that he needed a La La Girl, Gary told him, "Let's not even call anybody else until we see this one girl I know. She's perfect."

I really nailed the audition. Paul and I had worked up three hits—"Don't It Make My Brown Eyes Blue," "I Just Want to Be Your Everything," and, of course, "You Light Up My Life," a huge pop-gospel crossover hit for Debby Boone. Before I left the room I was the new La La Girl. It's scary how fast your luck and stature can change in a place like Hollywood.

We taped a whole fall season of twenty-six shows in five high-pressure weeks during May and June. During a break after one taping, a producer asked with a skeptical smirk, "How would you feel about changing Epstein? It's not especially lyrical."

"You mean it's too ethnic?" I retorted.

"What about your married name?" Paul and I had preferred to keep our names separate. We checked the Screen Actors Guild and found that a Kathie Johnson had beaten me to it, so I added my middle name.

I got scale for the twenty-six episodes—but was I complaining? I was a lead vocalist on a top-rated nationwide secular TV show. I was ecstatic. And it made me crazy. A little old lady would get in the booth and after a few bars she'd yell out, "Some Day My Prince Will Come," and then she'd walk off with $100,000. Life just isn't fair sometimes!

But life was good to my sister—or so it appeared. On June 18, 1977, during my taping schedule, she married her prince, Craig Mader, her college sweetheart after she followed me to ORU. Talk about things falling into place. Wasn't there a song about how you can't hurry love? She had met Craig—a strapping jock from Kansas City, Missouri, who was on a full athletic scholarship—on *orientation* day in the fall of 1973. Their relationship had survived plenty of travel and distance. After I finished my book and left Tulsa in March 1975, Michie quit school and went to Miami for the second half of the year to sing with Anita. Then she moved to L.A. to sing on my LP, to be a Paul Johnson Singer, and to take a shot at commercials. But Michie just couldn't hack the go-sees. As she said, *"You* get rejected and come out pumped. *I* come out wiped. We're so different. I just don't have the stomach for this."* It turned out to be an eerily prophetic comment.

Craig finished ORU that spring and came to L.A. just before they married. They'd been mostly apart for three years before their marriage. Craig played baseball and had been scouted by the major leagues until an injury shattered his dreams of playing pro ball. So when he came west he had to switch gears, hit the pavement running, and take whatever job he could get to make ends meet.

I was thrilled for Michie but not all that crazy about Craig. He seemed cocky and young, not yet ready to be Michie's partner for life. Chances are *no one* would have won my approval for such a big job. But I was rough on Craig early on and made no secret of my feelings. They took an apartment in Canoga Park, and Craig worked as a salesclerk with the Big 5 sporting goods chain.

Neither my chilly ties to Craig nor my clearly troubled marriage to Paul affected us as sisters. Michie and I made our film debuts as sisters in a Christian feature called *Jana.* The film was based on the story of a girl who died of leukemia. My dying scene was incredible, with a life-support system and everything. The reason it was so realistic is that Michie and I had gone to Lincoln, Nebraska, the weekend before that scene was shot. We'd stayed just long enough for a gospel booking—and a lunch that gave me the worst case of food poisoning I've ever had. We flew back all night with what seemed like more layovers than there are airports between Nebraska and California. My death scene was filmed right after that ordeal, while I was still so weak and dehydrated I thought I was going to die. My misery must have come across onscreen. I still get letters from girls who see that film today.

So you see, serendipity played a big part in my life back then. A remark to Anita's husband had shifted my life to Miami and then to Tulsa. Anita had told me to look up a cute guy in L.A., and I had married his roommate. Then a case of food poisoning in Nebraska helped my film debut in L.A.

Then there was the surreal coincidence that led to getting a new manager and some great career opportunities. An agent of mine was trying to "position" me as the next Dinah Shore—upbeat, inspirational, yet not gospel per se. But Dinah's musical director, Norman Martin, already had a Dinah and wouldn't book me on her show. Unknown to me, Dinah's own manager, Henry Jaffe, had been so impressed by a young gospel singer he'd seen doing "Isn't That Just like Jesus" on TV that he tracked down a video, learned the singer's name, and sent the tape to Norman Martin, urging him to book the young singer for Dinah's show.

Norman checked out the tape Jaffe had sent him and he loved what he saw. Meanwhile, as he listened, he was on two calls at once. On one line was my agent, pitching me again; on the other, Jaffe.

"No, no, no," Norman repeated to my agent. "I am NOT interested. I can't book her if she hasn't done anything. Who is she? I don't even know what this what's-her-name looks like."

"Her *name* is Kathie Lee Johnson."

"Whatever. The answer is no. I'm sorry."

Then, to Jaffe, he gushed, "She's amazing. I love it. She'd be great for the show. Sign her up as a client! What's her name?"

"Kathie Lee Johnson."

Isn't that just like show biz?

I did sign with Jaffe's firm and things started happening. I did a pilot that later turned into a slick, naughty knockoff of "Hee Haw" called "Hee Haw Honeys." I worked hard with Norman Martin to put together a solid nightclub act that utilized my strengths. He combined a big band sound and my brand of shtick and stage patter to work a crowd. I was already getting plenty of vocal coaching in L.A. from the same people who taught Barbra Streisand, Lee and Sally Sweetland. But Norman taught me pacing and showed me how to take my time when I get nervous.

Meanwhile the gospel career was in full swing under Paul's masterful guidance. We did two more albums on Petra Records:

"Kathie and Michie . . . Friends" in 1977; and "Finders Keepers," written almost entirely by Paul, which came out a year later. I'm proud of all the work I did with Paul, especially "Friends." That was such a labor of love for Michie and me. We were glorifying the Lord with our voices, and because we were keeping costs down, we did many tracks in one or two takes.

By the fall of 1978 I was getting airplay on Christian radio stations *and* airtime on national TV with "Hee Haw Honeys." The pilot had been taped before "Name That Tune" had even aired. (Ironically, it got preempted in a lot of local markets by a Billy Graham crusade.) Henry Jaffe's management firm—his son Michael was handling me—negotiated an incredible contract for me. And not a moment too soon. My La La days were over when the show's producers opted not to renew my contract for the 1978 season for reasons I never really understood.

Now, on "Hee Haw Honeys," I was Kathie Honey of the Honey family, which owned the Honey Club diner. My cohorts were all "Hee Haw" graduates—the late Kenny Price, Lulu Roman, Misty Rowe, and Gailard Sartain, one of the funniest men alive. I had to go to Nashville four or five times for a month each time to shoot the episodes.

I loved Nashville and I loved getting away from my life in L.A. Each week we had another country music guest, which was a hoot. Larry Gatlin, actually, was much more than a hoot. Larry was a doll when he and his brothers, Steve and Rudy, were featured. I loved those guys. When I waited on them at the club in our sketch, I was supposed to play the scene so flustered that I could barely get it together to give them menus. During the taping I said my line: "You must be Larry Gatlin." And then, star struck, I went on: "And your brothers, Reve and Study." I wasn't just *supposed* to be flustered; I *was* flustered. There was an instant rapport between Larry and me that has turned into a long and wonderful friendship.

It was also a relief to get away from gospel music and experience a new kind of performance. I didn't like the fact that the show was so tightly scripted, but I learned something new every week with my absolutely insane new partners. I got a lot of grief from Christian colleagues about doing a show like that, but I felt no shame doing it. I was proud to finally be making a good living in show business.

At home, Paul and I just weren't connecting, but he visited Nashville twice while I was shooting. I felt that he might have been a little threatened by my new success in the secular field, and that he basically hated it.

Mom and Dad, however, became fixtures on the set. They came down for most of the shoots and even got into a few as extras, laughing or clapping for the country music guest we had each week at the Honey Club.

But their last visit to Nashville in late May 1978 was no laughing matter. We were all tense. Michie was eight months pregnant back in California and she had had a very difficult time. She had had fainting spells. She had been to three gastroenterologists and been misdiagnosed each time. Before I went to Nashville, she was so weak and intestinally sick one day that she came out of the bathroom and asked me to look in the toilet. I almost fainted. It looked as if someone had died. At one point Michie was so ill, it nearly aborted her pregnancy. No one could diagnose her properly. We were just praying that she'd make it through the last weeks.

On June 2, before the taping, Mom and Dad went downstairs to the coffee shop for breakfast. Just then I got a call. It was Michie. I gasped with panic. She sounded drugged, disoriented. I thought she was dying. "Mich, are you all right? What's hap—"

"Kaaath," she mumbled weakly, "you have a baby niece."

I burst into tears of relief and joy and bolted downstairs to tell Mom and Daddy that they were grandparents to Shannan Michele Mader.

Her birth was premature, but it was a miracle Shannie was born at all, let alone by natural childbirth. One doctor had ominously told Michie, "That's the quietest colon I've ever seen."

We found out why three months later, over Labor Day weekend. Michie, Paul, and I were touring the Northwest with the Singers. Michie had Shannie with her and was breast-feeding her, though her weight had dropped to a scary ninety pounds. She hadn't been able to keep a meal down in six weeks. After we sang in Eugene, Oregon, she was too weak to even join us for dinner. In the middle of the night, Michie had a terrifying premonition that she was dying of cancer. She knew, of course, that Paul's dad, Dr. Paul Johnson, was a fine abdominal surgeon in Seattle, one of the stops on our tour.

When we got to Seattle, Dr. Paul urged Michie not to sing in church that night but Michie insisted. Her skin color was a ghastly grayish yellow. But she went on, leaving Shannie in the care of a local woman in a church nursery. During the show, Michie had to sit and nearly collapsed as her eyes rolled in her head. As she remembers it, she was "more gone than there."

She was so delirious that after the show she ran to the nursery, completely pulled off her dress, grabbed Shannie, plopped in a rocker, and nursed her infant. Dr. Paul had seen enough. He insisted she stay at his house on Lake Washington. She lay on a couch and he hung an I.V. hookup from a movie screen to restore her electrolytes and body fluids. He checked in on her every two hours.

Daddy Paul took Michie to a specialist at his hospital the very next day. He took one look inside her, and the way he said "Oh, my God" told her that her life was in danger. Michie's colon wasn't quiet; it was *gone*. A normal colon is eight to twelve feet long and firm. Michie's was two feet long, massively perforated, and had the consistency of wet toilet paper. The diagnosis: acute ulcerative colitis. Treatment: surgical removal of the colon and rectum, replaced with an ileostomy, over which is worn a surgical prosthesis, for life.

With a gorgeous, sexually vibrant twenty-three-year-old woman, you do everything you can to save the colon and avoid the radical surgical procedure of an ileostomy. Maybe it's different when you're eighty, but at twenty-three you're thinking, What will this look like? Will my husband ever want to make love to me? But we had to save Michie's life. There was neither the time nor the need for a second opinion—just prayers for her survival.

I was such a nervous wreck the morning of the surgery. Daddy Paul walked me onto the unit as they were prepping Michie. When he left me on my own I saw a nurse manhandling Michie, grabbing her skinny arms, shaking her, trying to poke her with some kind of shot. Michie was standing there rocking, half zonked like a rag doll. I walked over and smacked the nurse. I tried to push her away from Michie. "You get away from my sister," I snapped. I was furious.

I saw Dr. Johnson and told him, "She doesn't deserve the privilege of taking care of sick people." I tried to have her fired and I was told she was. Seeing somebody pushed around like that makes me so angry to this day I could punch her again now. She made a travesty of the commitment medical professionals make to heal and comfort the sick and dying.

My heart just broke for my baby sister. I saw her ileostomy bag. And I saw the stub of intestine that protrudes through the opening and is surgically appended to the outside of her abdomen. And I thought of Craig. He was going through his own hell. When a nurse asked him if he would help clean Michie's dressing and rebandage her, which they had to keep doing, he lifted her up, gently set her down, and helped out. Here's a tough, strong jock who runs at the sight of blood. But he hung in there.

When the task was finished, he asked, "Can I go now?" Then he raced to the bathroom and threw up. He came out pale and distraught and collapsed in Mom's arms. He started to weep. "Oh, Joanie," he moaned, "what a number they did on my baby."

"They" weren't finished. We left the hospital and returned to Dr. Johnson's home for rest. While Michie was being walked around to prevent clotting and get her going again, she suffered three grand mal seizures. One of these can kill you or leave you brain damaged. Michie lapsed into a coma and was rushed to intensive care. We were called back and bluntly informed that she might not make it through the night. I was crazed with sadness and fear, unable to imagine her gone.

It was now a life-and-death vigil. We sent up an endless stream of prayers to keep Michie with us. Mom and Dad were trying to be like rocks for the rest of us. This was the darkest time I have ever known in my entire life. Michie had been such a good and giving and decent person. I could think of a thousand people, including myself, who deserved this agony more than she did. She's just such a rare, rare special human being.

I knew she and Craig had had problems that first year of marriage. They were battling and, I thought, on the road to divorce. I felt he had not been much of a husband to her. I didn't like him, had no respect for him. But I was the most protective person in the world when it came to Michie. I've since come to love him very dearly as my brother-in-law, but it took a long time. They were telling us that this disease is stress-related, and I thought that he was a big part of the reason she'd lost her colon. But I wasn't about to berate him at that time. We all needed to find strength in each other.

The truth was Michie had always held things in, long before Craig. Her love-hate thing with me was never openly expressed. She came behind two overachievers. She felt overshadowed by me; everything I touched turned to gold in her mind. She had so little self-confidence. More than with Mom and Dad, she craved my approval and dreaded my disapproval. She hid and internalized her anger. She relished her role as confidante with her friends who sought her advice, but she was shut down to herself. She never felt she could admit her own vulnerabilities, never let her guard down. She could wipe anyone off a tennis court, could outrun anyone on a track, but in her self-denigrating way, she said, Who cares?

Singing came easiest to her and was what she wanted to do more than anything. She'd always been told that she'd be the star of the family, but while I recorded three LPs, she got turned down by Word Records. People told her she had "a look" for modeling, but she was devastated by the rejections; meanwhile I was on TV series and in commercials. She'd go to gospel conventions and see pictures of Paul and me and other Petra artists but none of her, though she was a Paul Johnson Singer, too. Her unspoken feelings had been literally eating away at her for so long that they nearly consumed her.

"I always cried alone," Michie later told me. "No one would ever have known what bothered me. I was always too embarrassed to admit I wasn't cutting it in the world I wanted to break into."

But I didn't know all this as Michie lay in a coma. I focused my anger on Craig and fought my emotions as he sat across from me. And as I battled the feelings of rage and injustice, I cursed God. For the first time in my life, I was so mad at God for doing this to my sister, making her live with this grotesque stub on the outside of her beautiful body for the rest of her life, that I cursed him. She had brought this beautiful little baby into the world and should have been looking forward to the joys of motherhood, but instead she had nearly died and had this thing on the side of her body.

"This is an obscenity. I hate it," I said. I was just so angry. Then, miraculously, Michie came out of it, back to consciousness, and began to stir. She had made it! As she got her bearings, she looked straight at me—I will never forget this for the rest of my life—and said: "Kathie, don't curse God for this bag. I thank God for it. It means I get to live the rest of my life."

This was not believable. It was mystical. She was *inside my mind?* Yes, she was, and she was right.

Now I went from rage to shame—that Michie, with all her devastating pain and suffering, could maintain that kind of faith and I could not. I don't know where that kind of wisdom comes from in a twenty-three-year-old person. I don't have that kind of wisdom or grace even now.

We went home to Daddy Paul's house when they said Michie was going to make it. I remember gazing out the windows over Lake Washington. Everybody had gone to bed except Craig and me. I was haunted by Michie's astonishing remark to me, and all of a sudden my hatred simply gave way. I let go and melted. We all needed each other now more than ever.

In that moment at the window Craig started to sob. The full pain and sadness of what had happened seemed finally to be sinking in. I'd never seen anything but phony strength from him before the surgery. I went to him and silently put my arms around him. "Kathie," he said, "I'm so sorry for Michie. I'm going to lose the best thing that ever happened to me."

He finally knew just how precious she was. I told him I understood, that we both were desperately afraid of losing her.

That night changed everything between Craig and me. He and Michie still went through a lot of hell after that, but things changed for the better for them, too. As Michie has said to me: "Craig was at a crossroads. He became a man that day. If he had rejected me, if he'd looked at that thing and said, 'Hey, I'm a young, good-looking guy, no way I'm gonna be strapped to some woman with a bag on her thigh,' I never would have been able to love myself, to be whole again. In the privacy of our bedroom he could have made it a real nightmare for me. But he has said to me, 'I love you more for all you've had to go through.'"

Michie stayed in the hospital for about ten days. My mom stayed at Daddy Paul and Genevieve's house, and I went over to stay with Paul's sister, Karen. Daddy Paul and O.G. (for Old Genevieve) were unbelievable; they were saints. They gave us their home and he watched over Michie's treatment in the hospital.

Significantly, I cannot even remember if Paul was present for the surgery and vigil or if he had gone home. But there is no doubt that his father saved Michie's life. And if the only higher purpose of my marriage was so that Dr. Paul would be in our lives and in Seattle that night to save Michie's life, then it was absolutely worth all the unhappiness we ever felt. I think Paul would agree.

By yet another bizarre coincidence, after my eighteen-month return to the work force, I had long before planned to take September off to recharge my batteries. So now I was able to take Shannie for several weeks, as Mom and I took turns feeding her. Karen and her husband, Ron, had an upstairs rec room and I was sleeping there on a cot, with Shannie on a mattress on the floor. She had to be instantly weaned and she was totally traumatized by the abrupt loss of mother's milk. I remember her crying in the middle of the night every couple of hours, and I'd crawl across the room in the dark to give her a bottle. And then I'd hear that magical, unforgettable sound—the gurgling, gooey noise all babies make when they're sucking and satisfied. This was the first time I'd ever felt that somebody needed me. And the one thing I could do for my sister was take care of her child.

In the morning I'd give Shannie a bath, get her dressed up real sweet, and take her to see Michie in the hospital every single day. Michie couldn't even hold her. I remember she said, "I just want to smell her." And so I'd hold her over to Michie and she'd just breathe her in. She'd inhale her. And I'd lay her on Michie's chest. It was everything I could do not to break down and cry in front of her.

In October, Michie and Craig moved in with my parents in Bowie and stayed for almost a year. Davy and his wife, Sandy, were then living a few miles away with their children. So there was plenty of family to support them and help get their lives back to normal.

With the rest of my family pulling together more fiercely than ever back east, I resumed life in L.A. It wasn't going to be the same without Michie there. I could have used a lot of support myself. I was keeping some pretty heavy secrets of my own, and in the aftermath of Michie's tragedy, I seemed to be nearing a crossroads as well. Right at home.

There's No Business
Like Show Business

By the end of 1978, Paul and I were a hot couple in the Christian entertainment media. We were regulars on shows like "The PTL Club" and "The 700 Club," and we performed gospel ministries all over the country. We were on Christian magazine covers together and I was on some of them alone. Some cheerfully proclaimed, "Kathie Lee Johnson: A Hee Haw Honey Who Has It All Together" or "Career and Marriage, 'It Works for Us.'" A *Rolling Stone*-like gospel music paper hailed us as "A Rare Blend: Paul and Kathie Johnson."

It was a rare blend, all right—of illusion and reality.

The irony was that this image of our union was exactly what I had once dreamed it could be: a ministry beyond marriage. The ministry was working beautifully, but the marriage wasn't. It didn't help that I had some strange experiences with men in my work life that only mirrored—and intensified—how out of whack things were for me as a woman.

At least we had a nice home to show for our efforts. We had bought a house in Woodland Hills for what seemed like a fortune: $140,000. The payoffs in show biz seemed as random as a slot machine. I lived frugally, planning for a rainy day. The way my career went in streaks, I should have been saving for a rainy *life*. Our payments were $600 a month and we wondered if we were nuts—but we took the plunge.

We were far more brazen in real estate than in our marital state. At home we were polite, never abusive or ugly with each other. We were not screamers. We were good friends and companions and brother and sister in the Lord. I still had this unstinting faith that our problems could be solved. Without knowing exactly what those problems were, I tended to shift the blame, the responsibility, onto myself. I didn't see our lack of intimacy as permanent. I once told him—and we can laugh about it now—"You're the best friend a person could have in life. You're just a lousy husband." He thought I was a pretty lousy wife, too.

I always believed that in a marriage two people coming together made one new entity. But Paul disagreed.

I came to my career by default because I wasn't getting much applause at home and went elsewhere to get it. You tend to go where you are affirmed. And so, as my marriage began to bog down, my career started to take off. I had once been willing to give up anything to have Yancy in my life. I had been willing to give up my career for Paul—which he, mercifully, did not want.

My career was (and still is) hard work, and I paid dues with my share of rejection. My bread-and-butter jobs were still the church and banquet gospel bookings all over the country with the Paul Johnson Singers. I sang everywhere, from funky cinder-block churches to the famous Crystal Cathedral of Reverend Robert Shuller. Once, when I taped a show there, the cathedral was packed like a stadium. And I couldn't hit the highest note in "Isn't It Just like Jesus." I wasn't having what we called "a good voice day." Since it was taped, I asked to do it over and over. I'm telling you, that glass was *rattling*. Every time I opened my mouth to sing "He opened up my eyes again," the members of that vast congregation rose off their chairs to help nudge my voice to the peak of its range. It was hysterical, but, dear Lord, I was devastated.

Of all the gospel shows I did, none was more bizarre than the visit to the federal maximum-security prison at San Luis Obispo, California—a gospel booking made through a prison ministry organized out of Texas by a man named Chaplain Ray. Prison concerts at the intersection of Jesus and criminal justice were always a bit weird.

Chaplain Ray believed that even those souls at the edge of life's spectrum of darkness—rapists, murderers, madmen—could be saved. Criminals could be rehabilitated, he felt, through authentic "Road to Damascus" conversions. The term comes from the story of Saul, who, on his way to Damascus to persecute Christians, was "blinded by the light" and accepted Jesus as the Son of God.

I had sung and testified before for Chaplain Ray in the 1970s, usually with my sister. "Pat Boone will be there, too," he said, encouraging me to accept this particular invitation.

"Great," I said. But I knew this was a rough place and expressed concern for our safety.

"That won't be a problem," he said calmly. "Your bodyguard will be Tex Watson."

"You're kidding me." The memory of his name sent chills down my spine. Tex Watson was one of the Manson Family killers convicted in the brutal 1969 murders of actress Sharon Tate and several friends.

"No," he assured me. "He's accepted the Lord and totally repented."

"Chaplain Ray, are you kidding me?" Jailhouse conversions were common enough, but Watson, many thought, had been under Manson's demonic spell.

"You'll see," he said. I thought to myself: Well, if Tex Watson's soul can be redeemed, then I guess *anyone's* can. Such is the limitless power of God to forgive.

We arrived in 114-degree heat with no air conditioning, dressed in what we called our Katherine Kuhlman outfits—no makeup and covered from neck to wrists to toes.

Escorted by Tex, I attended a brief chapel service and signed autographs. I was struck by his gentle, clear-eyed manner. He had been sentenced to life, but he no longer seemed like the monster of the "Helter-Skelter" rampage. Then he, the warden and his wife, the chaplain, Pat, Michie, and I walked into the stifling gym—and already several muscle-bound guys with no shirts on were masturbating in the bleachers. I leaned over and said to Michie, "I guess we're not in Kansas anymore."

Each of us found a safe place to look as we proceeded with the program, but in the middle of the show the power went out. I was sure there was going to be a riot—or a breakout. So we all joined hands—Michie, Tex Watson, Pat Boone, Chaplain Ray, and me— and sang "What a Friend We Have in Jesus." It was one of the most bizarre moments I've ever experienced, trying to get murderers, rapists, kidnappers, armed robbers, and *masturbators* to join us in *singing* instead of *killing* us.

Back in Kansas, so to speak, my secular career began to gain some momentum as I started getting more commercials, for everything from Red Lobster and Carl Jr.'s to Piccadilly Clothes. I filled in openings in my schedule with extended bookings as a twenty-minute opening act in Vegas for comedians like Shecky Greene, Rich Little, and Bill Cosby. I was on "Cross Wits" once, and I was booked for what must have been hundreds of corporate and industrial shows, where I did my nightclub act with a ten-piece band. Most of the jobs were uninspired, but they were a much-needed source of income. When I couldn't get arrested in commercials, I'd do ten TV pilots that didn't go to series. I didn't have a TV series going and was no longer on the gospel or nightclub circuits.

It would have killed Mom and Dad to think I led people to a casino where they would lose their life savings. But I went to the casinos to entertain, not to minister, and I had no qualms about accepting those engagements. I didn't enjoy gambling, of course (except when Bill Cosby gave me *his* money!), and I did not encourage it.

I did a zillion telethons, endless conventions. I did everything from the ABA (bankers, not basketball) to the NRA (restaurant, not rifle). I didn't do IBM because I refused to send them lyric sheets ahead of time for approval. Must have been my famous *crotch-grabbing, boob-baring, pelvis-thrusting* rendition of "Send in the Clowns" they feared. *Just kidding!* They were completely paranoid about lyrical content, no matter who performed. It was absurd. They even made Debby Boone send lyrics ahead of time. I worked from a repertoire of a hundred songs and chose my material on site once I got a feel for the people who were there, their age, and where they were from.

I did some real Mickey Mouse performances but none like the two-weeker at Disney World. As a last-second fill-in, I flew to Orlando with my charts and my conductor (it wasn't Paul this time). I took one look at the top-floor two-bedroom hotel suite they had me in, immediately called Michie, and said, "Come on down!" I sent her a plane ticket so she and Shannie, who was still crawling, could come down from Bowie to be with me. Aside from the two evening shows, I was free to hang out with them and we had a blast.

Then there was Sutmiller's in Dayton, Ohio. The Jaffes had put me with Buster Davis, Judy Garland's onetime arranger-conductor, to work up a new show. I adored Buster, one of the most flamboyant characters I've ever worked with. It seemed as if he'd had an unhappy life, so we went to church a few times as I tried to lead him to the Lord. Buster led me to Dayton—he got the better end of that deal.

Everybody in show biz knows Sutmiller's as a place to try out new acts. I opened there on the night of the Academy Awards show. There was one drunk in the audience. All of Dayton was home watching the Oscars. But I had flowers opening night from my parents. My endless

Dayton engagement was so rough that Mom and Dad even drove out to see me.

My nightclub jobs in Las Vegas began right around the time of my disaster at Sutmiller's.

"How would you like to do Vegas?" my agent asked one day.

"I'd love to," I said, suffering at home with laryngitis and the flu.

"Great," he said. "You're on tomorrow night. Sandy Duncan's had a death in her family and you'll be opening for Rich Little at the MGM Grand."

I got my charts and my voice together and flew to Las Vegas. There were three thousand people in this enormous showroom. I went into my dressing room before the show and there was this big bouquet of flowers for me with a little note: "Dear Kathie, If you're better than I am, I'll kill you. Love, Sandy."

I thought that note was the sweetest, classiest thing anyone had ever done for me in show business. One of the little, but meaningful, kindnesses you never forget. I only did two shows for Sandy that night, but it's not easy to come into an established show where people love—or at least *expect*—the scheduled performer. To this day, if Joy Philbin or someone else is filling in for me, I always try to remember to leave flowers and a note to wish her well. *And to let her know that if she gets better ratings than I do, she's history!*

Just kidding.

The corporate conventions didn't exactly teach me kindness, but they did force me to learn how to turn on a roomful of brain-dead executives who have been hammered all day with deadly speeches, graphs, and charts. Talk about hostile takeovers: you're up against an indifferent crowd of corporate types who are stuck in a ballroom, having neither *chosen* nor *paid* to hear you. Some are angry because they're not with their wives; others are angry because they *are*. Bottom line: they're there—and you're there—to honor the fiscal bottom line. And as the headliner, you get a wobbly stage set up an hour earlier with the world's worst acoustics and a little tin can band behind you. That's where I learned my craft, learned how to work a room and come across.

I worked hard for the $500 to $1,000 I might get for a corporate show. I remember one time when I was on my way to Dallas, I ran into Bill Cosby at the airport. I was schlepping all my costumes and charts, I had my backup singers—Michie and Denise Carley. And Cos strode up with his cigar and one garment bag slung over his shoulder. He nicknamed me "Roots" because when we played tennis, he always said I didn't move my feet. He looked at all my paraphernalia and said, "Roots, I told you, you should've been a comedian."

Bill should have been there in Kansas City the night I had them rolling in the aisles for Coca-Cola. I did a TV spot for Coke and then became a longtime spokesperson, showing up at private parties and promotional events. At a big event for diet Coke, I'd rehearsed in the afternoon as workers built what looked like a very temporary stage. When showtime started, someone announced, "Ladies and gentlemen, for diet Coke, Kansas City welcomes . . . Kathie Lee Johnson!"

I strut out to a brassy fanfare, everyone's applauding, and as I trot up the steps to the stage the top step gives way and I go flying, my legs poking up in the air, my butt sliding across the floor maybe twelve, fifteen feet.

Well, at least I had their *attention*. It was unbelievable. The audience was just stunned silent.

I got up and I did a "da-dah!" I realized the audience must have thought the fall was part of my act—because they didn't really think I could sing. I decided to do a few bars to hook them. The problem was: I looked over to the band and my conductor wasn't there. I had not only mooned this entire audience of corporate honchos and civic leaders, but now there was no one to conduct the band.

"Isn't show business glamorous, folks?" I said into the mike. "I'd love to sing for you, but we're first going to have to find my conductor, who appears to be lost. I'll be back as soon as we can find him."

And I walked off. We found him—he had a drinking problem and had been on a binge. I got a standing ovation and people were great to me. It was one of those crazy times when I learned how rewarding it can be to just allow people to see your humanity and your frailty. It endears you to them in a way perfection never can. I earned people's respect that night as much for my honesty about my imperfections as for any talent I might have had. People may be in awe of perfection, but they warm to humanity.

Paul, however, didn't warm to some playfully flirty promotional photos taken of me for Coca-Cola. Raised as a Seventh-Day Adventist, Paul had a much stricter upbringing than I did. During a four-hour session with Dick Zimmerman, a photographer known for glitzy, sexy pictures of women celebrities, I'd done all the cutesy girl-next-door poses. Just before I left, Dick said, "Just for fun, can I mess you up a little bit and go for a fun picture, get you crawling on the floor with a totally different look?"

Totally different look? You mean I didn't look like a woman who'd crawl along the floor with wet hair? Why not? It was a lark. He shpritzed me and got me looking, well, moist. I wasn't naked. I wasn't even *half* naked. I was draped in a fur and wore nylons and underwear. So I got down on the floor and slithered toward him, eyeing the lens—the old "make love to the camera" thing—but I couldn't stop laughing. It was a riot, with the wet hair, the dewy soft focus, the parted-lips pout. My *animal* look. You remember Kim Basinger in *9½ Weeks?* This was *9½ Seconds. Pull-eeeze! In my dreams!* The pictures came out great—fun and innocent—but Paul wasn't crazy about them.

If I wasn't getting the kind of reinforcement I needed in my marriage, I certainly wasn't getting it on the road. Worse, I had unnerving encounters with men that ranged from what I considered embezzlement to sexual harassment to agonizing sexual temptation. They only left me feeling more frustrated and restless, since my home was hardly the haven it should have been.

I changed business managers and went with one who was pretty well connected and married to a well-known actress. He didn't last long. Coca-Cola sent me a check for $25,000 against road expenses, which were piling up and which I'd been paying out of pocket before being reimbursed. Shortly after opening this account, I wrote a check for $100 to my backup singer and the check bounced. I wrote another and *it* bounced. This guy had removed the $25,000 from my account and put it all in a money market in his name without letting me know. I fired him—and *he* threatened to sue *me* for future earnings. He denied any wrongdoing and told me he was doing me a favor by earning interest for me. Yeah, right. He just happened to *lose interest* in telling me about it.

But for every sleazeball in the business there are plenty of decent and wonderful people. Back then I had mostly good luck with agents and managers. Henry Jaffe did an awful lot for my career, but he came to feel he wasn't able to give me the kind of attention my career then needed. For a time he shared managerial duties of my career with a terrific business manager named David Martin, with whom I worked quite well until I moved to New York to do "Good Morning America." After that, it was just too hard to keep up a long-distance managerial relationship, but we parted as—and remain—friends.

I was also represented back then by APA, the Agency for the Performing Arts. APA was a big place and you were either an A-list, B-list, C-list, or Lucky-to-be-Here-list client. I was in that last group.

Henry helped me to get an assistant named Susie Cole, who had come out to L.A. to be a choreographer. She introduced me to a young friend of hers named Sam Haskell, who was from Mississippi but was now working in the mail room at the William Morris Agency. Sam and I became friends, and he always used to say, "I'm going to get important enough in this agency someday and bring you over here. You're going to be my first client and we're going to make it together."

Sure enough, Sam did make it at Morris, and he did take me on as one of his first clients. He fought hard for me, put me up for absolutely everything. Fourteen years later he is still my agent, my dear friend, and a powerhouse at the agency.

Overall, I've been lucky. But I do know that, as a woman, nothing anyone does to you in a business deal can match the feeling of rage and humiliation you feel when you are a victim of sexual harassment. I learned that the hard way.

In the late seventies I did a "700 Club" telethon in Virginia. At the end of the show I got a call from California, which in itself was weird. It was a well-known Hollywood "player"—a producer-manager—whose wife was a very popular TV and movie star. "Listen," he said cheerfully, "you're the most talented thing I've seen in years. You've *got* to call me when you get back to town. How come I've never heard of you before? Where have you *been?* Do you just work in gospel?"

I called him when I returned to L.A., and we met. He was not unpleasant—but he was unattractive. We discussed my career. I had some more pictures made, and when they were developed, we set up a meeting.

I sensed something seemed just a little off here. "I want my husband to be there," I said. Was it a protective instinct or a maneuver to help Paul make an inroad into secular entertainment?

"Well, tell me about him," he said.

I did.

"I'll tell you what," he said. "Don't bring your husband this time. That might be awkward. But I think I've got some ideas to help him."

So, idiot that I was at the time, I drove to this man's Beverly Hills home. From the minute I walked in, I knew things were weird. It was not an appropriate place for me to be. And this is the main reason why most women don't speak out on sexual harassment: even if you haven't done a thing wrong, you're still seen as guilty. People say, "Well, she should have been smart enough not to put herself in that position." But I was, what, twenty-five, twenty-six? I was relatively new to Hollywood, and I was naïve. This was strictly business on my part.

As we went through the motions of looking at the pictures, he asked me to stand and turn around. This wasn't a modeling agency like Zoli or Ford; there was no reason for him to check out my body. It continued to feel not right. But his conduct wasn't so blatant that I could say, Forget it.

Next thing I knew he had to show me his fancy sports car—and take me for one of those mindlessly macho I'll-show-you-what-this-baby-can-do drives. As we drove, he pointed out Paul Newman and Joanne Woodward's place, among others. I was thinking, I've really got to get home now.

He parked the car in front of Paul and Joanne's place (they lived mostly in Connecticut but must have been spending time in L.A.), and I said, "Look, I've got to be getting home. My husband's waiting up." I was getting edgy, looking for an exit, and of course I knew by now that working with him was out of the question.

He was wearing a sweat suit. Just as I was getting out of the car, he suddenly grabbed my hand and forced it on his lap. I freaked. Blood rushed to my head. "Stop it!" I demanded. "I have to GO!" I tried to pull back, but just that much contact was all this deviate needed. This was what his whole demeaning charade had been leading up to. I felt like throwing up.

Then I got frightened. I was in Beverly Hills. I still had to go back inside this man's house and get my purse and keys. Boy, I learned my lesson. It was dark, there were no streetlights, and I didn't know my way around. Plus, I was trapped in his car and had no guarantee this pervert wouldn't get rough with me.

But he let me go. All this took only two or three minutes, but by then, the damage was done. He had subjected me to an unspeakably humiliating and disgusting violation.

It was chilling to ponder what else he might have done to others, and what more he might have done to me. I might have gotten off lightly. He could have raped me—who knows? There were others at home upstairs. Maybe that was why he forced that trip in the car.

When I watched the Clarence Thomas and Anita Hill hearings, I thought to myself, You know, it happened to me, and nobody would believe that I hadn't provoked him or encouraged him or in any way come on to him. I could imagine jurors letting themselves believe I was just there to get what I wanted, to get a break, be a star, tantalize him with my pictures, and use him. So then it would just be part of the deal that he would use me. A good defense lawyer could do that—and rake me over the coals in the process. I felt that if all that *did* happen to Anita Hill—and I believe there was some truth to what she claimed—I had no problem understanding why she hadn't spoken up for so long.

Who would have believed her? What decent, moral person could imagine that these grotesque events are everyday occurrences for women in all walks of life—in the offices of dark-suited corporate executives, top elected officials, even so-called "men of God"? It's mind-boggling—and shameful—to contemplate.

In less harrowing forms, sexual harassment is rampant on our streets. One woman against a pack of hard hats hooting and hollering can feel outnumbered, demeaned, and vulnerable. And I was pretty daggone vulnerable that night in Beverly Hills. I just didn't know this about men. My brother, father, and male friends never talked about or treated women disrespectfully. If a girlfriend had ever warned me, say, to stay away from the old casting couch before an audition, I probably would have gone in, taken a look around, and suggested fabric ideas for new slipcovers. I mean, we're talking *clueless.*

But after that incident I was no longer an innocent. I was learning the ways of this world. I was learning that I wanted to make it in my field, but I knew I would never give away sexual favors to get there. I got smart in a hurry. I agreed to meetings only in offices. I agreed to "do" lunch, never dinner, and I learned never to let the man drive me to the restaurant but to meet him there.

That sleazoid actually had the gall to call me again and casually ask, "Well, so what do you think?"

"I think I never want to see you again as long as I live," I said, and I slammed the phone down.

Men know what kind of power they have over women, especially if they're in control. I'm sure it happens the other way, too, with women who are in control. It happens everywhere. In Frank's world. The Mets' world. Magic's world. "Women Who Harass Men"—I know, it sounds like Oprah's next show.

Frank says he's been sexually harassed all his life. He had women chase him and send him notes. Or he'd be at a party and some of his friends' wives, or the wives of business partners or associates, would slyly pass him notes and things like that. That's sexual harassment, though without the workplace issue of power and—unless you're talking about a wacko like the woman in *Fatal Attraction*—without the physical jeopardy a woman almost always experiences. But that sort of behavior is awkward, and it's unbelievably rude.

A man can walk away, not see the woman again, or if he's the boss, he can just avoid her or fire her. And some men would probably admit that they enjoy the flattery and ego-stroking of such direct and aggressive pursuit—partly because that behavior cuts against the culturally ingrained stereotype of women as coy and passive.

But a woman isn't flattered by sexual harassment; she's diminished and insulted. She has to confront it and fight. I was just lucky I didn't owe this man anything in terms of my career.

Another Hollywood slimeball tried something similar on my sister. This guy was a onetime partner of one of the most successful TV personalities and entrepreneurs in the business. He tried to seduce Michie one night by putting amyl nitrate up her nose. "Poppers" were a big thing at discos in the late 1970s. It was like the orange juice pitch: Poppers—They're Not Just for Cardiac Arrest Anymore. Back then, amyl nitrate was a party drug. Men would jam poppers up a girl's nostrils for this unbelievable (so I was *told*) thirty-second rush that heightened orgasms like you wouldn't believe. And then heightened (so I was *told*) headaches like you wouldn't believe. My sister didn't get the high or the headache—she ran off before he could do anything to her.

Sexual harassment is complex, subtle, and highly subjective. But you know when it's happening. When you're standing in an elevator and somebody's a little too close, you sense it, sense that intrusion into your space. It's very much the same issue with sexual harassment. I can tease and flirt with the best of them, but for somebody to say, "You've got a great body," or "Say, would I like to get you alone"—that's a violation.

And I came to believe that the producer was no worse than some of the pastors whose homes I would go into. Some tried to turn women on with poppers, others with prayers. In church it was "Let's pray together," but sometimes it felt more like "let's *play* together." They'd put their arm around you and suddenly they were sending up a prayer you felt might just be a bit too familiar.

And I had one of *those*, too—a "psalm-enchanted evening"—with a man on the road. It was enchantment mixed with madness and prayer, it was anything but adulterous and, though drugs were indirectly involved, it had nothing to do with the dark perils of harassment. On the contrary. It was the night country singer Larry Gatlin says I really might have saved his life.

Shortly after I began my affiliation with Coca-Cola, my agent Henry Jaffe finally got me booked on "The Dinah Show." The taping was at Burt Reynolds's dinner theater in Jupiter, Florida. It was a big event. We were using the show to announce my signing on as the new "Coca-Cola Girl," replacing Dottie West. Some Coke people flew down from Atlanta. Mom and Dad flew in. I was so nervous and excited at the afternoon rehearsal. I saw Burt sitting in his restaurant. I'd always loved Burt's work, and I'd heard so many great things about him: "Gonna love Burt," "Burt's a sweetie," "Burt's gonna love you." I went up to Burt awkwardly because he just looked so sullen. I had no idea what to say. I introduced myself and blurted, "So nice to meet you. Gee, we're really gonna have some fun today." And he looked at me with those sarcastic eyebrows and said, "Oh, yeah? You think so?" And that was it. That's all he had to say.

I stumbled off, wondering, Oh, dear, what did I just do?

The theme of this show was "What Is Macho?" Dinah's guests were all men—Burt, James Brolin, Lee Majors, Joe Namath, Paul Williams, and the Gatlin Brothers—except me. I had met Larry when he and the brothers guested on "Hee Haw Honeys" and found him very cute and sexy. Nothing had changed on that score—and, as the country tune said, we were both still "married, but not to each other."

I was supposed to come on right after Namath. And I stood waiting, my heart racing, in the hallway outside the greenroom as each guest went on and each guest came off.

The taping ended and I never got on. I stood there wondering what had gone wrong. Had they run out of time? Were Burt and Dinah, who were still in love, having a bad day? Was it a colossal dingbat boo-boo to cavalierly assume to Burt that we were "gonna have some fun"? Did Dinah fear me as the "next Dinah"? All I know is that I felt it was time, as Dinah might have put it, for me to see the U.S.A. in my Chevrolet and get outta Florida quick. And, with the Coca-Cola people and my parents on hand, it was one of the most painful, humiliating moments of my life. I was deeply hurt.

But Larry and his brothers were incredibly sweet and sensitive to me and helped talk me through it. The show asked me to stay and tape my segment the next day. That night I walked into a restaurant in town with the reps from Coke. A lot of people from the show were there. I freaked. But the instant they saw me, they all stood and started clapping for me.

I just totally lost it. I ran to the ladies' room and sobbed my eyes out. I was touched by this stirring vote of confidence. They knew I had tried to be a class act through a very touchy and painful time. I'd been rejected a zillion times; but this had insulted me beyond words.

Larry and I, among others, stayed on for the next day's taping, and Dinah was great with me on the air. Everything went fine, and afterward Larry said casually, "Give me a call when you get back to the room and we'll all go get a drink."

We arranged to meet in the downstairs lounge of the hotel at a certain time and I went down. Steve and Rudy Gatlin were there with a bunch of their friends, but Larry was gone. I finally asked Rudy what was going on. "Larry's upstairs," he said, "and I think he's really out of it. You oughta give him a call."

I called and couldn't tell *what* condition he was in. I had never been around drugs, except for a little marijuana when the surfers were hanging out. It had made the surfers mellow, but Larry was crazed and incoherent. "I'll be right up," I said.

When he opened the door to his room, Larry stood there with nothing on but a towel around his waist. The room was totally dark, and he staggered in, bumping into things. I guided him to the bed and just sat there with him. I talked to him, I held his hand, I got cold washcloths from the bathroom and pressed them against his forehead. He'd be fine for a few minutes and then he'd go rambling on kind of crazy. It was one of the most bizarre nights of my life. We sat there in the dark together, praying. I just wanted to keep him from going to sleep. I thought he'd never wake up.

Larry was, as they say, wired. He'd been partying with members of the show staff and hangers-on whom he'd collected at the bar downstairs. Larry was, by his own admission, "absolutely crazy, loaded up, and drunk." And for years, he later acknowledged, his entire life had been "a daily matter of going insane" like this. That night he'd been bingeing on a potentially lethal mix of what he called "Siberian Comas"—tall half-vodka, half-soda drinks with lime— and "Peruvian marching powder," which I figured out was cocaine. He and his buddies would down their Comas, then bump their way to the men's room to "toot up," then down more Comas before "tooting up" some more.

Larry had gone off the deep end, with the sweats, the chills, the shakes, and the verbal rambling. Then, as he told it, tragedy struck: he ran out of coke. He was in the bar screaming and boasting about how he was about to call his pilot, "pack his cokehead pals" into the Gatlins' private jet, and fly from Jupiter to Miami "for a score." Larry said he was ready to do anything "to score more drugs." He said he could have killed himself or someone else in the process. He was really gone.

The craziest part was that Larry was still very attractive to me. He was—and is—a gorgeous, talented guy. There was a point where Larry made a move to kiss me. Nothing more.

But in all honesty, there was nothing I would rather have done that night than go to bed with Larry, even in his condition. Larry was very physical, tactile—and I am very much like that.

But he was a brother in the Lord. I was a Christian. It wasn't right, and he needed my help. But believe me, I could have used some of *his* help. Could I have had a satisfying sexual experience with Larry? Hey, I could have had a satisfying sexual experience with *Godzilla* at that time in my life. Larry didn't need sex. He needed a friend. And that, in my way of sizing up the moment, took precedence over my needs and wants. But I know I was capable of a transgression.

That night, we just held each other for a very long long time, praying and crying together until he passed out.

Some people write country tunes about one-night stands. Larry now had material for a tune about a one-night standoff.

Since then Larry has gotten his life back together. In fact, when "Good Morning America" got the word that he was finally detoxing in December 1984, he agreed to head off the tabloids and go public on the show. As it happened—and we both believe this was a divine bit of booking—I was in for Joan Lunden the third week of January 1985 when he came on to do his two-part piece. It certainly made for a dramatic interview, since the interviewer happened to know something about her subject.

It was amazing I didn't actually know *more* about the subject, in fact. That night in Jupiter I was in an unhappy marriage. I had been roughed up and was vulnerable and needy. So there he was—this guy who could have had any woman he wanted, though he is married—almost naked on the bed. I was keeping him alive, going back and forth to the bathroom with the cold cloths. And we never stopped praying. We prayed for my marriage; he knew mine was a disaster. We prayed for his, and Lord knows his drug and drink binges weren't helping life with Janice, his high school sweetheart from Odessa, Texas, and their beautiful kids.

We got through it, and we bonded for a long and sweet friendship. Larry saved his marriage, and I have come to adore and respect Janice Gatlin. They are frequent houseguests of ours. Janice is a terrific and very funny lady. She has been a steadying influence for Larry, the rock he has needed. In that way, she is like Frank for me. She stood by him through Larry's four or five years of madness and I give her enormous credit.

Back then I tried to stand by Paul. It was miraculous that I didn't lapse. I didn't even fantasize. I wasn't living in denial. That's psychology. I knew what my problems were. But fooling around was forbidden. And that's spirituality. The same strong unbending will that allowed me to keep my virginity twenty-three-plus years allowed me to remain technically faithful.

I had amazing inner strength then. And I would need every bit of it, because things were going to get a lot worse before they got better.

Smile When Your Heart Is Breaking, Smile Even Though It's Aching

When people have built their lives on the transcendent power of spiritual faith, they cannot help but feel that God looks for ways to test that faith. My mother's childhood was filled with brutal tests of her heart and soul. Davy's "disappearing act" had tested us; Michie's illness was a terrifying yet rewarding trial—a wakeup call from above that shook us forever from spiritual lethargy. Never again could any of us take for granted the sweetest treasure of all—life itself—or the love that held our family together. In that Jupiter, Florida, hotel room, I was given a brief but challenging spot quiz by the Lord covering the subject of fidelity. And, Lord knows, my marriage was turning into a daily test of my embrace of the beliefs and values I had grown up with and which had shaped my life. My career was a series of tests of my self-esteem, which, in turn, was anchored in the precious belief that had dwelt within me since I accepted the Lord—that He would love me and help me make something beautiful of my life.

There was indeed no shortage of ways for God to get our attention. We learned that humbling, if inspiring, lesson all over again with startling clarity on June 2, 1980, the day my blue-eyed, angel-faced niece Shannie had her second birthday. It was a day filled with moments and images I will never be able to get out of my mind. None of us who were there will, either.

It was no ordinary second birthday. I flew in from California, while Craig's mom and dad flew in from Missouri. Michie, Craig, and

115

my parents, of course, all came down from Bowie. And Shannie had a whole bunch of new little friends to celebrate with: the other gravely ill children who, like Shannie, were patients on the pediatric care wing of Children's Hospital in Washington.

Shannie, we had learned, had been born with a condition known as pulmonary stenosis. Due, most likely, to Michie's illness during pregnancy, the pulmonary valve to Shannie's heart was constricted, and as a result she had an enlarged, overworked muscle in her heart that caused loud, labored breathing at night. We had noticed the breathing, but we didn't know why it was happening. One chamber of her heart, we learned, was clogged, and too little blood was flowing in. As a result she needed open heart surgery—the day after her second birthday.

Just a few years ago—and in many other parts of the country in 1980—children simply died from this disorder. Still, Michie asked: "What'll happen if she doesn't have the surgery?"

"By the age of five," a doctor said, "the odds are good that one day you'll walk in on her, she'll be blue, and she'll die."

As I looked around at these other children on that ward, many of whom were without family, I kept thinking, Thank God our little Shannie is surrounded by so many people who love her. We visited several times and realized many of those children—heart cases as well as cancer patients facing surgery or chemo—had no visitors. Or their single moms could come only in the evenings after work. The children just stayed by themselves, looking so lost and lonely. Each of us "adopted" a child to spend time with. I remember sitting in a little playroom with one little boy on chemotherapy who suddenly threw up all over me. And to me it was like a baptism, a privilege, and a blessing. That's the only way to say it. His mother had other kids and a job, and I thought, How do they get through it? You can't fail to examine your own life at a time like that. Then you realize what an obligation we have to serve others, to give back and to love those who most need it.

So we decided to throw a party on Shannie's birthday. The children were so excited and happy to have a little party in a playroom, the one place they knew was off limits to M.D.'s and medical procedures. It just broke my heart because I knew that some of these children were going to die before Shannie turned three. And some did.

Shannie was far more fortunate. I gave her a pull-toy we called Timmy Turtle, and as we walked through the hall to the surgery unit, this toddler in her hospital smock was pulling Timmy Turtle, happy, oblivious to the awful trauma her soft little body was about to undergo. Behind her was her entourage of eleven adults. It's a moment, and an image, I will always cherish.

The next day, when they bathed her prior to surgery, we tried not to show our fears. But I pictured the team slicing open her little chest. That and my time with Craig after Michie's ordeal were the darkest moments I've ever known in my life.

The surgery took a lot longer than anticipated. There was a complication: the surgeons found a hole in her heart. This more extensive damage required an extra procedure and more waiting. Now we were freaked out.

The operation finally ended, but it took Shannie a long while to come off the anesthesia. Michie and I were standing by her side, this small and delicate little angel with this tiny baby blanket over her, hooked up to tubes in her nose and her little arms. And I just kept thinking, This can't be happening. And when she came out of it—it was just like Michie coming out of her coma—she looked right at me first and said, "Aunt Kath, want Coke."

That's why when I now perform and I see my sister singing and Shannie standing in the wings I feel like crying for joy, for they are walking miracles. They are so much more precious to me because we almost lost them. I could never, ever take them, or anyone I love, for granted after that. Never. It was another test of our faith. We searched for reasons why Shannie would have to endure such an ordeal. We tried to contain our anger at the Lord. We sent up constant prayer and we were bonded as one in our anguish—and bonded as one in our relief when it was over.

I don't remember being close to my husband through all this. This crisis was driving another huge nail into the coffin of our marriage. Paul wasn't around for the surgery. He had asked my father to take him to the airport that morning—he had some reason to go. I said, "Can't you wait at least until she's out of surgery?" The last thing my daddy wanted to do was drive Paul to the airport. He wanted to be with his granddaughter. I always sensed Paul was embarrassed by the demonstrative emotionality of my family. Paul and Michie always had a keen affection for each other; they were, in fact, linked more compatibly in some ways than Paul and I were. But I felt he never wanted to be a part of my family.

The past year and a half had been an incredibly tough test for us. We had been through years of therapy and counseling with pastors and therapists. We saw our pastor, Jack Hayford, at the Church of the Way in Hollywood. We saw the respected Dr. James Dobson in

Orange County quite a few times. He was an expert on Christian marriage and therapy, with radio shows and numerous books to his credit. We'd drive two and a half hours so Dr. Dobson could tell me he thought everything was my fault. I'll never forget that. If I just gave up my career and stayed home and was the wife Paul needed me to be, then we'd be fine, he said.

Paul was on my side on that score. "You're wrong," he'd tell Dobson. "I don't want her at home. If I wanted a maid and a cook I'd hire one."

We took a vacation to Hawaii in 1980 that I had hoped would be a wonderful, romantic rekindling between us. The weather was fine; the vibes were cold and raw. Paul went off on his own a lot and there was nothing physical between us. We had a big blowup and I said something like "What on earth are we married for?"

When we got back home we were walking on eggshells. I'm going to disappoint him, I'd think, or I'll say something wrong. You can't live like that and sustain a healthy self-image. This was a marriage I believed was made not only in but *for* heaven. Yet I had spent some five years trying to be perfect and even that wasn't enough. That can really do a brutal number on your self-esteem.

I had tried to be everything for Paul, including a successful entertainer whose talents he would respect. I also cared for Paul during his awful migraine attacks when he suffered horrendous, disabling pain. In the throes of these "auras" he needed careful attention and medication. I felt so sorry for Paul. I remember one time we were visiting my family in Bowie and Paul awoke in the middle of the night with the pain coming on. He asked me to get up and take him to the airport at 4:00 or 5:00 A.M. so he could catch a plane to Seattle, where his doctor father could help him. That happened more than once.

Sometimes I'd drive him to Glendale in the middle of the night—again, this happened more than once—to a doctor friend of ours. Paul would be bent over in the passenger seat, holding his head in agony. The doctor would give him medicine which gave Paul some relief, but it also made him sleepy. I'd drive him home, undress him, and put him to bed. He'd sleep like a baby and then he'd be fine again. And he'd barely remember anything the next day.

The migraines were heartbreaking and disruptive of his life, and they made me feel helpless. He could never predict the onset of these auras. How many dinners with friends were we forced to cancel because he got an attack and had to stay in a blacked-out room? He suffered tremendously. I could not relate to the pain Paul endured, but I know it was a terrible thing for him to have to live with. And who knows what effect that pain had on our life?

But there was no killing the emotional pain of our failing marriage. At Paul's suggestion, we searched beyond conventional therapy for some relief. We made five or six trips to a counseling center in New York, which Paul felt did good work.

I found it very weird. Their premise was this: once we come to grips with contempt—that was the buzzword—toward a father, mother, or church, say, we can deal with our problem and get help.

In some sessions clients were triple-teamed by counselors. I attended a female group led by a trio of married women. They tried to tell me that I hated my mother, and they tried to manipulate me into denouncing her and saying horrendous things about her. I got angry and defensive. "I *love* my mother," I said. "Don't try to make me hate her. Aren't you thrilled to meet somebody who doesn't hate her mother?"

If I was ever going to have my big breakthrough analyzing Mom, this was the time. And *this* is the horrible secret I'd been hiding: While Michie and I were at ORU, Mom and Dad visited Tulsa and drove us to Dallas, where we had a Campus Crusade for Christ concert. It was hot and late, and we had had car trouble. We were tired and starved. But at every pit stop and McDonald's we'd go, Naw, we'll eat at the hotel.

By the time we got to our hotel close to midnight, everything was shut tight and "room service" was but a fantasy. Mom, as always, beelined for the bathtub "to bathe this body beautiful," as she liked to say. Daddy unwound by watching TV. As Michie and I unpacked, I recalled that I had brought Carnation Breakfast Squares for the trip and was down to the last two-square packet. Perfect, I figured. We'll all share them and it'll at least hold us over till tomorrow.

I looked everywhere. They were gone. I combed the suitcases for them to no avail. Then Michie and I slowly looked up at each other and it hit us at the same instant: Mom.

We shook our heads. "No, she wouldn't do that to us."

"No way. Come on, get real. *She's our mother!*"

We burst into the bathroom just in time to catch Mom contentedly smacking her lips and trying to pick the last floating crumbs off the bathwater. She calmly looked at us and shrugged innocently: "I was hungry."

"What kind of mother," I said, "takes food *out of* her children's mouths? You're supposed to feed us. You could've at least *shared* them with us."

"Oh, you girls are always on a diet anyway."

Okay. She scarfed down my last two Carnation Breakfast Squares. For that I should be filled with *hatred* and *contempt* for the woman? *Get a life!*

I always walked out of those counseling sessions thinking, I really hate this. Why do we need this? Can't we just go home and be married and be happy? It was like outtakes from a Woody Allen movie to me. And not one of the good ones, either. Here we had bougainvillea all over our new house, a beautiful pool, and a garden—we gardened constantly. And as if we weren't already having enough problems, we'd leave that 70-degree sun-drenched California garden in the middle of winter to go to New York City, walk up those weird steps and into that cold and manipulative place in the dreary bowels of SoHo where I'd sit with these gnarly strangers who'd look at me funny and say, "Have you always hated your mother?"

Did I need this aggravation? It was so horrible. When I go to New York I like to walk around, visit the galleries, go to the theater, shop at the fine department stores and fancy boutiques, eat lunch at Sardi's. Don't drag me down to this place and subject me to "You don't love your mother, you hate your mother."

But Paul respected his therapists' approach. He read up, he listened to audiotapes, he even met with the center's founder. He attended night sessions where people "testified" about how they explored their various "issues." And Paul—a cerebral, sensitive, and excruciatingly complicated person—explored his. I do believe the sessions were helpful for him intellectually. That help never translated into dramatic improvements at home, but I felt it important to stand behind him and support him. This was my Mother Teresa martyr role. I was trying to save my marriage. I thought it was going to give him some insight and I tried to be a sport.

The irony was: I really needed a trusting, comforting outlet for sharing my feelings, and none of the therapies worked for me. I could never admit to my parents and close friends then how bad things were. I was ashamed—and afraid for the longest time that they'd hate Paul. When they later found out, they were deeply upset. It's hard for parents. It would kill me for Cody to go through what I went through. I know it was very tough on Paul's family, too. It's got to be devastating for a parent to watch a child in an unhappy relationship.

At times, I felt worse than unhappy; I was annihilated. I once asked

Paul why he didn't seem to love me. He simply said, "I can't love you because I don't respect you."

There were, in fairness, two sides to the story. I believe Paul came to see me as a spiritual phony. I think he lost some respect for me when my secular career took off. He openly resented the fact that I had aggressive agents and managers who were guiding my career and making me "a star." Ironically, Paul, who had urged me to strike out on my own and make it as a high-energy entertainer, felt singed by those same 220 volts when he began to feel that his own stature in the Christian musical community was slipping.

"It was overpowering me. She was no longer my wife," Paul later said. "She was this show-business property. That felt sleazy. It pulled me off my spiritual path, my center. It wasn't what we had dreamed about. I felt damaged."

Clearly we were both hurting. But in my home you didn't go sniveling to Mama. As I said, you make your bed and you lie in it. Or, in my case, for much of the previous two years I had been making the *guest room bed* and lying in it. And I had felt cheapened every day of my life when I woke up in that room. I had believed I was marrying a man who would love me and care for me and be a husband to me. I had earlier come to see that the greatest distance in the world is the one between two people in bed who don't love each other, and that distance certainly didn't get any shorter once I began sleeping in the guest room. That was degrading to me as a woman. I had had twenty-two years of a positive upbringing that told me I was worthy of love and a good, kind person, not an inadequate one.

Paul would wait until I was asleep to come upstairs, and he'd get up before I did. I felt like such a dirt rag. I'd come down in the morning; he'd come down in the morning. We'd have coffee and read the papers. He'd go to the studio or office; I'd water the plants. I couldn't wait for a job so I could leave the house.

If we had begun our marriage with a shared dream—the marriage as a ministry—we were now living what had once been our worst nightmare: the Christian sham marriage. The wicked irony was that I *was*, after all, turning into Anita's handpicked protégée, though hardly in the role either of us expected.

Also ironic was the fact that Michie and I had begun doing seminars for young Christian women around the country—when my private life was beginning to feel like a facade. We saw some disturbing trends in Christendom with the rise of the born-again movement, and we hoped to send out a message of our own about the quality and purpose of the walk with God.

We felt many Christians, in their righteous, sometimes arrogant, fervor, were far removed from what was happening in the secular world. Faith in the Lord was being mass-marketed on Christian talk shows and "I Found It" bumper stickers. There was an insidious and anti-scriptural "Name it and claim it" mentality—you merely professed yourself to be a true believer and that entitled you to material gains or instant healing. "In the name of Jesus, by the blood of Jesus, I am healed!" Or "I name it and I claim it in the name of Jesus!" My reading of Scripture had taught me that people who loved Christ were destined to suffer, not clean up at the races or in business. "Getting it" or "Finding it" seemed to be taking on the shady glibness of a chain letter or a late-night mail-order miracle cure. "It" wasn't about winning the lottery or beating cancer overnight. It was about enduring surgery or chemo; it was about understanding why Michie and Shannie had been asked by the Lord to suffer. It was supposed to offer the blessing of true faith—which meant tests and trials and the resultant wonder of God's miracles.

So many young Christians were simply missing the point, losing touch with the world around them—the same world to which they are supposed to minister. And in particular, Michie and I felt the need to help our young sisters in Christ integrate themselves into the real world without having to become the minister's wife or the church organist, unless that was what they *wanted*. They had such a limited scope of what they could be in God's world, and we hoped to expand their vision and encourage them to explore other paths.

At our seminars Michie would testify about her own suffering, Shannie's condition, and how God had healed them by guiding them through their pain. It's so easy to spew "Praise God"'s when you've had an instantaneous cure or when something wonderful occurs. It's a little harder to praise God and cling to the belief that He loves you when you're in the throes of a disease, during radiation and chemotherapy and rehab, and when you're barfing your guts out and in physical agony.

We wanted to instill some practical uses for the values we had developed through our walk with the Lord: to not simply see others as potential trophies to win for the Lord; to live in harmony with people rather than feel superior and self-righteous in their midst simply because they didn't share our faith.

We had seen this arrogance and elitism in "good Christians" all along the gospel highway. But we got brutally hurt by it in, of all places, the PTL (Praise the Lord) Club in Charlotte, North Carolina. Michie and I had agreed that we would appear with Jim and Tammy

Faye Bakker before we knew when Shannie's surgery would be. I felt we should just cancel the appearance, but Michie's feeling was: My word is my word and I must honor it or it has no value. We wanted to discuss how a disease or loss doesn't nullify God's power, but glorifies it. What an amazing testimony Michie had! I called the PTL producers and said, "My sister's baby has just had heart surgery. We will come only if we can talk about how God has healed in the midst of suffering rather than *gotten rid* of the suffering." They said okay.

Shannie had been home from the hospital just one day when we left Bowie. It was agony for Michie to leave. Some people would say she was a bad mother. But because of the world we grew up in, we saw this as a higher calling. Jim Bakker was not there then, just Tammy. I had been a guest several times, but I'd never felt comfortable. Something about their ministry felt wrong. I never believed Jimmy Swaggart either, with all his manipulative sobbing.

Tammy Bakker has never been happy sharing the spotlight, especially with other women whom she considers more talented or attractive—which, excuse me, had me worried: "What were Michie and I doing on her show?" I'm sorry, she may be lovely underneath it all, but pounds of mascara, false eyelashes, tons of pancake makeup, teased hair, and quivering cleavage is my idea of a caricature of a woman.

I was ashamed that they were the hottest thing going in Christian TV. It was all unbelievably *shallow*. I felt many of these evangelists probably had started out sincerely, loving God, wanting to serve Him. But then they get rich, and they get lost. They start believing their own press. It's just like Hollywood or sports or any field driven by a star system.

And there were no bigger stars in the new evangelism than the Bakkers. We had gone to Charlotte with the assurance that we would do four songs and then share our testimony about suffering and God's healing in the midst of it. Tammy kept looking over at us in the wings throughout her appearance, but the show just went on and on and on, and in the end there was time only for us to sing "What a Friend We Have in Jesus," and we did no witnessing. And Michie had left her bandaged-up baby with open-heart surgery for *this?* This seemed to me to be the very definition of obscenity.

My sister—my loving, giving, gracious, kind, and forgiving sister —had come to share her life with others and had been treated so unkindly and with so little sensitivity to what she'd just endured. As the credits were running at the close of the show, Tammy asked Michie how Shannie was doing. Tammy had seen the little red light and knew the camera was on her. And so she was nodding and half listening as Michie tried to tell her about Shannie pulling through her surgery.

Then the red light went off and, while Michie was *in mid-sentence,* Tammy walked off. At that moment I said to myself, I will never be a part of this again as long as I live. That was it for me. And this was years before their scandal blew open. I know this sounds self-righteous of me, but the truth is, I didn't want to make one more dollar in the name of God after that. I did not want to buy a dress, buy mascara, pay my mortgage with one dollar made from God. I did not want to have anything to do with that world again. Sure, there were still men like Billy Graham in the world, but this was not Billy Graham's world. It was a world full of people seeking power, ego gratification, and monetary and material wealth in the name of serving God. Yes, I love nice things as much as the next person; but I wasn't going to earn money and acquire goods by climbing over the backs of people like my Michie and Shannie. I can't explain how much it bothered me that they could get the poor and vulnerable to fork over their fixed incomes and pensions and Social Security payments as a way of praising the Lord, when in fact the money wasn't going to much of God's work at all. Many PTL workers were loving, truly caring people, but others were caricatures of people of God. Michie, bless her, was the genuine article.

Believe it or not, the Bakkers asked me to do a promo after that and say how wonderful the PTL Club was. After one of the most upsetting experiences I'd ever had *in my life?*

No way, Tammy Faye! If I raised a *penny* for them, then I too would be responsible for what they were doing.

The PTL disaster was a sign that it was time for me to graduate from the world of Christian entertainment, where the dream had always been about our serving the Lord with our musical ministry through marriage.

I had no idea that graduation day was coming up so soon.

I Shall Be Released

In October of 1981 I left town for three weeks of work—two weeks on my own, doing the nightclub act at the Atlanta Hyatt Regency, and a week in Reno, where I opened for Bill Cosby at Harrah's. Shortly before leaving I had filled in for two days as a substitute host on "A.M. Los Angeles," a local talk show. The first day, a Thursday, I hosted with local weatherman Johnny Mountain and on Friday with a newscaster named Harold Green. All kinds of people had been filling in since the departure of the show's regular hosts—a droll, acerbic talk show veteran named Regis Philbin and Cindy Garvey, then the wife and later ex-wife of Dodger baseball great Steve Garvey. Regis left the show to do a national NBC show, which was canceled; then he went on to New York to do "The Morning Show."

I felt right at home with the format. There was no pressure, and after all, I wasn't pursuing a talk show career. I laughed a lot with both my co-hosts, took some teasing about my La La Girl days, and did an interesting interview with Erica Jong. Her new book, out just in time for Halloween, was called *Witches*. In my eagerness to do well, I had prayed to the Lord the night before for insight on how to handle this interview, and the Lord's answer was: get her to explain the paradox between feminism—which is all about will and autonomy—and witchcraft, which is about sticking voodoo pins and casting spells and taking people's choice away. The Lord would make quite the segment producer. We struck gold—that's when you create a great moment on air. And Erica herself was gold—gregarious, campy, funny, and extremely intelligent.

The producers wanted me to come back on Monday, but by then I would be on my way to Atlanta. Later on, while I was at Harrah's in Reno, I got an excited call from my agent, Sam Haskell. The executive producer of "Good Morning America," Susan Winston, had just called him to say she had seen me on "A.M. Los Angeles" and wanted to meet with me. My agent's impression was that they were looking for someone to take over for Joan Lunden. *Yeah, right.* After *two days* as a fill-in morning host.

"I'm an actress, I'm a singer—I can't do that," I said. "Are they crazy?" But I must admit I was flattered, and I agreed to meet with her.

When I flew back to L.A. from Reno I took a cab to my house. I was exhausted from the long road trip and living out of suitcases. I paid the cabbie, hauled my luggage up the front walk, and found the door was closed but unlocked. The lock had been broken and it was still not fixed.

Or else we had been robbed. I pushed the door open and warily looked inside. My heart stopped. We *had* been robbed. GRAND THEFT—MARRIAGE. Five and a half years of our lives were suddenly missing.

Half the stuff in my house was gone. The piano was gone. The TV and stereo were gone. Pictures had been taken off the walls. Closet doors were open. Clothes had been yanked off hangers and removed. But surprisingly, Petula Sue was still there.

It was over.

I was in shock. My mouth hung open as I stared around. I don't know how long I stood there with my bags, feeling like an idiot, not a friend in the world. I walked around to inspect.

Paul was gone, all right. I couldn't believe it.

I found a short note on the kitchen counter that said, in effect, that Paul felt it best that we live apart; that he needed time to figure out what he wanted to do; that he would never get my attention until he did something like this to show me how desperate things were. Actually, it wasn't being apart but being *together* that had shown me how desperate things were. His note didn't make a whole lot of sense to me. I didn't know what he wanted to shock me *into*. I didn't want the marriage to end. I just wanted an end to the *kind* of marriage we had. I didn't want to keep living the lie.

Reaching out to touch someone was out of the question. My parents had no idea how bad it had been. I needed to get centered before I acted like a maniac and unloaded on everyone.

The house was a half-empty wreck, the marriage was over, and it was now time to vacuum. I figured that would pull me together. First

I rearranged furniture, moved things around, filled in the empty spaces to make a new home.

But the vacuum was gone from the hall closet. No problem. Head high and determined, I went to a discount store and bought my own vacuum cleaner. I always figured you buy a vacuum cleaner, take it out of the box fully assembled, and go. Wrong. This thing was like in a thousand pieces. Our tool chest was still there, but I am not exactly Ms. Fix-it, so this was like Outward Bound survival training for me. I got out the tools, plunked myself down on the floor with the dumb little screws, washers, and manual and—as tears streamed down my face—put the daggone thing together in about an hour.

And let me tell you, when I plugged that monster in, heard that wheezing motor kick over, and saw that hose actually sucking up dirt, it was like, "I am woman, hear me *roar!*" I believed all over again in miracles.

I was sobbing my eyes out as I worked. It was just like the good old early-retirement days after we married: I vacuumed, I cried. I waxed, I wept. I scrubbed, I screamed.

Vacuuming, which had once been the symbol of my failure as a dependent Total Woman, became that day a symbol of my (astonishing) ability to rebuild my life as an independent woman.

Thinking back to my parents' stories of childhood, I realized that I had inherited their survival genes. Those lifelong images of my parents that had haunted me now took on a new significance: my father asking his mom to let him leave dreary Baltimore for his cherished Chesapeake shore; Mom stepping off that lonely train with one suitcase and walking up to her sister's apartment. They had made it, and I knew I would make it. I would not be crushed by this, no way, no how. But I *was* crushed in three ways that mattered most to me: as a wife, since Paul had left me; as a woman, because he didn't want me; and as a Christian, because my so-called godly union had failed. Everything that should have made me feel good about myself was now gone. I had, for the first time in my life, *no* self-esteem whatsoever. It was like losing my skin. It was time to admit we'd been enduring a non-marriage marriage, a "union" that existed in a legal sense only. I had the painful realization that it had probably been an equally sad and lonely and empty experience for Paul.

I eventually learned that he had moved into a nearby condo. He gave me the phone number but not the address. In my deepening disorientation I figured that if he wanted to come back he would. I had the impression he was uncertain about all this and was renting a place while he sorted things out. I didn't learn until later that his parents had *bought* this condo for him—which, I must say, lent a certain ring of finality to the proceedings. I think a person looking to save a marriage sees a counselor, not a broker.

I was not going to let him ruin my life. And I didn't want to ruin his. I tried to focus on my feelings of relief rather than loss. A loveless marriage is much worse than being single. I'd rather be single for the rest of my life than be stuck in a bad marriage ever again. There's nothing so lonely as being in the same bed and worlds apart. Nuclear physicists can debate the feasibility of cold fusion in the lab all they want. I *know* it can be accomplished in the bedroom. That can be the coldest place in the world.

This was five and a half years into our marriage. And I had been unhappy for all five and a half of those years. Suddenly it was easier for me to see and admit the truth: that it had been a non-life. We were both lost in that marriage.

My family was extremely supportive, because although they didn't believe in divorce, they also didn't believe in misery. Mine or Paul's. And I know it takes two to make a lousy marriage. Of course my mother had seen it coming all along. We certainly loved Paul's family, and a strong bond still exists between Paul and Michie; but the strain of our marriage had taken effect.

I probably would have stayed in that marriage a long, long time if Paul hadn't left. I never imagined we'd divorce. We'd have likely stayed together because of the pressure on us to be the perfect Christian couple. As we grew older, though, something would have come along to end it. I had not had an affair; my heart was clean. But I probably would have had one eventually to provoke the end of the marriage.

I saw no hope for our marriage and I found myself quietly hoping that Paul would just disappear. I longed for an instant solution so that I wouldn't have to spend my one and only life with him. It's terrible to feel so trapped.

When I look back now I can honestly say that the kindest thing Paul ever did for me was to leave, to give me the wings to fly away and find a new life. Though my self-image was demolished at that time, his departure gave me another chance to have real love in my life. He didn't really want children, so I would never have had Cody. I would never have had a man like Frank in my life who unconditionally loves me for myself—no ifs, ands, or buts.

I am really very grateful to Paul. I know he was equally hurt, and I am to this day truly sorry for causing him pain, for not being "the one" for him. But when the marriage ended, the matter was settled in my heart. I am not bombarded by his image the way he is by mine today. I know it causes him anguish to see me on magazine covers and TV shows and to hear about me from friends. I wish nothing for him but the best life he can find. I bear no animosity whatsoever toward him, for he made it possible, ultimately, for me to search for—and find—the most precious gift a human being can receive in life.

After the marriage ended, I threw myself into my career with a vengeance. My mother—who may have stolen my last two breakfast squares—was on the next plane out to L.A. to spiritually nourish me and to be there for me. And she *stayed* there for me for three tumultuous, draining weeks. Mom's one of the world's great listeners. When I finally told her the whole story of my marriage, what she heard devastated her.

But life goes on, and in November mine went on to the Polo Lounge at the Beverly Hills Hotel for a meeting with Susan Winston, the exec producer of "Good Morning America" ("GMA"). We hit it off right away. She had been out several times and seen, as she put it, "every blonde in L.A." My understanding had been they were looking not only for on-air "talent," meaning a field correspondent, but for a fill-in host for Joan Lunden. From "GMA" insiders I would later hear stories of friction between her and David Hartman, and I inferred that the new person would be considered as a possible permanent replacement for Joan. When I met with Susan, she said they wanted someone "willing to travel and to do Purina dog food commercials in the studio."

I told Susan she was barking up the wrong talent. "I'm not a reporter. I don't want to be a reporter. Surely you can find someone," I said, "who has worked as long and as hard as I have, but in the right field."

Susan said she saw me as a lively, relaxed, and uninhibited person with "real good energy in front of the camera." Star quality. They were not, she added, hung up on finding "a seasoned, slick journalist." They wanted "a natural communicator who makes people feel at ease." So now I'd have to be good with people, learn how to be a TV reporter, *maybe* fill in for Joan, maybe *replace* Joan, *and* get along with pooches at six in the morning. *And* move to New York. This was turning into a big job.

At that point I felt it only fair to inform Susan that this uninhibited, live-wire schmoozmeister sitting opposite her in the Polo Lounge 90210 was just beginning to dig out from under the rubble of an 8.0

domestic earthquake whose spiritual epicenter was situated directly beneath Woodland Hills. I didn't want to just get lured to New York with a bogus prospect that would lead me nowhere, I told her. Having honed my singing career for ten years with gospel appearances and nightclub shtick, would I now want to become an overnight TV correspondent? Then again, if that could lead to a hosting spot, I was istening.

My full-disclosure approach actually warmed things up between us. "Look," I said. "My husband's just left me, and I have no idea what's happening in my marriage or my life. This isn't the greatest time for me to change careers, much less pick up and move to New York—unless I have a sense that the move is permanent and the new position has some stature. I don't need a job. I've got work that I love." I made it clear I wasn't going to turn my life inside out and move without some sort of a commitment, or at least an understanding that I'd be groomed to sit next to David Hartman someday. (For the record, Susan, who remains a friend to both Frank and me, strenuously denies ever mentioning that she was looking to replace Joan.)

When I asked her point-blank how serious this plan was, her exact words were: "I'm not shitting you." I'll never forget that, because it surprised me that this dynamic New York media woman would use language like that. I had come from a totally different world where people, especially women, *never* spoke that way. I'm crazy about her anyway!

Then I told Susan that no matter what happened to me at "GMA," there was no way I was going to give up singing, which was my first love.

"Is there any way I can talk you out of that?" she asked.

"Well, singing has brought me more pleasure and creative satisfaction than anything else, so I guess the answer is no."

We set up an audition for late December in New York.

Meanwhile, before Thanksgiving, I went up for a magazine-format TV pilot in L.A. called "Weekday." There was no way I could count on the "GMA" job, so I went for this one too. It would be two male hosts and me. The show was produced for NBC by Bob Banner Associates. I passed the audition, and we slated the field piece for right before Christmas.

The piece was on heli-skiing at a swanky ski resort in Utah. I was lowered by a rope from a chopper at the top of a mountain in deep virgin powder. I was out of my element. I was no longer a deep virgin, nor could I ski on powder. The crazy stuff you do in the name of "the show must go on."

But this is the really crazy part: right before going to Utah I had surgery on my eyes to correct serious nearsightedness. Three friends I'd run into recently had all undergone the same procedure—radial kerototomy—performed by the same renowned specialist, Dr. Ronald Jensen. And their eyes were perfect. So I saw Jensen and he decided to do the operation right away. I told Mom and Dad to pray, because I was going under the knife on my eyes. They freaked. So after taking half a Valium (my first) and with liquid cocaine on my clamped-open eye that got me feeling a bit strange, I had my left eye corrected in about five minutes. I went from 20/400 vision to 20/20 and let me tell you, this really *was* a miracle.

And not a day too soon. When I went for my "Weekday" audition at the studio, this absolutely adorable young man introduced himself to me as the associate producer. He was four years younger than I was, and I could not believe they made associate producers that young— or that friendly. His name was Don Weiner and he had the kindest smile I'd ever seen in my life.

By the time I had finished the Utah heli-ski field piece and the studio segments back in Hollywood, Don and I had become buddies. I felt incredibly comfortable around him, in part because he seemed mellow and self-assured. We spent time together hanging out, going for coffee breaks, lunches, even a couple of dinners. I couldn't be sure, but I was starting to feel there was *something* going on between us. I felt more alive, more womanly and attractive around Don than I had in a *long* time. He even came to my house a couple of times while Mom was in town. After church one day, the three of us went to brunch at the Polo Lounge.

Mom's eyesight was as good as mine. "I know," she said to me later. "A woman needs the affirmation that she is loved—and desired."

A woman in my situation also needed to know she was legally separated, but I hadn't talked to Paul since I'd been back, and I had no idea what our status was.

I went to New York and taped an audition for "GMA" that went pretty well—considering that the lights in the studio shut down. I didn't meet David and Joan, but I was sure Joan knew they were auditioning people to sit in for her. Susan waited until everyone was out of the studio except the crew. In the middle of my interview all the lights went out for a mandatory union break—a "technical five," as they say. No warning, just *boom!* Darkness. I just kept talking as if nothing had happened.

Christmas in Bowie that year was a bit weird. I didn't know if my "GMA" deal was going ahead, if the "Weekday" pilot would be picked up by NBC for a series—they had a six-month option on it and on me—or what Paul's next move would be.

But the New Year brought some clarity and movement. My legal separation went into effect on New Year's Day 1982, and Paul decided to begin the divorce proceeding.

Figuring that the odds of "GMA" coming through were slim to get-a-life, I moved out of our Woodland Hills home and bought my own adorable little town house in Coldwater Canyon.

The "Weekday" pilot was not picked up by NBC.

"GMA" offered me the job in May, to begin in June.

And I fell in love with Don Weiner.

The more time Don and I spent with each other, the harder I tried to keep the reins on my heart. But I adored him. He came over after work and helped me paint my new place, which was a fifth the size of the house I owned with Paul. But I didn't care. I'm a nester. I decorated it and made a little home, to move on with my life.

Thinking back, I thank God I met Don and not some jerk who would have taken advantage of my vulnerability. Don was the best thing that could have happened to me: he made me feel I was a treasure, not a trophy. As much as I wanted to, one of the hardest things I've ever done is not sleep with Don. I hadn't ever slept with anyone but my husband, and even then, well, it was never really happening. I was sick of this and beginning to wonder, Where's mine? What does it *take?* The Bible talks about sex between two people who are devoted and committed to each other as being the most beautiful thing in the world. The Song of Solomon is the sexiest thing I've ever read, and I longed for this kind of fulfillment.

I was in an almost paralyzing bind. I was terrified of marrying again or even getting involved *without* sleeping together first because of what I had just survived. But I didn't want to open up the complex issue of premarital sex. I felt I should follow the Bible, but I was shell-shocked from six years of following the Bible right into a loveless marriage. And I was in love with one man while still legally married to another.

But the upside was pretty terrific. Don loved children, so for the first time I could conceive, as it were, of having children together. A woman's maternal urges don't tend to surface when she's with a man who does not want children. It's amazing how far down humans can bury things in order to survive.

Not that I was looking to *rush* anything. He was so understanding and took great care to let me set the pace. We didn't go out in public together, but rather spent evenings in front of a fire all winter long (you need to snuggle through those brutal L.A. winters). Don's tender side melted me down when I desperately needed a friend, when my wounds were still so raw. It was the first time a person had preferred being with me over anybody else on the face of the earth. Don was a best friend who fell in love with me, the soul mate I'd never had in my life before. I cried a lot with him, talked a lot, and opened up to a man like never before.

In other words, and I mean this as the ultimate compliment: Don had many of the qualities that Frank Gifford embodies.

Had I not met Don, I don't know what I'd have done with myself. I honestly believe I would have been directionless, and I might have looked for love in all the wrong places. Don was safe, kind, and sweet at a time when I was terrified of a physical relationship, absolutely terrified. And though it was too soon for the kind of intimacy I craved, I can say that Don loved me back to life.

Don's family background was similar to mine. Like me, he was part Jewish; another part was Japanese. He had a beautiful heart. I once asked my niece, who was about three, if she knew why Don's eyes were just a little bit different from other people's. I said, "His mommy comes from a country far, far away called Japan, and everybody there has eyes like this." I pulled up the corners of my eyes, and Shannie said, "But, Aunt Kath, can they ever put their arms down?" Picture a whole nation of people walking around holding their fingers to their eyes. Michie and I screamed!

Don's father was the son of an Orthodox Jewish rabbi. After World War II, his dad was stationed in Japan and fell in love with Hiroko, who was Catholic. When he brought her home his family basically disowned him. But he and Hiroko married and had three children. Then while Don's dad was getting an advanced degree in journalism at Columbia University, he dropped dead from a brain hemorrhage, just like that. Don's mom, a courageous and resourceful woman, could barely speak English, but she got a job in a library on Long Island and raised three phenomenal kids. I believe she runs the library today.

Don went to Northwestern and was a dynamic go-getter, but hardly the typical raving Hollywood hustler. He never lost his temper, he was excellent under fire, and he had a great instinct for handling people in stressful situations.

If my new heartthrob was the good news, the bad news was the Ogre and Ogrette. Mom and Dad wasted no time in weighing in against the idea of the relationship, even though I knew Mom adored Don. They didn't even want me to *date* until the divorce was final. They also felt he was too young and that I had strayed from God's "excellent way." This made me crazy. In their opinion it was fine for me to be joylessly married in the eyes of God and the Golden State, but it was wrong for me to fall for someone who, for once in my adult life, truly cared for me. For the first time I seriously began to question all the sacred values I had grown up with. I knew that God understood me; people didn't.

Daddy didn't want to hear about rapture and romance and womanly needs. His feeling was that our family's divine laws, enforced by the parents, "narrowed a lot of choices" in life, as he put it, and left me with but one issue: "the urge and the challenge to be as good as you can be."

It felt like "molding" all over again, and my parents' love, for this brief time, didn't seem unconditional any longer. In my view, love survives despite disagreements, if it is a pure love. It shouldn't be "I love you, but get off my planet if you don't agree with me." Love is about accepting somebody without trying to impose your ideas, your religion, hopes, fears, values, whatever, onto another human being. It's just not fair.

Mom knew I was beaten down, Daddy knew that emotions could overpower the mind. But he was adamant and would not accept that I was in a relationship. God's excellent way meant gutting it out alone until I was legally sprung. Mom was closer to the middle ground than Dad. When Don and Mom and I had brunch together, she fell in love with him too, this greatest Christian woman of all time. She said he was the most physically beautiful man she'd ever seen, that he was more gorgeous than Tyrone Power. But she was struggling, too. "Your father's being better [meaning tougher] about this than I am," she said.

Mom, to whatever degree she condoned, or even understood, my attraction to Don, was filled with turmoil and spiritual compromise. As my mother she desperately prayed for my happiness, but she didn't see why part of my happiness had to involve a man. I'm not sure what she and Daddy thought would make me happy at that point—season tickets to the Lakers? Another season as a Hee Haw Honey? When Mom got home after her stay with me, she and Daddy were virtually at each other's throats over this. "People have far bigger problems than this in life," he said, "and they deal with them. Just because she's your daughter doesn't give you or her the right to accept this kind of behavior."

When I called home, Daddy sometimes got so mad that he actually hung up on me. At one point my parents even refused to take my calls. And that was fine with me. I could not believe that—given the unhappiness they now knew I'd endured in my marriage—they didn't want me to have happiness now. The truth was, at that time Don and I fully intended to marry when my divorce became final—when the state of California said I could, which was just bunk to me. I adored him and am still fond of him to this day.

My parents felt that if I wasn't living the Christian life I claimed to live, then they had to disassociate themselves from me.

At that time, as much as my family mattered to me, I was not going to be the dutiful, obedient daughter for the sake of fellowship with them. I thought they were wrong. I thought if I was going to make mistakes—and it was Daddy himself who'd always told me "we love you too much to deny you the privilege of making mistakes"—then they were really going to have to love me through them. I was twenty-eight. My rebellious teens had finally kicked in.

I was spiritually orphaned for just three days. Then my mother called, sobbing her eyes out, and said, "I can no more disown you than I can cut off my arm and not miss it. I do not under any circumstances condone your life-style, but you are and will always be my daughter, and I love you."

In late May the call came from Susan Winston's office that I had a new career as "on-air talent" in the media capital of the world and would start in June 1982. My life as a gospel singer, actress, and suburban wife in a spacious home had ended; a new life, as a single woman and an untested TV journalist in the biggest, craziest city in America, was about to begin.

I was elated, but I was also terrified of living in New York. Though I was in love and had been in my new town house less than a month, the offer could not have come at a better time. For while Don was a soul mate, he was, after all, a rebound soul mate. It was just too soon for me. In my heart I was afraid of making another huge mistake. The new job would put some healthy distance between us. I'd sort things out, wipe the slate clean, and begin all over again—with a whole new way of seeing the world. My way.

Yesterday All My Troubles
Seemed So Far Away

Shortly after I came to "GMA" in late June, I was about to do a puppy food commercial at sunrise when my new 20/20 eyes swept past an open dressing room—and locked on a man with an incredible set of buns. He was leaning over a sink, struggling with contact lenses. He was also extremely handsome and in better shape than me.

I looked like a chipmunk, a chubbette with chubby cheeks and little chubby buns. But nerves of steel.

"Have I got an operation for you!" I said, or some lame opener like that. This gorgeous man looked at me in the mirror like I was slightly cuckoo. It was then I learned that that tight end was none other than Frank Gifford's.

Frank had been subbing for David Hartman for a few years by then, an extension of his "ABC's Wide World of Sports" and "Monday Night Football" work. I knew all about number 16 from the old Giants-Colts rivalry my brother and father followed when we were kids and which culminated in what they now call "the greatest game ever played." To put it another way, Frank was an American legend long before I began shaving my legs.

Our first conversation was about contacts versus surgery—and we did not see eye to eye. I was pro-surgery and said it was a miracle cure. He was dead set against it. "My doctor," he said with a smirk, "says a scalpel is an instrument with a fool on each end. Surgery is dangerous and stupid."

Even with 20/20 vision I never saw much of Frank in those early days. I couldn't focus on much of anything once the culture shock, travel, and exhaustion set in. I saw departure and arrival gates, hotel rooms, field-piece locations, editing rooms around the country, and the network's studios in Manhattan's West Sixties. It was a brutal adjustment. I was crazed.

I did once dump lunch plans with my assistant to go for a three-hour lunch with Frank. I was going out the door when the phone rang. "Kathie, it's Frank," he said. "The Cowboy's in town. We're going to get some lunch, and you're coming with us."

All right! The Cowboy was, of course, Dandy Don Meredith, the onetime Dallas Cowboy quarterback and Frank's "Monday Night Football" buddy. These guys were a scream together. I had the greatest time and drank a little more wine than I should have. (Thanks to Frank I do that too often now, but he says he weaned me from margaritas and saved my life because I was turning into Pancho Villa.)

I was their little mascot. I kept saying to myself, What am I doing here? *I am out of my league.* They teased me relentlessly about my younger boyfriend across the country and how I was sure it would all work out. "Y'know, Kathie," Don drawled, "you know whatcha need to do?" I can see Frank has heard this good ole boy routine a million times. "Ya need t' have an affaih with a rilly nice *olduh* man." Don, who's happily married, assumed Frank was already putting the moves on me. "And you know how you'll know when you've seen him?" he went on.

"No, Don, how will I know when I've seen him?"

"He's gonna say t' you, 'Kathie, darlin', I'm gonna take a tour of you . . . from the top of your head to the tip of your toes . . . with lots of intermittent stops.'"

These two guys had been around the block several times and I hadn't even set foot on the curb. But they were charming and treated me like their little sister.

New York was lonely those first six weeks. I was holed up at the St. Moritz, which, okay, you could do worse, but I hated it. I hated New York. I am not a hotel person. I nest. I like my own things around. My ABC guru, Susan Winston, reassured me, "Kathie, just give the city a year. You'll never want to live anywhere else"—which is a scream because *she* later moved to California.

My first "home" was a furnished thirty-seventh-floor sublet on the West Side, but I didn't like subletting, either. A year later I bought a sweet ground floor–basement duplex in a West Seventieth Street brownstone near the studios and Central Park. It had brick walls, a fireplace, a garden in the back, and water in the basement. I fixed it up so it was just so charming, so Laura Ashley, so precious—so me!

But I was never there. One year I flew a quarter-million miles on American Airlines alone. In August 1984, during the L.A. Olympics, I made four coast-to-coast trips in nine days. On some trips I'd lug research and outfits for three different pieces in three different cities. Or I'd swoop in to New York just long enough between assignments to edit a piece and check my mail. Instead of miles, American should have just given me my own plane.

Being "home" meant sitting in bed with one eye on the news and the other on a loathsome foot-high stack of research for stories or guest interviews. I'd read until 10:00 P.M. and get up at four for rehearsals. I was often awakened at 3:00 A.M. to come in for Joan or to fly off for a piece.

Or I'd go to some black-tie event in the city, get my sound bites, race right to the studio, rip off my gown and toss it to the floor, change into jeans and sweatshirt, write my piece, and sit with an editor until 7:00 A.M. to make my deadline.

Over the next three hazy-blue years, I did dozens of field pieces and hundreds of celebrity interviews, and I spent more than thirty weeks sitting in for Joan. It sounded glamorous to other people, but it was not fun.

I seemed to be making a career of not fitting in. Most of my colleagues were incredibly helpful, and I was *such* a novice. But many of the women there were tough radical or liberal New York feminist types. And some New York women have a special look—and sound—to them. They're well read, highly opinionated, smart-mouthed, a tad abrasive, and not always well groomed. Intimidation seemed to come so naturally to many of them.

I did make a couple of close women friends at "GMA," though, like Chris Tardio, who was my travel coordinator before becoming a producer, and producers Tory Baker, Amy Hirsh, Sheila Bowe, and Phyllis McGrady. They were wonderful, compassionate, talented, giving women. The producers and I were in many trenches together on the road; Chris and I quickly became sushi-and-shopping sisters when we could squeeze in a long lunch. Those women were there for me to cry with and unload on. It's amazing they ever found time to do their jobs.

I am not a political animal, but I was viewed with tremendous—if understandable—resentment at first. Staffers saw me in a cushy, plum job in TV journalism for which I was ludicrously unqualified.

Because I'd never been on that career track, I didn't know from cushy. To me this territory was merely unknown and terrifying. But Susan had gone with me because I was "fresh" and "telecommunicative."

I was a 100 percent flamboyant sunny Californian, and they were hard-edged don't-screw-with-me New Yorkers. The sweeter I was, the more suspicious they became. But they didn't hate me. They just didn't know what I was *doing* there. I just cooled it and said I was a correspondent who might fill in now and then.

The smartest thing I did was stay low-key, admit my limits, and ask the experts for help. I was too clueless to be intimidating, so most people were unfailingly generous. (I didn't even know a "stand-up" in TV was the copy a reporter reads on camera. I thought it was a comedy routine.)

The transition was hell, and I was lonely, rootless, and vulnerable. I wondered if maybe I should have just married Don and had babies like my mother. It hadn't worked out so badly for her. Why did I want so much? Why wasn't it enough for me to find a good man? But then I'd get post-stress Total Woman flashbacks and say, How many bubble baths can you take? You can't make more than seven dinners a week. Twenty-four hours is never enough for a busy person and way too much for somebody with nothing to do. Plus, I'd resolved never to give up my career again for any man.

Five weeks after I started, I sat in for Joan. I learned by doing— and by doing *wrong*. The show was rigidly scripted. I was supposed to interview top spy novelist Jack Higgins, whose latest book had just come out. Of course I was miked and everybody in the booth could hear what I was saying. "GMA" interviews were three minutes, not the leisurely ten Reege and I now have. At "GMA" the pacing and patter were surgically precise from segment to segment.

Just to be honest, I told Higgins I hadn't read the book. "The topic sounds fascinating. I look forward to reading it."

I wasn't raised to lie, but my producers later clued me in: "Don't admit you haven't read it."

That advice came too late. Jack Higgins was incensed: "You don't even do me the courtesy of reading my book?"

I explained that he'd only been booked a day before, and I'd been given the book the night before.

Joan and David were real professionals. Joan was like the Earth Mother on the show, a survivor, a trailblazer in bringing her child in and making the transition to motherhood work for her. (She was pregnant with her second child when I first worked there.) Though never close friends, we have shared a warm and cordial bond as colleagues.

David was a sweetheart. The Friday before I spent that first week in Joan's chair, he was watching me as everybody was making me crazy prepping me for Monday morning. I'd studied the show's flow and formula and done a warm-up piece on the Bluegrass Festival in Kentucky, which never aired. So when David came over to me and said, "Come into my office, I want to talk to you," I went in with fear and trembling.

"I just want you to know," he said, "you're here because you're the best person we could find in this whole country. We looked at hundreds of tapes and we all agreed you were what we wanted for this show. We're delighted you're here. Just forget everything everybody said to you today and be yourself." It was the kindest, most gracious advice he could have given me. And as I was walking out the door he suddenly said, "Oh, Kathie Lee, there is one thing you do have to do on Monday."

"What's that?" I asked.

"Just show up." He smiled.

I was soon suffering from Multiple Job Description Disorder—a crazed double life. Studio work was tightly scripted with split-second precision. Road life was chaotic, grueling, and unpredictable. Time zones? Who knew? I couldn't even schedule a lunch date or a dental appointment. Besides, what was my dentist going to work on—my sound bites?

I was all over America looking for warm, funny, revealing stories covering a vast range of people on camera. I did stories slugged "Midair Refueler," "Ghost Fleet," "Cheerleader Clinic," "Ballooning," "Child Find," "Flying Doctor," " 'Dynasty' " (a sizzling week backstage), "Steeplejacks," "Men of Rock," "Boy out of Bubble," "Jacksons on Tour," " 'Love Boat' Reunion," and "Breakdance Champ." In the studio I interviewed leaders from the worlds of sports, politics, the arts, and show biz. Grammys, Oscars, Kennedy Center honors, premieres, opening nights, benefit galas, you name it—I was there foraging for sound bites.

I covered the Grammys and went Madonna-hunting backstage after she'd been nominated for her first award. I'd never met anybody so outrageously sure of herself with, at that time, very little to be cocky about.

Her attitude was "What do I need this for? Maybe I'll talk to you, maybe I won't." And I was thinking, Who is this woman? Of course, this was about $300 million ago, so what do I know?

I never had the killer instinct for getting sound bites. You break too many nails, right? I was always getting knocked all over the place by these tabloid terrors—some of the same people who are at events that I now attend as a guest. I'd wear my prettiest shoes and they'd get all bruised up. But once I had someone on camera, I knew how to zero in and get good bite.

I did enjoy that journalist's rush—getting a midnight call from a producer, dropping everything, packing, doing crash research, flying off, and nailing the story. Susan called me one day early on and said, "Go to Bloomingdale's, pick up a few leotards. You're going to L.A. tomorrow. Victoria Principal has a new book out called *The Body Principal*, and you're doing a health thing with her." Okay, so it wasn't three weeks in the jungle with the Sandinistas.

"One day's notice you're giving me?" I shot back. "You give a woman at least a *month* to prepare for something like this."

Victoria is stunning; her body is to die for. And this chubbette is just overflowing with positive body image and self-confidence while taping this segment in her wuggie-hugging leotard.

Victoria goes, "Kathie, you have a beautiful body, but you love cheese, don't you?"

"Huh?" She read minds, too? "Well, I do like cheese. Why?"

"Women don't digest milk products well and it always just sort of lands right *there*. (Hands slapping wuggies!) I promise," she went on, "if you give up milk products it'll disappear."

"Like mozzarella, pizza—all that good stuff?"

Yes, she said, all the things I love most. Give them up.

Dairy products never passed that woman's lips. The backs of her thighs were firm and perfect with no creases. Her boobs were magnificent. So what the Body Principal says, goes. I gave them all up for a month. Gained two pounds.

Meanwhile I was working my butt off just to prove to the veteran producers that I could cut it. As with singing, commercials, soap work, I loved a challenge. I'd show up on my early locations dressed for success—on a golf course. Tory Baker Masters and her husband (she married another "GMA" producer friend, Howie Masters) still tease me about the Buster Brown hair and the matching Kelly green Lacoste shirt, slacks, espadrilles, lip gloss, and perfect nails. And this is on the decks of the mothballed navy "ghost fleet" out of San Francisco, or hanging from a steeple with steeplejacks, or kicking up dirt with a family of crop dusters in farm country; or at a survival-rehab camp in sweltering Florida for hardened juvenile delinquents. (Howie, whose father is the renowned sex researcher, Dr. William Masters, and I used to check into motels as Masters and Johnson, which usually got a few laughs.)

My stories were almost always soft- rather than hard-breaking news—light on issues, heavy on heart and soul. In the very beginning I pretty much read whatever stand-ups a producer like Tory wrote and handed me.

But that changed on the "Vision Quest" survival camp piece. I trotted alongside the wagon trains and did my interviews with these teenage criminals. Then I sat in the grass as Tory finished writing my stand-up. "Here," she said, "memorize this and let's do it." For the first time it didn't feel, didn't read, like me.

"I'm not comfortable with it," I told her. And so I changed it, tried to put my own voice into it. It worked well. That was a breakthrough for me.

Writing and editing was creative, fascinating, and challenging. I was proud of myself for figuring all that stuff out. Only months earlier, it had been all I could do to put together a vacuum cleaner. This was growth.

If I was trying to find an on-air personality in the Florida heat, I almost lost it with Paul Newman at a Tavern on the Green tribute for Yves Montand. Paul's distaste for, and distrust of, the media is famous. He did not want to be there with all the cameras. I wanted a one-on-one with him for three minutes. Once the producer yells, "You've got speed" and the camera rolls, that kind of interview feels like both a split second and an eternity. The instant before you ask that first question of a celebrity can be an incredibly awkward moment.

I was trying to be cool, professional, detached. I was doing what you'd call sound-bite Lamaze exercises. Deep breaths, focusing, organizing. What was I supposed to do, make small talk about how the single most repugnant event of my life occurred in a sleazy producer's car outside Paul's home in Beverly Hills?

Finally I had "speed," so I looked right into those eyes of his and—nothing came out. I froze. Went blank. I said, "Oh, my God," and I looked up at the sky, lost in space for a second or two—and at that moment he melted. He saw I was being so real, so *excited*, so useless! He's probably surrounded by so many people who try to out-cool him that he was drawn in by my rather obvious haplessness. But on my part, this was no device; it was closer to a *demise*. So I snapped out of my star-struck trance, and he came through for me and gave me a fine interview.

On most pieces with hunks, however, a little detachment goes a long way. When I interviewed Don Johnson in Fort Lauderdale for one of his power boat races, I introduced myself and joked, "Maybe we're related." And he gave me this incredibly suggestive, titillating once-over and said, "I hope not." I froze. I wasn't used to men being that overt with me. I was *way* out of my league. I thought, I will never get through this interview. That look was so blatantly sexual and disconcerting, and he was so gorgeous. Of course that was before he remarried Melanie Griffith, who, by the way, is really delightful.

He behaved for the interview, though, and I hightailed it home as fast as I could. Certain people you just knew: Don't mess.

Warren Beatty, same thing. Don't mess. He was once in the full upright position right near me all night—on a red-eye to New York. He just made eye contact and, boy, I dived right back into whatever book I was reading—probably a Jack Higgins novel. I wasn't going to give that one a chance.

I did have my share of small victories on the celebrity circuit, though, even when I was out of my league. One of my special moments with "GMA" came while I was covering an opening-night party at Tavern on the Green for the Broadway show *Private Lives* with Elizabeth Taylor and Richard Burton. As usual, I had to scramble around for on-air quotes. Wherever Liz went, hordes of camera crews and paparazzi followed. For some reason she saw me and allowed me in close enough to do my interview. I was the only one who even got a sound bite, not to mention a close-up look at a smudge of pink lipstick across her teeth.

She was so exquisitely gorgeous standing there—except for the lipstick. Ordinarily, I'd mention the smudge so it wouldn't show up on camera. But I was going nuts, wondering if I should tell her. I was so afraid of losing the sound bite—and of offending her—that I didn't even mention it. I figured if I stopped and told her, she'd lose her concentration, get irritated, and say, *"Who the hell are you?"* Then she'd walk off. So I said nothing. We ran that piece, and because of shadows and dim light, you could hardly see the stain.

That, of course, is never the case with Liz's world-class cleavage, which is always very much in evidence in *any* amount of light. When this woman goes to an early-morning event, you could set your tray down and have *breakfast* off it. I'm so-o-o jealous.

A couple of years ago I saw Liz again at a Fragrance Foundation benefit dinner at the Waldorf. Naturally she was decked out and looked spectacular in some revealing, low-cut number. I was doing Jean Naté commercials for Revlon then, but it was peculiar that Frank and I were even there. The foundation was honoring several so-called quintessential New York couples, and we lived in Connecticut. That was close enough, I suppose, so we agreed to be included on a special guest list. We were trotted around for photo ops with Liz, as was just about everyone else in the crush around her.

Frank could have given a royal rip about being there and being seen. As we walked up toward Liz, I felt so awkward. What do you say to Elizabeth Taylor? You stand there looking buddy-buddy, smiling for the paparazzi, and feeling like the world's biggest dork.

So I'm looking at her, and suddenly I blurted out, "You know, my husband hates these things just as much as you do."

She looked at me with her piercing violet eyes, paused, and said, "I *doubt* that." And then she turned away.

I felt like such an idiot.

In those days I saw reporting as an excellent learning experience until the right thing came along. Barbara Walters I was not. I was never a news-oriented person. Statistics mean nothing to me, except as they affect people. I always went for the human aspect of a story. Most women in TV scream for equal time in the news area. Can I tell you, those women can have the budget deficit, they can have Social Security, and they can have the Clarence Thomas–Anita Hill hearings. They have their place, but so did math and science in school—and they were agony for me, too.

Incredibly, I had very few real screwups. I remember one, though. It started on a Friday when my producer said, "Kathie, take David's work home with you over the weekend and be well versed in his interview subjects for Monday. He'll be at the ground-breaking dedication of the Betty Ford Center in Rancho Mirage and he'll also be interviewing Lou Piniella and Tug McGraw, who will be in the New York studio. There's always a chance of losing satellite."

"Losing satellite? I've heard of losing cellulite, but what exactly are we talking about here?"

"If we lose the bird—the satellite—then we'll have no way of communicating with David and *you'll* have to do his interviews."

"Fine. Whatever." Now my stack of homework's two feet high.

David's Betty Ford stuff was going fine on Monday. Until I heard the nastiest words ever spoken: "We've lost satellite, Kathie. You're in."

At that moment I was greeting the women I was supposed to interview next—Wilma Rudolph and Billie Jean King, both of whom had just won the annual Women's Sports Awards. But instead I had to quickly switch to Tug McGraw and Lou Piniella on the set. There were no cue cards for me, no TelePrompTer, nothing. I had to rely on my wits. And they were in short supply.

Usually when the red light goes on you have a TelePrompTer intro saying, "You've seen him before many times on live television but now he's in"—and you've got an intro, right? I went totally blank. The Paul Newman Syndrome was getting worse. I muttered: "Well, it's that time of year again. World Series time. And if you're like me, you haven't followed baseball all season, so we've invited two experts here to tell us today what's going on with the World Series."

And then I said, "We have from the Philadelphia Phillies, Tug McGraw. And Lou Piniella." I had no idea what team Piniella played for. I just said, "Good morning, gentlemen. Tug, what's happening?" God bless them. They took over. And at one point Tug McGraw said on air, "Is this where you want me to talk about the Atlanta Braves?" I said, "Good, yes, exactly. Talk about the Atlanta Braves."

In the midst of this, David Hartman broke in. The bird, it seemed, was back. "Kathie? Kathie!" I heard him say. And I gasped, "Oh, thank God, David!" And I was miked. I got creamed for that by TV critics. "She was doing just fine," feminists said. "She didn't need David to save her." The heck I didn't. I needed him like crazy.

Next up was my interview with Wilma and Billie Jean. That went fine. Then someone said, "Kathie, we've lost satellite again."

By now I don't need a satellite, I need a martini. And a new blouse—those sticky armpit rings were now the size of dinner plates. Plus, now I was supposed to do an interview with Mary Kay Ash of Mary Kay Cosmetics, who was waiting in the Green Room. But no, they're telling me, "Kathie, we've lost satellite. Instead of Mary Kay we're going live to Kathmandu with Jack Smith."

Cat Man Who? Thank God I had watched "Nightline" the Friday before while I was studying. That's how I knew about the Canadian expedition reaching the peak of Mount Everest with a camera crew. One member of the party had died. So I said, "Well, we were going to bring you an interview with Mary Kay Ash of Mary Kay Cosmetics. We'll bring that to you at another time." I was totally winging it. "Instead we're going live to Kathmandu, Nepal—that's near India— where they're about to mount . . . Mount Everest."

Well, that just sounded so ridiculous you could see my lips starting to quiver as I bit hard to stifle a laugh. I couldn't believe I said "mount Mount Everest." Sounded like the fourth race at Aqueduct.

The show finally ended, the crew gave me a standing ovation with cheers and howls—and my beautiful blue silk blouse was history. And I post-taped Mary Kay. Somehow "GMA" kept me on.

The show's scripted rituals, I felt, squelched spontaneity and forced phony "happy talk" on viewers; but in the field I learned about a richer creative challenge—"striking gold." I made my first strike with a family that was sort of the Flying Wallendas of crop dusting, one of my first pieces. I interviewed two young guys whose father had been killed in an accident. They were carrying on his high-risk tradition. As I interviewed them, I thought of *my* dad and zeroed in on a place in their hearts. I hit pay dirt. These robust cowboy types opened up and cried. It was a precious and genuine moment.

When the tape stopped rolling, Howie Masters said, "Kathie, now you know about gold." And that's what they meant.

In my New York love life, though, I struck out more than I struck gold. The move put some much-needed distance between Don and me. But Don soon followed me to New York to work for a Broadway producer. In L.A. he had been on the road to great success; in New York, I was always literally on the road. He gave up a lot for me and got far too little in return.

He was miserable. Living together was absolutely out of the question, and getting his own place was so expensive. Everything was a step down for him when he moved. And I wasn't in town much. I would've seen him more if he'd stayed in L.A.

I was still afraid of the relationship, and age was also an issue. Don, as I said before, was four years younger. Also, I was further along in my career. For most men that's a problem. For Don it wasn't, but our lives didn't mesh. Had he been ten years older—or had we met five or ten years later—he'd have been more established, more confident in the world. The relationship wasn't meant to last, but being with him was the beginning of my healing. It was a powerful awakening and catharsis for me not only because we were so affectionate, but because we were so *caring*. The beginning of the end came when I took Don home to my family on Thanksgiving Day 1983.

With my brother leading the charge, my family essentially ran Don out of their home because I didn't have a piece of paper with the word "Divorced" stamped on it by a California court. It shouldn't take eighteen months to get a divorce in California. It should take eighteen months to get *married* and one day to get divorced. Make it tough to get in, real quick and simple to get out if you have to.

That was the only time I have ever been ashamed of and humiliated by my family. Except for Gram!

Forget remorse. My father was glad that Davy, who could do no wrong in his eyes, had expressed what everyone had apparently been feeling. Whatever my brother said became gospel to my parents. I adore Davy but he *is* fallible; he is as imperfect as the rest of us. To Mom and Dad he seems perfect. He paid his dues, he put them through far more hell than I ever did, and now he's serving God. Which gave me all the more reason to be mortified that they—and Davy—could treat a wonderful, loving sweetheart of a human being so badly. And on Thanksgiving, no less.

But as angry as I was, I knew I could never choose someone over my family's objections. They meant the world to me. I could be angry with them, but I could never dump them. I was furious; and I would, over the next two years, turn my anger inward, in startlingly ugly ways. If it was my weird way of punishing my family, I ended up hurting no one more than myself.

Ironically, it was on Thanksgiving Day, the year before, that I was paired with the man who *would* become the man of my dreams.

Early that morning, because David Hartman was on vacation and Joan Lunden called in sick at the last minute, I'd had to race in and work with a co-host I had never worked with before—that gorgeous fox with the great buns and dumb contact lenses.

"Good morning once again," Frank said to me on-air after the 7:00 A.M. news.

"Good morning, Frank."

"Great to be with you."

"Same here."

We weren't even striking *tin*.

It was a strange, low-key show. We aired my nostalgia segment on Buffalo Bob ("There were so many terrific characters on the [Howdy Doody] show. One of the most unusual was Flubbadub. Tell me about him!"); my "Dynasty" location piece; drawings and wishes from second graders in New Jersey; and my touchy-feely field piece about the harvesting of leftover crops for the needy in central California. Frank introduced that one by saying: "Kathaleen has a Thanksgiving story . . ." No one's perfect.

Our scripted chemistry was more fizzle than sizzle. "Good morning once again to you, Kathie," he said on the air after a break.

"Good morning, Frank," I said.

"You look great today," he said.

"Thank you, same to you," I said.

"Having a big turkey—" he started to say.

"Not bad at all," I said, cutting in too soon.

147

"—day today," he finished.

"Yes, I do. How 'bout you?" I asked.

"Oh, yeah. Lots of friends," he said.

"Lots of drumsticks," I said.

"Yessss." Dead pause. "It's Thursday, November twenty-fifth . . ."
After the show, Frank told me he was distracted by my hair, which
earned me the nickname Helmet Head. I said it was my Dorothy
Hamill look. He said I looked more like Boston Bruins hockey great
Bobby Orr.

Later Frank came back on the air after another break and said,
rather curiously, "I'm Frank Gifford, sitting in with the number one
draft pick in every respect, Kathie Lee Johnson."

"Well, thank you Frank. From you that's quite a compliment."

"No question. Top pick."

If anyone had seen that show and predicted we'd end up husband
and wife, he or she should have been heavily sedated.

Anyone but Mom.

Right around the time Frank was making happy talk about draft
picks and top choices, Mom, who never misses a thing, was home in
Bowie, taking it all in as she prepared the big turkey. She said, "Look
at that, Ep! Will you just *look* at that."

And Daddy said, "What?"

She said, "Would you look at that?"

"What?"

"Look at the way he's *looking* at her."

Daddy looked. "Yeah, so? What are you talking about, Joanie?"

"He's *crazy* about her. He's absolutely *smitten*." Only Mom gets
away with using biblical words like "smitten." But she saw something happening. She was sure I smote number 16 right there on
network television.

And Daddy said, "Oh, Joanie, you're crazy, you know that?"

On My Way to You

I've never been an in-between type woman in romance. If I'm in love I want to get married.

That's how stupid I am.

You can fall in love with a lot of people in this world, but that doesn't mean you should marry every one of them. Unless you're Elizabeth Taylor. Once in love I could always envision life with somebody. I don't necessarily believe in finding your "one and only"—just "one and only one at a time."

As I approached thirty, the idea of having babies and settling down was looking better and better all the time. But the reality was still scary—and more remote than ever.

At least by then I was free of my marriage. The night my divorce became final, in 1983, I ran into Paul at our favorite restaurant. He was with his family; I was with my father and my faithful friend and agent, Sam Haskell. I was so relieved. Marriage was the only thing that had gotten in the way of our otherwise loving friendship and fellowship, and now maybe some of that could be restored between us. But Daddy leaned over to me and poignantly muttered, "You have no idea how much this man has hurt you."

Paul had bought back and moved into the first house we had shared. That seemed sad to me. I wasn't stuck in the past. I was stuck in-between for two painful, turbulent years. I wasn't nesting. I was gliding. As Don and I began to drift, we broke up several times and tried messy experiments with dating other people after he moved back to L.A. Relationships were hard under the same roof; they weren't any easier three thousand miles apart.

He sublet my L.A. town house, and we agreed to see other people but would get together whenever "GMA" sent me to L.A. He was too decent and caring to lose, too young, and now too far away to marry. So I started to see new people—interesting, attractive men who never became serious involvements.

But this was not my style. It was two years of a hectic, depressing, sometimes shameful life-style that made me feel, for the first time, that I had abandoned the Lord and everything my faith in Him had meant. The dream of a secure Christian family seemed incongruous as my work life got more frenetic and exhausting and my love life got more reckless and unfulfilling.

I'd wake up with a surge of anxiety in the night, without the right man in my life, with that biological clock ticking loud and clear in the dark. And that's one clock that keeps on ticking as you keep taking a licking in the trenches of singledom.

And these were the trenches of the trendy. Through a charming and fascinating Dutch woman friend, who "adopted" me, I was invited into the sophisticated, well-heeled world of Régine's in New York. "Dahling," she would say, "you simply must come tonight," or "You're having lunch with me tomorrow at Régine's." Suddenly I was at posh dinners with Régine and her husband, Roger, with a European prince on one side of me, a Saudi sheikh on the other, a dapper financier or global entrepreneur opposite me. There was no shortage of smooth-talking Continental playboys who did God-knows-what all day to bankroll their nocturnal mating rituals. As many single-woman mistakes as I made in the big city, I passed on the playboys. I was *way* out of their league.

I hardly had time to play in my *own* league. Chris Tardio at "GMA" became a trusted buddy. We'd do weekend movie marathons—two or three in a row on a Saturday—go for lunch, hit Bloomie's, cruise the boutiques at the South Street seaport, get our nails done together, girl things. She was a real anchor for me.

Chris wasn't my only well-manicured, stylish friend. I was beginning to nurture and prize a warm, thoroughly platonic friendship with my fellow Turkey Day host. I adored Frank as an older brother. We tried to schedule lunch about once a month, but even that was hard with our schedules. Frank was then still married to his second wife, Astrid. (His three children are from first wife, Maxine.)

I had heard around the office that Frank's marriage to Astrid, a statuesque blond aerobics instructor, was on the rocks, but that was water-cooler talk, and so I didn't pay much attention to it. It turned out to be true, but Frank never discussed her in a disparaging way and he *never* came on to me, so I had no overt signs from him that he was especially unhappy. I did think he seemed to be away from her a lot. Now that we're married there's no way I'd have lunch with a man unless it was strictly business. Frank wouldn't understand lunch or drinks with a guy friend. Yet here I was, a woman friend, going out for lunches and dinners.

My connection to Frank was always unique and special. Frank is my Mom's age, and I'm a year younger than his son Jeff. (Kyle is two years younger and Vicki is three years younger.) He was past fifty then, but looked more than a decade younger. Frank was—and is—gorgeous and manly and, without being fussy or vain, perfectly groomed, down to his nails and pocket kerchief. More importantly, his background—he grew up poor in the oil fields of California— was fascinating to me, and he had had a career full of remarkable accomplishments as a genuine American hero.

He was like nobody I'd ever known—worldly yet casual, effortlessly sexy but deeply spiritual, and quick with an earthy, playful humor that easily disguised his sorrows, his wisdom, and his compassion. Wherever we went, Frank, who had been a mainstay of "Monday Night Football" since 1971, drew lots of attention, yet he remained totally focused. He didn't work the room; the room worked Frank. Even when we were just friends, he made me feel that being together meant something special to him.

Frank was the first man I knew in the high-powered media world who really seemed to have it all. Including a wife. But an affair was the last thing on our minds then. As we grew more comfortable with each other, I cherished the bantering and the protective way he related to me without ever giving a thought to moving beyond that.

In fact, Frank was always trying to fix me up with two of his best buddies. He said something like, "Both of these guys have a lot of money and, well, you seem to like nice things." I was leery of this. I loved Frank as a friend and knew his buddies weren't jerks. But I really hated fix-ups with friends of friends. I did go to lunch with these two men, but I insisted that Frank come along as insurance, or protection. As I said, it was so much like my brother Davy when we were kids. Maybe that's why I fell into this kind of relationship with Frank so easily.

Both times I ignored my prospective suitors, both wonderful men, and talked to Frank the whole time. These were blind dates that certain women would have married sight unseen: Jonathan Tisch of the Tisch fortune and Tim Mara of the Mara fortune. Tim owned the New York Giants. A few years ago, when Jonathan Tisch married

Laura Steinberg, whose father is financier Saul Steinberg, it was called the wedding of the century. During the wedding ceremony, Frank—by then, fortunately, my husband—leaned toward me. *"Honey,"* he whispered, *"all this could have been yours."*

"All this" never mattered to me. But then again, I didn't have in my life then what *did* matter most—a man who loved and treasured me. Far from it. But as I look back on those two years "in between" serious involvements, it's clear that I didn't love or treasure myself. Let's just say I was not the best little girl in the world anymore.

Excuses? I had plenty. I felt: bitterly disillusioned and defeated (because of my marriage); angry (at my parents); confused and tentative (about Don); crazed and weary (from work); lonely, vulnerable, and needy (from life itself). I lost my inner compass and strayed from the Lord, paying a huge price in self-respect. I realized I was capable of the very indiscretions I was so quick to condemn in others, actions that did not make me feel safe or virtuous or at one with the values I grew up with. I deeply disappointed myself. To put it bluntly, I was a real jerk in a lot of ways, because I felt so wounded. I came to feel that my pain entitled me to live my life the way I wanted to live it.

And I lived it a day at a time. I dated a lot, often with disastrous results. When you're a young, reasonably attractive woman in New York, there's an abundance of wealthy, successful men at your doorstep. It sounds crass, but they're everywhere. I wasn't ever interested in marrying someone else's career or bank account.

I struggled with the grim fact of life that most men I dated were seeking a sexual partner with no commitment. Some just wanted a sexual *experience,* never mind the "partner" thing. They wanted a trophy, not a treasure. And I vowed never to settle again until I was somebody's treasure.

And I knew what it felt like to be a trophy. I went out with one man who didn't bother to tell me he was married. I felt disgusted when I finally found out. I felt borrowed, used.

Before I went to New Orleans for a piece on Julio Iglesias a friend warned me, "Julio's going to love you." He was charming but did not come on to me at all. The word was he'd been with ten thousand women, which made him, what, *half the man* Wilt Chamberlain was? Even if a man is the sexiest man on the planet, I would never want to be number 10,001. I'm not thrilled about being number 3! My heart's desire has always been to be special to somebody.

A lot of the men I met boasted of fulfillment. These were famous, charismatic, wealthy, successful people. Sure, I saw how women could be seduced by a man's image, wealth, or sheer physical beauty. I mean, let's face it, Warren Beatty didn't conquer as many women as he did because he bears an eerie resemblance to the Hunchback of Notre Dame.

But I got to know some people in this crowd, and they proved to be some of the loneliest people I'd ever met. Some existed in a moral, ethical void. They had not been humanized but rather desensitized by their success, power, and conquests.

I was raised to believe in the basic goodness of people, and to trust. That trust was seriously broken one night. I'd gone on a dinner date with a European clothing executive whom I had met on the Paris trip with my parents. After dinner I wanted to avoid the typical "may I come in for a nightcap" routine at *my* apartment, so I agreed to say good night at his hotel and then catch a taxi home . . . alone! In retrospect that was stupid, but at the time it didn't seem wrong or risky.

In his suite, I took a sip of the wine he offered me, which was definitely spiked, drugged. And then I just blacked out. I have no idea what happened, which scares the heck out of me. I'd never passed out before, and I haven't since. I *swooned* when Frank kissed me, that's just about it.

Later, I somehow made it home in a taxi, though I don't remember any of that. The worst part is not knowing what happened. At the time I felt that this could only happen to someone who has stopped loving herself. Daddy had never tolerated sloppiness in our values at home. Was I in revolt against my parents' repressive regime, the years of "molding"? Was my self-esteem still damaged by the marriage? We try to excuse too much of our behavior and take too little responsibility for its consequences.

I needed somebody to say, "You're beautiful. You've got worth. I love you." I questioned my faith in God again, but this crisis was self-inflicted, not a reaction to a disease afflicting a loved one, like the genuine crises I faced with Michie and Shannie. At least when I was married I knew what I was, and there was some moral order in my life. Once on my own, I lost that.

I was smart enough to remove myself from any sort of a public ministry. I had been telling young girls how to live their lives through writing books and articles, giving concerts, giving my Christian Girl testimonial. Now I was a hypocrite and I quit.

This moral crisis was between me and me. Regarding sex outside of marriage, men are so different from women. I don't think most men feel as if something precious is stolen from them. But most women feel differently. I know I did.

I no longer felt comfortable about sharing my faith in relationships. I had helped lead Yancy and Don to the Lord. Now I was more intent on fleeing the Lord. I was, for once, living in the same world as everybody else. I was crushed that that *godly* world I'd given myself to in every way imaginable had let me down so badly. By the time I got to New York, I felt that I'd been sold a bill of goods. But the Lord did not stray from me. I was the one who strayed. He was still there, as He had been all along, to help me make something beautiful of my life. But I was bent on making it ugly. Our bodies, the Bible says, are temples of the Holy Spirit. That's why we care for our bodies, cleanse them, purify them.

Looking back, of course, I see I was a fool not to be courageous and trust God a little longer. God blessed me in a miraculous way with His mercy—and by making something exquisite of my life when He brought me Frank. I hadn't forgiven myself yet. But God forgave me. I didn't even feel remorse until my baby boy was born. I'm overwhelmed that despite all I've sinned and done to let God down, He could bless me with a little guy like Cody and a husband like Frank. But that's the essence of the Gospel, that there's forgiveness for all who come and ask.

For the longest time after I fell in love with Frank, my favorite song was "On My Way to You" by Marilyn and Alan Bergman and Michel Legrand. It's a gorgeous song with incredible lyrics that include: "If I could change a single day, what went amiss or went astray, I may have never found my way to you."

Maybe it *was* all meant to be—the bumpy, twisting, dimly lit itinerary God had chosen for me. But sometimes I think back and say, No, the lyrics are wrong. I would change *a lot of things* on my way to Frank. And many of them took place during that dark, rootless time when I had lost my way to *me*.

The Long and Winding Road
That Leads to Your Door

☆

At the end of March 1984 I covered Gloria Steinem's fiftieth birthday celebration at the Waldorf-Astoria Hotel. It was quite an assignment. I interviewed Bette Midler, Alan Alda, Phil Donahue, Marlo Thomas, and a man I would soon fall in love with—the birthday girl's boyfriend of nine years.

I worked the celebrity-packed room for sound bites and got ready to leave. Just then someone pointed out the man in Gloria's life, and I decided it would be interesting to get him on camera. His name was Stan Pottinger, and he had made a name for himself as a brilliant young assistant attorney general under Nixon and Ford before going into investment banking. I was surprised at how attractive he was—tall, slender, very sharp-looking with dark hair graying at the temples. Not manly gorgeous the way Frank is, but more chic, smooth, and dangerous.

I put my mike up and started talking, but he wouldn't meet my eyes. He wasn't even close. Missed by about a foot.

"Excuse me," I wisecracked. "Those are my breasts. My eyes are up here." He laughed. I was wearing a chartreuse silk dress that crisscrossed on top and tied at the waist. It was much more flowy than showy. You couldn't wear anything even vaguely seductive at "GMA." There should have been a sign posted on the studio door: No Cleavage Allowed. Did you ever notice how Joan has nothing but smooth area from the neck down? There were no erogenous zones on any of us at "Good Morning America." It was unnerving that my

155

viewers might think there was actually *something* there *to look at.* Anyway, I got the interview out of him, and as we were leaving, a girlfriend of mine whom I'd invited along said to me: "That man is crazy about you."

"You're crazy!" I shot back. "He's been with Gloria nine years for goodness' sake. Gloria founded *Ms.* magazine; she's the best-known feminist in America. I doubt he's crazy about me."

I guess I was *Ms.*-taken.

In June I signed a contract to be Carnival Cruise Lines' pitch woman. It was a perfect departure for me since I wasn't exactly expressing my musicality on "GMA." Having a celebrity name and face was a first for a cruise line and Carnival had committed something like $10 million to the ad campaign. I was, as always, not the first choice. For this I was number five. Sandy Duncan was number one, but she was already with Nabisco and, well, that's the way the cookie crumbles.

Then they wanted Bernadette Peters, but she wanted ten times more money than I ultimately signed for. Not to mention that she got seasick or that her perfect milky complexion couldn't take the sun.

Then they wanted Joyce DeWitt because "Three's Company" was a big hit, but Joyce couldn't sing a lick. So Carnival was thinking four's a crowd when they tried to nail down Cathy Lee Crosby. The story I heard is that she had just a few weeks earlier helped christen a celebrity sidewalk at the Nassau Beach Hotel in the Bahamas. Celebrities were asked to put their hand- or footprints in cement. A full-page picture in *People* magazine revealed her shapely cleavage and, as I heard it, this was not the image Carnival associated with "In the morning . . . in the evening . . . ain't we got fun!"

Number five was the charm. But by the time I shot my first commercial on the Mexican Riviera, I was more despondent than thrilled. I was on a tight schedule and was able to see Don just long enough to break up with him—again. Now it was over a Japanese woman who was coming on real strong with him and trying like crazy to break us up by doing things like calling me in New York and describing in intimate detail what my town house looked like. And the other issues weren't going away. So I was in *great* emotional shape as I danced across the cruise ship deck, singing, "Ain't we got fun."

I came home and, as the 1984 Olympics were gearing up, there was an enormous amount of travel and work. I grabbed a lunch or two with Frank and gave him the up-to-the-minute reports from the singles wars. He was, as always, supportive and helped me keep my sense of humor.

He was swamped with Olympics work, too—he'd be covering the games for ABC Sports—but there was news on his end. He and Astrid were getting a legal separation and he was moving into an apartment just five blocks from mine on the West Side. And the divorce was getting acrimonious, as he put it. As always, it was a hit-and-run lunch—and we were off.

A month later, as I was running out the door to catch yet another plane to L.A., my assistant told me I had a call. "It's Stan Pottinger." Hmmmm, Gloria's boyfriend, I thought. He surprised me by saying he had been thinking about me and wanted to get together. It turned out that Gloria's fiftieth birthday had marked the end of their relationship. This was Monday; I was due back on Thursday. We made a date for Thursday night.

Out in L.A. I saw Don, and we had just enough time to get back together. This was getting crazy. I called Stan to cancel, explaining that I was still clearly invested in a relationship. Which was true. There are two things a single New York woman should never get rid of—her apartment and a decent guy. Don was three thousand miles away, but I couldn't imagine really letting him go.

Stan, the brilliant attorney, made a counteroffer: "If you're like me, that doesn't mean you don't need a friend in New York. No harm in a friendly dinner."

Yeah, right. Friendly. And charming. And sexy, articulate, worldly, sophisticated. Stan had just had a very successful year. He had a great apartment on Lexington Avenue. He was a mover and shaker, that was clear. But he was divorced and had three children. Paul and Katie, who were teenagers, lived with him. Matt, who was then eleven or twelve, stayed with his mom in Fairfield, Connecticut. Don didn't have Stan's powerful edge and energy; Stan, though, didn't seem to have Don's heart and soul. Stan was ten years older than I was. He and Don could not have been more different—or spoken to such separate parts of my being.

After our friendly dinner in New York, Stan took me home. I made some coffee, and he asked if he could use the phone to call his older son. My brownstone apartment, like most, had a tiny living room. A guy in my living room was like the beast in "Beauty and the Beast." They all seemed so big, and everything I had was so tiny and delicate. I couldn't help but overhear Stan's warm, touching fifteen-minute talk with his son. This was not staged. He had called to say he'd be a little while longer and not to worry. That genuine affection between a father and child melted me.

Stan had grown up in Dayton, Ohio, with a Pentecostal upbringing that he had long since renounced. He got his undergraduate and law degrees at Harvard and married his college sweetheart along the way. As Stan talked, I realized this was a whole new world for me: political hardball, legislation, litigation, the women's movement, Wall Street. And children. I had never dated a man who was somebody's daddy.

Bottom-line: I saw no future. So we went out dancing the next night until four in the morning at the Red Parrot with my brother-in-law, Craig, who had come to New York to drop off some outdoor furniture for me, and Chris Tardio, my good friend. It wasn't a romantic evening, but it was a real hoot. It was a Friday and I had the weekend off; I almost never went out dancing like that. Then Stan asked me to join him—platonically—for a weekend at Alan and Arlene Alda's beach house in Water Mill a few weeks from then. Forget it, I told him. I was still involved with Don. And besides, I just didn't *do* weekends.

Stan made a strong case. He promised I'd have my *own* room. He just needed a date. The Aldas were close friends, he said. It would be fun.

My defense collapsed with the appearance of a surprise witness that stunned the courtroom in my head: "Are you crazy?" Mom squealed when I told her. Was I hearing this right? Miss Born Again urging me to spend a *weekend* with a guy I've gone out with twice? In my DREAMS! But, hey, anything to get me back into circulation. Plus, she loved Alan from "M*A*S*H" and figured an O*R*G*Y was out of the question.

"You'll be a lady, now, won't you?" she said.

"Yes, Mom."

It was weird being nearly thirty-one and telling Stan, "My mom thinks I should go away with you for the weekend."

"Your mother sounds like a smart woman."

Camp Alda, as I called it, was fabulous, and I fell in love—with the Aldas. Alan had this little dinghy motorboat that had two speeds—slow and what Alan called megathrust, which was just as slow as slow but louder. It was hilarious. We played tennis, swam, listened to Arlene play beautiful classical clarinet and piano, and we cooked with everybody chopping and blocking. It reminded me so much of my own home—and of *The Four Seasons*, one of my favorite movies of all time. Stan was pretty much a gentleman. He wasn't pushing. We laughed nonstop from Friday night to late Sunday.

I then fell in love with Stan's two older kids. They were such sharp, liberal, knowing city kids, but with an adorable needy side. After two years of emotional and often lonely confusion, I savored the "instant family" warmth around Stan. I adored my connection with Katie and Paul. She and I did the girl things—shopping and lunch. Paul had a girlfriend, and we spent some great time talking about guy stuff, high school stuff. I remember one especially sweet day when I was over at the apartment and we just had one of those fun Sunday afternoons. We had all gone out to lunch and then sat around and listened to music. I'd given Katie some voice lessons and we suddenly just were real at ease around each other. It wasn't just Stan I fell in love with. If it had just been Stan it would have never happened. He had such dear kids who made me feel needed.

In September Stan asked me to ride with him when he dropped Katie off at her boarding school upstate. It was the first time she was ever going to live away from her daddy for so long, and he anticipated an emotionally rough time. I figured: it's a two-hour drive on a crisp, early fall day, how rough can it get?

We settled her in at the school, had lunch, strolled through horse country, and met her teachers. Then Stan and I said a tearful good-bye and came back to the car, where Stan promptly started sobbing. I was deeply touched—to see how free he felt with me. Those moments push some heavy buttons for me—a father's affection for his daughter—and can rip me to shreds. As sexy as he was, nothing he could have done indoors by candlelight could have seduced me any more powerfully than his tears by the car for Katie. It's a quality I love in a person. It was clear I was falling very deeply in love with Stan and beginning to see myself in the role of ready-made mother-wife-lover.

Beyond the children, Stan brought me into a fascinating world of high-powered feminist comrades, power brokers, financial tycoons, national politicians, and Washington lawyers. I shied away from politics because Washington seemed like a predatory environment. I'd always take a moral rather than a political stand. But I was stimulated and enlightened by these people and never got the feeling they considered me a dingbat. I found their lives more interesting than mine, and they found mine more interesting than theirs.

Stan was amazing at parties, dinners, fund-raisers, and political events. He was a master at working the room and could be quite the flirt without being a cad. He was a political animal. But he would often leave me at the door and schmooze his way through a crowded black-tie room, shaking one hand here, eyeing someone's entrance there. Me, I'm sorry. I'm a romantic. I like to stand by my guy's side, greet people together, and be a couple. Frank's the kind of guy who's been known to go into a dining room and switch names around so that we end up next to each other. Stan was a smooth and charming operator, in the positive sense, though, and he thrived in that climate.

I thrived on the love boats. When I went to L.A. to shoot another spot for Carnival that year I met Don for lunch at the Beverly Wilshire and broke the news to him—for the zillionth time—that it was finally over.

Then I gave him the *bad* news: I've met somebody.

Don cried, I cried. He wasn't surprised, but he was crushed. Stan aside, the broken trust was a deal-breaker for me. You don't come back from that. I was heartbroken for both of us. I hated losing him, but through my tears I told him, "You'll be my friend forever." And I meant it.

Of course I soon got the big picture: I had exchanged a man who was young and commitment-crazy for a man who was older and commitment-phobic. Stan seemed unwilling—incapable, ultimately—of talking about marriage, setting a date, building toward a real future. Plus, his old girlfriends had a habit of passing through his life all the time. Gloria, for instance, was often at the same events or dinners, and it was clear that she and Stan would remain in touch, which was fine.

In September that year I co-hosted the Miss America pageant for the first time. I heard through a friend that Gloria was outraged that I would participate in such an event. She felt that it was demeaning to women. I strongly disagreed with her. I believe that feminism is about choice and about women taking advantage of all the same opportunities men have to realize their dreams. The pageant served those purposes for young women. *They* didn't feel demeaned. They were fighting for something. They were there out of *choice*. If Gloria's disapproval had something to do with women getting all lacquered up and made up and putting their physiques on display, all I can say is that Peter Jennings, Frank Gifford, and other male television personalities and politicians get their hair and makeup done before airtime and no one tells *them* what they do is demeaning.

It wasn't just Gloria. Stan's other ex-lovers also made their presence felt. One night really blew my mind. We went to dinner at Jack's on Lexington Avenue with one of Stan's old flames from his Washington days. She was absolutely Grace Kelly–gorgeous. And she was going out with a big movie mogul. "And another old friend of hers is going to join us," Stan had said.

The old pal was Mikhail Baryshnikov. So here's this knockout beauty sitting at dinner with three of her lovers—and me. And I'm sitting there thinking, *This is either the most mature, urbane, sophisticated group of people I've ever been with, or I'm dining out this evening with a table full of Looney Tunes!* In any event, I *knew* I wasn't in Kansas anymore. Nothing in my life had prepared me for such experiences—my mom had been with my father from the time she was nineteen.

I liked those people. But I'm sorry, I don't feel we were meant to have that many sexual partners in a *lifetime*, much less at a dinner. God did not design and build me for life's fast lane. There's no way I would ever live with a man without being his wife. I had no desire even to be seen as a man's mistress, girlfriend, or appendage. As it was, I stayed at Stan's place way too much for my own comfort. If somebody doesn't care about you enough to marry you and give you a baby, then he doesn't really care about you that much at all. That's one of those laws of life I grew up with.

So long before "Married . . . with Children" was a sitcom, I knew it only as a deal-breaker. I wanted to reserve the right, the choice, to have children. And the reason Stan was reluctant to remarry was that he didn't want more kids. So our second year together was a roller coaster. We broke up no fewer than eight times. Early in the game with Stan, a former law firm partner of his from Washington took me aside at a party and said, rather curiously, "I want to warn you: just be careful. Stan's great but he's the kind of guy who always has to know the back door's open." Just what you want to hear when you're in love.

I was either miserable or ecstatic. Where I came from, after a year you're either engaged or gone. Typically, I was neither.

But Stan had a vibrant sense of humor, a wonderful laugh, a brilliant mind, and fascinating friends. It was a very substantial and challenging world for me, filled with people like Elliot Richardson and John Ehrlichman. Sure, I floated through the A-list party crowds of politics and pop culture as part of my work, but those people were not social friends, and that was never my real world. Still, there was a lot I loved about this man's life. We were a good fit intellectually and personality-wise. And he was drawn to my world of show business and the media, with long-range hopes of getting into filmmaking.

My big problem was that I just never knew exactly where we stood, and ultimately, that's one thing that has to fall into place securely for a woman, especially once those child-bearing years start flying by.

Our happiest times, really, were when we all would go down to Stan's place in the Virgin Islands away from the pressures of our lives. I remember once, though, I had a wild trip down there. He and the kids were already in Saint Thomas, and I was to fly down after work to join them. I flew first to Puerto Rico, where I was to catch a connecting private flight from San Juan to Saint Thomas. But by the time my plane arrived late in San Juan, it was past midnight and the airport lights had been turned off. No one spoke English and I had no idea where to go. I was a basket case. The pilot finally showed up and we got into this two-seater for the twenty-minute flight.

As we were taking off the small hatch on the copilot side flew open. I freaked out. I grabbed it and pulled it shut, but it wouldn't latch properly. So I held the door shut for the entire flight. It was terrifying. And I broke a nail.

By the time I arrived, Stan had been waiting a while for me at the small airport in Saint Thomas, and it was like, *Are we having fun yet?* Stan tried to make light of it. "Breaking a nail's not the biggest tragedy in life, Kathie," he said. That remark bugged me, as if nothing that happened to me could ever be as important as anything in *his* life.

By mid-1985, my friends—Frank included—had all heard enough of my nail-breaking adventures. But two grave losses in Frank's life gave me a chance to show him I could be a good listener in times of trouble for him.

The first occurred after his brother Waine had a massive heart attack and died suddenly. I was the first person Frank called when he got home to New York after the funeral. This was a whole other Frank, who needed to talk. We went, as always, to the restaurant Santa Fe and talked about it. And tears came to Frank's eyes as I listened to him reminisce about his family and the meaning he was searching for in the loss of his brother.

Frank also came to me for comfort when a pilot friend of his had a fatal coronary in flight. Frank was an in-house personal-appearance spokesman for Nabisco. Ross Johnson, then chairman of RJR Nabisco, is one of Frank's oldest and dearest friends—and was best man at our wedding a year or so later.

Frank made many appearances for Nabisco and often used the company jet to attend Nabisco-related conventions, golf tournaments, benefits, dinners, whatever. He knew the company pilots very well.

So this time he and Ross and Laurie Johnson were returning from a funeral in the plane when they felt a turbulence-type bump in the cabin. But then the copilot came back, told them that the pilot had just had a massive heart attack, and asked Frank to come up and help. Frank tried desperately to do CPR on the pilot in his seat while the copilot got clearance to land safely wherever he could find a runway. But the pilot was already gone; he had died instantly.

Frank was devastated. When he got home he called me, needing to be with a friend and talk through his sadness and shock. It was peculiar, because we could go for a couple months without even seeing each other or even talking on the phone. Yet it seemed that there was a warmth and a closeness between us that didn't require constant chatter to flourish. Our friendship seemed to be taking on an unspoken, almost indefinable depth and life of its own no matter how much time we actually logged in the real world.

And given our respective circumstances, we didn't even know why the friendship was there at all. There was no real reason for it to be. We were at such different stages of life. He was a jock who loved fishing, golfing, and tennis; I was more the movie maven–shopping bag queen. There certainly didn't seem to be a whole lot of stuff we could actually *do* together. But both of us must have sensed that *something* was going on between us on *some* level, because we prized those times we were together.

I hardly ever saw Frank socially, except for our warm table-for-two moments and a few raucous three-hour fiestas with the Cowboy. There was one exception: a lunch at which Frank, who never bad-mouths anyone, truly shocked me. That was the day I introduced him to Stan.

Stan had invited me to a Sunday brunch at Mortimer's with his friends Herb and Ann Siegel. Herb was then chairman of the board of Criss-Craft Industries. In the morning they called to ask Stan if it was all right if they brought a friend of theirs who had been playing tennis with Herb all morning. Stan asked me, "Is it all right if the Siegels bring Frank Gifford?"

I said, "Sure, Frank's a good friend of mine, and I haven't seen him in a while. It'll be nice to see him."

We greeted each other at the restaurant with everybody kissy-facey, Bloody Mary, yapping away, and catching up. Frank was on my left taking it all in; Stan was on my right. It went well, actually. When we left Mortimer's, Frank guided me through the door and leaning into my ear said, "You're not going to *marry* this jerk, are you?"

I was taken aback. First of all, I thought we'd had a lovely brunch. Stan hadn't been unkind or jerky. But by Frank's standards, he'd treated me atrociously. As we were waiting on the sidewalk I asked, "What are you talking about?"

"He's not in love with you. All he did was work the room. He just cares about impressing Herb Siegel. He didn't talk to you once."

I couldn't believe what I was hearing. I didn't remember it that way at all. I looked at him indignantly and defensively and snapped, "Well, I *might* marry him. What's it to you?" I felt like adding, "And who asked you, anyway?" I hadn't sensed any tension whatsoever between the two men, but then again, I trusted Frank's insight so much. He had clearly picked up on something he did not like. I guess as my friend he was on my side, and this didn't look like his idea of a love affair.

Frank might have been extra-critical because of his acrimonious divorce proceedings. He wanted out, but the lawyers were just "beating up on each other." So he decided to get away.

He took off and spent more than two months in Santa Fe, doing *The Odd Couple* with his close buddy Don Meredith. Don and his wife, Susan, were living there. Susan was a member of the Theatre Guild, and they were trying to raise money for the Greer Garson Theater. They did three or four weeks of rehearsals, working for free, and then a two-week sellout run. Frank said it was the hardest he'd ever worked in his life.

There was no way "Good Morning America" could resist this story. I flew to Santa Fe to cover the previews. By this time Frank and I had known each other for three years. I'd never seen him nervous, but he was actually sweating before the performance. I stayed for the show, and Frank and Don were adorable. To see Frank come out as Felix, looking and acting prissy and domesticated in his apron, was hysterical.

I did a backstage piece, and they invited me to the Merediths' home. I definitely got the sense there was a young local lady kind of sniffing around Frank out there. I know he took her to the cast party on opening night, but she was nowhere in sight at the Merediths'. There had always been gossip-column items about Frank running around when he was married, but I knew them to be false. And there were stories around the studio that Frank was having a torrid affair with a well-known married media executive who, the rumors went, was ready to ditch her husband for him. Frank told me the stories were bogus. He and the executive were good friends who found some solace in each other when they were both hurting at home. The woman is still married, and knowing Frank, I think he probably encouraged her to stay with her husband.

Whatever, Frank was still off-limits in my mind. Besides, Frank was never the predatory type around me. We had some wine and did a lot of laughing. He took me upstairs to show me "the Frank Gifford Suite" or "the Memorial Wing"—whatever they called the guest room where he always stayed out there. I remember standing in the doorway, feeling weird, being in Frank's bedroom.

Later on, Don and Frank drove me to my hotel. I sat scrunched between the Odd Couple. Then Frank walked me up to my room and said good night. By this time Frank was legally separated, living in his own place. I was in the "off" mode with Stan at the moment. So we were both technically available. Frank asked me if I was sure I couldn't stay the weekend; it was going to be a lot of fun. I couldn't.

He gave me a sweet, gentle kiss on the cheek as he said good-bye—and we both had the same flash as he walked off, kind of a "Hmmm-now-*that*-was-interesting" sensation. An odd "couple" sensation.

When Frank got in the car, Dandy Don of course was ready to tease him. "You're just *leaving* her there?" he ranted in mock disbelief. Frank shrugged. And they had this running gag I later heard about: if Frank EVER considered getting married again, Don was authorized to simply cut "It" off before Frank could say "I do."

The play and seeing me in Santa Fe gave him a lift, he said, and a feeling that the worst was behind him. Though that was the last time I saw Frank for a few months, I must have been on his mind. One Monday night early in the football season, Frank was in Seattle and did a live halftime hookup with Washington Redskins quarterback Joe Theismann from his hospital bed, where he was recovering from a savage thigh fracture the Sunday before. That week I had gotten a message from Frank to schedule lunch but we had missed each other.

I came home that night and found twenty-two messages on my machine. They were all from different people who said the same thing: "Frank talked about you tonight" or "Didja hear what Frank said on the air?" Mom had weighed in, too. What happened was that Frank began his piece by saying: "Now joining us live from the hospital is Joe Theismann, and with him is Kathie Lee Johnson." Of course he meant Cathy Lee Crosby—she and Joe were engaged, and

Frank had known her for years. By then, not only Mom but also Don and Sue Meredith were lobbying for *something* to happen between us. It seemed inevitable to everyone but us.

In fact, I had had lunch with my dear friend Eva Mohr the summer before, and even she saw it. We were at a restaurant near Lincoln Center, sitting at a sidewalk table on Broadway. As was usual for my closest friends then, Eva was getting her share of my whining and moaning about my love life.

Eva's a real character; she and her husband, Stanley, are Cody's East Coast godparents. Every year they go on a safari. Eva's a cultured, worldly woman who traipses off into the bush with her Chanels and Yves Saint Laurents. Most people on safari get up at 5:00 A.M.; Eva gets up at four to do her hair and makeup. She lights a candle in the dark and puts on her false eyelashes. When I ask her why, she always says the same thing: "Because you never know who you're going to run into."

Well, she ought to know. She once ran into Robert Redford at the Mount Kenya Safari Club.

As Eva listened to one of my sob stories, her eyes suddenly spotted some big game right there behind me. She exclaimed, *"Oh, my God! Oh! My! God!"*

I said, "What? What is it?"

"Don't look. Don't *look!*" she whispered, and of course I wheeled around to look.

"Frank Gifford's walking right this way," she said excitedly.

I had never mentioned my friendship with Frank to Eva. "Frank's a friend of mine," I said. She was stunned. Frank came over to the table, and of course he looked so put together and sexy in his jeans and shirt and smelled so good. He gave me a kiss, I introduced him to Eva, and we had a brief chat. Then he walked off as Eva's eyes followed him. She looked at me, leaned forward, and grabbed my hand.

"Now *that's* the man you should be married to!"

Everyone thought Frank was my Mr. Right. Everyone but me. I didn't have a clue. I can see now how I might have missed what was happening. The situation with Stan getting more tense and confused. My own career was in a fair amount of upheaval that spring. Regis Philbin had come to New York in the early eighties after six years with "A.M. Los Angeles" to do "The Morning Show" in the local New York market. He had tried a thirteen-week show for a national program with Mary Hart but ended up again with his former L.A. partner, Cindy Garvey. But Cindy got into a very messy and public contract dispute, not to mention her rather messy and public split from baseball star Steve Garvey, and she left the show.

Now, Regis, who had been in show biz for three decades, needed a new co-host with whom he could build an on-air chemistry. I had really OD'd on the scripted formula of "GMA," and it was clear Joan was going to outlast the planet. I wasn't exactly on the war or White House correspondent track; and yet I had struck gold more often than anyone figured I would. I had brought to my correspondent work my best assets—my personality, an innate curiosity, a heart for people, a certain amount of wit and wisdom rooted in a staunchly traditional take on life.

Ironically, that made me something of an anomaly, since the producers of TV's "reality programs" were digging in gutters for sensational, topical pieces to keep up with the unrelenting ugliness of the tabloids.

In short, my time—our time—had come.

An agent of mine, who also happened to be Regis's agent at the William Morris Agency, began some behind-the-scenes discussions with WABC, which owned the show. I was still under contract to "GMA" and would have to continue for nearly a year. That didn't bother me.

Friends, colleagues, even my good and wise buddy Frank, told me I was crazy to leave what was then the highest-rated network morning show for a local show. But I detected a downward trend. I felt the "GMA" audience was getting older, and the show was also too rehearsed and dull for me. And the truth was, my career was at a plateau.

I attended a luncheon at Le Cirque while all of this was going on, and I ran into Barbara Walters, who told me she had read some gossip items about the possible jump. "Come over here," she said. "I've been reading you might go, might not go."

I was still undecided, so I asked her what she thought.

"You *have* to do it," she said.

"You're the only one who thinks that," I told her. "What about the fact that it's local?" She held my hand and gave me a long, wise look. "Kathie. New York is not local and this is a wonderful showcase for you." She meant that if I clicked and found the right vehicle in New York, where all the entertainment and media firms are concentrated, then I could go national in a New York minute.

We started in June of 1985 on one station—WABC. Two months later we knocked Phil Donahue out of first place for the first time in fourteen years, and eventually we chased him to four o'clock.

I knew we'd clicked from day one.

I was in for Joan that week and did double duty. The two studios were a minute and half apart along West Sixty-seventh Street, so I made a big deal of putting on my running shoes and racing, during the credits and commercials, to Reege's set. (Actually, a car drove me, but it made for a cute gag.)

That set up an edge between Regis and me right off the bat. That same animated (mostly!) jabbing-teasing repartee between us has made the show work—on some two hundred stations now. That first day I ran in, and already he was set with the taunts: "Oh, great! Is this what it's going to be like? My new co-host and she can't even get here on time?"

I went with it. I'd sort of race in, even if we were faking it, and they'd make a big show of my lateness and I'd say, "I'm HEEEERE! Da-daaaa!" and they'd pan down and show my sneakers. It was a ready-made shtick that just *worked* between us.

We had our own kind of reality programming. I called Reege a jerk that first week. Nobody had ever called the King a jerk on the air. And we were off and running. I just loved the guy. He was terrific to work with, and I had nothing but respect for his genius for that format. So when I called him a jerk, people loved it. It was unscripted and spontaneous and outrageous. And affectionate. Many people felt I was his first co-host who set her own guidelines and fully intended to be her own person.

Unfortunately, that same clarity was missing from my love life. Love and marriage—that was always the goal for me. But Stan's children had stopped hoping he'd ever get married again, even though they really wanted him to. His reason was always the same: he didn't want any more kids.

In November Frank and I had another one of our friendly dinners at Santa Fe on West Sixty-ninth Street, our favorite Mexican hangout, where I once again cried the blues about my love life. I had hardly seen Frank lately, yet the warmth was a constant, especially in the wake of his two recent losses, when he had turned to me for solace.

Now I was the one who needed comfort. I was heading into the holiday season with a troubled heart. New York can be a magical place between Thanksgiving and New Year's—but it can also be a miserable place. So over chips and dips and margaritas, Frank said, "Look, I'm getting out of here for the whole Christmas vacation. I've got this new place down in Jupiter, a great boat. You can get away and clear your head. The front yard's the ocean, the backyard's the waterway. I know lots of nice guys. You can have your own room."

I said I'd think about it. (I didn't go and got back with Stan.) Frank walked me home and we said good night. He took my face in his hands and gave me the sweetest kiss on my lips. It wasn't a sexual kiss; it was just a tender kiss. A *tender, devastating, unbelievable, unforgettable* kiss. And as I stood there, frozen, watching him walk away, I remember for the first time in my life almost fainting. I was actually spinning, so dramatic and intense was that one brief kiss from Frank.

And then I barfed my brains out all night long.

The next morning it was obvious I had been *somewhere* the night before, and Reege was merciless with the host chat teasing. I finally admitted I had been out with "a friend." Then I said it was Frank and swore it was harmless. From that point on, the rumors and gossip never stopped.

Stan and I seemed to have gotten nowhere by the end of the winter and early spring of 1986. In his view it was fine for me to love and be a "mother" to his three children, and to be like a wife to him. But he didn't love me enough to let me have my own child with him. It struck me as rather hypocritical that such an active self-proclaimed feminist wasn't so gung-ho pro-choice when it came to *my* choice to bear children. But he had a right to his reasons, which I understood and respected.

Our relationship ended for the umpteenth and final time after a big fight in early May of 1986. I went home that night to my apartment, tossed and turned. Then I had a breakthrough. I would later claim it came from God but other people would just say I came to my senses and got smart. I still believe God spoke straight to my heart: *If you settle for what you've got, you deserve what you get.*

In Stan's politically correct feminist environment you can change your life, you have power over your choices, you can do and be anything you choose to be. Which sounded great on the New York cocktail party circuit. But how did all that seductive rhetoric translate into living my life?

Then it hit me: *It didn't. I was miserable almost all the time. I was in another romantic rut. And I was two child-bearing years older.* My choices had been taken from me—except the choice to end the relationship. I should have broken up with Stan at least a year earlier. I'd stayed mostly out of love for his children and out of my own pride. I had invested a lot in his family.

He finally came out and told me that absolutely and positively there was no way he'd ever have any more kids. I was heartbroken again, but Daddy put it all in perspective for me when he said very,

very clearly: "Kathie, any man who will not marry a woman and give her a child, if he can, doesn't love her. Just flat out doesn't love her." I hated hearing that. But I would never forget it.

If there was ever any doubt in my mind that God was watching over me, it was dispelled the next day. Weeks before this final blowup with Stan, Frank and I had scheduled a lunch at the Santa Fe.

I didn't look too bad for someone who had just broken up for the ninth time in two years. I wore a real short and tight denim mini and a crisp white linen blouse. I'd lost a lot of weight because I was so crazed over Stan. Frank hadn't seen me in a while, and I guess I looked better to him than before. I'd burned and worried off all ten or twelve pounds of my baby fat. I had cheekbones now, and I looked and felt more womanly. None of which was lost on Frank. He later admitted he saw the dramatic change—and he commented on my "ever-decreasing bun structure," which was looking better and better. "You used to have a fat bottom," he said. (So *that's* what took us so long!)

One thing hadn't changed, though. I was still pouring my heart out to him. For the umpteenth time I started talking about Stan and about commitments, babies, freedom, choice, blah-blah-blah, but by then Frank had had it.

By now Frank's divorce was just weeks away. He was getting his own life in order. He had this beautiful place in Jupiter, Florida, and a great boat for fishing. He had talked some of his good friends into buying places down there. Frank didn't have to retire, exactly, but he didn't have to work out of New York, either.

Looking back, I think *he* was lonely, *I* was lonely, and *we* were clinging to each other as friends. So Frank took charge and took a stand.

"You know what?" he said firmly. "You're going to hang out with me until you get over this guy. There are some fun things coming up we can do. I'm not going to let you be alone long enough to miss that guy and go back to him. Now that my divorce is almost final, there's no problem with us being seen together. Plus, I think you're making a big mistake with him. You're being hurt. So that's it. You're hanging out with me now."

After lunch we walked across Columbus Avenue and said good-bye. I had walked halfway up the block when I suddenly felt self-conscious, *which is a rare state for me.* I looked over my shoulder and there he was, simply smiling at me. Now number 16 was *really* in The Greatest Game Ever Played.

Please Don't Let This Feeling End

Looking back, you'd think that with our marital histories, we just might have taken a *little* bit longer, given it a chance to build, *made sure we weren't making a huge mistake.*

As Cody would say, *"Forget about it!"*

This was a May–October courtship, and we really didn't need much longer than that to discover that it was real, it was love, and it was forever.

Frank and I began to emerge as a public couple. It just felt so easy and natural after what each of us had been through. After a dinner date Frank walked me the ten or so blocks down to my place. It was one of those warm and lazy spring evenings when it stays light later, everybody's out, and the city is charged up like one huge street fair. Frank sweetly draped his arm around me and pulled me closer. I was surprised and thought, Isn't he worried that someone from "Good Morning America" will see us? What would they think? That we were more than friends? The farther we walked, the less I cared.

Frank then had to go to Florida and on to Santa Fe for two weeks. When he called me from Florida early one morning, I invited him to a black-tie party ABC was throwing for media tycoon Walter Annenberg at the Waldorf. I didn't have anybody to ask and I just couldn't deal with showing up alone.

Frank shot me down. He'd be out west. "Listen," he said with a little edge, "you're not going to take somebody tall, dark, and handsome, are you?"

"I just might, if I can find one. You never know," I said coyly. Five minutes after we hung up, the phone rang again. "On second thought," Frank said, "I'm coming back to take you to that party."

Frank flew in from Santa Fe for the party. When he picked me up he had a gift-wrapped box with him. Inside was a gorgeous Rolex sport watch. I was stunned. He said he was tired of looking at the Bulgari snake watch he thought Stan had given me. This, he said, was a friendship watch.

"It's quite a friendship," I said.

"I had a good year," he said.

"These things go for thousands of dollars!"

"Well," he said, shrugging, "they made this one in Haiti."

Maybe that was his way of telling me it was time. That night was our first public night out, and we danced and sat together with the whole media world—including many of our bosses and producers—surrounding us. For once, we didn't care.

Frank had been wary of gossip columnists and colleagues getting the wrong idea. He didn't need to fan the flames with Astrid, but he was quite the eligible bachelor. The word was that Angie Dickinson, Priscilla Presley, and Shirley Fonda all had feelers out for Frank through friends. He was seeing people in Santa Fe and Jupiter. He'd had a couple dates with actress Susan Sullivan of "Falcon Crest" and a friendly lunch or two with Diane Sawyer.

After one lunch, Diane canceled plans she and Frank had made to go out again and decided instead to go to Connecticut for a weekend of reading Emily Dickinson or something like that. Years later, after Diane had married director Mike Nichols, she was making a speech at a fund-raiser for the American Paralysis Association, and she was so adorable. She told the story of their date, her change of plans, and her expecting to reschedule the date with Frank.

"But by the time I got back to town," she joked at the luncheon, "that woman had him checked out, bagged, in the cart, out the door, and in her car driving off." It was hysterical.

Early in the spring, I had spent my last penny on a cute summer house in Southampton. But instead of relaxing and reading books with Stan and his kids—the original concept—I was most often accompanied by Frank. On Fridays he'd pick me up in his Jaguar and his tight jeans and sexy shirts, and we'd drive out for our weekends "together." He stayed in a guest room at the beachfront home of Ron Konecky, his attorney, and his wife, Isobel.

There aren't many men at any age, particularly past thirty-five or forty, who can get away with tight jeans, but I've never seen *any* man look sexier in tight, faded Levi's than Frank does. God made jeans with Frank in mind. He puts them on, I go crazy.

Frank not only helped me through this healing time. He also helped with gardening, plumbing, rigging outdoor lights, and antiquing. We proceeded cautiously, more intent on companionship than courtship. But a whole other part of him was emerging. It was a side of Frank millions of Americans don't see when he appears as a sportscaster in a network blazer. He is so much more multidimensional. He's funny, he's incredibly bright, he's an extremely tender person with a delightfully playful, keen sense of humor, which, of course, is very attractive. I was falling deeper and deeper into *something*.

Then one day it just whacked me over the head: I'd probably been in love with him for years and hadn't realized it—and if I had realized, I'd have promptly repressed it.

After all the shaky, on-off, and no-win situations I had been in, I felt totally *safe and taken care of*. It makes such a difference when you fall in love with a man you've already shared four years of friendship with. The trust and the caring are already in place. I knew this was someone who wasn't going to hurt me. There was no uncertainty, anxiety, or skepticism, no complex defenses against getting blind-sided in love. As you get older and survive your share of knocks, life gets complicated; you're not looking for teen heat but rather for a soothing grown-up comfort zone. With Frank, I didn't even have to give up all of one to have the other.

And yet there were valid reasons to stay away from Frank as a mate. The twenty-three-year age difference was a big one. Frank was my mother's age. Also, I'd been in and out of two turbulent relationships since meeting Frank. And we were both on the rebound. He was still legally married, *and* he was occasionally co-hosting for Regis on "The Morning Show." I did not want to be seen as a home-wrecker, because I wasn't one.

So while I'd always shut down any sexy notions about Frank, now little things I'd seen for years *were driving me wild* when he'd drive out to the beach—like his beautiful hands, the powerful muscles in his arms, his striking profile, the little dimple in his chin. And I was thinking, *God, he's gorgeous. What's wrong with me? I never saw that?*

I finally got zapped by the bolt of lightning during the weekend of the U.S. Open golf tournament in late June. We went to a big dinner party in the Hamptons home of Frank's friends, David and Hillie Mahoney. Frank and I were there as buddies more than anything, but it sure didn't seem that way to his friends.

To this day they tease him about the point in the evening when we wandered out to the deck. As they tell it, Frank gently pulled me toward his heaving masculine hairy chest, pointed heavenward, and said, "Look, Kathie, there's the moon."

To which I, femininity pouring from my every pore, responded breathlessly, "Oh, really Frank?" We don't remember this incident as reported, but they never let us forget it.

I do remember what happened the following weekend, though. Frank took me to another party at Tony and Marianne Ittelson's house in Southampton. Now, I was used to Stan disappearing to work the room the minute we arrived at a big party. But this time it was Frank who said, "Let me say hello to a few friends, and then I'll be back." Yeah, right.

Five minutes later he came back, put his arm around my waist, and said, "I've done my duty. Now I've come home." And he never left my side the rest of the night. I was just knocked out by those words—and they set the tone for the rest of the evening.

At one point, he said, "You realize everyone in this room is drooling over you. You're the most beautiful sight in the house. You look gorgeous."

Was I arguing, in my lacy feminine off-the-shoulder thing with tight ankle-length pants and sandals? Frank always made me feel so feminine. Don was sweet, but he was like a little boy. Stan rarely made me feel I was precious. Frank was very seductive in his own strong, silent way.

And yet, who knows? It might never have happened for us were it not for the Ittelsons' Singing Machine. This gizmo allows you to sing and record your own vocals over the instrumental backing of your favorite artists (sheet music came with these specially doctored tapes). Everybody took turns singing, and it was a complete riot. Frank, who had never heard me really sing, and I, decided to play Barbra Streisand and Neil Diamond singing "You Don't Bring Me Flowers."

So, with all the feeling I could muster, I sang, "You don't bring me flowers," and then Frank, without missing a beat—and he was supposed to miss eight—blurted, all in one breath, "You-hardly-ever-talk-to-me-anymore-and-you-don't-come-to-the-door-at-the-end-of-the-daaaay!!!" Well, I died. DIED! It was hysterical. I simply had no idea people could sing that badly. I had never seen this tone-deaf side of Frank.

We did it three times, and each time was funnier than the last. I literally fell off the sofa, tears streaming down my face, holding my sides I was laughing so hard, clutching the mike and looking up at him. Frank was howling and crying, too.

That was the big breakthrough for me. I looked up at him—and to this day I feel this way—and realized, I don't ever want to go through one day of my life without that man in it. I knew it then and I still feel it now.

I didn't need a Rolex to know our time had come. That night Frank took me back home to my little house, stayed up with me until three o'clock, and, well, I never looked back. I'd been an absolute fool. This gorgeous, funny, tender, gentle, sexy, wise, and spiritual man had been under my nose all that time.

The truth is, I didn't steal someone's husband. But if I'd been smart, if I'd known how wonderful he was four years earlier, I don't know what I would have done. But our time had finally come.

If I sometimes felt like a trophy to other men before, I truly felt like a treasure in Frank's life. I came to feel so loved and protected and cared for and safe. That's what it was. I felt safe. I'd left my parents' home exactly half my life ago—and for the first time since then, I felt emotionally secure.

God knows I'd paid my dues and felt adrift. I went through high school and ORU feeling that no one understood me. I was out of place in Anita's home and unhappily married in my own home. I searched frantically for an artistic home between the secular and gospel worlds; I uprooted myself and came to New York for a new career and life-style. I hadn't exactly mastered life as either a total woman or a single woman. I'd spent four romantically shaky years in two relationships that went on too long and were doomed to fail.

Despite the incredibly loving home that had produced me, I had spent all those years feeling, for the most part, lost and alone. Frank and I found each other at a time when we were both emotionally crippled. I had lost my direction, lost my faith, and was asking, Why am I here? Do I have any talent? Am I worth anything? Will I ever feel valued by a man? Frank came along at the perfect time to save me from wallowing in my misery.

And I came along for him when he had pretty much lost faith in everything. Frank told me—and he meant no offense to the mother of his three children—that he felt he had never allowed himself to be truly in love. When we fell in love he let me know I had brought to his life a dimension of playful exuberance and joy that he had never known before. I made it safe for Frank to be silly, to lighten up, to have a good time. I had never seen that side of him in our four years of platonic friendship. Like the movie *When Harry Met Sally*, the transition from friendship to love was scary and risky. We both needed the romance, but we were afraid it would ruin the friendship.

Frank had withheld himself emotionally far more than I had. He was leery, almost cynical, about being "used" to make Stan jealous. He was at times sure that was my hidden agenda. He had been over a couple times when I played back Stan's messages. He sensed that I was really stuck on Stan, and that he—Frank—would be a perfect one to "use," because the news would certainly get back to Stan that we were seeing each other.

I finally made it clear that I had not been in love with Stan for a long time. I believe love dies slowly. You don't just wake up one morning and you're not in love anymore. It's a dynamic progression where love dies piece by piece, day by day, just the way it builds. And that's why I'm more in love with Frank now than I was at the height of romantic passion. I know him better now, I respect him so much more, I like him more.

Most often the opposite occurs. First you flame; then you burn out when the passion cools with nothing behind it. Your whole personal life seems to revolve around this one person. A lot of people stay in bad relationships because at least it's a relationship they know and understand. A fear of the unknown keeps a lot of people from leaving bad situations.

I had been stuck in an unfulfilling, one-sided relationship, staying on because I loved Stan's kids and enjoyed his network of friends. Frank had given up and was ready to go fishing and golfing in Florida. It wasn't until that night in front of the Singing Machine that we both discovered a joyful, romantic ease in simply being together. Curiously, that was the one component each of us had always missed in the other. Now, suddenly, there it was.

My parents were hearing more and more about Frank and me and got concerned. Four years earlier it had amused Mom that Frank seemed "smitten" on Turkey Day. Now I wasn't sure they were giving thanks so readily. But they knew Frank was more than a concierge out there at the beach.

The age gap was one problem. Frank, gorgeous as he was, also embodied all that was seductive about the fast-track media world that had always seemed remote and threatening to Mom and Dad. "Kathie," Mom said once, "could this be serious with him?"

"Yes, I really think it could."

"You're kidding. Here we go again."

"No," I said calmly, "it just seems so right to have him in my life. You'll see."

She got her chance over July Fourth weekend, when my parents, Craig, Michie, and Shannie came out to my modest Hamptons house. The next day Frank drove up after stopping off at Babinski's, our favorite market in the Hamptons, to buy corn, scones, fruit, bagels, croissants, fish, and chicken for a barbecue—I mean, this man came bearing gifts. He was taking *no* chances.

It took exactly five minutes for him to totally disarm my conservative, watchful parents—to show them how absolutely right he was in my life. "I saw right away," Mom later confided, "that he loves you and that he's a *real* man. And like your father he's a man of action who takes charge. So you know you can bend me."

As for Daddy, he was so cute—and, for once, realistic. It looked as if the Ogre was finally ready to retire: "Well," he said sardonically, "that leaves the question of divorce, and at this point we can't argue about track record, because he's only had one more than you."

From that weekend on, my parents felt that Frank was definitely the wonderful, fabulous man I should spend my life with.

I knew things were going well when we had a noise problem with some young kids who took over the house across the way for the weekend. Their music was blaring so loud we could hardly converse. When Frank said, "I guess I'll go over there and talk to them," my dad, who had been kind of lying back, taking it all in, saw an opportunity to bond—and break the tension. "Hey, I've got a better idea. Let me get my bazooka and I'll *blow* 'em away."

For a second or two Frank was thinking: "Oh, no! I've fallen in love with the daughter of an NRA maniac who's gonna kill me." Daddy blew *us* away with the joke, and from that point on, the soldier of fortune's daughter could stop sweating bullets.

Any lingering qualms my no-nonsense parents had over Frank's "intentions" vanished three weeks later. Frank and I went to London, where he was covering an exhibition between two American football teams in Wembley Stadium. While Frank did an interview at a radio station, I waited in an anteroom but could hear the broadcast.

I thought maybe I was hearing voices when Frank said, "I'm here in London with my fiancée."

I just thought, "fiancée," isn't *that* a lovely word? We had begun to talk in the abstract about "when we get married" and "if we ever got married." But nothing concrete. Until now. Afterward, I said, "Frank, I can't be your fiancée because you haven't asked me."

He shrugged. "Well, you are."

I was confused.

Frank had pulled strings through American friends so we could have dinner that night at Annabel's, a super-chic private club. But they had said they could only give us a table at eight-thirty. Fine.

When we got there the place looked closed. We banged on the door and walked around to see if there was another entrance. The door opened and the maître d' appeared with his tie askew and his vest unbuttoned. We could see a bunch of waiters chowing down at a table in the rear, but there was *no one* in the dining room. The maître d' finally explained that no halfway-fashionable Londoner would be caught *dead* inside Annabel's much before eleven, but we were welcome to stay and enjoy London's hottest hot spot all by ourselves.

We sat at the bar and had a drink before going to our table, thinking maybe someone else would come in and we wouldn't be the only ones there.

We sat down, and a strolling violinist promptly waltzed over to our table. Of course he came to our table: there was *nowhere else* for him to stroll because there were no other people there. The food arrived, and it looked great, but I was so in love I didn't taste food for four months. I have no idea if I ate. I always know when I'm in love. I'm skinny when I'm in love, and by that time I was down to 104 and Frank weighed only 175. It's the least either of us had weighed since we were born. When you're just madly in love, you don't see straight. You just live on love.

Things got bittersweet because this guy was just standing there serenading us and Frank still hadn't popped the question—despite blabbing to a London DJ that I was his fiancée. I started crying—and of course none of the waiters and busboys had *anything* to do but watch me weep. So they stared at us. The poor violinist couldn't figure out what was wrong with his playing, and Frank was squirming and looking around with major discomfort. Finally he leaned forward and whispered, "Will you marry me?"

I sniffed, stopped crying, and gushed, "YYYESSS!"

I had told Frank I did not want an ostentatious engagement ring, just a simple gold wedding band. I knew people would make a big deal out of it.

Once back home, we were determined to spend every possible minute together. The football training camp and exhibition season were under way, however, and I had a bunch of solo nightclub bookings. So when I had a concert at Mount Airy Lodge in the Poconos over a summer weekend, we had to get there from the

Hamptons. Frank wanted me to hurry out and back so he chartered a plane out of Easthampton Airport.

One of the world's worst storms hit the shore. It was so fierce that even the birds were grounded. So Frank offered to drive me to the Poconos—five hours through gusty winds and thunderstorms. Talk about a close, bonding experience.

On the way , as we drove through Buttsville, Pennsylvania, Frank said to me, "'You know, ever since I fell in love with you, I'm a mess, I'm a mush-head. I can't eat, I can't think straight, I can't do anything. I'm a total mush-head!"

"You're not a mush-head," I said in my favorite yiddish accent. *"You're a Moishe-head,"* I said, spitting on him. *"From now on, you're my Moishe."*

He laughed, "Well, then you're my Golda." From that moment on, we were Golda and Moishe of Buttsville, Pennsylvania. To this day, even though I tend to call him Lambchop more than Moishe, he'll sign any card or gift or Valentine, "Love you, Moishe." And he still calls me Golda, because it reminds both of us of such a sweet, loving time.

But that was also a busy and disjointed time that had us pinching ourselves. Was this really going anywhere? we wondered. Were we crazy? Dreaming? How was this *really* going to work, with all the travel and disruptions?

I had a week of stage shows scheduled in August at the Trump Plaza in Atlantic City. Frank chartered choppers to take me down and back so I could do the morning show with Reege and not have to spend six hours a day commuting. I was getting kind of spoiled. But I was also in a lot of pain with bad vocal problems due to strain, fatigue, and New York allergies.

Between my two shows the first night, I wanted to cancel my remaining engagements. "I can't do them," I moaned to Frank. "I can't sing. My voice is gone. I'd rather not sing than do less than my best."

Frank was tough. "That's bull," he said. "This laryngitis is about everything else. You get dressed up, you go back out, and you tell *them* you can't sing. You croak if you have to." He told me he thought the problem was psychological.

I knew he was referring to what I felt was a vicious review I'd gotten a year or so earlier when I sang at Freddy's nightclub in New York. I shouldn't have let it affect me but this reviewer crucified me, which means he didn't adore me. I'd worked for this a long time, and it was my first real New York engagement. Frank said, "I hate to see some jerk like that hurt you this way. You've got to believe in yourself." Frank had been through it all before and had a real healthy view.

"Look," Frank went on, "the first time I read that somebody didn't like me was when I threw an interception in high school when I was sixteen. I lived through it. And even now the TV sports critics think I can't do anything right. So what?"

Frank was great at helping me handle critics. But I'd really been burned. So when I got to Atlantic City I went out there and won one for the Giffer!

I came, I croaked, I conquered. I got standing ovations. *No accounting for taste!* They loved that I was so hoarse, so game. It was a huge breakthrough for me, and it chased away the ghosts of Freddy's.

One day, before another performance at the Trump Plaza Frank came to a rehearsal but was unusually quiet, almost solemn. He'd asked me a few times if he could speak to me privately during a break. I was absolutely sure he wanted to tell me it was over. My mind raced.

Yes, he'd tell me he loved me, I was wonderful, and all that. He'd had the best time in his life. But he didn't see himself fitting into this kind of life right now. Couldn't share me with all these people putting demands on my time and energies. Couldn't deal with me being on display, sitting in guys' laps during shows as part of the playful working-the-crowd shtick (always a guy with far less hair and far more pounds than Frank).

It would not have shocked me. It had been a real tough few months for Frank. His mom had been ill and he had been shuttling back and forth to Ventura, California, to look after her. Frank suffered plenty of guilt about his mom and his dad, whom he had lost several years before, and blamed himself for not having spent more time with them later in their lives. The divorce proceedings had also been emotionally draining for him.

Moreover, Frank was wrestling with his situation at ABC that spring. There were major changes in the air at "Monday Night." Don Meredith was gone, and Frank was mulling over a big offer to jump to CBS to do something new. Though he never got crazy about his age and certainly didn't feel it, he *was* fifty-six years old. He had never missed a single Monday game in fifteen years and had seen just about all the hotel lobbies and airports a man could ask for in one lifetime. Financially, he really didn't need to work anymore, and for the first time in his life, he thought about quitting.

He had gone soul-searching with the Merediths out in Santa Fe, and in late April he had signed a multi-year contract with ABC, which involved, as he puts it, "a lot of zeros and a lot of promises" to stay on. Even so, he wasn't happy with much of what was going on in his life then.

If part of me feared I was becoming just another problem for him to deal with—another involvement that didn't fit into Frank's life—a widely read New York gossip column that appeared in mid-July didn't help. The *Post*'s Page Six devoted its lead story to Frank, his impending divorce, and me. It quoted Astrid angrily accusing us of having an affair for "quite a while" and for "openly and rather disgustingly" talking about the "affair" when Frank sat in for Reege that week. The implication was that I'd stolen her husband, which of course, was just one of many misstatements of fact in the piece. My feeling was that only the truth can hurt. The lies stung only momentarily.

Anyone who knew Frank considered him divorced months and months earlier. Only an agreement on the property settlement was hanging up the paperwork. My parents had met Frank just two weeks before the item ran and if his marital status was good enough for my staunch born-again Christian parents, it should have been good enough for *anyone*. The Page Six story was pure, laughable fantasy. But now I thought maybe it had upset Frank and convinced him to back away.

It was a sad thought. Frank had loved my act, though he'd ask, "Who's that guy smiling at her?" He'd beat to a pulp the first guy who laid a paw on me. I needed that. I needed to know I was that important to somebody. Now I feared that Frank didn't need it. He's a traditional guy and his attitude was, "You're mah woman." Some women regard that as a Neanderthal approach and find it appalling; I found it appealing and sexy because I knew Frank was no caveman. But now I was scared to talk to him, certain it was curtains for the Moishe and Golda Show.

We finally got upstairs to my suite and I cut to the chase. "You want out, don't you?" I said. "You want to tell me you can't live this way."

He didn't say anything and looked at me curiously. Then he reached into his pocket and said, "No, actually I just wanted a moment with you so I could tell you I want you to be mine forever."

And when his hand came out he was holding a gorgeous ring.

I shrieked. Did I actually sit there and let him kiss me and hold me? Yeah, right. "I gotta show Michie," I said and blasted out of the room in search of my sister.

It was a five-carat emerald-cut diamond with a baguette on either side. It's amazing what they can do with cubic zirconiums these days!

The irony, of course, is that I had honestly believed I didn't want an engagement ring. I had insisted that I didn't want to be pretentious. And I really did want Frank to know I loved him for the love he gave me, not for the things he gave me. I could buy all of the worldly things I wanted. The gifts men had given me before usually found their way to the fingers, wrists, necks, and backs of my mother, my sister, and my sister-in-law. But not *this* ring. They'd have to cut my hand off to get *this*.

I asked Moishe why he gave me the ring. He said, typically, "It's not so much for you, Golda. It's for Menachem Begin and Yitzhak Shamir—your parents. I want them to know how serious I am about you and that I'm not using their little girl."

Frank was also eager to show my parents that the ring was mightier than the pen—that the bogus gossip item could never tear us apart. It was his way of validating our relationship and of assuring everyone that we, not some item they'd read in the press, were the genuine article.

Once I knew we were getting married, the age difference ceased to matter. I once said to Frank, "I only wish, Lamb, that we could have met and fallen in love when we were both twenty, both virgins, and had our entire lives ahead of us." I didn't need a calculator to figure out that happily-ever-after was all well and good but the reality is that we will never celebrate our fiftieth wedding anniversary.

But Frank said simply, "Golda, you wouldn't have wanted me then. I had too much to prove—to myself, to my father, to the world. I could never have loved a woman then the way I love you now, or given to a woman then the way I can give to you now."

On September 18, early in the football season, Frank did a Monday night game with the Cleveland Browns—but it was the Cleveland Blues that made my day.

As usual, he had left on Sunday. Frank always spent a day before a game walking around the city, getting the flavor of the place and people and studying the two teams. The strolls helped him fight jet lag and gave him some exercise. But Cleveland was rainy that day, and he got depressed—of course, without me! After our dreamy summer of sun and romance in the city and at the beach, the thought of life on the road for another long season made him lonely and miserable.

I couldn't wait to get his phone call. "What's one month from today?" he asked.

"October eighteenth," I said.

"Fine. I miss you so much. Let's get married one month from today."

And that's as complicated as the date-setting decision ever got.

Just days before the wedding, Ron Konecky, Frank's attorney and our wedding day host, Frank, and I were sitting in the sand at Ron's home on the ocean. It was one of those gloriously crisp Canadian-high fall days, and we were watching the sparkling surf curl and crash in the brilliant sun—as we discussed a prenuptial agreement. I had no problem with signing a prenup. I had my own career; I was no gold digger; I wasn't after Frank's money.

As we sat on the beach, Ron's little poodle, Monsieur Claude, scampered over to me and began madly humping my arm. He just wouldn't quit. The talks bogged down.

Frank said it best: "Claude feels the same way about you as I do." And at that point, we decided that a prenuptial was a sacrilege that had no bearing on the way we felt toward each other. I expected Ron to fight harder for a deal, but seeing how strongly Frank identified with Monsieur Claude, we all agreed that an agreement was unnecessary.

Once we got over that last hump, as it were, we planned a small, simple one-o'clock wedding at Ron and Isobel's spectacular glass house on the deck over the dunes. We invited about seventy of our family and friends.

I went to Bergdorf Goodman and Saks looking for a magnificent wedding dress. They asked me when the big day was. I said October. They said fine. October next year? I said no, October three weeks. Forget it, they said, no way. They needed a year. I ended up going to Kleinfeld's in Brooklyn—the bridal assembly-line place—and picked out something.

It was wild. They've got a room just for bridesmaids, a room just for veils, a room just for full-figured mothers-in-law. I picked out a dress I liked and had them shorten and tighten it. I didn't think I should wear a billowing, flowing white lacy gown with five marriages between us. Seemed just a bit tacky.

Yet I felt no stigma whatsoever in being the third Mrs. Gifford. On the contrary, I became more merciful, less judgmental about other people. There's a human story behind every statistic. It's people and what's in their hearts that matter. I'm sure even Liz Taylor, as outrageous as eight marriages sounds, has eight stories and they all make perfect sense to her.

Now it was time for me to meet Frank's family. I met his sons—Jeff, who is a year older than I am, and Kyle, who is one year younger—in Jupiter, and they were both warm and terrific to me. Frank's daughter, Vicki, who is three years younger than I, couldn't come, and I did not meet her until the night before our marriage.

I met his mom, Lola Mae, just before the weekend of the wedding. I'd never been so nervous in all my life. Mama was eighty-two, and I had gotten along with her on the phone. She knew I was a born-again Christian, and she had grown up in the church and gone to services all her life. Frank's dad had passed away a few years earlier, and Mama was now with her boyfriend, George Byers.

I was so worked up as we waited for them at the Regency Hotel that I said, "Honey, I want a martini." I don't remember ever ordering a martini in my life. Frank did a double take, as if he thought I was nuts, but he ordered me one. I took two sips of it and I gagged.

By the time Mama, a teetotaler, arrived, I'd pushed the martini away, but it was still in plain sight. We met and were getting along just fine until Frank ordered wine for dinner. She looked at me and said, "You're having wine for dinner, too?" Well, I was off to a great start with her.

On October 17, the night before the wedding, many of our friends joined us for an informal, high-energy dinner and party at a funky place called the Salty Dog near Sag Harbor out at the beach. There was a guy who played "Feelings" on the piano and kazoo. We passed pumpkins all around, danced and sang, and had a great old time until one in the morning with everybody from the little grandchildren to captains of industry.

Reege graciously took time from his busy, hot, and ever-happening show-biz career to hear me say the fewest words he'd ever heard from *this* mouth: "*I do.*"

It's hard on children when their parents remarry, and it's particularly hard on daughters. Frank's daughter, Vicki, was not entirely comfortable with the new marriage. I can understand Vicki's initial aloofness. I tried to put myself in her shoes: What if my daddy had divorced my mother and married someone close to my age, someone I didn't know and about whom I'd heard some weird things? It would have been real tough on me, that's for sure. Vicki knew I was on TV. She'd heard I had a big mouth. Maybe she'd also heard I was a gold digger. I knew she was closer to Astrid than the boys were, so I'm sure there was some pressure on her there. I knew we would have to work on the awkwardness between us, and eventually it all worked out wonderfully.

Frank encouraged me to give it time, assuring me that when Vicki and I got to know each other things would work out. They did. Vicki, who married Bobby and Ethel Kennedy's son Michael, is a fabulous person. But there were moments of chilliness and real conflict between us. Nobody ever threw anything, but there were tears and healing. It was a complicated process for the two of us and for her and Frank, who also had some patching up to do. As they came to grips with their lifelong issues, our relationships evolved and fell slowly, sweetly into place.

I think that once she saw how much I adored her father, saw that I had my own life and made my own way, understood I was not *after* anything, not trying to manipulate him or keep him from his children, once the caring and trusting were in place, we were fine.

Things changed considerably after Cody was born. Then we had in common motherhood and all the joys and pains early infancy can bring. Vicki's a sensational mother. Her children liked me, and that helped. They always came away with a story I'd told them or we'd go shopping together.

Our wedding day started out cold and overcast, and I was worried to death that it wouldn't be so great out there on the deck. By noon the skies opened up, however, and God gave us a spectacular Indian summer afternoon with dry, crisp ocean breezes and warm sunshine. Our friends mingled and sipped champagne before the ceremony.

It was a simple, brief, and beautiful wedding. My brother Davy presided over the ceremony, and Frank and I wrote our own vows to each other. I almost killed myself in my high heels as I wobbled out on the planks of Ron's deck, because they're spaced apart like a boardwalk and are made for flat shoes or no shoes.

Looking back on it now I'm sure Don Meredith and Frank's other friends were glad we had moved too fast for anyone to have a chance to cut us off; but some trepidation about the age gap and getting hitched so quickly was understandable. Yet they all made me feel accepted. At some point in life you meet someone and decide you're going to do whatever it takes to make your relationship work and to be together. Just do it. To complicate love with "I'm not ready yet" or "This isn't a good time for me" is, frankly, as Cody would say, "poo-poo." He's *such* a genius! There's no such thing as a bad time for true love. You don't always get to choose when you'll fall in love, and sometimes it's best to just get out of your own crazy way and let it happen.

When you're ready, you'll know it. And heaven help the person who gets in the way.

I remember saying to the friends on the deck during the ceremony, "To so many of you gathered here this glorious afternoon, Frank has through the years been 'Giff.' I just want to say that to me the man I'm standing next to today isn't Giff but a *gift*. He's been a gift from God who's restored the goodness I was missing in my life for so long."

The wedding broke up around four in the afternoon after a beautiful brunch of grilled swordfish, baby lamb, an assortment of pastas, rosemary potatoes, wedding cake, fruit, and lots of champagne. And then the chase was on to Gurney's Inn in Montauk at the eastern tip of Long Island. Frank had a Giants game that Monday, but at least we had the weekend.

The paparazzi had been camped out front and crawling through the dunes all afternoon as if they thought this was the Normandy landing or something. We ducked out of Ron's and raced off in Frank's red Jag before anyone could fire a shot. Then they chased us all the way out to Montauk. It was getting dangerous on the narrow highway. We knew they wouldn't leave us alone until Frank pulled over so they could get a shot.

As they all piled out of their cars and set up their equipment, Frank and I jumped back in the Jag and tore off again. He was gunning it to Gurney's, and finally I said, "Honey, someone's going to get hurt."

So we stopped to let them get their roadside shot. By the time we got to Gurney's charming, romantic inn, we were totally exhausted. We caught the last magic hour of sunlight as we strolled along the beach. We were lying down, half unpacked, absolutely exhausted, trying to relax. We both felt such exquisite relief at the end of these last two or three emotion-filled months that we both dozed off in the middle of the Mets' World Series game against the Red Sox.

When I look back at that exhilarating autumn day, I remember being not the least bit nervous. I was grateful. I had stopped believing in fairy tales, in happy endings, and so had Frank. I honestly wonder if I'd be alive today without Frank. I had slipped into an abyss and lost so much of my self-respect. After a while in life you rack up so many hurts—and do your share of hurting—that you become cynical, jaded. Experience gradually wears away the rosy hue of life's glasses. You get less sentimental, tougher. You just say, Well, I'll take whatever pleasure I can in what's handed to me, but I'd be a fool to feel entitled to much more than that.

We were both so wrong. All of a sudden my sweetest and most intimate dreams in life had come true. How could I be nervous and apprehensive when I was feeling such gratitude to the Lord for the healing process He had brought me through?

And for letting us believe again that happy endings happen.

It Don't Mean a Thing
If It Ain't Got That Swing

☆

The fall and winter of 1986 was a strange time. Living with Frank and working with Reege was like having two partners in life. But now that I had Frank, it looked as if I might lose Regis. Or, more accurately, as if he might lose me. After a little more than a year with him on "The Morning Show," I was tired of the business aspects of my career, sick of struggling for everything I had worked toward for so long. I didn't want to continue doing the show, and quite honestly, I was ready to quit working.

My voice was gone after a busy summer filled with strain, allergy problems, and fatigue. I didn't want to sing anymore. Just as Daddy had been for Mom, Frank was to be a knight in shining armor who would take me away from all that. Frank's fantasy was that I'd give it all up, be with him all the time, sit at his feet, and sort of worship him. *Just kidding!*

At home, life was happier than ever, but in my career, I was frustrated with everybody—except Reege—and ready to bail out. It was the reverse image of several years earlier, when, at "GMA," I flourished in a new career even though my private life, at times, was desolate.

My problems at the show were absolutely not about Reege or about clashes or personalities or dressing room size or any of that nonsense. I have worked seven years with this man without so much as an argument. That's miraculous. I love him like a friend and brother. We're open and honest enough so I can tell him if he's hurt me somehow and vice versa. The problem was certainly not about our ratings. By the fall of 1986 we were on top.

I was more surprised than anyone that I would actually consider quitting. I used to watch Reege on television in Los Angeles and think: He's incredible. He's fabulous. So fast, so funny, so *grating*. I couldn't decide if he was obnoxiously adorable or adorably obnoxious. (Now I think he's both! As I say to him, "You may be a pain in the butt, but you're *my* pain in the butt!) Every time I turned on his show he was doing something stupid. And I *loved* that! He's one of the most daring and creative people on TV. If I could only work with *him*." I thought.

And, aside from the times when I had legitimate reasons to consider leaving, the clash between our opposite on-air personalities has created a demand for something fresh and spontaneous and *positive*. He gets to taunt and tease me, be combative and vinegary, jab me about how tired he is of my treacly Frank and Cody stories, cut me *off* in the middle of a story so he can go and tell his *endless* stories about Notre Dame or about his dumb wrestlers. We just have the best time, and it's totally unrehearsed and genuine.

But my discontent early on wasn't about personality; it was about perception, agents, politics, and pride. It was about people's egos, too, which was new turf for me and not my most comfortable area.

It took me some time to realize that the perceptions of powerful people translate into money and respect. The basic issue was that the powers that be saw the show as "The Regis Show." The reality was that it was "our" show. This misperception on the part of management did not boost my bargaining power at contract renewal time.

Everyone in show business knows that Regis has a great track record. In fact, he'd done so many versions of "The Regis Philbin Show" over the years that I could understand why media veterans regarded ours as just the latest version. He had debuted with a "Regis Philbin Show" out of San Diego way back when JFK was President in 1961. That show was syndicated through the mid-1960s and ended up as a late-night show on KTTV in L.A. Regis spent two and a half years as the sidekick on "The Joey Bishop Show" and then had shows through the 1970s and early 1980s, with titles like "Philbin's People," "Regis Philbin's Saturday Night in St. Louis," "Regis Philbin's Health Styles," "Regis Philbin's Lifestyles," and my personal favorite, "That Regis Philbin Show."

After six years with "A.M. Los Angeles," co-hosted by Sarah Purcell for four years and then by Cindy Garvey for two years (and me for two days), Regis came to New York in April 1983 with "The

Morning Show." He was rejoined by Cindy Garvey. Ann Abernathy replaced her during the year before I came on board in June 1985.

In order to work well, all two-host shows require an on-camera spark, the chemistry that reporters drive us crazy about. Reege, gifted as he is, had survived an uneven flow of spark and fizzle through the years. Soon after he came to New York to do "The Morning Show," he became the first host in fourteen years to make a dent in the local ratings.

For any number of reasons, ratings really improved as soon as I came on board. I like to kid Reege *and* Frank that they both found the woman of their very different dreams at around the same time.

There has been, with all the teasing and taunting, only one incident between them when their respective agendas didn't mesh smoothly around me. Soon after we were married, Reege was encouraging our viewers to join us on a trip to Puerto Rico to watch us do the show from there. Reege said something like "It'll be great. We'll party by the pool, and who knows, maybe you'll get lucky and get invited up to Kathie's suite for happy hour."

That's not the kind of thing *anyone* says about Frank's woman. Despite his wonderful, sometimes frisky sense of humor, Frank, ultratraditional and superpossessive, draws a line on his turf, and Reege had inadvertently crossed it.

That turf was only two blocks from the studio. Frank walked over and confronted Reege. "How would you like it if during 'Monday Night Football' I said something like 'Why don't you rowdy football fans come on over and have a few beers with Joy?'" And he said it with some heat. Poor Reege was stunned. He'd been kibbitzing with co-hosts off the top of his head for so long it wasn't really something he ever thought about. And no one had ever spoken to him like this.

Frank's intensity brought Reege around to understanding how sensitive I am about family and people's feelings and that I, unlike so many show-biz veterans, am *not* totally jaded. I *do* hurt and I will not knowingly do or say anything just to get a laugh or extra ratings point if it's at someone else's expense. I have no problem with cute and self-mocking remarks, but there's a line of discretion and decency that should not be crossed.

That incident marked a shift with Reege. For us, walking on eggshells would be death on TV, but there was a new respect. I had spent a year being Reege's latest "gal about town" partner, as Frank saw it, a throwback to Regis's shtick with other women co-hosts. There were the coy references to my mystery-man dates (with Frank and others) and, later, the acknowledged dates with Frank for him to play off in our "about last night" host chats. Fine.

But by the fall of 1986 I was a married woman; I was fulfilled. Frank and I felt the back-and-forth should, without getting dull, always respect that. Our fans seemed to embrace my new identity and Frank's wake-up-to-reality call brought Reege up to speed. It was an important transition for all of us.

Frank has grown to like Reege, but it took a while. Reege can be an acquired taste. Sometimes he teases me and asks, "How can you like that jerk?" They are such opposites. Frank is quiet, with a gentlemanly manner. Reege is combative, aggressive, and rruff-rruff! Frank's a Great Dane, Reege is a Chihuahua nipping at your heels—you know, "You're cute, but get out of my way, and while you're at it, shut up!"

The truth is Frank, Reege, Joy, and I have all become good friends.

There's no question that my career blossomed because of the love and support I've always gotten from Frank and, indirectly, from the immense respect Frank enjoys among all his friends in high places throughout the broadcast industry. That can't hurt.

But nothing's been handed to me and it hasn't always been easy and fun to get what I felt entitled to. I still had to fight like crazy to be considered an equal partner, though we were clearly on to something unique and marketable.

I hate politics, hate deals, and deal-making, hate meeting with attorneys and agents. Put me on a stage, give me a mike, throw some lights or turn on the tube. I'm there. All the other stuff to me is wearying beyond belief.

So when I renewed my first contract, I did it, basically, under protest. I didn't feel appreciated. But I did make an important choice. I chose more vacation time over more money in the bank.

Meanwhile, we seemed to be making deals all over the place. Frank and I unloaded our separate West Side apartments on the last day of 1986 and bought a wonderful duplex together in the East Fifties. We stayed at a friend's place while the duplex underwent major—and much-needed—renovations. Frank sold his place in Jupiter, too, much to the dismay of my parents. They'd visited and fallen in love with it and kind of had their hearts set on some long-term winter house-sitting stints for us.

Then, before we knew it, it was time for more contract negotiations—and a huge turning point in my career. It was the middle of 1987 and talks were going on about the syndication of our local WABC show with Buena Vista Television, a division of Walt Disney Productions. That's when it became maddeningly clear that I was not getting the respect I felt I'd earned.

The syndicate pays a licensing fee to the station that produces and owns the show (WABC) in return for the right to sell it to other local stations. Buena Vista, I had heard, wanted to rename our show "The Regis Philbin Show," in part because it would air in the afternoon in some markets. I made it clear I'd leave if they used that title. Any woman would have been as offended as I was, if she felt she'd made the kind of contribution to the show's success I had. I didn't demand equal pay. I wanted equal respect.

One big problem was that Regis and I had the same agent (not Sam Haskell)—a situation with a potential conflict of interest. He was negotiating our individual contracts along with a separate deal with Buena Vista. The station had always paid our salaries, but Buena Vista would cut us in on "back end" syndication profits if there were any. Plus, WABC had to cut *its* deal with Buena Vista before we would even have a back end to negotiate. It was unbelievably complex.

It was the subtly sexist view of the syndicate that I'd be thrilled with the new name—as if I'd be thrilled *just to be on the show at all*. My agent also shared that view, and in retrospect, I can see why he didn't want to rock the boat. "You got a problem with 'The Regis Philbin Show'?" he asked. Yes, I did, and when he went to Regis and told him I had a problem, Reege said, "I don't blame her."

"I've got a big problem with it," I told the agent, standing my ground. That was really hard for me to do, but my career and my self-worth were at stake. "The show is going into syndication," I said, "because of Regis *and* me. If they want to call it 'The Regis Show,' then I'm happy for Regis, but I can't be on it."

Frank was frustrated with the condescending attitude that Regis was the show and I was just a nice little addition to it. I'm sure there isn't a woman co-host anywhere who hasn't felt at one point that she's like a lamp or a fixture to dress up the set—the next Barbie doll, a sidekick, a second banana. And always with the assumption that she's "not too bright," plus the inference that this is the male host's latest babe.

IN THEIR DREAMS!

I was upset and hurt. So I said the series had to have a generic title or both our names. And I was told, "Kathie, you really don't have that kind of strength to negotiate that."

"I'm not talking about strength," I'd say. "I'm talking about reality. About graciously leaving and wishing everyone well."

With all due respect to Reege, it would have been suicidal for me professionally to be on a show with that name. Already there was a far-reaching perception that "The Morning Show" was Reege's show. I couldn't pick up a newspaper or a *TV Guide* without seeing the show referred to as "The Regis Show." Sometimes the interns would answer the phone with one word: "Regis." Or a producer would write on a card, *"My* next guest is . . . "* I would nicely go up and say, "This is very harmful to me as a person. Am I the Invisible Woman out there? It's not *'my* next guest.' It's *'our* next guest,' please."

Of course objecting to the title was a risky move. I knew that, from the beginning, many people, from the general manager on down, had been dead set against my being Regis's co-host. I never felt I enjoyed total support from the station until the numbers started happening. I wondered if I had made a mistake by going local. Dennis Swanson, then head of the ABC-owned and -operated stations, had been responsible for Oprah Winfrey's success, and he became involved in the negotiations. Today we enjoy teasing each other. He says he made my career. I say he hated my voice—even though he asked me to sing at his daughter's wedding a few years later.

The new general manager of WABC, Walter Liss, *did* believe in me and wanted nothing more than to keep the top-rated morning show in the New York market.

The coup de grâce occurred when "my" agent came to me with a fait accompli—he'd already struck a "back end" deal for his other client with Buena Vista. As of September 1988 the show would be renamed, suitably enough, "Live with Regis and Kathie Lee." That was the good news. The bad news was that by this time the "back end" pie had been divvied up. Reege had his cut and they were offering me a crumb. The message was clear: I got my respect but I'd have to wait for a fair-sized slice of the pie.

In all honesty, I renewed largely because of my tremendous affection for Regis. There was no way the show could have been sold around the country with Regis and an unknown, unsigned, untested co-host. I also knew I'd miss the heck out of it if I left. I'd miss Reege. I'd miss the creative buzz, the crazy energy and wacky spontaneity of live TV. I'd miss the live audience applause and laughter. I'm a spontaneous person. If I sing a song on our show, I get immediate feedback. If I tell a joke and it gets a laugh, I'm a hit. If it lies there and dies in dead air, I'm a flop. I like that. I thrive on that kind of immediacy.

I also thrive on risk. There's nothing quite like being on the edge of catastrophe, and you spend a lot of time there when you do live TV. You have no script, no tape delay, no net. That's why I always send up a prayer just as that red light goes on.

Frank thought I'd been sold down the river on the deal. This kind of male-dominated arrogance is so prevalent in our industry, not to mention our society. The harder women strive for equality across the board—opportunity, pay, respect, mobility—the clearer it becomes that it's going to take a long, long time.

At least when I came home I knew Moishe and Golda were equal partners. Frank and I were very much as one on all this. I remember him being very wise and supportive, though he saw part of the problem as my fault for not having my own agent. He asked his attorney, Ron Konecky (he is now my attorney) to look the situation over. His conclusion was the same as Frank's, and we resolved to make some major changes next time around two years down the road.

Again, behind the very successful and buoyant chemistry that defined the show's core appeal, I agonized over quitting. But Frank helped me stay with it and taught me an awful lot that I needed to know about the way the world operated.

My decision to stay or leave would determine where and how we would live together. As supportive as Frank was, I sensed he was hoping I'd switch gears, give it all up and see the world with him. But his special strength has always been to give me the confidence to let me make my own decisions, to let me come to things on my own and not feel railroaded and, thus, resentful. That's the kind of man a woman needs: one who's secure and loving and trusting enough to let her use her own power to control her own life and achieve what she wants for herself. I think Frank knew that, behind my posturing and demands, I didn't want to leave. He was right.

Frank has at times expressed his disappointment that I didn't quit, but he never tried to impose his agenda on me and he never once got heavy-handed by trying to undercut my self-confidence for his own needs. He always made me feel I could get what I wanted by not quitting and just hanging tough. He never said: "I'm leaving you unless you quit this show."

Frank knew I had more than twenty years of performing experience at stake. I was no kid on a lark, no fluke. I'd worked hard since my teens and paid my own bills since I was seventeen to become a performer. This was a raw deal, and it angered him no end. He's still angry about it. So when we went into yet another round of talks at the end of my last contract, after Cody was born, no one was watching more closely than Frank. This time the message was clear: I was going to get what I wanted or I was gone. We were together on this one, and I had some solid leverage: the show was earning a profit and was the only steadily growing talk show in the country, up to close to two hundred markets.

They also knew that I had lots of other career options. I had been asked to do sitcoms and had met with writers to develop ideas for pilots and series. Reege and I had been considered for movie parts. I also had several informal discussions with a major Broadway producer about singing in musicals that were then in development and have since come to Broadway. There had been talks about signing a long-term record contract (I ultimately signed a six-record deal with Warner Brothers Records), and there's been interest in my having my own prime-time variety specials.

These options were all flattering and terrifying. But what if I jumped and then failed miserably at something? I'd be leaving a proven hit for the great unknown. So I wasn't *looking* to leave, I didn't *want* to leave. But I was ready to leave if they didn't treat me properly this time around.

Also, it was a whole new ball game for me. I had a son now. My work had taken on a totally different place in my life. I wouldn't have hesitated to leave this time. The negotiations were like a game of chess, a roll of the dice. If I issued an ultimatum, I'd better be ready to stand on it.

I was tough. I wasn't exactly raping and plundering, but I wasn't going to walk out of there feeling ripped off. You make a lot of concessions on the way up when no one knows who you are, you have no leverage, you're not seen as crucial to the project, or you're not skilled enough to ask for what you've worked for. This time I would settle for nothing less than an equal partnership because I *had* worked liked crazy to earn it.

Bottom line: I got more than what I asked for—and still felt I deserved all of it. WABC and Disney were more than fair, though. In that world, when Disney Chairman Michael Eisner and President Jeffrey Katzenberg get on the phone to thank you for re-signing, it means something. The last time I had renewed, maybe two executives called me. This time, when it was all over, almost a dozen called.

I had asked the station to let me bring Cody to the studio with me and, at my own expense, turn my dressing room into a nursery for Cody and his incredible nanny, Christine Gardner. They were fabulous about this. My wonderful staff bought Cody's crib, I papered the walls blue and white, had a Laura Ashley sofa made, and, as he got older, brought in his favorite toys and books. In the first fifteen months of Cody's life, his attendance record was probably better than that of most employees: he maybe missed four days. What a pro!

Working "9 to 10,"
What a Way to Make a Living!

☆

I've said that I pray every morning before I go on the air: "Lord, please help me today. Don't let me hurt anyone with my mouth." I say that prayer twice, actually—once before my feet hit the floor as I get out of bed, and again just as my bottom hits the seat in front of the cameras. Why do I pray? Because I never know what's going to pop out of my mouth.

Because I once said the queen of England could use some fashion advice.

Because when Reege asked me why I got invited to a state dinner at the White House for the president of South Korea, I said, "Because they have the greatest produce stands in the world."

Because when Regis held up a headline saying Ross Perot wouldn't hire gays or adulterers for his cabinet if elected President, I said, "Well, that's just about everybody in America."

Because when my producer Michael Gelman's hair was long and greasy I said he looked like a pervert—just like Pee Wee Herman's mug shot.

Because when a "semi-retired" trivia caller from Florida got on the line with a weird, static-filled connection that made her speech hard to understand, Reege asked her if she had just gotten a new phone—or, I blurted out, "a new set of teeth."

Because when Reege said, "Tell me about those two dresses Glenn Close wore [at the 1992 Tony Awards] last night," I said: "The second one I loved. The first one looked like Swamp Thing."

197

Because when Donald Trump, after running an angry full-page *New York Times* ad demanding hard-line justice in the Central Park jogger rape attack, boasted that he was "too controversial" to go into politics, I reminded him, "You can't live on what the President makes."

Reege and I have survived together, I'd guess, more than 7,500 live segments in all. That's a lot of edge. And a lot of prayer. We both love the challenge and unpredictability of live television. Reege felt safe going with me, when I was first hired as his co-host. I had been in the business one way or another since I was fourteen, almost as many years as he had. He knew I had what he called "savvy." He thought I could handle anything that was thrown at me—and learn how to throw back. He liked that. It was essential, in fact, for the partnership to work, because if you don't throw it back at Reege, he could seem mean and insulting, which he is not; if you do, he's a pussycat. It's wild. He needed someone with some spunk and speed who could take it *and* dish it out.

People told me early on, if you're looking for a three-ring circus, then Regis is your ringleader. And I don't mind walking the high wire, flying the trapeze without a net, or just plain being a clown.

After all those thousands of segments, I still love coming in to work with him. I don't know why I love the guy, but I do. He's like everybody's kid brother with his hand in the cookie jar and his foot in his mouth. You love him, but you can't take him anywhere.

When I get in at seven-thirty every morning I immediately go in for hair and makeup—and the older I get, the longer it takes. I use that time to read up on our guests for the day and get briefed by our producers. Reege, on the other hand, strolls into makeup at ten minutes to nine barking at Julian, our stage manager, to give him a back rub. It's at this point that I take his emotional temperature du jour. If I don't hear bellowing, singing, or yelling down the hall ("I feel strong, Don Pardo"), then I know my work is cut out for me.

We have our own equation for success, and we don't rely on sleaze or decadence to get people's attention. Instead, we find what's extraordinary and humorous in life's ordinary moments. I guess you could say I'm the Moral Majority's Madonna; and Reege is no Prince, he's the King. The meshing—or mashing—of our very distinct personalities and visions is what's so much fun.

When we're "on," the most normal and tacky and trifling incidents can become golden moments. So if I want to talk about my bichon frisé, Chardonnay, I do. Chardonnay gets spayed at the vet. Chardy gets sprayed by a skunk. Chardy falls in love. Chardy bites my face, chases a rabbit, chews my shoes. Chardy gets letters from two other bichons frisés—with snapshots. Chardy gets a baby-sitter when I go to Florida. Chardy gets a pooper-scooper from one viewer and a faux fur from another. I get another bichon, Chablis, to keep Chardy company. I take Chabby with me in the car to keep *me* company and she gets sick all over the seats. And on and on.

Reege has his Notre Dame thing, his Wrestlemania mania, and his Everyman view of the world. It's a perfect match: I've got Frank and Codesville, and he's got Joy and Randy "Macho Man" Savage.

And, of course, we've got each other. It's a dream job. We use absolutely anything from our lives or the headlines to make the show work. As I said, in an era when the mean-spirited sensational tabloids have infiltrated "reality programming," we've discovered the antidote to their poison. Its secret formula is: humility + humor = humanity.

You could put it this way: the tabloid shows are obsessed with highlighting what makes certain people most shocking and deviant; we're obsessed with highlighting what makes us feel most human, funny, and alive. And believe me, no one's laughing harder at us than we are at ourselves.

Our show is: Reege living out his jock dreams by racing across Columbus Avenue in traffic to catch passes from Joe Namath and Terry Bradshaw; it's Reege mussing up wrestling manager Freddie Blassie's hair and getting a chair tossed at him; shadow-boxing with Razor Ruddock; weight lifting with Joe Piscopo; jousting with American Gladiators Lace and Gemini; and dancing with Chippendale's hunks but not being able to get his pants off over his shoes, so he has to hop around with his pants around his feet in his underwear and a bow tie. Unbelievable stuff the man has done on that set.

We had a great moment, a golden moment, when Kareem Abdul-Jabbar and Julius "Dr. J" Erving came on before their one-on-one TV exhibition. We had an official NBA-height basket set up and everything. Well, Reege was in high-five heaven. He takes off his jacket and starts racing around the place like a total nerd. He makes about one out of fifteen shots. He's a joke! Throwing up nothing but air balls! So it's my turn. Now, I'm wearing heels, and I don't want to break a nail, right? I grab a ball, and feeling the weight of all of womanhood upon me, I LET IT FLY! *Swish!* Sheer perfection! I can hear Gloria Steinem, Betty Friedan, and Bella Abzug cheering me on. Now I'm pumped up. So Kareem comes over and I try to leap up and high-five him. It was a riot. These guys then do more of their testosterone stuff—the slapping, scratching, whatever. End of the segment, clock ticking away, I grab the ball, and from twenty feet, *swish!* Another victory for the women of America. Unbelievable! The crowd was going crazy by now. Reege was ready to kill me. At the end of the show, they rolled the tape in slo-mo, with the shot, the swish, and the high five in high heels. It was priceless. Those are the moments you live for—or, in Reege's case, die from.

He's a glutton for comic punishment. He'll do anything to make a gag work. Only Regis would eat a chocolate-dipped cricket live from London and take a bubble bath filled with herbs, oil, and perfume in an old-fashioned men's swimsuit. During a "Young Single Millionaires" segment, Regis poked inside the wallets of two of our guests. One contained $23; the other, no money at all. We once did a Valentine's Eve recipe using supposedly aphrodisiac spices—which Reege pocketed to take home. The next day Frank cooked our favorite lamb recipe, and Reege served us by the fire. Reege expressed outrage at being left off *People* magazine's list of the ten sexiest men. *Fred Savage* made it. And he was like ELEVEN YEARS OLD!

If Regis plays out Everyman's macho manqué act to perfection, I live out Everywoman's worst nightmares ad nauseum. I fly to Cleveland for a Monday Night game with Frank and forget my curling iron, so I have to go to a crummy local barbershop, where I get a hairstyle from hell; I travel to Kitzbühel, Austria, and hunt down a beauty salon; I slide off a chair at "21" and pop a button on my dress while dining with Ivana Trump at Le Cirque; I go to the White House for a benefit dinner and sport the biggest, juiciest zit of my life; we get a new phone system for the trivia call-in and when I try it out by phoning home, Frank's not in.

I've shared great Mom stories—like the time I got Mom and Dad tickets to see *The Will Rogers Follies* on Broadway and they came in for dinner at Neary's, our favorite place for steaks and chops. I showed up with Cody to join them for a cup of tea before the theater. Mom asked me if I had a little bag, and I said only Cody's diaper bag. "Why," I asked.

"Well, honey," she said, "I ate so much I don't think I can sit comfortably for three hours." So she went to the ladies' room, took off her panty girdle, and stuffed it inside my little purse. The purse was now bulging rather strangely. We howled.

"Mom," I said, "you just made the show." Those are the magic words now whenever anything happens in the family. The next day the whole world knew about Mom's panty girdle and no one laughed harder during host chat than Mom. She's a very secure woman—even out of her girdle. Of course, someone sent her a nice new one in the mail.

Then there was Mom's great Spam story. Frank, Mom, Dad, and I all went on the Slimfast diet after I quit breast-feeding Cody. Mom and Dad were at the house visiting. I walked into the kitchen at about eight at night, and there was Mom sizzling up something at the stove. We had already eaten dinner, and so I asked her what was going on. "I'm just a little hungry," she said. And what exactly are we making here? "Spam."

Spam? What was this, World War Two? We were dieting, not *rationing!* I hadn't heard the word "Spam" since childhood. Mom was frying *Spam!* I was nauseated. I didn't even know I had Spam in the house. It turned out that Ted, our housekeeper, a former navy chief petty officer, kept some around. He threw some in now and then with his eggs. So she scored a can from him. And she scarfed that down. Next we went into the living room to watch a movie, and I spotted this skinny wooden stick with a Häagen-Dazs wrapper around it. I gave her a look and she shrugged. "I was hungry."

Then, as the movie started, she walked out briefly, and I got a whiff of something from the kitchen. She came back in and asked, "Got any Molly McButter?" *Now* she was popping corn. I died.

"You just made the show, lady," I said. And she did. Well, Hormel sent boxes and boxes of Spam to the show. We sent them off to homeless shelters, saving one ceremonial can for Mom. They also sent Spam T-shirts, and I sent them to Mom. People relate powerfully to stuff like that. It's the way everybody lives. We're all trying to diet. Our mothers are trying to diet. Then they say, "I'll just have a little Spam." Then it's a little ice cream bar and just a taste of popcorn with a pound of Molly McButter.

That was the night I gave up on Mom and her dieting. Mom doesn't have to be slender. I tell her, "Mom, you're plump, but you're precious." I just want her to be happy. But I love the absurdity of it. Of all the things in the world to eat—and cheat! I always thought we should have a week of Spam recipes on the show and let Mom come in and judge the best one.

This was funny. When Frank and I were in Minneapolis for the 1992 Super Bowl, the people at Hormel, which is headquartered out there, honored me with my very own Spam wristwatch for making Spam semi-famous through the show. One of my associate producers was ready to kill for it, he wanted it so badly. "It's cooler than a Rolex," he said.

If I don't have a Mom or Dad story to tell, I dip into my endless supply of decorating-disaster tales. The fabric's wrong. My hands are smeared with green paint from painting wicker furniture. The construction is on a runaway budget and endless schedule; I come home one day and the azaleas are wrong, the fence is wrong, the stairs and floor are wrong, and I have to leave before I seriously hurt someone, not with my mouth but with a blunt instrument! I catch my gardener peeing in my bushes. I let my audience and viewers know that I find the toilet paper in Europe far too scratchy.

I tell how the secretary to Michael Eisner, the Disney chairman, leaves a message on my machine for Cathy Lee Crosby. I try to have lunch at Le Cirque wearing a veiled hat that I can't even eat through; I show up at a chichi fundraiser in a gorgeous one-of-a-kind designer dress that's identical to another one-of-a-kind worn by someone else.

And if I've cut back on tales of Chardonnay and Chablis, I've now got Cody stories that never stop: Cody's first steps, first fever, first "Mama," first molars, first haircut; Cody finds his wing-wang; Frank goes to the Grammys with me but doesn't recognize Ringo Starr until I tell him he's Mr. Conductor on "Shining Station," his favorite show with Cody. The wonders never cease.

Regis and I love to get outrageous-down-and-dirty, too. Nothing is off-limits, down to lipstick on my teeth, food *in* my teeth, "ungawa" on my face—Reege's word for any little scabs or lashes or soot he can pick off. He shares his cholesterol counts, colon checkups, and kidney stones, and I've got my oral surgery, mood swings, and infected nipples during breast-feeding.

And when it comes to guests, we've had our share of unusual personalities: the world's heaviest man, the late Walter Hudson, who weighed well over a thousand pounds and, when he lost hundreds, left his house for the first time in eighteen years on our show; the world's fastest reader; a bed-making champ; a bubble-blowing champ. Our thousands of guests have spanned the spectrum of American culture. In one show, we've gone from Hulk Hogan to Marilyn Chambers to Bobby Short; or from wrestling's Captain Lou Albano to actress Patricia Neal; from Judge Wapner to Martina Navratilova. It's been an amazing education, indeed, and you learn to roll with anything, hoping you don't self-destruct along the way with a slur or a slip.

The odds are against a perfect record. Hoping isn't enough. Praying isn't enough. It didn't keep me from insulting all Italian-Americans everywhere when I learned the hard way—meaning on live TV—that "Guido," when used in a certain way, is an ethnic slur.

I was telling a story about a plane ride with my sister and niece. During the flight, this guy with the open shirt, hairy chest, gold chain, and 'hey-baby' attitude wanted to hit on Michie, so he tried to endear himself to Shannie, who was three at the time. Shannie turned to Michie and said, "Mom, does he have bad breath?" It was a scream. Except that, in telling the story, I said the guy was a real "guido." I used that word because Cody's nanny, Christine, is always telling me about "gum snappers" and "maulers" she sees, and she calls these guys "guidos." What did I know? I thought it was the funniest thing I'd ever heard. Guidos.

Let me tell you, I was in more hot water than a pound of fettuccini. Gelman and my program director, Art Moore, immediately came over during the break and said that the switchboard was melting down like mozzarella with irate calls. An ethnic slur? I swear I had no idea. So I promptly apologized after the break if I offended anyone.

But I will say this: I think this "politically correct" thing has gone just about too far. I mean, it's gotten to the point where you can't say anything anymore without somebody claiming you're a bigot. There's bigotry and there's ignorance. I shot my mouth off in utter, if perhaps reckless, ignorance. So I blew it. I said I was sorry. I should fear for my life for using the G-word? The way things are going we're all gonna be one dull, humorless country once we've lost the ability to lighten up and poke a little dumb fun at ourselves.

That gaffe was a rare lapse. But in live TV you run the risk of airing bad taste and worse, because you just never know what's going to happen.

We had some real bad taste when we asked a bunch of Regis's nemeses—the hard hats who were building a high-rise blocking his office view—to come on with Jockey pitchman Jim Palmer and model the latest styles.

One of the construction workers was a crusty older fellow who must have been the foreman. We were told that he'd earned the nickname "Sockman" for stuffing that particular item of clothing where he might have *wanted* a size ten but, in fact, did not have one. That story wasn't bad enough. He then turned his back to the camera, and we were afraid he was going to moon us. Gelman looked as if the blood was draining from his head. But did he moon us? Noooo! He turned around and stuck his thumbs inside the waistband like he was going to strip. But did he? Noooo!

He reached into his Jockeys and pulled it out (the sock!)—then tossed it into the audience! *G-r-r-o-s-s-s!* I was disgusted! The audience was going wild! Our mouths were hanging open in shock. He was a decent enough guy, and he sent me flowers for three days with little cards signed, "Sorry, Kathie. Love, Sockman." Okay, but save that stuff for, you know, "Men Who Stuff Socks in Their Jocks—Today, on 'Geraldo'!"

Double entendres can be fun and all, but I'm just not comfortable with the sleazy stuff. We've had Chippendale's dancers in G-strings thrusting their pelvises into grandmothers' faces. Not everybody wants that—but some people clearly do. That's a little much for me.

This is my idea of a fun moment. On one of our fifth anniversary shows, we went to an inset of Joy in her robe at home, congratulating Reege and me. "Gee, it's gone by so fast," she says, "and this is where I sit and watch you two every morning at nine, having my cup of coffee." And then in walks Frank behind her, wearing a robe, saying, "Joy, I heated up your coffee, hon." We just howled. It was priceless.

In addition to Sockman, I had another amorous guest once who needed no stocking-stuffers to show me how happy he was to see me. This was pure gold. This was falling in love with Max!

Max, the co-star of a new Tarzan film, came out with Joe Lara, who played the title role. "Hello, darling," I said to Max as I greeted him. I had the feeling he gave me five and took a special liking to me right off. I was very direct.

I grabbed Max, put my arms around him, and held him close. Even Reege noticed. "You guys look good together," he said. "He's got your ears. He's cute, he's cute."

Max started to hold on tight and nuzzle, brushing his lips against mine as he eyed me intently with a look of—well, call me crazy—wild animal lust. Max's hand went for my right breast on camera. Things were heating up. "He's squeezing me like you can't believe," I said, getting a bit concerned things might get out of control on the air.

The audience roared, and Max clapped his hands together before stealing another smooch. Then he got a little rough and slapped me across the jaw. What a guy!

This was amazing: I was falling in love with a guest. "He's got lipstick all over him," Reege marveled to Joe. "He doesn't get this close to Jane, does he? I think Max is tired of hanging out with Tarzan."

"Yeah." Joe shrugged. "Max is a hardworking chimp and he's well-trained."

This adorable little Max was getting aroused right there as he wrapped his arms around my neck and brushed back my hair. It was unbelievable. I was afraid he was going to get an erection on me and pop right out through his shorts and diaper. Hysterical! One of my absolute favorite moments.

We've had great animal segments. We had Bunny Mania right before Easter when a little teeny rabbit took on a huge rabbit and started mating right there on the set. The other funny bunny incident happened when, in the middle of a cooking segment, the kitchen set caught fire. Our guest was a Playboy bunny in her costume, and Reege gallantly carried her out through the smoke, screaming, "Save the bunny, save the bunny!" It was fabulous.

There are two other animal stories: one involved a horse; the other, a professional wrestler.

Stephanie Powers came on to promote a horseback instructional video. She brought along Mickey the Horse. Now, I fell off a horse when I was five. How traumatized was I? My cousin married one of the nation's top trainers and I grew up in the shadow of Bowie racetrack, but I never rode again and I went to the races only once. In a word, I'm terrified of horses.

So Mickey came out with Stephanie. Now Mickey was a show-business horse. A horse that had been in *Aïda*. A horse that'd been on Broadway. Probably read *Backstage* and had an agent, too. I was trying to make nice when his mouth opened and all I saw were the ugliest, grossest teeth—he made Mister Ed look like Mr. Clean. This horse needed to roll through a car wash and get those teeth brushed and hot waxed.

I extended my hand very gingerly and suddenly he went KWONK! and bit down on my hand. I let out a screech you wouldn't believe. I was in shock. I made it through the segment, we went to commercial, and I ran to the prop room and sobbed hysterically. You'd never know it from watching, but I had black teeth marks on the back of my hand. I guess it was a little late for the instructional video at that point, but Stephanie did explain that you always show a horse your open palm, never the back of your hand.

Then there was the "animal" known as Ravishing Rick Rude. Now, I have a problem with Reege's wrestling thing. We aren't exactly McNeil-Lehrer out there, but I think the wrestlers' shtick lowers the quality of the show a notch or two. Some of them are pretty sleazy. Rick Rude was about as low as they get, right down there with the Bushwhackers. If there was a gold championship belt for the most horrible, disgusting-smelling people, the Bushwhackers would have been wearing it the day they came on. They tried to hold me and kiss me. First of all, I'm sorry but don't touch me, and second of all, I don't kiss people I don't want to kiss. And Cody was there with me that day. They chased me all over the set and I ran off, locked myself in my dressing room–nursery with Cody and refused to come out. I was afraid they'd come right in there after me to bushwhack Cody.

But the absolute low point was a year or so before, when Ravishing Rick Rude came out, bragging about his "Rude Awakening" at wrestling arenas. Young women are handpicked to go into the ring with him, where this muscle-bound baboon embraces and kisses them until they just pretend to faint dead away with ardor as he stands over his latest conquest.

It's a pathetic spectacle. So of course Gelman booked him.

The guy comes out in his "Simply Ravishing" sequined robe, kisses my hand ever so gently, and sits there giving me the eye like he'd been behind bars for a decade. Nonstop. It's not like we ask them the tough questions—like, "Duhh, howja get dose muscles?" We let them pretty much do their thing—which, cartoonish and entertaining as it is to some people, has its place in the world. But not this kind of stuff. I was so flustered I crossed my legs and one shoe dropped off my foot.

Gracious host that I am, I humored him ("Rick, you're sweet-talking me") while Reege sucked up to him by mooning over his title belt. "This guy," he said, "is the best-built of all the wrestlers. He's got a tremendous physique and great sex appeal."

With an ego to match. He asked me how tall I was and I told him "really short, I've got stumps for legs."

He leered at me and said, "Those don't look like no stubs I've ever seen before."

Regis egged him on. "Honest to God, I sense something going on here! Frank is out of town, isn't he?" Yeah, I said. Rick's manager now is on. "The guy is looking her over and making her very nervous," Reege tells him. "The woman is coming unglued."

"Kathie Lee needs a Rude Awakening," the manager says.

"Kathie Lee," I say, "has had a few rude awakenings."

"Not *this* rude, not this rude."

"Over the airwaves," Rick says, staring at my body, "I could see that Kathie Lee was the most beautiful woman on television. Now, as I draw closer and closer, I just can't believe it."

Rick gave a woman in the audience an "awakening" to stripper music and then dropped his robe in front of me. I was standing off now to the side. I didn't believe what I saw. This was absolutely unscripted.

On his clingy nothing-left-to-the-imagination Lycra tights, he had painted *my face over his crotch*. He stood there, hands behind his head, thrusting and flexing, half naked. It was so gross I didn't know what to do or where to go. I put my hands over my face and ran off up the stairs at the rear of the set.

Meanwhile, he turned his butt to the camera and, of course, there was Reege's face painted on his, Rick's, quivering, gyrating glutes. Talk about "back end participation"! This got my vote for the worst breach of taste in the history of the show.

Then Rick ran up the stairs after me and I came down, skipped over the couches, and dashed off the set, amazed that I didn't wipe out and hurt myself.

One of our regular viewers who caught the show on our New Orleans station was not at all amused by what he had just seen. He decided to call the show and express his rather strong feelings. This irate caller had been in a hotel room preparing for his job later that evening. He was seething and insisted on speaking directly to Gelman.

"If this kind of thing ever happens again," Frank fumed, "she will never be on the show again. And neither will you." As Frank later said, "The stupidity of putting that arrogant sleazeball on the show was due to Michael's immaturity in this business." Michael, in his defense, said he had no idea what Ravishing Rick was going to do.

It hardly helped that at the time, late August 1989, I was almost two months pregnant. I would have jumped from the stairwell to get away from him, risking my health and that of my unborn child. I never heard Frank use language like that, ever. He gave Gelman a Rude Awakening of his own.

I was not surprised, however. This is a husband who isn't thrilled that I wear clinging evening gowns onstage in Atlantic City. A husband who's uncomfortable if I have to do massage segments.

A husband who was angry when Dana Carvey, at the end of one of the funniest hours of TV I've ever been a part of, took Reege's place in late 1991, spontaneously leaned over, knocked me back on the couch as if surrendering to a long-pent-up urge to make out with me, and clumsily lifted his leg up over me. I didn't think it was on camera because it was right at the end. The camera caught it. Frank caught it at home. And I caught hell from Frank.

The audience shrieked, it was so funny. In fact, it was hysterical to just about everyone in America—except Frank. "Who's that underneath?" he had asked as he watched the show. "That couldn't be my wife," he said. Oh, yes, it could! And it was. He just doesn't want anyone touching me, kissing me, or messing with me—and that's a part of Frank I absolutely adore, that I could be so special to him.

Now, Dana adores his wife and baby boy. There was nothing there in terms of flirtation or heat. And he'd been amazing. I didn't do *anything* the whole time he was in for Regis. He did all his characters. He did Schwarzenegger, Church Lady, President Bush. He did Reege. But to Frank, it was, "Who is this jerk who thinks he can get on top of my wife?" And he has a point. But he wasn't angry with me, and he thought Dana was fabulous up to that moment. He doesn't blame me for these things. Early on, he did. In the past he'd have actually agonized for days over it. Now he understands that it's just show business—and only agonizes about it *for hours.*

I've had, incredibly, only one truly unpleasant encounter behind the scenes at the show. I do not like confrontation. I am not the Conflict Queen. I like everybody to like everybody and adore me and get along and have no awkwardness. In the early days, we had a producer before Gelman who was a great, fun guy I liked an awful lot, but he was volatile, a real firecracker that could go off any time. During a show he started screaming at me right in front of the audience for something I was doing.

I just glared at him and pointed. I said, "You. You come here." I went off the set to a private room and just let him have it. "Don't you ever, EVER raise your voice to me again like that, much less in front of people. Because if you do, you're the one who's going to be gone, not me."

On a personality-driven show like ours, if anyone's expendable it's the producer, not the talent. As I said, they could call the show "Regis and Rhonda Lee," but the dynamics would change and who knows how successfully? Lucy wasn't the same without Ricky, nor was George without Gracie. Regardless of whatever they went on to, the magic they had produced together was gone. I'm certainly not equating Reege and myself with them. And whatever else anyone can say about Regis and me, the show works. Tampering with the formula would change everything.

The tone of our show has changed, however, lightening up considerably in recent years. In the earlier days we had more heavy topical segments on diseases and heavier medical issues like new prosthetic limbs, multiple personality disorders, near-death experiences, coma survivors, and past lives—none of the last three to be confused with the thirtieth-anniversary tribute we gave Reege in May of 1992!

But that wasn't what we were about. The other talk shows were all trying to out-sleaze each other with transvestite rape victims or whatever. Reege, Gelman, and I went for counterprogramming and lightened the tone up, offering a solid and positive alternative to what was, unfortunately, becoming the norm.

Plus, the serious segments were inevitably slotted at the end, and we gave short shrift to many people with dramatic and important stories. I have a hard time knowing Billy Graham is waiting in our Green Room for the entire show listening to seven minutes on leaf raking and eight minutes on cooking Chicken Surprise. Then he comes on at the end just long enough to say, "God bless you." That drives me crazy. I feel responsible for our guests and hope that everyone gets treated well.

On the other hand, there was the segment we did with author C. David Heymann, who came on to hype his lurid, unauthorized book about Jacqueline Onassis. They should call those books slime-ographies because that's what they are. His aim, as he pretentiously put it, was, to "disimbue that facade of Camelot." It was, I believe, the only time I crossed the line and was ungracious to a guest. I unloaded on the guy. I strongly objected to booking him to begin with and could hardly bring myself to participate in the segment.

I sat there fuming, listening as he justified his "investigative" tactics while Regis carried the interview. Finally I'd had enough of his smugness.

"The world's gotten to be a tough place to live these days," I said. "A woman's desperately trying to have her own privacy, and this is not Madonna saying Buy My Records. Mrs. Onassis is trying to live her life, to raise her family in an impossible situation. It seems extremely parasitical to me that you're going to make a lot of money off another person's life and reputation and efforts and accomplishments."

I really could *not* believe I said that. Yet the audience erupted in wild cheers and applause for my stand. I'm very justice-oriented, and what he and the Kitty Kelleys of the world do is unjust. They murder people's reputations. I see people buying their books and I want to scream. They're rewriting history. Just because it makes money doesn't mean it's right. In some ways our society has become sick.

Then again for every David Heymann there is an Audrey Hepburn, and it's while sitting with a great lady like her that I realize how incredibly thrilling and humbling this job can be. Frank was in for Reege the day she came on, and when he's there the tone of the show is lower-key. If I were as naughty with Frank at home as I am with

Reege on the air, my marriage wouldn't have lasted a month. I'm on my best behavior around Frank. The same goes for Regis when he's with Joy. The key to Frank and me is lovey-dovey; with Reege and me it's kissy-killy. With Frank, that edge is smoothed.

But we didn't need any edge the day we had the honor of co-hosting when Audrey came on to tell about her recent trip to Africa. I admire few women as much as I do her. She is so classy and elegant and has given so much of herself to UNICEF to help poor children around the world.

I look at women like her and think, God, I wish I were like that. But there's no way. Does she wake up every morning and spend an hour with King Regis? Forget it. Me, I'm a hoofer, a Vaudevillian, a circus performer. I've got this three-ring act going. And she is so refined, so shy and private, so dignified, so in control all the time. She left me wanting to be a lot more like her.

I'm a clown and a part of me aches not to be. Many of us, I guess, would like to have a little more of the lady in us. Audrey Hepburn never bangs her funny bone. Mine's practically arthritic, I've used it so much through the years.

And, of course, for every Audrey there's a Zsa Zsa out there waiting to happen. And she happened on to our set one day unannounced, on a cue that existed only in her own Hungarian head. Reege was winding up host chat, giving the rundown for the day's show. He had just said, "Zsa Zsa creates excitement wherever she goes," and I'd said, "She's rather imperial." Boy, I got that right. At that instant, she waltzed onto the set ranting and raving. She was in a fury, muttering something about "that Revlon bitch." I knew she was referring to our entertainment reporter, Claudia Cohen, whose husband, Ron Perelman, basically owns Revlon.

Her tirade, we later learned, was over access to our makeup room before the show. Claudia had innocently opened the door only to discover that Zsa Zsa had commandeered the makeup room. Zsa Zsa threw a fit backstage and stormed out onto the set spewing very unprincesslike language. The audience was in shock. They had no idea what was going on, and neither did we. It was a disaster but great television, and *it was live*. She sat down, Reege tried to calm her, and our producer instantly went to a commercial. As we broke, I stood and said something like "I'll just go and get us all some coffee." At which point Reege said, "Oh, sure. And leave me here with Zsa Zsa!"

Zsa Zsa's just one of life's calculating, self-absorbed human beings. We calmed her down. Claudia, whom I love and respect, is a tough cookie, a real New Yorker who's proven she can go out and get what she wants. I was really proud of the way Claudia handled the situation. She's not a "princess," but she sure was the lady!

Here's the kicker. As a courtesy, the show drives guests by limo to their next appointment, which, for Zsa Zsa, was lunch at "21."

The show's driver, a sweet guy named Mike, later told us about his ride on the wild side with Zsa Zsa. She piled into the limo with all her dogs and bags and had no trouble finding the refreshments provided in the limo. On their way over she was, he claimed, still raving about "the bitch."

Then, at "21," Zsa Zsa demanded that Mike wait for her so he could then take her out to the airport. Mike, a Vietnam vet, wasn't about to take orders from her. He called the man who books the car for the show and he said, "no way." Instead, he instructed Mike to deposit all her dogs and bags with the restaurant's doorman and let her find her own ride out to the airport.

Zsa Zsa may have tried to be Queen for the Day but this Queen's Day was over by lunch.

Zsa Zsa proved that while live TV mainly hits its target, it sometimes backfires. Sometimes it does both at the same time. Like the time *TV Guide* included me in its "Most Beautiful Woman on Television" phone-in contest. We used the absurdity of the contest to create some of the wildest stuff we ever did on the show. That week confirmed for me: (1) just how vast and powerful TV is as a medium; (2) how strongly and graciously our viewers relate to what Reege and I do; (3) how easy it is for the press to misunderstand your success and then punish you for it; and (4) that, regardless of the press, we were—and continue to be—on the right track as entertainers.

I came home one Friday in mid-July 1990, and our nanny, Christine, said, "Did you see the new *TV Guide?* There's good news and bad news. The good news is you've been nominated as one of the most beautiful women on TV."

I screamed hysterically. "So what's the bad news?" I asked.

"The bad news is that you're number fifty out of fifty-one."

This was a riot. The numbers were actually not a ranking but were assigned arbitrarily so the callers could vote electronically. But I knew Regis was going to let me have it over this on Monday morning, and so I came prepared. I called Bobby Orsillo, one of my favorite prop guys, and asked him to get me an apple pie and American flag; and I had brought in a picture of Cody. So sure enough Reege did his thing.

I joked about how I really didn't want to win *anyway*—but "just in case you feel like calling," I announced that a vote for me was, after all, a vote for apple pie, motherhood, and the American way. It was complete tongue in cheek, and it was hysterical. The audience ate it up. Viewers started calling. And calling. I walked down the street in Connecticut and people were yelling, "Way to go!" "Go get 'em!" "I voted for you!" I just thought, this is so silly.

Gelmonster is from the school of "if it works once, let's drive it into the ground until it doesn't." We didn't want to let this gag die—the vote would continue until mid-week. So for two or three days we saved a segment for this girl-next-door-pageant shtick. I even got some pom-poms and led the audience in cheers.

The next day I pretended that I had gotten up with Cody at four in the morning to bake cookies for the entire studio audience. Tongue in cheek, I went on the air about what a wonderful person I was. Cody took his baby finger on camera and dialed the contest 900 number to vote for Mommy. I mean, this was a *joke!* No one watching could ever have thought in a million years that I was taking this seriously.

On the last day of the contest Frank came in with me, and we rolled out onto the set with Cody in a vintage convertible with banners and balloons. It was so stupid, so hokey-jokey, and it was done in the spirit of "so what's a beauty contest all about anyway? Let's have some fun with it." After all, the idea of a "Most Beautiful Woman on TV" wasn't ours to begin with, right? And how great a concept is *that?*

Well, I won. By a landslide. Or a mudslide, depending on whom you ask. I got 17,796 votes; the runner-up was Jaclyn Smith, with 3,603. Number 12, Phylicia Rashad, got 1,600. The magazine now wanted to put me on the cover of their August 25 contest-result issue, but only if I would agree to be shown karate chopping Candice Bergen and drawing a mustache on Connie Chung.

I refused. "These women are respected colleagues and friends and, frankly, far prettier than I am," I told the magazine. "It would be denigrating—plus, I did this as a joke. If you want a picture of me making fun of myself, fine."

They were angry now, because this obviously got in the way of their marketing scheme for the August 25 issue. So they came over and spent hours with me, getting a "who, me?" shot as I spoke on the phone. But the editors had clearly lost their sense of humor about the whole thing, and they dumped me from the cover. They ran photos of Vanna White, Nicolette Sheridan, and Jaclyn instead, with the question: "Is one of these the most beautiful woman on TV?

Turn the page. Kathie Lee Gifford. Perhaps there's been some mistake."

There'd been a mistake, all right. The mistake was: they didn't get the joke—but nearly 18,000 TV viewers did! Those people all paid two dollars to be in on it, in on the power of TV and the ability to make harmless fun of yourself. I don't think of myself as the most beautiful *anything*. To think I was serious about it is ludicrous. It was meant as total sarcasm and self-mockery.

So the magazine rewarded TV's "prettiest woman" with its nastiest piece. The writers said other contenders were "shocked" at my chutzpah; they claimed my "vote-for-me rampage" was "revenge" for my "Charlie's Angels" audition in the 1970s, when I was told, "We're looking for a drop-dead gorgeous girl."

I sent roses to Jaclyn Smith. "To the real most beautiful woman on television, lots of love, your friend, Kathie Lee." Nicolette Sheridan (number 3) may well be a physically perfect human being, but that doesn't drive people to their telephones to make a two-dollar vote. Those editors were so silly to miss the point of their own results. Nicolette doesn't have ladies stopping her in the grocery store asking her questions like, "How's Cody? . . . Is Frank okay? . . . I heard he had a cold . . . Are Christine's tonsils all right?" It's so sweet. I love that support.

It was like voting for Lucille Ball, or Carol Burnett, women who don't fit the classically beautiful stereotype. If Lucille Ball had gotten on with Ethel and said, "Ethel, how am I going to get people to vote for me?," viewers would have gone to their phones and voted for Lucy.

I don't want to protest too much. The point is, Lucy and Carol touched viewers on a level much deeper than transient physical beauty. And I hope in some way that I have a similar effect.

I was disappointed at the aftermath of what had started out as good clean fun. We're all so quick to pounce, to judge, to attack and blame. Maybe we're all just starting to take ourselves a little too seriously. We object to the shrewd, often mindless "packaging" of corrupt politicians in the sound-bite era, but we go ballistic over a spontaneous and innocuous faux pas. We complain about violence and moral decay in society but we glorify crime and decadence by making stars of "reality programming" personalities. Eighteen thousand good-natured viewers make the effort to express affection for a self-mocking TV personality and suddenly I'm on a vengeful "rampage" to bury my competition.

I was bruised a little, hurt by the misunderstanding. But I felt that "our" people knew exactly what had happened. What I was left with after that contest was the message those 18,000 people left when they called. We're obviously affecting people in a positive way that's been ignored for a long time. And I'd vote for that any time.

The following year, 1991, *TV Guide* ran a similar contest and I came in a respectable eighth, losing (surprise!) to Jaclyn Smith. I did it without campaigning, convertibles, cookies or Cody.

Well, in 1992 *TV Guide* changed its contest to "The Most Bodacious Woman in TV." When drop-dead gorgeous model and MTV hostess Cindy Crawford won, she laughed and said, "Kathie Lee Gifford is going to be crushed." I wasn't. I was thrilled to come in second to a twenty-six-year-old with no stretch marks.

In the Morning . . .
In the Evening . . .
Ain't We Got Fun!

In late autumn of 1989 I sat down one afternoon and wrote a poem:

> *I wanted ribbons and ruffles and rainbows and frills*
> *I'll get cowboys and Indians and bad guys and thrills*
> *Fat little fingers and bruised little knees*
> *And hanging by monkey arms high in the trees*
> *How will I handle him? What will I say?*
> *Will I be enough when his dad goes away?*
> *Will I understand him or be too quick to scold?*
> *Will I be patient or has patience grown old?*
> *His little-boy thoughts are a mystery to me*
> *Long before I know him, my little Cody*
> *Will I have wisdom when he longs for a reason*
> *Why grass grows and snow falls with every new season?*
> *Perhaps I can tell him when he longs to know*
> *How little girls feel when his love starts to grow*
> *He'll look at his mother and understand finally*
> *And maybe he'll think of me often and kindly.*

I wrote these couplets the day I had amniocentesis and learned the amazing news that I was pregnant with a little boy—and not the little girl I'd always hoped for. At the time—and this is so stupid—this was a big disappointment to both Frank and me. Looking back, you

215

see it doesn't matter. They're yours and you adore them. But I just couldn't think of myself as having anything in common with a little boy. I grew into accepting it. And grew. And accepted. Like when he started punching me like crazy in the stomach and being very active. I liked this kid's spunk. This guy was quite the little monkey in there.

He was there because his daddy and mommy had gotten a little spunky themselves during a five-day cruise off the French and Italian Rivieras in early July. Frank was covering the Tour de France for "Wide World" and had to be in Paris on two successive Saturdays. So between July Fourth and Bastille Day—July 14—while Joy Philbin and Leeza Gibbons sat in for me, I went to Europe with Frank so we could spend most of the intervening week aboard one of Carnival's 440-foot-long, triple-decked, four-masted sailing ships called the *Windstar*.

If we were destined for the dreamiest vacation of our lives, Frank set the tone before I arrived. He had flown from L.A. to New York, then from New York to Paris—two red-eyes in two days—before touching down in Paris. The next morning I got a call and he told me the whole incredible story of his episode of "transglobal amnesia."

He had stayed awake all day, eaten dinner alone in a quiet bistro with a bottle of wine, and was pretty much *pommes frites* by the time he got ready for bed. "Golda," he said, "you are not going to believe what happened next."

Frank was at the Hôtel George V, one of the world's great hotels. But when he awoke in the middle of the night, *tout nu*, he was absolutely certain he was in the Mount Kisco home of society bandleader Peter Duchin, listening to his band. What's strange is that Frank has never *been* to Peter Duchin's house in Mount Kisco.

He walked out of the hotel room, still naked, following the music. I'm just glad Frank didn't try to walk outside and catch the 7:25 to Grand Central. Like a zombie, he walked up steps and down steps and rode elevators until he wandered into the kitchen.

I had known about Frank's sleepwalking, which has gone on for fifteen years or so. It's sort of like *Night of the Living Dead*, except he usually just bangs into a wall like some radio-guided toy truck and bounces off, waking himself up. This time he wandered. He walked up to a little Balkan guy who was peeling potatoes and said, trancelike, "I need to find my room."

This guy, of course, did *not* think he was peeling potatoes in Peter Duchin's Mount Kisco kitchen. He spoke no English. So he wrapped a tablecloth around Frank's waist, guided him to the elevator and got him to the lobby one floor up. Frank walked right past two maids who must have thought they were hallucinating at 3:00 A.M. He found the concierge and told him, rather unnecessarily, that he needed to find his room.

The unruffled Frenchman took it in his stride and gave Frank an extra key. Then Frank went back to bed. When he awoke, he was sure the whole thing had been a dream—until he saw the tablecloth and second key lying by the bed. That's when he called me.

I caught the next plane over.

Of course, Frank's most widely publicized sleepwalk ended up as a tabloid cover story—"Kathie Lee's Hubby in Bed with Nanny!"—and a host chat tale. It happened when we were all getting up every two hours to feed Cody and I was on the breast pump. Usually Frank can sleep soundly through the dogs' barking, Cody's crying, anything.

But this night, after traveling across several time zones (which is the only time Frank sleepwalks) he got up and thought he was going to the bathroom. And he was stark naked. He got all mixed up and went in the other direction through Cody's room, knocking pictures off the wall as he went. He made it into the bathroom just off Cody's room and turned around to leave. That was when he saw Chablis at the foot of the bed—except it was our nanny's bed.

Back then Chabby slept with us, so Frank assumed he was in our room. He walked in, sat on the edge of the bed, and started petting Chabby. By now Christine understandably had one eye open and was trying to figure out exactly *what* was going on. Then Frank made moves to slip under the covers, whispering, "Hi, honey," in the dark.

Christine freaked. "FRANK!" she screamed.

That woke him up in a hurry. He shook off the cobwebs and hurried back into our room. "The weirdest thing just happened," he said.

For Christmas that year, I bought Frank a pair of pajamas, figuring that if he was going to keep doing this he ought to protect himself and all those concerned.

We joined the *Windstar* in Saint-Tropez on Sunday and cruised along the breathtakingly scenic waterfronts of Corsica, Sardinia, and Portofino. We'd dive off the ship into the glass-smooth water, swim to the beach, picnic on the sand, explore small inland villages, eat bowls of pasta in funky hole-in-the-wall cafés. It was a week of exquisite romance and privacy—no newspapers, no TV, no cameras, no phones, no watches, no schedules, no agents, no Reege!

It was easy to forget what day of the week it was, not to mention that my body obviously forgot what time of the month it was. We were not trying to conceive a baby. *Au contraire,* we were trying not to. I was thirty-five. I had gone off the pill that year at my gynecologist's urging to cleanse my body and get back on my own natural cycles. Alternative methods of birth control were recommended. I guess we used the "none of the above" alternative.

I had lost track of my ovulating, as I believe nine of ten women do, unless they're really working at conception. If someone wants to think I'm stupid for not keeping track, well, I'm delighted because I got the most glorious little creature in the world from that.

But was the timing great? Forget it. Unlike falling in love, I defy anyone who's in a two-career couple with commitments, contracts, and travel to show me when the "right time" is. And I defy any couple with pressures like ours to find time to make love with each other and really truly care for each other every day. It's pretty much impossible.

Some people use the rhythm method. We used the rock-and-roll method—relying on the seductive, lulling sea swells, vast, starry skies, and silvery moonlit water to reignite our passion and remind us how important intimacy is to the love between a man and woman. It's so easy for any couple to lose track of it in the often deadening day-to-day struggle to juggle complicated lives. We had had enough of the high-pressure New York whining and dining routine in our lives. It didn't hurt the cause one bit that in Italy you simply cannot get a bad meal and that we discovered many a fine local Italian wine along the way.

Any couple who can't rekindle their passion on a cruise like this, I'm sorry, I say it's time to check in for marital counseling. They don't call them the fun ships for nothing.

The nautical setting aside, that cruise showed us just how far we had drifted, how much we were already taking for granted. I think it's unavoidable because you do become so comfortable. When you're dating and you don't know where you stand with somebody, you play games; it's always showtime. Your hair and makeup are always done, you're never without fresh nails and a pedicure (unless you're Madonna), and the dry-cleaning bills are sky-high because you're dressed to the hilt. But courtship and dating can become a game, an act that has zero to do with reality.

Marriage brings an enormous relief in knowing that part of your life is settled. No more dates from hell. No more friends to terrorize you with the words, "I've got this really terrific person for you to meet who's going to call you." There's a lot to be said for settling into a nurturing, loving comfort zone. But the paradox is that because showtime's over and reality intrudes, the spark of romance that kicked the whole thing off can short-circuit.

Trust me, as we sailed along the Riviera at sunset, those sparks were flying.

That's why, when a couple can't conceive, I'm only half joking when I suggest a Mediterranean cruise. Too many people who fail at it end up taking a clinical, science-class approach, and they feel pressured to pass the test. I understand that. I'm not Dr. Ruth (and Dr. Ruth doesn't pitch for cruise lines), but I also feel there's nothing wrong between two caring people that making passionate love three times a day can't cure—or at least improve. If you could just fall in love again, with the sea air making your skin taste salty, the delicious, leisurely dinners together, the sloshing of the sea against the ship at night as the sails billow in the warm winds—it's daggone seductive. I wasn't there to shoot a commercial, but I discovered on my own time the cruise's best selling point of all.

A few weeks after we returned, I began to feel nauseated from drinking coffee and couldn't read the paper in the morning. I thought it was jet lag. Then I noticed in early August that my cycle—usually like clockwork—was, strangely, three days off. No. I recalculated and saw it was actually ten days off. I went and had an EPT. Mine turned clear immediately.

Frank was not a happy camper. He would turn fifty-nine that summer. His head was much more geared to life on Easy Street than on Sesame Street.

He knew I hadn't tricked him. I have far too much respect for him to do that. Frank's stance on "more kids" was similar to Stan's— with one very significant difference. Both men, fathers of three, had said to me, "Having children is not an experience you should miss out on." Both men had said, "I personally don't want any more." Only one of them, however, loved me and respected me enough to say: "It's your decision."

The truth was, I didn't think I wanted one then either. But as always, I wanted my options kept open. I was beginning to think we might never find "the right time." Our schedules were getting ludicrous because of our work lives. And my feeling is that people who are working *not* to have children very often succeed and then find, sadly, that their time has come and gone.

Our show was on hiatus during much of August, and I hardly ever got out of my bathrobe. I was concerned about word getting out before we had a chance to announce it ourselves. And sure enough, we were scooped. On Monday night, September 11, Al Michaels made the announcement on TV as he sat with Frank and Dan Dierdorf at a Giants game.

Reege's comic genius is such that the more he's hurt, the more hilarious he gets. We replayed the announcement from the night before and the audience went nuts with cheering and applause. He was in *agony* because he didn't get the scoop—and it was sitting right next to him. *Ooooh*, the indignity of learning he was to become Uncle Reege "from Al Michaels, in between grunts and blocks on a football game," as he put it.

"A little angry?" I teased. "Little hot under the collar? He was thrilled to scoop you, you know," I said, twisting the knife.

"It just hurt," said Reege. "Not only Al Michaels. Joan Lunden had it this morning. And Sally Jessy Raphael, on a *two-week tape delay*, she had it. Everybody got it but me."

"I didn't know they were going to do that," I assured him.

"Oh, please," said Reege, his pride gravely wounded, "this show isn't big enough. I understand."

It was a terrific bit.

From that day on, a woman's most intimate and sacred secret—the miracle of carrying her first baby—became an integral part of our "Live" shtick.

We received a colossal outpouring of love that none of us could have imagined. Five thousand cards, over a thousand gifts, many of them painstakingly handmade and precious—quilts, rockers, cradles, and bonnets and puppets and stuffed animals. I had never seen Frank so moved in all the time I'd known him.

We had obviously touched a nerve or two. People who couldn't quite get a handle on me before I was pregnant now related to me for the first time. I wasn't just this career woman with a glamorous man and a life of black-tie banquets, galas and singing with Frank Sinatra in Atlantic City. Now I was pregnant. I gained weight, and my ankles were swollen. I was tired. My hormones were running amok.

That endeared me to people. For maybe the first time ever on television a woman grew in front of the audience's eyes. Unlike Joan Lunden and Jane Pauley, I wasn't hidden behind a desk.

It was inevitable that my baby would become a celebrity long before his birth—like Lucy and Ricky Ricardo's kids in the 1950s. Our audience is largely women eighteen to forty-five, and it includes millions of young moms and older moms and they could relate to what I was about to go through.

The year of pregnancy and Cody's infancy marked a turning point. For the first time, people saw in me a depth and warmth that was always there but had not been a major element in the host chat chemistry. It's hard to come off as nurturing and maternal when Regis is leaning over flicking "ungawa" off my face. As I told Barbara Walters on our show, people tend to equate funny with shallow, particularly in women.

The closest I had ever come to showing a nesting instinct as I sat next to Reege was maybe laying a huge egg by telling some dumb story during host chat. But anyone who's ever come into my home sees that I spend a tremendous amount of time and attention and affection on creating a home. By sharing honestly the joys and hassles of motherhood on the air, I tapped into that vast spirit of kinship that exists in the hearts and memories of all the great women and mothers who had gone through pregnancy before or were going through it for the first time right there along with me.

Moreover, I had always stood up for certain values—strong, loving family values. It would have been hypocritical for me to hide this part of my life from the people who had come to "know" me and who had always thanked me for openly loving my husband or for being one or another kind of role model. Now it was "Thank you for letting the world know about the highs and lows women go through," and "Thank you for sharing this time of your life with us, because it's helping us go through it too."

The issue of whether Frank would or would not "give me" a baby was one of the running motifs we'd established in host chat. So it was normal for us just to go on with more. We'd had a psychic on the show, and she had predicted I would have a baby—at least three years in a row! I once told the story of the old Italian woman who whacked Frank on the head with her umbrella, saying, "Whatsamatta wichyou, you can't give your wife a bambino?"

After eight months of "Uncle Reege" brilliantly playing Mad Curmudgeon to my warm and fuzzy Earth Mother-to-Be, we did a wonderful Baby Week in March, right before my maternity leave. Gelman and program director Art Moore had monitored audience letters and calls to make sure our fans hadn't OD'ed on OB-GYN. *No way.*

We kicked off Baby Week on Monday when Uncle Regis became Ample Regis and strapped on a thirty-five-pound "empathy belly"—a big round belly and bosom for expectant daddies so they can get the hang of it, as it were, and understand why Mommy's always carrying on about carrying big. Reege taped a fabulous segment with a video crew, leaving the building and walking around town as "the world's first pregnant man." (This is a guy who still likes to claim that carrying an eight-and-a-half-pound child is a day at the beach compared to passing a microscopic kidney stone the size of a grain of sand.) Reege was a riot, tilting backward, waddling around short of breath, his overcoat buttons straining so hard they'd have killed someone if they'd popped loose. In the lobby of our studio, a passerby asked him if it was a boy or a girl. "I'm having twins," he said matter-of-factly. "Two boys and two girls." He made fun of me by tenderly calling his prosthesis Puddin' and talking to it. It was one of Reege's finest and funniest, bits.

By Tuesday he was back to normal. "Baby Week continues," he crabbed. "It's only Tuesday and it's *already* on my nerves."

"I want you all to know it was not my idea," I said sweetly.

"I can't TAKE much more of this! You have been *milking* it for all it's worth."

We did Lamaze exercises on one show, and for another, I bravely put on a form-fitting black leotard three weeks before Codes was born and exercised with *Callanetics* author Callan Pinckney. The funny thing was, I only looked pregnant from the side. I was lucky in that way. I had almost no swelling.

At one point I had to turn sideways and do squats while holding on to a chair. "Okay," I said. "You get a side view. Big *deal!*" And quite the view it was. Sideways, in my leotard, I had basically had the same proportions as the California Raisins. I looked like Empathy Mountain.

"I just wanted to make a statement," I said, "that pregnancy is a natural state and for too many centuries pregnant women were hidden away."

Reege, glaring with mock outrage, screamed, "Not ANYMORE! Not around HERE!"

I told a funny story that got back at Reege. Frank and I had attended his wonderful induction into the New York Sports Hall of Fame the night before. I left early because I was exhausted, so Frank cabbed it home, lugging this enormous plaque. He noticed the driver's unpronounceable name and asked him—Frank, man of the world that he is—if he was Ukrainian. "No," he said.

"Yugoslav?" Frank guessed.

The man nodded and smiled, eyeing Frank in the mirror. "What you do?" the amused driver asked.

Frank mentioned he'd covered the 1984 Games in Sarajevo.

"What your name?"

Frank told him. (By now, when I told this story on the air, Reege was giving me his "let's-get-this-over-with" look.)

"Oh, Frank Gifford," the driver said. "You married to lady on TV having baby."

The audience went nuts. But there was another punch line—the most bitter insult to Reege: "She work with Sregis," the cabbie said, "and he have this thing on his belly."

On the last day of Baby Week our audience was made up of pregnant women only. We mentioned it on the air once and had *thousands* of calls. We had ambulances waiting outside in case any women went into contractions. One woman's water actually broke in our studio, and we taped her getting wheeled out and put into an emergency vehicle.

We interviewed "Guiding Light" actress Kim Zimmer, mother of a newborn, and she mentioned taking one milligram of a new natural painkiller for births. I said, "I know, it's party time," on those drugs.

Reege went wild over that one: "I can't BELIEVE these two mothers are pushing DRUGS to America right here on our show! You got any of that stuff *on* you? I could use some now—to get me through Baby Week!"

Regis looked stricken when Kim mentioned her water breaking. He had had it. "Now, that's one expression I don't want to hear again on this show. I've heard it all my life, I really don't understand it, and I don't want to THINK about it! 'My water broke.'"

I wouldn't let it go, of course. "It's about a quart, Reege."

"PLEEEZE! That's all!"

But the pièce de résistance—actually, make that the pee-ece de résistance—was the baby-massage segment on our final day. Adrien Arpel of the cosmetics firm showed Reege and me tips on powdering, diapering, and massaging three adorable babies. Each of us worked with a baby; Reege was with Adrien's grandson, Phil. Before we even put the babies down for the diapering, Phil wet Reege's apron, leaving a huge dark spot. That was quite a crowd-pleaser.

Five minutes later, when Reege bent over to diaper Phil as he lay on his back, another stream shot up in a wild arc right toward Reege's face. The audience went absolutely crazy. Talk about striking gold! This was, you might say, pee-back time for Uncle Regis after his sourpuss posturing all week. "We're bonding now, Phil," he screamed. "Oh, yes, we're bonding!"

Reege was in rare form all week.

We were both in rare form, as a matter of fact.

Baby Week brought my two lives together. The numbers proved there was a market for our brand of reality programming. Reege mentioned our astounding 33 share for one show. "The U.S. Supreme Court," he said in host chat, "has difficulty defining obscenity. A thirty-three share in this business—IS OBSCENE!"

With Frank's football duties mostly done after Christmas, the third trimester was, happily, all ours. But I was appalled that he had to leave home on Christmas Eve to go do a game somewhere and miss Christmas. The rest of my family gathered around and did a terrific job of cheering me up while Frank was gone, but I still don't think I've ever had a worse Christmas.

I'm hopelessly sentimental about Christmas. I believe that some things in this world should remain holy. I don't think football has any place on television on Christmas Day, and I don't think people should be at football games on Christmas Day. Thanksgiving's different. It's not a religious holiday.

After that, though, Frank and I spent many a wintry evening at our new Connecticut home, cooking a nice dinner and then snuggling by the fire, talking and dreaming of our little guy. Frank knew far better than I did how much life was about to change for us, especially for me, and so we both treasured those last weeks together when we were just two.

Frank was so eager to be involved. "I want to know how it all happens," he said with Boy Scout–like exuberance. And, oh, did he learn, let me tell you. Frank became the Vince Lombardi of Lamaze coaches. Our nurse instructor, Emily Beck, became a close friend because of all the sweet connections to that time of our lives. On March 22, 1990, at 1:28 A.M. I gave birth to Cody Newton Gifford. He barreled into this world a week ahead of schedule but tipped the scales at one ounce shy of nine pounds. And, boy, was he shy. After sixteen hours of labor, the little guy simply would not come out so I had a C-section.

I remember my very first visit to my doctor, Dr. Michael Langan. I repeated stories Mom had told us as kids about how she almost *died* from each of her pregnancies. I'd heard nothing but horror stories my whole life. Dr. Langan assured me that everything was fine and I would be able to bear a normal-sized baby. To which I responded, "Oh, you mean like a seven-and-a-half-pound baby?"

"No," he said. "I'll be happy with a six-pound baby."

A week before the birth I saw the doctor, and we learned that Cody was already eight and a half pounds. I asked Dr. Langan if we should just schedule a C-section.

"Nature says you can have this baby," he said. "You are dropped, effaced, and dilated."

"What am I, an eyeball?" I said.

I had an appointment a week later with Dr. Langan so that he could, for the third time, manipulate and soften my cervix—kind of mush it up to ease the birth. He did not want to induce labor, and it didn't seem as if he'd have to.

The night before Cody was born—*this was smart*—we went to see a movie, *The Handmaid's Tale*, which contained one of the most graphic birth scenes of all time. During that scene, I had my first contraction. *Who says movies don't have a profound influence on your psyche?*

After I got to the hospital, I was administered Petocin, which induces labor. A couple of hours later—*cover your eyes, Regis*—my water broke. Lamaze teaches you to focus on something during the breathing. We'd always called the baby Puddin'. Frank did a stick drawing, and whenever I'd turn over he'd put his drawing of Puddin' where I could see it, so I had this little picture to concentrate on. It was very sweet of him. He never left my side. And he was having horrendous back agony at the time, too. (In fact, he had back surgery six weeks later.) The experience must have been almost as painful for Frank as it was for me.

I thought I was dying, and I really took the Lamaze seriously. The only rough moment we had as a team happened when Frank lost his rhythm (as he did when we were singing together) and temporarily got his breathing wrong. I WANTED TO KILL HIM! We managed to get back on course and continued together as the contractions became more severe. No one could figure out why the anesthesiologist hadn't arrived. We learned later that his own baby had been born weeks before and he was happily at home having a leisurely and, may I add, completely painless dinner with his family.

I kept moaning, "He's not coming. I hate you. You lied to me. He's not coming." By the time the anesthesiologist arrived, I was ten centimeters dilated. I was finished, *thank you very much*, with the really hard, really painful, really *excruciating* part. He gave me an epidural and I proceeded to push for the next three hours.

Finally, at one in the morning, Dr. Langan, Emily, and especially Frank decided I had had enough. Frank was the one to break the news to me. "I'm sorry, honey. Dr. Langan says you have to have a C-section. Are you disappointed?"

With my last ounce of strength I managed to raise my throbbing head and, with matted hair and rivers of perspiration rolling down my face, I grimaced with pain and screamed, *"ARE YOU CRAZY!!! GET THIS THING OUT OF ME!!!"*

I was awake for the whole unbelievable birth. It was so emotional I

sobbed through the entire experience. My head was tilted way back so all my tears were running up my nose. I needed to lift my head and let them drain out. I could hardly breathe. But I could feel. And then I saw the doctor lift him up. It is the single most amazing experience a human being could ever have.

Frank was there, and then the nurses took Cody and cleaned him up. He was screaming at the top of his baby lungs until Frank held him. And he immediately calmed down completely in his arms—because, I truly believe, he was so used to hearing Frank's voice from inside the womb. They say babies get very accustomed to voices and dogs barking. That's why they can sleep once they come back to the home. And that's why Cody has always been able to sleep through Chard's and Chab's barking—he's known their sound-bites since he was conceived.

This was bizarre, too. This small, attractive blond woman came into the room and told me she was an associate of Dr. Langan's. "I'm your pediatrician. My name is Dr. Cody." And I'm going, Yeah, right.

We had already named our baby, of course. Newton was Frank's middle name, a family name. Cody was the unusual part. On Thanksgiving—I was four months pregnant—I was cooking with my mom in their kitchen, and Frank and Daddy were watching a Cleveland Browns game on TV. Frank yelled to me out of nowhere, "What do you think of the name 'Cody'?"

"Love it." Frank had heard someone mention Cody Riesen, who played for the Browns. He'd been playing a dozen or so years and Frank had never even met the guy, but when he heard the name, he knew. When Cody was born, publicist Kathleen Gold-Singer called the Browns to find out how to spell his name. It turned out that Cody Riesen had announced his retirement on March 22, 1990—and that it was his birthday too. That was a pretty unbelievable set of coincidences.

The morning of the birth, Uncle Regis finally had his big scoop. He made the announcement on the air, with Joy filling in for me. Then he got me on the phone in my hospital room.

I was real groggy and my speech was slurred. "I'm holding the most precious little boy," I said. I was about as cognizant as a human can be on morphine. "You find out every woman, every pregnancy, every little baby's so unique," I said. "It was an experience I will never forget. A gift from God, that's the only thing you can say. He's got the Gifford cleft in the chin and he's got Frank's nose before it was broken four times. And—God bless you, Cody! He just sneezed."

Proud Papa Frank then got on the phone. "I'll just say it flat out,"

he told the audience. "He is really a good-lookin' little guy. He's got a lot of hair, and it's parted on the right side. He's some baby. He's asked for the keys to the car."

It wasn't long before I had to face a more traumatic "C" than my own "C" (section): Cody's circumcision.

I couldn't bear the thought of my child leaving my arms, much less going under the knife. To deal with my anxiety I nursed Cody right before, wrote this little note, and stuck it in his diaper:

> Dear Dr. Langan:
>
> Just take a tad.
> Please leave me most of what I already had.
> Life is too short, so don't make ME that way!
> Now please hold steady and have a nice day.
>
> Love,
> Cody

In the forty years of Dr. Langan's practice, no one had ever left a message in a baby's diaper. The nurse said it was so funny that the doctor screamed. I wanted the note back for Cody's baby book but he said, "No, make your own copy." The nurse told me Cody didn't even cry and that it was the best circumcision Dr. Langan had ever done—*of course.* Painless and perfect.

Before Cody's "C" and my own unforeseen C-section, I was wiped out, so I made a deal with the show. Sweeps month was coming up in May, and that's when ratings count the most. I agreed to come back early, on April 30, if they would give me most of June off. They agreed.

Those five weeks after Cody was born were, as any new mom knows, incredibly exhausting. I was so sore I could hardly sit up. My nine-pound baby kept nestling on my scar. My breasts became infected. It was pretty daggone gross. It's about then that the thought crosses every woman's mind: I will never feel or be a desirable creature again.

My breasts were just huge. Poor Frank. Once when I was getting dressed I turned around. He looked at me and said, "Don't aim those things at me." They were like torpedoes.

How bad was my body? Well, I had always felt uncomfortable with my body *before*—and now I was praying I could get *that* one back! Your waistline's history—forget it. Your legs will always be jelly, your breasts will always be brown, your nipples will always be six inches in diameter, and your belly button's days as an "inny" are over.

227

For the first time in my life I felt totally out of control. Most of us have been dieting since we were twelve years old. We know all the tricks, right? Eat a little less, our tummy's a little flatter. Do leg lifts, we get that nice little line right there. Let me tell you: pregnancy is a one-way ticket to Bigger. You can't control your appetite, you can't control your mood swings. And that's the *fun* part.

Then came breast-feeding. I had a horrendous time. I was really looking forward to what every mother said was such a precious time with her child, so intimate, so sweet. Just like Gerber's serene, peaceful shot of mother and child. Forget it. I didn't know from serene, don't tell me about precious.

For some reason, Cody would take milk only from my right breast. He did double duty on my right. So now I was hooked up to a breast pump for the left breast.

Frank felt I should breast-feed for a year, but Cody was so big and voracious that I couldn't feed him fast enough. He was just sucking like crazy. Tears would stream down my face when I breast-fed; the pain was excruciating. My breasts became chapped; the skin cracked, and blood and pus formed. I developed horrendous mastitis, an infection that gives you big red lines leading down your breast right to your nipple. I couldn't believe my nipples could get that huge. Then you crack, literally, and bleed. It gets disgusting. Those veins are infected, inflamed, and you are engorged with all this milk. I'll never forget the sound of that pump at four o'clock in the morning. I had to do Lamaze breathing just to get through the pain of nursing. God bless our nanny, Christine Gardner. I could never have gotten through it without her. Once I'd finish with the breast pump, she'd fill the little bottle that came with it and give the milk to Cody. She performed miracles. I was covered with lanolin to moisturize and soothe the skin. Poor Christine. She says she'll *never* get pregnant as long as she lives, after watching me go through that ordeal.

It gets worse. The pump must be dismantled, sterilized, and reassembled every time it's used, and there are a few little parts to it, so it's a huge to-do. Over one weekend, Chabby, who must have been in a jealous rage over all the attention Cody was getting, gnawed and chewed the pump to bits, and all of the drugstores were closed. At that point I lost it. I remember standing there holding this chewed-up piece of breast pump, weeping, quivering, helpless: "Chabby ate m-my p-p-pump. How could sh-sh-she eat my br-br-breast p-pump?"

I *had* to pump. If you don't pump the pain is even more

excruciating. You're basically a cow. I started mooing through the house. I'd always had a normal-size bust. I had no idea cup sizes went so far along in the alphabet. *Who knew from E cups?* I look at my old nursing bras now and I just laugh. My underwear was huge because I had to get it around my middle. That was one period I was *not* sorry to see end. I stopped nursing after five weeks, when I went back to the show.

And yet, despite all I had gone through, I felt I had somehow failed Frank and Cody.

Interestingly, after I announced my pregnancy, the Slimfast company asked me to do a postpartum pitch for their weight-loss drink. I said no. I had never used it so it seemed a little tacky. Plus, I figured I should be focused on caring for my baby. I thanked them and that was the end of it.

But that was then, and this was twenty pounds later. After I stopped nursing, Christine, Cody, and I went straight from the doctor's office one day to Grand Union and picked up six months' worth of Slimfast. Christine had lost fifteen pounds on it. I was going back to work, and I wanted to be slimmer. Frank, with his bad back, had stopped working out and had added a few pounds to his sympathy weight. He was up fifteen. I had gained thirty during my pregnancy and had lost only the Cody pounds. I had never before been twenty big ones overweight in my life.

I eventually dropped ten while breast-feeding. (You can't diet when you're breast-feeding. You're supposed to consume extra calories each day just because everything goes to the baby.) That left ten. Every woman will tell you the last ten are torture. I was committed to shooting some new Carnival spots three months after the birth. The heat was on to take it off.

On Slimfast I lost it all within one month and got down to 110 pounds. Frank and I tried to make the diet fun. We'd put flowers on the table and light candles, and Frank and Christine and I would sit there with our crystal glasses and toast each other and do everything we could to make our drinks last. It was silly, but we pulled together and it worked for all of us. (I ended up feeling great about the product, so I signed to do some spots with Frank.)

On April 30, after five weeks away, it was time to become a working mom. By then my dressing room had been done over in Laura Ashley and equipped with a crib so I could ride in every morning with Christine and Cody.

It took ten seconds for Regis and me to hit our stride.

"Is there any sense of recognition at this early stage?" Reege asked.

"There must be," I said, "because the minute he heard your voice, Cody went, OUUAHHHHH! He was totally content, totally calm, wonderful, like the little Simpson baby, right? All of a sudden Christine says, 'Look, there's Uncle Regis,' and OUUAHHHHH!"

I showed Cody on the air the next morning. It was a very touching experience, but Reege kept the mood playful. He mentioned that the staff had chipped in and bought Cody a crib for the nursery. "Which, incidentally," he said, "I use in the afternoon when Cody's gone. What a sleep I get on that crib! Pull the blanket over me and nobody can get me, you know what I mean?"

We showed the inside of the nursery and some close-ups of my yawning, handsome Cody. Then I cradled him in my arms and walked out onstage so that everyone could see him. The audience reaction was so warm and loving.

At the end of the opening segment, Reege said we had had huge numbers for my return. "Yes, ma'am," he said with unusual warmth and pride. "The only show to tie us in share-of-audience was the lost 'Lucy' episode. How do you like that?"

"Well, that's nice to know."

"Stomping over every prime-time show," he said with comic fierceness, "over everything. How can that be, this little tiny show, y'know what I'm saying? Stomping on those big shows. It's a JUGGERNAUT coming down a hill. I CAN'T EXPLAIN IT!"

"Be grateful," I said. "Be *very* grateful."

With my beautiful baby boy nearby and my career reaching a new peak, I wasn't just grateful. I felt blessed.

Many a Tear Has to Fall,
But It's All in the Game

Frank has been married most of his adult life, and yet he has said to me more than once, rather poignantly, "All I've ever wanted in my life is a home."

I've been married or in serious relationships most of my adult life, and I've said to Frank more than once, "I didn't feel whole until I had you and Cody in my life."

I believe God sent Frank to me to save me from myself, from my own selfish, desperate abandonment of His love. I believe God brought me to Frank because He saw Frank needed one of life's nesters to help him build the home he'd been searching for all his life.

It was one sweet deal. Until Frank came into my life, I had no one with whom I could create and share the home I'd always wanted. Instead of nesting, I'd just been winging it, emotionally and spiritually. When Davy, Michie, and I were children, that warm and fuzzy bubble of family love enclosed and protected us wherever we went, whatever we did. That was all I had ever known. I felt empty and aimless without it. I yearned to have that back in my life as a woman, wife, and mother. I'm a person who needs to be surrounded constantly by people I love and who love me.

But Frank was more realistic. He'd made it clear he did not want more children. He was not one to idealize parenthood. He knew its pleasures came wrapped up with heartache, loss, and regret. Yet Frank is old-fashioned enough to cling to the notion that the sex drive exists primarily as an instinct to propagate, to replace ourselves on earth and ensure our survival. All his other accomplishments in his lifetime, in his mind, pale before the creation and raising of four wonderful human beings.

When Frank left the baby decision up to me, it was especially poignant for what it told me about the way he felt. When you love somebody unselfishly, unconditionally, you want him or her to be happy. You care more about that person's happiness than about your own because making a loved one happy ultimately makes you so much happier. The more you give away, the more you receive in return. It's an old biblical truth that I firmly believe in, and it's the foundation of all my deepest relationships and of my charity work. To give of yourself and serve others is to serve the Lord.

Still, there was no way for me to really know how Frank would adapt to our new life as parents. You can go away for a weekend with someone to test romance and compatibility, but you can't rehearse raising children. A part of me wondered what effect this baby would have on our absolutely wonderful, fulfilling marriage. I wanted to rock the cradle; I didn't want to rock the boat. I couldn't help thinking that it could really break either way for us.

We were obviously at very different stages of life. That didn't seem to matter when we got married. But with the demands of my career being what they were, and with Frank being more home-oriented than I was at that point, a child could easily have magnified the underlying differences in our game plans.

Trophies meant nothing to Frank anymore because he had won so many. There was nothing left for him to prove to the world about who Frank Gifford was. What he didn't have in his life then was a treasure—and a home.

I still had plenty to prove—at least to myself. My career was just taking off after many years of struggle. When Cody was born, Frank was at the exact age—fifty-nine and a half—when many men cash in their certificates of deposit. Now Frank was taking courses in diapering. Before we got married, Frank was looking to retire, to move to Jupiter for golf, tennis, fishing, and boating with old cronies. Now he had a nine-pound linebacker of a bambino he couldn't even lift because of a deteriorating intervertebral disc—and a thirty-six-year-old wife with infected nipples and a 44 share.

The way I saw it, as secure as I was in his love for me, I sensed this wasn't exactly what he had bargained for—and that we could be in for a real test. Frank had seen how my life got taken up entirely by the pregnancy plus work; now it was going to be infancy plus work. So here was this ultratraditional man, nearing sixty, whose son Jeff was born a year before I was, coming off the sidelines to suit up in the radically altered culture of fatherhood—and feminism—in the 1990s. It was a whole new ball game this time around, and, as in any other he'd ever played, Frank would have to want it if he was going to win it.

I don't know what odds Vegas would have given us, but I know I still felt it could turn into a disaster. If he didn't love Cody to pieces, he could resent him for disrupting what we had built in our first three or four years together. And from my point of view, knowing what I now know about motherhood, that would have been the ball game right there.

But Giff had come to play, as they say, and he came through in the clutch. This time the stakes were high, but the outcome was never seriously in doubt. It wasn't that he played like there was no tomorrow; Frank played like there was no yesterday. It was joyous to watch him. I've never seen anyone so determined to get it right.

The first time Frank ever saw the inside of a gynecologist's office was with me. He went along to all my baby appointments. He heard Cody's heartbeat the same moment I did. He saw the sonogram when I did. He was there beside me for amniocentesis. He was, as I said, the Vince Lombardi of Lamaze coaches, and he never missed a class, even though all of the other parents-to-be were in their twenties and thirties. He was absolutely fascinated, and he soaked up information like a sponge. He was adorable. He quickly mastered the jargon—"dilated," "dropped," "effaced," centimeters, water breaking. The whole nine yards . . . or pounds, I should say.

"It's incredible," he once said in a tone of awe and self-mocking amusement as he gazed at my belly. "I've had three children of my own already and I had no idea what goes on in there. *None*."

Frank didn't know "warm and fuzzy" as a boy. Where Frank came from it was more like "parched and gritty." Frank was a child of the Depression, born into abject poverty in southern California. If I had perfect stability in childhood, Frank had none. His family shuffled through more than forty-seven places before settling in Bakersfield, which Frank now calls his hometown. He did grow up with a strong spiritual anchor, though: his parents raised him in a strict hellfire-and-brimstone Pentecostal milieu.

Frank would eventually lose his faith because of the same hypocrisies—greed, ego, cruelty—I had witnessed among so-called

233

Bible-believing people. We could both relate to the Elmer Gantrys of that world. The Giffords, like their neighbors, were so poor that church was their recreation and the center of their social life. Even if they could have afforded movies, it was considered a sin to watch them. So they attended prayer meetings, revivals, picnics, and softball games. Frank had his first boyhood crush not on a movie starlet but on an evangelist Aimee Semple McPherson, whose flowing chiffon dresses and stunning face had little Frank's eyes bulging.

Frank was the baby of the family and a devoted, loving son to his mom, Lola Mae. She was an extremely religious—and, ultimately, bitter—woman who never accepted the frailties and vices of her husband, Weldon. Weldon Waine Gifford was a stern, gentle, rugged man who was loving but often absent from home, looking for work.

Men were so tough in the Gifford clan that football was seen as a sissy game. "Real men" didn't play it, but Frank had a natural gift for the sport (did I mention he was a perfect physical specimen as well?), and he pursued the dream that would carry him far beyond the despair of the California oil rigs. He was a star halfback and the first male member of the Gifford clan to graduate from high school, much less go to college. Here was a kid who flunked shop class in high school but went on to All-American glory at USC, where he also won the Trojan Award, presented to the athlete with the highest scholastic achievement.

Frank showed up at USC on a full football scholarship with only one pair of jeans and one shirt to his name—and ended up on *Life* magazine's cover as an All-American. (Can I tell you, if this man spent the rest of our *life* together in one pair of jeans and a work shirt, I'd still find him the Sexiest Man Alive.)

Frank was a rookie with the Giants in 1952, the year before I was born. By then he was married to Maxine Ewart, his college sweetheart (and, naturally, the Homecoming Queen). By 1956 they had three children, and Yankee Stadium had become the field of dreams for number 16's glory days of autumn. That same year, Frank was the NFL's Most Valuable Player as a member of the fabled Giants team made up of Charley Conerly, Kyle Rote, Sam Huff, Harlan Svare, Rosie Grier, Andy Robustelli, and Pat Summerall, among others. And, of course, he was in the Greatest Game Ever Played—the NFL championship game against the Colts and Johnny Unitas, which the Giants lost 23 to 16 in a sudden-death overtime in December 1958.

But Frank took his share of hits and realized that football wasn't forever. So, even in the off-seasons, Frank spent plenty of time away from home. He went out west, studied acting, and was under contract to Warner Brothers. He appeared in *Darby's Rangers* with James Garner and in *All-American* with Tony Curtis. (Frank likes to tell how Tony's baby daughter, Jamie Lee, peed on him when he held her.) When he left the game in 1965, Frank was one of the very first professional athletes to make a smooth and successful transition to broadcasting. He won an Emmy in 1977 for Sports Broadcasting in the days when they gave out only one.

But while Frank was becoming a sports legend to an entire generation of American men and boys, he hardly knew the three children who called him Daddy. He was gone too much of the time, and he came to feel he had paid an enormous price for glory.

Frank's children came of age in the tumultuous 1960s when many kids were antiestablishment and rebellious. He loved his children deeply, but between a football career and broadcasting career, he was working night and day. He says today that there is no question that his family life suffered immensely as a result. At a time when children really need their parents, Frank feels he simply wasn't there. (His children don't agree.)

But it was in 1979 that Frank suffered his deepest anguish as a parent. He had been best man at Ross Johnson's wedding on March 1, 1979, and was flying to the Olympic site in Lake Placid when he got the terrible news that his son Kyle, then in his mid-twenties, had been seriously injured in a car accident. Two of Kyle's friends were killed instantly in the crash. It was a miracle that Kyle lived. Frank was devastated.

The friends had been sitting in the front seat of Frank's car and Kyle was asleep in the back as they tore up the Palisades Parkway in New Jersey. Kyle was a young Frank—a handsome young man, great high school athlete, and, at the time, a promising law student in Colorado. Police said the car was going 90 miles an hour. The boys had not been drinking, but the driver lost control of the car. At that speed they never had a chance. The bodies of the two other boys were crushed on impact.

When police examined the wreckage they were certain there were only two victims. They were leaving the site when they heard moaning from what was now a heap of scrap metal so severely mangled they couldn't believe a human was compressed inside.

They extricated Kyle and learned he was, miraculously, neither paralyzed nor internally injured. But a severe head injury impaired his short-term memory. After several years of painstaking rehabilitation, Kyle was able to resume his life and live on his own.

Frank suffers regret and guilt over his performance as a parent the first time around, and he says, "I don't want to do that with Cody."

I don't believe the core of who we are changes once it develops early on. You take your hits and things eat away at you on the outside, but your essence is always there. At Frank's core family and church had always been the refuge in the face of grim adversity. But life, career, society—all of it can take us away from our true nature. With Cody and me in his life, Frank found the path that would lead him back to that vital core.

I got a brief but vivid glimpse into that part of Frank's life just a month after we got married. It was right around Thanksgiving 1986. Much as a document or ring symbolizes a bond between man and wife, this was a moment that made that bond a deeply shared reality for us.

We got word that Lola Mae had suffered a major heart attack.

We flew out to California, where Frank had bought for his Mom the only home she ever owned.

Poor Mom was hooked up to all kinds of tubes, but she was conscious, so we talked about faith, the Lord, life, and beyond. I was doing everything I knew to keep her spirits buoyant, though we sensed the end was near. Mom was a gorgeous, slender, very elegant woman with beautiful skin and hands and fingers. She was still so sharp and vibrant.

"You know, Mom," I said, trying to lighten things up, "you really should hang on for a couple more years."

"Why is that?" she asked.

"Because Frank and I will probably give you another grandchild."

With that she lifted herself up in the bed and said, "Now, what do you want to do a stupid thing like *that* for?"

I was taken aback. "Mom, don't you think it's a great idea?"

She looked away and, in a feisty tone, said, "What's the kid gonna do—walk Frank to the Social Security office?" I died. I couldn't stop giggling. Her presence of mind was astounding.

Then she sank back in her pillows and gave me a long, hard look that betrayed some of the pain of her long life of struggle. "Kathie," she said solemnly, "let me tell you something. You have a baby, you lose your love. You lose your life." It sounded so cold, so empty and heartless. But that was what had happened to her. She had married Frank's dad when she was seventeen years old. She'd had three babies. Every penny had gone to feeding and clothing those children. The romance and excitement of life had left her when she was still a teenager. And for the next sixty years of her life she knew nothing but disappointment. Frank and her grandchildren were the only joys in her life.

I understood. She was trying to tell me, "Don't do that. You've got a chance to have something more than I had in life." Her words and her sadness at the end of her life devastated me.

Mom's two older children had been a major disappointment to her, but Frank had always been devoted, had always been there when she was sick, and had taken care of things. He'd been a true son to her.

About a week later Mom left us. We buried her on Thanksgiving Day. Frank and I went to our hotel, got turkey sandwiches, and sat on the beach eating turkey and dressing, talking quietly for hours about Mom and Frank's fondest memories of her.

At the service I sang two of Mom's favorite hymns, "What a Friend We Have in Jesus" and "Amazing Grace." I was so glad to have known her, even if it was just for a month. I found it remarkable that, given his own tests of faith and trials, Frank felt none of her bitterness toward life. I certainly hoped he would not share her views on having children.

Frank doesn't know how he would have gotten through his mother's illness and death if I hadn't been there for him. Mom was his last real link with his own family. His brother and father had died, and he'd been estranged from his sister Winona for years and years.

Frank had always been everybody else's rock in difficult times. For maybe the first time in our young marriage, he saw me as someone who could be a rock for him.

I don't know if anything could have changed Mom's grim, cynical views, but I sure would have loved for her to see Frank and Cody together. It made me a believer in Frank's ability to learn, to adapt, and to work for something he treasured.

When Cody was an infant, Frank was so sweet with him. He'd hold him and love him and help me with everything. But a father doesn't have a "relationship" the way a mother does as the newborn's main caretaker, nurturer, source of everything. I was the one who breast-fed, I got up when Cody cried in the night. What was Frank going to do? He couldn't exactly give Cody what he wanted. Cody was just this gorgeous little creature to Frank, but it takes a father a much longer time to create a real bond.

There was no way I wasn't taking Cody with me to the studio after

I returned to work. Then, with summer upon us and Cody hitting fifteen months, Frank came to me out of the blue and said: "The morning should really be my time with him." Frank had a lot of time off between football seasons, and besides, he was right. So they began a beautiful little routine that has continued ever since.

In those first weeks after I stopped taking Cody to the studio, Frank would get up with him and fix him his favorite breakfast. Frank would heat up the Mickey Mouse waffle machine and serve waffles, cereal, juice, and eggs. Oh . . . And the baba (Cody's bottle). I mean, at fifteen months this kid was on a Giants training camp breakfast— everything but the cup of coffee and the morning papers.

Then Frank would take him across the street to what we call "the secret garden," which sounds a lot nicer than "the real estate nightmare," which is what it is—three huge mansions that were built in high times and then never sold as the recession flattened the market. They'd hold hands and wander over on their nature walks, looking for deer, talking about the flowers and trees, listening to the birdies, discussing interest rates on thirty-year fixed mortgages.

It's a sweet time for them to bond. By the time I get home from the show it's time for lunch and a dip in the pool or another walk with Mommy, and then a nap. It seemed selfish of me to take Cody away from that.

When Cody ran his first fever, I, of course, wanted to get the National Institutes of Health on the case. I freaked. I heard my little boy at 4:00 A.M. calling out for Mommy, and there was no way I wasn't getting up. And, boy, did it show. I looked like hell that morning from crying and caring for Cody. My eyes were puffy and everything. But I've got a wonderful outlet. I share those moments on the air, knowing that every mother who's listening understands— whether she works or not—being with her sick child all night long.

Frank was doing a game out of town. He called six times the day he left for fever updates. He called before game time; he called at halftime. He rushed home on the earliest flight the next morning just so we could all have lunch together before Cody and I lay down for a nap. Normally Frank would be awake till two in the morning after a game, winding down. Then he'd sleep till ten, eat brunch, catch a noon flight, and get home when Cody's asleep. He rushed home because he cared so much.

Once Cody began walking, babbling curiously, and throwing egg rolls around at dinner, visions of us as a genuine "family" began to come into joyful focus. There were so many new things to do together, like visit Sesame Street studios, see all the wonderful

Disney animated features, rent all the wonderful Disney animated features, listen to the sound track albums for all the wonderful Disney animated features. If Cody has seen *Beauty and the Beast* and *The Little Mermaid* once, he's seen each of them fifty times. He could recite the dialogue by heart and sing every song. We just love to sit with him and watch and read and sing together.

And there was our first Halloween night out.

I am not into cowboys. But when Frank and I took Cody out for his first year of trick-or-treating, Frank went as a cowboy—jeans, boots, a little cowboy hat of mine, and one of his work shirts.

But that wasn't the point. We had been asked to spend Halloween at the "Black & White" charity ball for Alzheimer's disease hosted by Princess Yasmin Aga Khan. That year I was supposed to model a dress by Fabrice, but I just had to say no. It was one of the first of countless decisions I have since made to just say no to something in order to find time for Codes. I decided I wasn't going to go anywhere ever again on Halloween as long as he's a little boy. This was one of those moments when you see that your desires have simply changed as you matured.

Well, not entirely. I left the house in this stupid outfit I called Little Bo Creep—a little kid with lipstick slopped all over my face. Cody went as Phil Simms, with his tiny adorable Giants number 11 jersey. He was dancing and was so happy in his little shoulder pads and Giants slippers with the fake cleats. Frank was going to use tape to change the 11 to Daddy's number 16. But Frank figured Phil had been sidelined in favor of Jeff Hostetler most of the 1991 season and needed a little action. So we let Cody wear Phil Simms's number.

Cody's nanny, Christine, was a Fig Newton, and with her sister Colleen and her sister's kids, Cailin and Robby, we had a pumpkin and a ballerina. We jumped into our Jeep and drove around the neighborhood. It was the first shift of trick-or-treat, like five o'clock; I wanted to go before it got dark. We drove and drove. And nobody but dogs were home. I was the designated knocker, the one who always had to get out of the car in my ridiculous outfit, with lipstick smeared all over my goofy face, and knock on the door and wait. I'd look back and see these adorable little expectant faces going, Is anybody home? Does anybody have any candy? We went to then-WCBS sportscaster Warner Wolf's home. Nothing. Everywhere we drove, no one. Just their dogs. They'd come up to your butt, sniff you, lose interest, and run off. And I'm going, "That's it? That's Halloween?"

It was the saddest, most humiliating Halloween of my life. No, seriously, we howled our buns off, it was so pitiful.

Finally we went to Christine's mom's house around the corner. She didn't have any candy for us, but she did give us Mama Gardner's fabulous lasagna. So we came home and we all sat around eating our Halloween lasagna.

The kids didn't care about the candy. What mattered was that we did it as an extended family, and we had our boy out for his first Halloween. What can I say? My son was the most adorable little thing in the world to me, and his daddy was the most handsome little thing in the world to me.

The truth is, you just never know what hands life is going to deal you. Frank had come through so much. He didn't know he'd marry three times, have five grandchildren who were all older than his youngest son and marry a woman who was younger than his oldest son. And I hadn't exactly gone around saying, Well, now, when am I gonna meet some great guy I can marry who's *Mom's* age? But you know something? None of that matters. If life always went according to plan, how boring would that be? I know God loves to hear our prayers just so He can then figure out something even better for us, something our fears or hang-ups or limited imaginations had kept us from scripting for ourselves. Frank, me, and Cody? Who'd have figured?

But there we were: the ageless cowboy in a silly gaucho hat, a teeny towheaded Giants quarterback, and a lipstick-smeared Little Bo Creep, piling into their stupid Jeep, making home videos. Well, it sure was *our* idea of a precious good time. And it sure beat spending another night out on the town.

Frank lets me know it means the world to him to have this chance to be a father to Cody and apply some of the amazing, hard-won wisdom he's gained through his own triumphs and tragedies. As reluctant as he might have been in the beginning, Frank is insane about this child, absolutely adores him. I'm so overjoyed, so grateful he feels such a fierce attachment and commitment to both of us, particularly Cody. I've seen a beautiful father-son bond grow and deepen—and become part of our own warm and fuzzy bubble.

In that way we've both found our way back home to each other—and to ourselves.

Isn't It "Loverly"? The Epstein girls: Mom, Michie, and me in 1957 . . .
photos courtesy of Kathie Lee Gifford

. . . and again in London, dressed My Fair Lady*–style, 1989.*

1979: My sex-goddess stage . . . it lasted for fifteen minutes, and, as you can see, it gave me gas and a headache.

photos by Dick Zimmerman

This is more like it: my cover-girl photo for Christian Life, *1978.*

© James M. Goss

Paul Johnson (my talented ex-husband) and me, when we were making gospel music in the 1970s.

In the morning . . .

(and you thought show business was glamorous)

photo courtesy of Kathie Lee Gifford

In the evening . . .

(my Manhattan cabaret debut)

© Jeff Sleppin

Ain't we got fun!

(one of my favorite Carnival Cruise shots)

property of Carnival Cruise Lines, Inc.

▲

*October 18, 1986:
Sharing our wedding
day with family and
friends. I would agree
with what Don
Meredith would say:
"Frank is #16 in
your program but #1
in my heart."*

© 1986 David M. Spindel

▶

*Scenes from my TV
marriage: Oh, Reege,
where would you be
without me?*

© 1987 David M. Spindel

Birth or bust . . . and the next day I did both! Our two dogs, Chardonnay and Chablis, are not looking forward to Cody's arrival at all!

photos courtesy of Kathie Lee Gifford

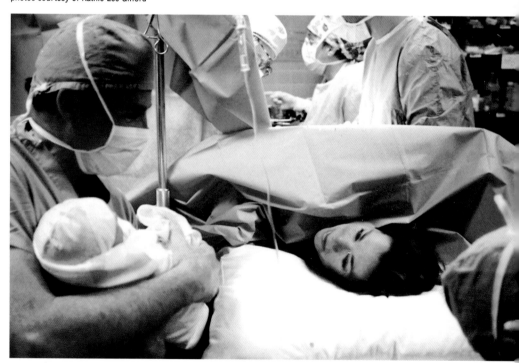

March 22, 1990, 1:28 A.M. Frank and I welcome Cody Newton Gifford into the world. Next time I want Frank's job.

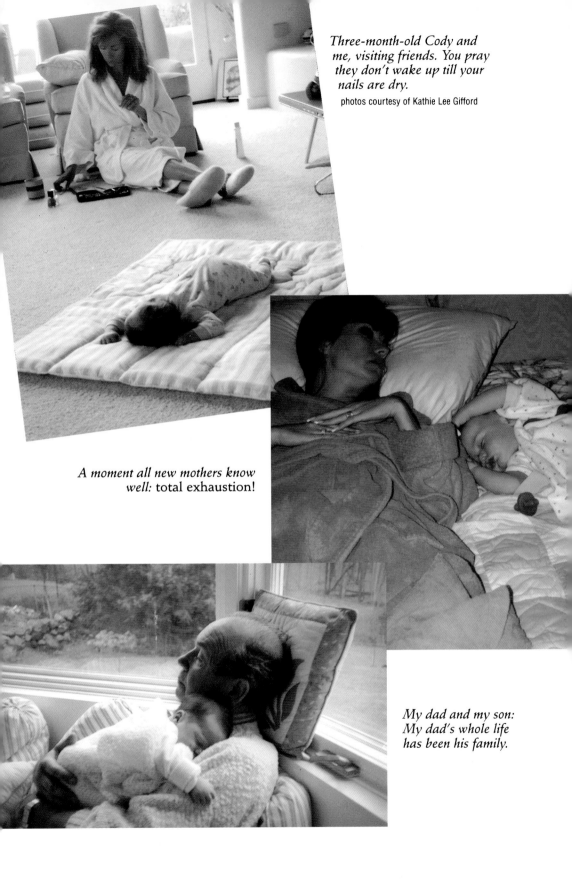

Three-month-old Cody and me, visiting friends. You pray they don't wake up till your nails are dry.

photos courtesy of Kathie Lee Gifford

A moment all new mothers know well: total exhaustion!

My dad and my son: My dad's whole life has been his family.

All in the Family

photos courtesy of Kathie Lee Gifford

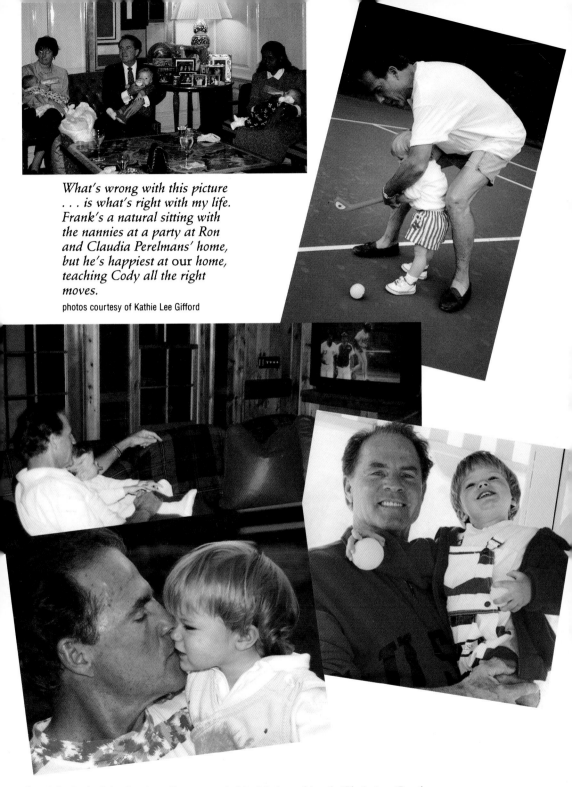

*What's wrong with this picture
. . . is what's right with my life.
Frank's a natural sitting with
the nannies at a party at Ron
and Claudia Perelmans' home,
but he's happiest at our home,
teaching Cody all the right
moves.*

photos courtesy of Kathie Lee Gifford

◀ *With Cody (clockwise, from top left): his best friend, Christine Gardner;
Frank and me; Frank's older sons, Jeff and Kyle; my adorable niece, Shannie;
my brother, David, his wife, Sandy, and me; and my mom and dad.*

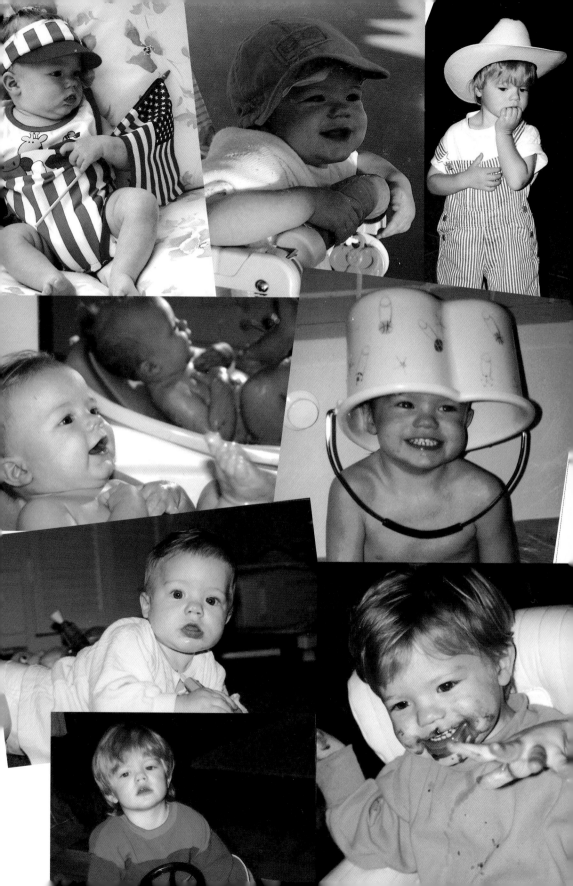

Cody, Frank's favorite photo subject, and my favorite subject.
photos by Frank Gifford

Who said Halloween was just for kids? The cowboy, the quarterback, and Little Bo Creep . . . The family that laughs together lasts together.

photo courtesy of Kathie Lee Gifford

I Can Only Give You Love
That Lasts Forever . . . That's All

☆

What working mother really has time to have it all?

For me the concept is simply impossible. No matter what sacrifices you make to juggle your time as wife, career woman, and mother, you pay a price—at home, in your career, or both.

But even if it's an unrealistic goal worth pursuing, a woman needs plenty of very real support from the man in her life—in the form of trust, respect, compromise, and a desire to communicate from the heart. A two-career couple with children is a complex, sensitive piece of machinery with lots of moving parts. Anything less than total cooperation will throw it out of whack and shut it down. A couple can wind up paying the ultimate price for trying to have it all—losing it all.

Whatever Frank and I have going for us can't be taught, can't be bought, and certainly can't be leveraged with junk bonds, so to speak. It comes from within, from faith and values, and from trusting, unconditional love.

The "having it all" trap snares every woman the moment she says, "I want to be the best mother and wife possible—*and* be challenged, respected, and fulfilled in my profession." A woman simply cannot be in two places at once and give her all to everything. This issue has pushed women's buttons from day one of the feminist movement through today's backlash era, when many women are coping with disillusionment at the end of the career rainbow, hitting the "glass ceiling" of corporate sexism in high places, getting trapped lower down the ladder on the "mommy track," or putting off children for career moves until it's, sadly, too late.

No wonder women have achieved a more equal footing with men in areas they never fought for—ulcers, hypertension, and heart attacks. We're racing around trying to be all things to all people, burdened by a brutal mix of ambition, anxiety, and guilt.

Then there's dependency. After three decades of feminism, "dependency" has somehow become a synonym for victimization; "compromise" means surrender, defeat. I don't accept that. A successful couple, to use biblical imagery, must be "equally yoked" —in all ways, including spiritual. A husband and wife can only pull together in a field of trust. Their two lives are so deeply entwined that suspicion—let alone infidelity—would throw them out of line. They wouldn't be harvesting as a team; they'd just be digging up each other's dirt.

A true partnership shouldn't stifle a woman's personality and autonomy—and I don't mean to make light of the destructive patterns in so-called co-dependent relationships where abuse occurs. But the truth is, in marriage you are *mutually* dependent. If I wanted a boarder who came and went as he pleased, I'd post the rent, find a quiet, clean guy, and give him a room and his own key. That's independence. Why would I want that?

Frank is my husband, my confidant, lover, therapist, parenting partner, and my best friend. We depend on each other for security, for emotional, sexual, and spiritual fulfillment, and for companionship. Our lives are thoroughly interdependent. That's *the whole point, isn't it?* That's what those vows mean when you get married.

I still get to have my own life—but that doesn't keep me from feeling that something's missing when Frank leaves the room. It doesn't feel right until he returns. If that's dependent, then I say it's a lovely dependency. I've been in relationships that weren't "dependent" and I ached for it. What good is a friend or lover you can't depend on? I'm talking about bonding, not bondage. I'm talking about the kind of mutual dependency that brings joy, safety, strength, and a sexy, cozy intimacy all its own.

And it's getting better. I am more in love with my husband now than I was in the early months of our love. When we married we both had career discontent to sort out and were coming out of rough relationships. Frank lost his mother a month after we married. But the turbulent peaks and valleys have smoothed and deepened.

Not that we've sunk into a crater of uncaring distance. On the contrary. It's now a mellower comingling, like two narrow streams flowing together to make a river that rushes with far greater force. It makes me never want to flow alone again. And trust is the riverbank that contains the flow, harnessing and guiding its power. Frank told me early on, "I will never ever be unfaithful to you, because if I'm unfaithful to you I will already have left." He's right. Happy, sexually satisfied people don't have affairs. You don't threaten something as wonderful as this. How can somebody offer me more than I already have?

Cheating is out of the question. Sure, Frank sees sexy flight attendants and businesswomen when he flies around the country. But the only come-on he gets anymore is "C'mon, Frank, show me a picture of Cody."

Last year Frank was in San Diego to cover the America's Cup races and went to a gym to work out, as he usually does. There was this great-looking younger woman on the StairMaster. He said she had the most fabulous body he'd ever seen. Incredible, totally dolled up and put together in this perfect, sexy gym outfit. And, of course, *no sweat!*

When she finished, she draped a towel around her neck and strutted over toward Frank, who, I'm *sure*, was already in his target heart zone. He was probably thinking this gorgeous woman was ready to flirt with him.

"I just loooove Kathie's show," she said in a southern drawl. "And how's Cody?" With that, she took out a picture of her own young daughter. "Brittany wants to meet Cody," she said. And Frank was standing there thinking, Wow, times sure have changed.

You bet they have!

As for me cheating on Frank, forget it! I work hard to find quality time with the one man who *belongs* in my life. Anyway, how would I do it? A quickie to me is changing Cody's diaper on the floor in an airplane. Besides, I've never met a man who could take me away from Frank. I have, however, *noticed* Kevin Costner—I may be married but I'm not blind. I think he's adorable. But that's because he reminds me of Frank. I blew my one chance to meet him when I rescued Cody from a bees' nest the day before Whitney Houston's wedding. We were both scheduled to attend, but there was no way I was going to go, looking like the Terminator. So many bees had stung me that my forearms were the size of my thighs—minus the cellulite.

But would I have an affair with him? Sorry, Kevin. I know you're just sitting home, pining away. Why would I long for him when I already have a better vintage—the wiser, more mature version—at home? Why threaten everything I've built with Frank and Cody?

When you cheat, you pay harsh consequences. The repercussions go way beyond that one night. It's easy to say no out of respect for the one you love.

When Frank assured me, "Nobody on the outside can hurt us," he meant not only third parties but also rumors, gossips, critics. "The only people who can hurt this marriage are you and me."

Which is exactly the feeling I often get when I spread myself too thin. Even the short list of requirements for "having it all" includes romance; but that's the first to go when work pressure builds up or when a baby comes into your lives. Frank felt that he lost me physically—and, to some extent, emotionally—for a year and a half before and after Cody came along. He felt excluded. Romantic, whimsical things we took for granted—a late night out on the town, staying in our city place overnight, flying off together for a Monday night game—were ancient history once the baby became top priority.

Frank isn't into excess flesh on a body. He likes a firm, healthy, fit body. He didn't like my body when I was pregnant, though he didn't stop loving or cuddling me and taking care of me. He realized it was a temporary thing. He'd been through it three times before. A lot of men apparently think pregnant women are sexy. But was I a turn-on to my husband? Absolutely not. Wrong guy. No one was happier to see me slip back into a size four than Frank.

I actually wanted to have a bosom lift after Cody was born. I used to have such nice perky breasts. They stood up and saluted and sang "The Star-Spangled Banner." Now they're basically humming "Go Down, Moses." They sag, they've got slight stretch marks. But in a peculiar twist my husband doesn't want me to have them surgically altered. Frank says, "Are you crazy? Those are your trophies."

"They're like hounds' ears, Lamb," I say. But he's right. It's wonderful that I nursed Cody, but I'm not twenty years old anymore and I haven't had a career that depends on my image as a sex symbol—well, not *entirely*. (Although I am, remember, the second most bodacious woman on television.) But while we're on this subject, I would love to have liposuction on my thighs, and I'll get my eyes done if I ever start to look haggard on TV. I had my eyeteeth filed down and laminated a couple of years ago. Was I going to wear braces for two years on TV? Not next to Regis I wasn't.

I change my hairstyle every day for the show, I'm fastidious and vain about my nails and teeth and grooming and makeup, but a perfect body, forget it. Dust to dust, wuggies to wuggies. The closest

I'll come to appearing in public in a bathing suit is my own pool. I just don't want to display my body, particularly those chunky thighs. Then again, if I had Raquel Welch's body I just might not mind parading it around. I don't. But I also don't live with the pressure to maintain a sexpot look or a young and virginal ingenue look at forty and beyond. The truth is, we all hate the treadmills and step classes with beauties half our age; but we still want better thighs, firmer tone, ageless skin, and perfect teeth.

Does that make me an egomaniac? A narcissist? It makes me a woman who doesn't want to miss out on living a full and happy life because of her hang-ups. It makes me *normal*.

That's why it seemed so crazy when Revlon asked me to join Claudia Schiffer and Cindy Crawford as a long-term pitchwoman. Yeah, right. The three world-class cover girls. "You are not hiring me because this face is the best face in the business," I said. "This face is going, and it's going fast! How soon do you want this deal?"

They laughed. "Don't worry. Your face is hanging in there. We're hiring you for your attitude."

"Attitude I've got. And lots of it." Their research was classic: Women thirty to forty-five years old want to look like Claudia and Cindy and go *shopping* with me. In other words, I win the Miss Congeniality award at the pageant. I'm the one they trust and like, want to hang with—uhh, sorry, "be around." This must be the kinder, gentler approach to growing older: The new Charles of the Ritz lady with the sore nipples, varicose veins, zits and all, pitching a line of de-aging skin-care products.

After Codes was born, I actually got my body back in shape, but I was exhausted. Cody didn't sleep through the night for a year. I was recuperating from surgery. Yes, I felt exquisitely close to the person I'd created this child with. But it was more wonderment than sensuality. I didn't look at my newborn and remember a wild night of passionate lovemaking on the Riviera; I just felt what an awesome miracle life is. Now, that's the ultimate turn-on, but sexy it isn't. I wistfully recalled those simpler days when Frank and I could go somewhere exotic and uninhibitedly zero in on each other's emotional and physical needs.

During those long postpartum months, that feeling seems totally out of reach forever. You have to work to get it back, whether that means working out, toning up, or sitting down together with your appointment books and penciling in passion and romance. Bliss isn't handed to you. Once you start sharing mortgage payments, night feedings, diapering, breast pumps, and basement leaks, everything changes. It's hard to think "sensuous" once your pillow talk turns to "I did the windows, you take out the garbage" and "I love you, my agent says it's a done deal, what do you think?"

I do beat myself up for this. I get the guilts from hurting Frank or ignoring Cody, and Frank feels guilty and selfish if he thinks he's stopping me from having my day in the sun. He's seen his dreams come true, and he sees how hard I've worked for mine. But he's wise enough to know a day in the sun can give you skin cancer or sunstroke.

It's tricky. If I gave up my career now, I would hate to think that someday I might blame Cody and say, "You kept my dreams from coming true." It's tough to strike a balance between regretting what I'd miss at home if I work hard, and resenting what's *at* home if I don't work. It makes me crazy.

These Big Questions seem to hit me hardest after the smallest moments. I remember how awful I felt when Cody and Christine went off to see Santa Claus and I had to stay home and work. And I had a rough time when he started swimming classes at 9:00 A.M. on Wednesdays. Just as I was going on the air, I'd picture him getting into the water, knowing I would never share that experience with him. This is a parent's endless conflict: Is it his need or *mine* to insist on us being together?

All my life I had sold other people's products, using other people's storyboards and camera angles. Then, when I launched my clothing line, Kathie Lee for Plaza South, in the fall of 1991, I finally had an opportunity to make my own creative decisions and be solely responsible for the success or failure of a new venture. More important, a percentage of my gross profits goes straight to my favorite charity—the Variety Club International's Children's Charity, for whom I feel I never give or do enough.

Flying around the country to visit department stores, I met hundreds of women who would bring their little children and say, "You are *such* a wonderful mother. We can relate." And I'd say to myself, No. *You guys* are the wonderful mothers. You've come with your babies. I had to leave mine home today.

I'm sure the guilt will lessen once Cody gets to be—oh, I don't know—sixty or seventy, and then he can wheel me to my store appearances. Something for him to look forward to!

But then there are the "feminists" who think I'm a sellout for "shamelessly" expressing affection for my husband and child on the air—as if, what, it's shameful? These are the same women who get on my case for hosting the Miss America Pageant.

At the 1991 pageant I brought Cody to a press conference. A woman reporter wrote that I had "dragged" my baby along. She also called me a "perky cupcake." I had been called perky and been called a cupcake; this lady laid a triple whammy on me: a perky cupcake who *drags* her kid to work. What a monster!

The writer was either childless, clueless, or both, since any working mother tries to spend every minute she can with her young child. Sour grapes? Jealousy? Who knows? If I'd come *without* Cody, someone else—or maybe the same woman—would have written that the "well-heeled mom" had "dumped" him with "her high-priced staff."

When *TV Guide* published its "Top Ten TV Blunders of the Year" in 1990, I made the list: For the hospital-room interview I did with Reege eight hours after Cody was born. Okay, my work will never be confused with Ted Koppel's. I can live with that. But given TV's toxic megadoses of "reality"—the parade of publicity-hungry weirdos on the talk shows, the crime, all those ridiculous rock videos—it's hard to imagine that only nine other programming moments blundered as badly as my calling Cody "the most precious little boy." We must really be in trouble as a civilization.

I'm not asking anybody to shed any tears for me. But it must drive critics crazy that someone as goony, sentimental, and happy as I am has succeeded. I'm like Doris Day on diet pills. It's the I'm-happy-therefore-I'm-shallow syndrome. But I don't gloat. I share. I try to articulate the joys and struggles and calamities that bond us all as human beings. I weep inside for women who have to leave their kids in awful day-care facilities. I weep inside for women who worry about having enough money to feed the kids. Maybe I can't solve their problems; but I don't want to *ignore* their problems either.

I, for one, neither deserve nor want to be idolized. In my heart I would love to be a perfect person—wife, woman, mother, Christian, entertainer. But I am unbelievably imperfect. Pedestals rock, and things that are on them fall and smash. I never set myself up as a standard for moral righteousness or as a measure for how to live your life. When I'm described as a devout Christian I shudder. I'm a struggling Christian. I know how much I have failed the Lord in the past.

But I also know what brings me life's purest joy and pleasure: being home when we're all a family. That may be the last thing the feminists want to hear, but that's the truth. It wasn't my master plan that my career would shift into high gear after Cody came along. I thought I'd find the time and energy to do everything that mattered —and still have a good marriage and be a good mother. I'm trying, like anyone else, to get along and find a way to make it work. The cynics aside (another female writer once snidely hinted I was "using Cody as fodder for my career"), the real hindrance was internal. I was missing out on quality time with Cody. I was getting home too late to see him before his nap. Then when he got up, after 4:00 P.M., I'd be wiped, having started my day at 6:00 A.M. By then I want to relax, sit in front of the fire or on the patio, and catch up on the news. It's a time when Mommy, the perfect caretaker, needs to be taken care of herself.

Yes, I'm incredibly lucky Cody has a nanny who'd give her life for him. He barely notices that I'm gone. I honestly don't believe Cody suffers when I'm gone or too pooped to play. But I do.

Frank has trusted all along that I'd come to these realizations on my own—and not because he imposed them. He sensed success would drive me back to the nest, not propel me into a doomed "star trip" trajectory.

I don't think I damaged Cody in his first two years, but I'll probably have to put the brakes on sooner or later. My career has, I feel, hurt Frank in that he thought I was ready to leave the show and cut back on my other commitments. But I was a wounded bird then, and we both had some healing to do. Frank was set to play and travel and see the world when we married. He feels he's making a sacrifice by letting me have my career. But he's stuck. I'm not going to give him a way out by screwing up the marriage. No way. I'd sacrifice some of my dreams in a heartbeat to save my marriage. Never the other way around.

Frank helped get me back to my roots, my most sacred values. He gave me a place to bloom where I was planted. He helped reanimate my self-confidence to make something beautiful of my life. We helped each other build a home. My career blossomed after we married. I relaxed. I'd been trying too hard. When I could finally let go of ambition, things started coming to me.

Of course, then I wanted to give my career everything I had and see where it could take me. And where it takes me too often is away from my husband and son. I had to get a big dose of success before I realized how relatively meaningless it can be in the big scheme of things. No matter where I am, what I'm sent to do, I always want to go running home. But I don't want to give up my show. All of us need one area in life where we can say, "Hey, I'm one of the best at that." For me, it's the show. I've proven myself every day for years. I'm a survivor—and a proud one, too.

It's been invaluable for me to have a man who's so much more successful than I am and who sloughs off his success like, so what? I can ask Frank, "What's it like to be the greatest in the world at something?" He was the NFL's 1956 MVP, a Hall of Famer, the Emmy-winning Outstanding Sports Personality of 1977. But Frank has lasted in his field because he is so simple and modest. He's no prima donna. He doesn't need the chauffeured stretch limo at the airport. Just send an intern in a car. And forget the big suite. Just a decent room with a window. His perspective has become my own shortcut for survival; it's kept me centered and grounded and prevented me from taking it all too seriously.

He's complicated in truly preferring to be home with me and his boy. He feels cheated. He was expecting, ultimately, a traditional marriage. I can't make that big a compromise. Yet. I'd resent him if I quit. But I can, in positive and challenging ways, streamline my act. I owe him that. He's given up a lot for me. I don't think any happy marriage survives because one person does all the giving up. With a child, the stakes rise urgently; every hour of a working mom's life has to count like never before.

But it can be rough. Not long ago I went to California on business with what Reege calls my power entourage—Cody's nanny, my assistant (Mickey "the Warden" Kaufman), and Cody. They went on to our hotel in L.A., and I waited at LAX for a connecting flight to Palm Springs, where I had a solo concert. When I say I do not thrive when I'm alone for long periods of time, we're talking about two hours, okay? I was surrounded by people affirming me with their affection, but I was truly miserable. I was soon overcome by the most poignant aloneness.

I had no reason to feel that way. I can't imagine how hard it must be for working moms who aren't in a position to bring their children along on business trips! I couldn't reach Frank by phone. He wasn't handling the separation much better than I was. Frank ordinarily savors our fall Saturdays together before he leaves for his "Monday Night" destinations. He was so unhappy being home alone that he left for Minneapolis a day early to see close friends there. Our home, as beautiful as it is, is just a house without the three of us.

It was more than just jet lag. I felt disconnected. Why should I be apart from those I love? For another standing ovation? For more money? We have enough money. I've had lots of standing ovations, but they're nothing compared to your little boy spotting you in a crowded room and running to you with his arms out going, "Mama! Mama!"

Frank had been upset and distant before I left. He knew I had to do "Live" in L.A. that week, but he didn't think the concert was necessary. I agreed with him and was resentful. Frank doesn't want to punish me for the choices I make. But it hurts him to think that something might mean more to me than he does at that time.

Yet it's hard for me not to ride this present momentum, wherever it leads. I always want to be open to new, creative challenges. But this is where a twenty-three-year age gap becomes a *life* gap. Two lives may be on track professionally, spiritually, emotionally, and sexually, but they'll *never* be on the same *schedule*. The arrival and departure times are just too far apart.

That was a rough weekend. I read the Bible, which comforted and chastened me. I met lots more women after my show—"You're such a great mom, wonderful wife, such an inspiration to us, the way you love your home so much." All of it made me look honestly through my own denial, past the public persona, and straight into the truth: which was that I felt like a complete fraud.

Why, I asked myself, if the love I express for Frank and Cody is real, am I here? Why am I always choosing other things over them? That kind of soul-searching leads to images of Mom, the ultimate role model. She sold eggs door-to-door and showed model homes a few miles away to make extra cash, but nothing could take her away from her family. Her life was homemaking, and she did it proudly and beautifully. When I started this career thing, it didn't even mean that much to me. I was compensating. Once it was painfully clear that Paul didn't want the total homemaker, work became my solace and a substitute for the love I didn't have in my marriage. If I'd married a different kind of man, I'd have likely had a life much closer to Mom's, with a much-scaled-down version of my career. High-powered was never the master plan. I'd have sold stuff door-to-door instead of tube-to-tube.

What helps me to deal with it is knowing how long and hard I worked for it. Everything that is happening now occurred only in my early fantasies. You hear all your life how you should be careful what you wish for because you might get it. It's the longing and the working for and the getting there that are so exciting. I'm learning that being there can be a major disappointment, not to mention the pressure and hard knocks of staying there. I ask myself every day if I can afford to meet these challenges now.

What if my drifting meant the demise of my marriage? What if it damaged my son's development? How could I bear to look at the balance sheet years down the road and say, Wow, what a genius I was to hold out for gross instead of net on that deal, or boy, remember that 37 share I got for my prime-time special in 1994?

I've pondered putting everything on hold for five or ten years and spending the time with Frank and Cody and any other gorgeous little creatures that may come along. Frank's been very tough with me on many, many occasions, and there's an ongoing tension between us over this. He's lost respect and patience at times because I've wanted some things so badly.

We usually agree, though, like when Regis and I read for and were offered the roles as parents in the 1991 Disney comedy, *Encino Man*. Though I'd been dreaming of acting in a Disney film since first grade, *Encino Man* wasn't the film I had in mind. It would have been an ego trip to see my face that big on the screen—and my bottom too, unfortunately. But it would also have taken me away from home at a time when I was exhausted. Frank made no secret of his preference for me to pass up the offer—and I had no problem doing so. (Regis agreed.) But what if somebody offers me three months in an exotic location as Kevin Costner's love interest, a great script, and a brilliant director? IN MY DREAMS!

Frank is not a screamer. He's fair, he'll listen; he's tough and he's tender. And he is teachable—what I love most in any person. He's learned that I value his input enormously, but he accepts that I'm ultimately going to make my own decision from my own heart. Our marriage has never been in trouble, but I know he'd be happier if I didn't work. And I've wondered: If I quit, would I be running home to a man? I know I can't live with feeling kept, even by my husband. So I keep at it, and we work together to strike a balance. When I was unhappy doing concerts on the road, he said, "Don't do 'em," and he was right. When I was mad and disappointed in the show, he said, "Don't do it anymore," and he was right. So with his support, I took a strong stand and came out a winner.

It's important never to go to bed angry. The Bible says, "Don't let the sun set on your anger." You don't want to toss and turn all night and end up glaring awkwardly at each other in the mirror the next morning as you brush your teeth. We've spent many an evening talking things out and ending the night with a warm hug. Maybe three times we've ended it with frosty glares.

The work in a working mother's life is like interference on a cluttered radio dial. Sometimes Frank and I are on the right wavelength and our signals are beamed steady and clear. But other times our signals get drowned out by static in an overloaded atmosphere. That's when Frank and I need to be alone and get our signals on the beam again. That's what makes the relationship work—direct communication in a clear-channel atmosphere of love, trust, and commitment. It *usually* works. Occasionally it backfires.

"Let's go out on a date Saturday night," I said to Frank one night. I was burned out from working weekends, and so was Frank. A quiet, romantic evening out would pull things back together for us.

We went to a trendy new Italian bistro in Greenwich that serves wafer-thin pizzas and great pastas. But it was noisy and we attracted too much attention at an important moment. I was opening up to Frank, letting him know I was aware things had gotten out of hand and that it bothered me—not a time to be interrupted by well-intentioned fans.

It was a frustrating and wasted night. My fantasy of a sweet, romantic evening—eating great pasta, then listening to our favorite music by the fire, making love, dropping off to sleep—was blown.

We ended up with just the pasta—and heartburn.

We slid back into talking about careers instead of what we talked about when we fell in love—how much you mean to me, how close we feel tonight, how lucky we are to have each other. The only thing missing was our agents. It got really uncomfortable. I was exhausted, down on myself, self-involved.

Driving home in silence, Frank was mad. I am a classic approval-driven person, and no one's approval means more to me than Frank's. So when I've lost that, even for an evening, I'm destroyed. Finally I said, "I can never please you enough. You're always mad at me. I'm happy with you, but you're never happy with me." The sun set—and rose—on our anger that time.

Prayer, as always, pulled us out of that nosedive. I was so upset I had to wear sunglasses and stuff Kleenex up both nostrils from crying. You're never more vulnerable to each other than you are in prayer. Frank was so loving. It's impossible to hold on to anger during prayer. Prayer is a magical, mysterious thing. You cannot pray for God's will, God's peace and joy, without being softened in your heart toward the person you are praying with. It's a surrender to a higher power that briefly takes control of your life. The Bible says, "Come to the Lord in prayer. Seek and ye shall find." And on that

Sunday after our ruined "date," we sought, we found, and the clouds above us lifted once again.

Then there was the time Frank and I vowed to get away for our fifth anniversary, an important milestone for us. It was coming up on Saturday, October 18, 1991, and we couldn't seem to find a time for a brief getaway. Meanwhile, Ethel Kennedy had asked us to participate in an RFK, Jr., golf event in Hyannis Port, but she couldn't find a good time, either, and hadn't set the date. We were eager to help Ethel, whose son Michael is married to Vicki Gifford. The tournament would raise money for human-rights groups around the world.

Ethel finally called with a date: October 18.

I felt so selfish because I didn't want to work on our anniversary. So I made a deal. I agreed to go to Hyannis Port on Saturday, but only if Frank and I could steal away on Friday and go somewhere romantic and secluded on the way. I took Friday off, and we drove up through the glorious fall foliage to the deliciously quaint New England Inn of Blantyre in Lenox, Massachusetts, in the Berkshires.

This hit the spot—clear fall air, a rustic setting, a gorgeous crisp fall afternoon and evening. It was like going back in time to when we were so in love and had our whole married life in front of us.

Then Frank did the most adorable thing as we dined at the inn. Ever the romantic, he whipped out a couple snapshots of Cody and set them up against the bottle of our favorite wine. Like moonstruck kids, we gazed at our little guy and babbled on about how much he's meant to us. We'd been away less than twelve hours, and already we missed him like crazy. That was all we talked about—no contracts, no career, no stress. We talked about love.

"Is he the most gorgeous thing you've ever seen?" I'd say.

"He's so smart, you know, and he has such terrific musculature for his age," Frank would note.

This time, when fans stopped by to tell us how much they loved their kids, it wasn't miserable, it was magical. Our hearts burned, all right, but not from the seafood special. I realized that I was more in love with Frank that night and felt more passionate toward him than I had the night we married. I had always heard that in a good marriage the romance deepens and gets better. In a bad one it just gets worse and dies. Now, thank God, I'd had both kinds of marriages.

After dinner we went up to our room, got a fire going, and enjoyed all the romance we had hoped for to honor our first five amazing years together.

It was a weekend that proved how lucky I am to have a man who treasures me, respects my drive to excel, and shares my spiritual faith and my need to give something back to society. We've got a beautiful, healthy son we both adore. And I've got a career that's taken me beyond anything I ever imagined.

Maybe a woman can't have it all. But if this is not having the best of it, then I don't even want to know what's missing.

Baby, Baby,
I'm Taken with the Notion
to Love You with
the Sweetest of Devotion

☆

You never know what your child's going to look like. You can only hope that if he's a boy he's going to be very Robert Redford-ish. Or Frank Gifford-ish. While I was pregnant I, like all women, had my share of birth anxieties. And I don't know if it's just an excess of estrogen or what they call gestational anxiety. But I had a very weird dream while I was carrying Cody.

In my dream I give birth to a lobster.

In my dream I'm diapering a lobster with all of its claws and its tentacles and its little eyes and I'm going, "Okay. I know it isn't pretty, but it's mine. It's my lobster."

Maybe it was from one of the first commercials I ever did—Red Lobster restaurants. So I gave birth to a red lobster—"for the seafood mother in me," as they might say.

As powerful and dramatic as giving birth is, life can seem awfully fragile once you hold your newborn baby in your arms.

Once, when Cody was five months old, I heard the worst sound a parent can hear: a deadly thud followed by what seemed to be an endless silence before he started to scream.

Cody had been sitting in his favorite little rocking chair on the kitchen counter, and I had just said to him, "Cody and Mommy are going to have a special day together." Then I turned around to give Chard and Chabby their breakfast. The next thing I knew, Cody was on the floor crumpled underneath his chair, bleeding from his mouth and screaming his lungs out.

Frank was literally on his way out the door to catch a plane for a football game when it happened. We rushed Cody to the doctor's office, holding his sweet little sobbing body as our own hearts pounded with fear.

Thank God he was okay, but I learned a hard lesson that day: *life can change in an instant; you really can't let your guard down for a moment.*

In a way, it's easier when children are small. You can control their environment and stand guard over their every move. Frank, who has loads of experience in this department, says it gets a lot harder in the years ahead. I dread the day when Cody goes off with his friends in a car or when he's offered drugs by a stranger.

More recently Christine, Cody, and I went out onto our upstairs deck. Christine and I were looking at the garden below when we heard a sudden shriek from Cody at the other end of the porch. He was bent over, wailing with fear and flailing helplessly as hundreds of hornets swarmed around him. I didn't stop to think. I plunged right in, grabbed Cody, cradled him in my arms, and ran for safety. The hornets followed us into the house. I grabbed Frank's favorite silk jacket and flailed frantically at the swarm. I was merciless.

Cody had been stung several times on the leg but appeared to be fine. I, on the other hand, had a violent reaction. My arms, covered with sting marks, began to swell to twice their size and stayed that way for days.

This was certainly no tragedy in the big scheme of things. In fact, the big scheme of things had been unusually tragic when this incident occurred. My wonderful and talented friend Peter Allen had died of AIDS; Olivia Newton-John had undergone surgery for breast cancer; Annette Funicello announced she was battling multiple sclerosis; Mamas and Papas founder John Phillips had a liver transplant operation to save his life; Pope John Paul II had a malignancy removed from his colon; Ben Vereen had been hit and nearly killed by a car; and Billy Graham, my spiritual mentor, had been diagnosed with Parkinson's disease.

All these terrible events had made me see with great urgency the fragility of life. How quickly things can happen.

For every day of the rest of my life I will worry—worry that I'm doing the right thing, worry that Cody's doing the wrong thing. I'll worry even when I know he's okay.

That's another reason why a sense of humor is an absolute necessity for a parent's survival. The day after Cody fell, I told the story on the air, still shaken from the incident. After the show I stopped at the fish market on my way home. A lady I'd never seen before walked right up to me and simply said, "I dropped mine right on his head," and walked away.

Codes shows every sign of being a strong, tough, and totally lovable little guy. I never imagined that Cody, at almost two and a half, would already be so verbal, such an astute observer and mimic, such a clearly defined human being. That blows my mind. I thought I'd have to wait till he was five to see his real personality. But, oh, has he got one! He's flirtatious, mischievous. He's a little con man, he's very straightforward, he can be very, very bullheaded, like his father. And he's extremely entertaining; like his mother, he loves to perform.

I came in recently and he had his little Mr. Microphone and he was yelling, "Spoonful of sugar make the medicine go down." Just like the song in *Mary Poppins*, which he watches about five times every day. Then, more like Mick Jagger, he threw his mike on the floor and jumped around. I think, Oh, *no*, I've got a rock star in my future.

One day about two months ago, Christine and I were in the kitchen and Cody was acting like a maniac. Now, Cody's usually pretty mild-mannered. He's not hyperactive. But this particular day he was just buzzing around like a banshee. Finally I sat him down. "Cody Newton Gifford," I said, "what has gotten into you?"

And he looked directly at me and he said, "Too much shuh-gah!" I had never told him he'd had too much sugar. He must have heard it somewhere along the way.

He embarrasses us when anybody tries to give him a kiss. He'll let them get real close and then spray them noisily by blowing out of his pursed lips. I say, "I'm so sorry. He just doesn't . . ." Most people know you lean in to kiss a terrible two at your own risk.

A child rarely performs when you want him to. But Cody's a ham like me, no question. He likes the reaction he gets. Then he grins and goes, "I so funny," because I've been telling him he so funny all his life. Now he puts a diaper on his head and says: "I diaper head. Diaper head."

Potty-training has been a real education—for me. I can bribe Cody to do almost anything with a Twizzler licorice stick. I am a

Twizzler and pickle freak and so is Cody. He loves everything I love. It's really funny. The kid's got my taste buds. So I say, "Cody, you're going to sit on the potty today and Mommy's going to give you licorice."

"I do it, Mommy." So he sits down and he's got the Twizzler in his hand, right, and we're in the bathroom together. He looks at me and says, "I want pwivacy!"

So I say, "All right, all right," and I turn around. I go in the other room, just behind the door, and I wait. "Are you doing it?" I finally ask.

"I doin' it."

I hear his little sounds and I'm thinking this kid's fabulous. *What a great kid!*

Finally he says, "Mommy, I did it, I did it."

I go in, I look down in the toilet, and there's the Twizzler at the bottom.

I say, "Well, that's sort of the idea, Codes, but you have to eat the Twizzler first, you know." He's so sweet. He wants to please.

Now he's at the point where he says, "I help you." Everything is, "I help you, Mommy," so every chore now takes ten times longer. If he waters a plant, let me tell you, he *waters* a plant. Which leads to a long lesson on how not to *drown* plants.

Cody loves to learn. He can count, and he knows all of the Disney characters and what their names are and their fathers' names and their sisters' names and what they say in the movies. I thought *Beauty and the Beast* might be too violent for him, but he wasn't afraid of the beast or the wolves. The thing that concerned him was that Belle, Beauty's father, was sick, and that he was lost in the woods. When that scene ended and we didn't see the father again for a few more scenes, Cody kept looking and saying, "Mommy, her daddy, her daddy." He was very, very concerned.

I said, "We're going to see him in a minute. I'm sure he's okay."

Then he'd look a little bit more and ask, "where her daddy?" I just love it that he felt compassion instead of fear.

Cody may have to change his own name to Cody Lawn Mower Man Gifford. He has always had a thing for lawn mowers, which has slowly expanded into a thing for firemen and fire trucks. Everywhere he goes, he has to have something with a fireman motif. A baseball bat becomes a fire hose in Cody's hands. He has a great imagination and my love for hats. Every waking hour of his day he has a hat on. Sometimes he's the captain of a ship or a cowboy or a pirate. But most of the time he's a fireman. "I a fireman," he says. He's hysterical. The kid's a maniac.

He'll look at someone and say, "There's a fire on you," and start putting out the imaginary fire. We have four-alarmers every hour in my house. Or he'll yell, "Save the monster," because in one of his "Sesame Street" videos, they save the monster. And at the end the monster says, "you're a lifesaver," so Cody goes around saying, "I a lifesaver."

Cody's not perfect. He's no little saint. But I'm working on it. I've got him in Sunday school. He says his prayers every night. He'll know from his earliest memory that he had a personal relationship with God. And I'm just hoping that will be his heart's desire as he gets older and that it will be a source of joy and comfort in his life, the way it's always been in mine.

Like any kid, he needs his share of disciplining, which often falls to me because Frank's much more lax. Frank's attitude is always: He's only two, Kathie. My attitude is: He already knows right from wrong.

I know he does because I see the way he acts. He knows. And if I say, "Cody, you're going to bed now," he cons me: "Mommy, just one book." And I'll say, "Cody, no books," and he'll nudge me: "Mommy, just one. Just one book, Mommy." He knows how to push buttons. If I say, "No licorice before dinner, Cody," he'll shoot back: "Just a wittle piece, Mommy." Everything's bartered. And he's great at it. He's probably going to be an agent. *Heaven forbid!*

If he's doing something that might hurt him, I smack his little hand, not hard enough to hurt him, but hard enough to get his attention. If he's reaching over the flame of a burner or doing some other dangerous things, I definitely believe in making him know that it's going to be much more painful than what I do.

I have little tolerance for his behavior when he's rude. Or when he's in his biting mode. A viewer recommended that I take his own little finger when he wanted to bite, so I tried it. I put his finger in his mouth, and he saw that it hurt. He never bit anyone again. Sometimes he gets a little rough with other children and I have to say, "Cody, no children are going to want to play with you if you can't be nice." He knows he'll pay a price for his actions.

Cody's a very social little guy. He wants to be liked, he wants to be with his friends, he wants to have fun. And it's clear he loves little girls. At our friend Bob Beattie's wedding recently in Colorado, Cody tackled every little girl. We went to a hoedown theme party at the groom's house in Woody Creek. It was so cute. Cody danced every single dance in his red cowboy boots, blue jeans, white shirt, red bandanna, and cowboy hat. And when the band stopped and announced the next number, Cody stood there and yelled, "Stop talking. I want mookis, I want mookis." That's Cody's word for music.

Kids are such great mimics, and it's so funny when they're not quite sure what exactly they're mimicking. We used to have a little clown in the back seat of the car. Once kids stop sleeping in the car you need to entertain them or they're miserable and so are you. For a while it was the job of Harvey the Diving Clown to keep Cody amused in the car. Wherever we traveled, Harvey would sit with Cody in his car seat. We'd say, "Ladies and gentlemen, doing a three-and-a-half forward in a pike position in a layout with a double twist, it's Harvey the Diving Clown! Degree of difficulty, four point nine." Then Christine would take Harvey's little hand and thrust it in the air and yell, "Judges!" and Harvey would make his dramatic dive. Cody was fascinated. One time Frank said to Cody, "I'll just show you how a big boy goes potty. Come with Daddy." He took him into our bathroom and was right in the middle of showing him when Cody looked at Frank, shot his hand in the air, and yelled, "Judges!" Frank cracked up so hard he totally missed his target.

Much of my life as a parent—from birthing on—has been made much easier and more enjoyable because we're blessed with a young, fabulous nanny with a terrific sense of humor. I honestly don't know how I'd have made it without Christine Gardner. I once mentioned on the show how we'd just moved to Connecticut, just gotten Chardonnay, and didn't have a dog-sitter for our upcoming trip to Disney World to do the show. A couple days later I got a letter in our mailbox. It was from a young woman who had just graduated from Fairfield University and lived right around the corner. She was the sixth of seven children, and she said she had done plenty of house-sitting in our neighborhood. I loved the sunny, heartfelt spirit—and the beautiful penmanship—of the note, and we hired Christine as our house- and dog-sitter.

Two years later, a few weeks before Cody was born, we hired Christine away from her job at *Rolling Stone* to be our nanny—one of the best moves we've ever made. I never wanted some Gestapo-style nanny helping to raise my child. I knew I was going to bring the baby to the studio, so that meant I was going to spend a lot of time with this person. She had to be fun to be around. I didn't want some tyrant going: "Time for das Nap! Dis child vill sleep now for TVENTY minutes." I wanted to give my baby security, not regimentation.

We lucked out with Christine. Clearly, the woman's single greatest strength is that she laughs at my jokes. She even laughs when there *is* no joke. Everything I say she howls. I go, "Hiya, Christine," she howls. You've got to love someone like that! If she didn't have a sense of humor, she'd have been gone once I started breast-feeding. Going through that nightmare may have ruined Christine's desire to be a mother, but she saved motherhood for me. She and Cody now have an unbelievably strong bond. *Really* strong. So strong that Cody sometimes wants Christine over me. That hurts, but I know he's loved by both of us and he feels secure, which is most important. Frank claims that he wants no more children, but we've repeatedly tried to adopt her. I can't *believe* her parents won't let us. We also have an extended family that includes Amanda Malin, and Ted and Frances Kessler who take wonderful care of all of us.

Important, too, for Cody is Saturday eggs with Daddy, which is where "The Saturday Egg Song" came from.

I live for Saturday mornings when I get to sleep late. Sunday we go to church, and I'm up before dawn every weekday morning to do the show, but Saturday mornings are Frank and Cody time.

I went into the kitchen one Saturday morning, awakened by their screaming and howling. I had no idea *what* was going on. Talk about male bonding through waffle batter—the stuff was everywhere! Frank's Mickey Mouse waffle iron was *smoking*. There were Cheerios on the floor, chunks of bruised banana smeared all over Cody's face, eggshells and yolks and milk and flour wherever I looked. A cyclone had hit the kitchen. And they were having the time of their lives. That's when I wrote the song:

> It's a Saturday egg,
> It's a Saturday egg,
> my egg, my daddy and me;
> It's a Saturday egg,
> I don't have to beg
> for my egg, my daddy and me. Everybody!
> It's a Saturday egg . . .

I sang it on the show, just to be gooney, and everywhere I went after that people said, "Sing 'The Saturday Egg Song,'" or "I taught my kid the egg song."

And now I go to my concerts or my appearances, and people start yelling out, "Sing 'The Saturday Egg Song.'"

I just say I can't, that I sold the rights to Madonna.

I sing all kinds of stupid songs for Codes. It turns out that I write very good stupid songs. I don't write any good *good* songs, just good gooney ones:

> *I have a pup named Chablis Laurie.*
> *She is as precious as puppies can be;*
> *She has a sister named Chardon—nay*
> *They smell each other's butts all through the day.*
> *They wake up in the morning and jump on our bed,*
> *Then go out to poo-poo with Frances and Ted;*
> *They bark at the strangers that come to the do-o-o-r;*
> *They have their lunch, then they poo on the floor.*

I mean dumb stuff like that, but Cody loves them.

And what's better than to know your little boy loves his mom? I was taking a bath not long ago, having just put Cody to sleep. I had a really dorky shower cap on as I was washing, shaving my legs, and all that. I suddenly heard Cody screaming, so I jumped up, threw a towel around me, and rushed downstairs. He was holding on to the side of the crib, wailing at the top of his lungs. He took one look at me, instantly stopped bawling, and said, "You wook pwetty, Mommy," then promptly resumed his wailing. He'd rolled over, banged his head on the crib rail, and, though he was okay, it had scared him.

I consoled him, still wearing my ugly shower cap, dripping wet, and looking like a rag doll.

But to Codesville, I was pretty.

It made my day! *I can just hear Reege gagging as he reads this*, but IT MADE MY DAY!

I'm Just a Girl Who Can't Say No, I'm in a Terrible Fix

☆

If you want the white picket fence and all that," I told Marla Maples right off the bat, "then you'll have to marry Farmer Jones. You'll never have that with Donald. If you think that's ever going to change after getting married, you're wrong."

Not that I was ever the world's leading strategist when it came to "getting your man." I've never been that kind of woman. I never said, "Gee, well tonight I'm going to wear the push-up bra and the fishnet stockings, and that'll hook him, and I'll cook for him and then just reel him in." I never knew how to do that stuff. If it didn't happen naturally between two people, it didn't happen. I wasn't one to force things. I didn't show up at parties I wasn't invited to. I'm not one of life's gate-crashers. Or husband-stealers. Or home-wreckers.

Once Frank and I fell in love, we took no prisoners, we took no *parishioners*. We just up and married by the ocean. Talk about *The Art of the Deal*. When it came to closing on marriage, it was Frank Gifford, not Donald Trump, who wrote the book.

Whether life was going smoothly in Trumpville or not, Marla Maples always expressed envy of what Frank and I had going for us—the very private farmhouse outside the city, devotion, trust, communication, nurturing, the child, the home, the haven, the work of pulling together day in and day out to make it work.

To her, we *did* have it all. She was living my idea of a nightmare. Day one was sometime in August 1990, when Regis and I were appearing at the Trump Castle in Atlantic City and Donald and Marla were appearing daily in every tabloid headline in the city. They were putting on quite a show, what with the divorce deliberations between Donald and Ivana and the rabid, rumormongering about Marla, whom I, like everyone else following the stories, figured was your basic gold-digging, home-wrecking drop-dead gorgeous fox.

Well, I got that last part right.

I did not *want* to like Marla. Frank and Donald had been golf buddies for years at the Winged Foot Country Club in Westchester. We had been guests of Donald and Ivana's on their yacht and had run into Donald and the very gracious, glamorous Ivana at charity events around town and at the casinos when Reege and I performed. I always enjoyed spending time around Ivana, a lovely, hardworking, and effortlessly amusing woman.

I especially remember lunch at the Jockey Club with Ivana, my friend and colleague Claudia Cohen Perelman, and Joy Philbin. Cody was still a daily companion at the studio. We were talking babies. "I told de doctor," Ivana said in her brisk, inimitable accent, "vut time each child should be born because I had to be out of de hospital de next day." She was hilarious—and gorgeous in her svelte and impossibly chic Ungaro suit. It was impossible to think she'd been pregnant three times. "I vas in, dey take de baby, and I vas out. Den I go home."

I liked her and was saddened by all the sordid details once the tabloids were off on a rampage of rumor and misinformation. It hit the fan with a shouting match in Aspen the previous Christmas between Ivana and Marla, the "other woman." Editors were dying and going to headline heaven—from "IVANA BETTER DEAL" (than the $25 million prenup) to "BEST SEX I EVER HAD" (Marla whispered about Donald).

Every day Regis would hold up another front page and I'd feel bad that their private life was so maliciously and mercilessly exposed. I openly backed Ivana and felt she carried herself through the whole media circus with great elegance and dignity. It was a humiliating position for her to be in. No one could figure out how much of it Donald was orchestrating. He, at times, seemed to be amused by it all.

The truth was, I didn't even *know* the truth—until one night at the Castle in August 1990 when I had just finished my portion of our show. I raced off to my dressing room, took a quick shower, and sat barefoot and soaking wet in my robe, gearing up for the show's finale. I heard a knock on my door.

"Mrs. Gifford," someone called from the hallway, "Donald Trump would like to say hello."

"Just a second!" I shouted.

A half second later, in strode Donald with Marla, even more drop-dead dazzling and taller than she looked in her pictures—one of the most gorgeous creatures on the planet. "Hi. We watch you and Regis all the time," she said in a girlish, low-pitched Georgia drawl.

I wanted to dislike her but couldn't. There was something vulnerable about her that defied her rather racy image. Donald asked me to keep their visit—and the obvious fact of their very real relationship —off the record and off the air. I agreed.

I sensed Marla wanted to get together with me, but there was no way I would pursue a friendship until Donald and Ivana had reconciled or divorced. I'm all for saving a marriage, especially when there are children involved, and I was still holding out hope for the Trumps. Actually it was none of my business or anyone else's.

I didn't see Marla again until March of 1991, when Regis and I played the Trump Taj Mahal. By then the divorce was final and Donald and Marla were out in the open. I was warned, however, by a Trump official not to take it personally if they didn't stay for the entire Friday-night show for high rollers. "Mr. Trump can't sit still that long," they told me. But they did stay, and they even came back on Saturday. I teased Regis, telling him it was because Donald loved his singing.

Then we got it. Between shows, they came backstage. Marla, her mom, Ann Ogletree, and a friend chatted me up for an hour while Donald cornered Frank for an intense *mano-a-mano*. Again, Marla impressed me as a small-town girl at heart with none of the jaded, jagged edge of a gold-digger. Ironically, I felt *Donald* had struck gold and Marla had fallen in love with the wrong guy.

I later asked Frank what plays were called in the huddle. I learned that Donald had admitted there was trouble in paradise but felt that Marla was "the greatest thing that had ever happened" to him. But he was afraid all the "good stuff" of an affair would get ruined if they married, and he wanted Frank's take. So did I.

"I told him I had the same concerns before we got married," he said, "but that I love you much more now than I did five years ago. So I said you've got to commit or risk losing her. Don't play games and blow it. Marry her if you love her. Think long and hard," Frank warned him. "You can find a different beautiful body every night of the year if that's what you want. But Marla loves you. If you play games with that, you're a fool."

Donald clearly was still reeling from his messy divorce—not to mention his crumbling real estate kingdom. But if he walked in scared of *marrying* Marla, Frank now had him terrified of *losing* her. They left, walked through the Taj lobby into Tiffany's, and Donald bought her her first engagement ring. By Monday morning the headlines were shrieking the news—though Donald was hedging, unsure of his commitment to Marla and of his obligations to his bankers.

Marla called a couple weeks later and we agreed to have lunch at Neary's, off the paparazzi path, in late April. I showed up with Christine, Cody, and my assistant, Mickey, and we were seated way in the back. Ten minutes later life as we knew it in Neary's stood still as Marla breezed through the place in a very short, skintight, lime leather skirt and jacket, her honey-colored mane piled on top of her head. I mean, a hundred mouths full of turkey stuffing and lamb chops dropped open.

"I wondered if I should even come today," she said breathlessly before she even got to the table. She was so cute. "Cracked my nose in the middle of the night." Turned out she'd eaten scampi and OD'd on garlic. When she awoke in the dark to get some water she walked into the edge of the bathroom door and had a quarter-inch cut across the bridge of her nose. She leaned forward for all of us to inspect. "Think I broke it? First thing Donald says is, 'Oh, no, not your *nose!* My favorite part.'"

"Yeah, right," I said.

"Of my face." She giggled.

That's Marla. She doesn't always know what'll come out next. Reminds me of someone I know well.

I was struggling with their affair and my loyalty to Ivana. To clear the air, I came right out and told her that I did not condone what she and Donald had done. I told her that I believe adultery is wrong—not because I'm superior or because I'd never done the same thing myself. But I didn't believe in breaking up people's homes. I told her we could never have a friendship unless "as a Christian, you understand where I'm coming from. I understand how it could have happened but now you have to seek the Lord's guidance in your life."

She sighed. "I feel the same way as you. I never dreamed this could happen." It was clear she'd been raised with a strong Christian heart. I felt sorry for the choices she had made, but her honesty helped us forge a more solid spiritual basis for friendship than I might have imagined.

Marla was there, however, not to discuss the spirit with me, but, in fact, to talk about the flesh—more specifically, Donald's. She asked me how Frank stayed in such incredible shape. Marla was concerned that Donald, like his bank debt, was growing puffier day by day. She called him her Pillsbury Dough Boy. She was worried about stress and had been trying to get Donald away from the room service carts and closer to the treadmills in the Taj spa. Marla is a real health nut with an impossibly perfect leggy, busty body. She hoped The Frank's fitness fetish would rub off on the Donald.

She opened up about all sorts of problems plaguing her—the media hounds, her communication with Donald, his ambition, his collapsing realm, her concern for Ivana and the three children, her distress about her own family being caught in the crossfire, and her genuine worry about her own career.

Oh, and one other: Marla's Pillsbury Dough Boy had his eye on a new cupcake. This time it was ravishing swimsuit model Rowanne Brewer. Marla told me Donald had assured her he wasn't sleeping with her, but that it "was important to keep up the image as a player." This, of course, was devastating to Marla, who's an old-fashioned one-man girl. She had, after all, been living underground at Donald's beck and call, waiting for phone calls to arrange clandestine meetings. To me, that's a horrendous, hurtful life. Yet Marla didn't feel demeaned; she felt it was time for him to tell the world he loved her.

We hardly knew each other, really, and I was struck by her openness. I felt compassion and fondness for her. She was struggling with her own values, as I had once done in the years between my divorce from Paul and my marriage to Frank, when I was fed up with living by the Book but ended up ashamed of my new life-style. She said she never planned to fall in love with a married man, just as I had never planned on marrying the wrong man the first time around. Or marrying a divorced man, or being single at thirty, or remarrying a man twenty-three years older than I. But I told her we don't pick and choose the people or times we fall in love. It just happens. And while it was clear she loved Donald, she was chained to him, too. I tried to share with her my belief that when you fall in love, you must fall in love with a man the way he is now, because marriage won't change anything, except maybe your tax deductions.

I sensed I was one of the few new people outside the Trump organization who had shown Marla any kindness and whom she felt she could trust. At the Taj, she and Donald didn't seem to have friends around them, only Trump employees. She seemed trapped in the Trump bubble. Donald seemed to want her with him around the clock, although he professed to support her career. She was in a no-win situation.

At the end of lunch, I was exhausted. As those sexy, perfectly toned legs disappeared into the long black Trump limo outside Neary's (I wasn't *so* tired that I didn't notice), I waved good-bye with a heavy heart for Marla's plight, thinking, Things are never as they seem and realizing how grateful I am that my own life really is so simple and fulfilling next to hers.

How did I end up a confidante? It was a strange position for me. Frank didn't understand this new friendship at first. Later he came to genuinely like Marla, but she's the type of woman he would have totally discounted in the past as a bimbo. Yet now Marla trusted me as a fellow Christian. She also saw the support I get from Frank to do my own thing, and she longed for that in her own life. She also saw the respect Donald had for Frank. She said more than once that if she could have anyone else's type of marriage it would be ours. I am not comfortable with other people's envy, which is usually misplaced or misinformed. But in this matter I couldn't honestly blame her. Lives like hers and mine tend to appear glitzy and perfect. But that's just surface. I never see our life as perfect. Nor is hers. But she'd seen Donald through the divorce and the demise of his manipulated image of invincibility. Marla was in a bind: She wanted the picket fence, but she also wanted the stone wall around the mansion, the glitter and glamour, too.

It's awfully rare to successfully combine the two. If anyone imagined Frank and I had done it, it was because no more than two percent of our lives glitters and glimmers. The other ninety-eight percent is getting up in the morning, going off to work, rushing home to see the little guy, catching up with each other, and going to bed. And so, as simple and dull as that may seem to outsiders compared to jetting all over the world in private planes, my life started to look better to me all the time. You can't put a price on the simple joys and the inner peace they bring.

Marla's big mistake was seeing herself as Donald's spiritual salvation at a time when he needed debt restructuring as much as religious conversion. Still, Marla clung to the notion that she could lead Donald to the Lord.

That spring the tabloids were almost always wrong, but I managed, against all odds, to keep my mouth shut on and off the air. Donald and Marla were not happy, that was for sure. If we ever ran into them, Marla would mutter, "I'm so angry with him. Can you believe what he just did?" I once called her to ask her how she was, and she picked up the phone screaming: "I HATE you! I don't want to have anything to DO with you! Just leave me ALONE!"

I said, "Marla?"

A mortified gasp. "Oh, my God, I'm so sorry. I thought it was Donald, and I was having a fight with him."

Oh? I'd have never guessed. And I'm thinking, *This is hopeless.*

Donald has his boyish, even humble, moments behind the armor of brashness. But there was something pitiful about the way Marla, like so many women, latched on to the man as if she were an appendage. Back then Donald was not the end of her rainbow; he was the thunderstorm beforehand. What she truly wanted, Donald did not have to offer. Donald and Frank had utterly distinct game plans in life. Apples and oranges. Hardballs and footballs.

It wasn't as if I was pleading with Marla to hang in there, either. I found myself hoping she would move on and find a man who truly loved and treasured her and would allow her to be what she could be. That's why, I think, she felt that I was "so perfect," to use her words.

In late June, Susan and Don Meredith visited us from Santa Fe. We had put an addition on our old farmhouse, and it was completed ten minutes before they arrived, literally. I almost asked the carpenters and painters to stay for lunch and tennis. I wanted to honor the Merediths with a big lunch and have a ladies' tennis day for Susan, an ace for whom our court was informally named. Frank planned a golf outing for the Dandy Donald and the husbands of my Connecticut friends, all really fine ladies who are very settled and very married with children, some of them with grandkids.

Frank included Donald for golf, and he brought Marla. The ladies were all nervous about her coming for lunch—and about "How am I gonna look in my tennis outfit compared to her?" If such insecurity was *ever* well founded, this was the day.

"Please be fair," I asked them. "Give her a chance. But forget the tennis outfits, girls!"

Marla breezed in, adorable, gorgeous, *to die.* In two hours she'd warmed and disarmed everyone: How old are your kids? Do you like the schools here? I love your outfit. (Sure. Thanks, sweetie.) She was so radiant and happy. And I'd never seen Donald so relaxed and ebullient. He and Frank had won the eighteen-hole round. He had probably never been in such modest surroundings, nor had I ever before seen him without a tie.

Donald showered and put his suit back on. Then Marla joined us, having showered and dressed for dinner, and he became tense and competitive. He demanded she join him on the tennis court. She refused. Then he insisted Susan play him. He borrowed Frank's tennis shoes and made a big show of whipping her 6 to 1. Then he badgered Marla until she caved in too.

Some of our guests stayed until midnight and played pool. That was more of the same. Marla was furious because Donald got crazed whenever she missed a shot. Pool was life or death for him, like everything else. "That's going to be the longest ride home to Manhattan in the history of the world," I said to Frank as the Trump limo left.

Days later, on June 26, a Wednesday, the *Post* stunned tabloid readers everywhere with its headline, "Donald Dumps Marla for Carla," and a story about Carla Bruni, a sultry Italian model Donald was alleged to be dating. But then Sue Carswell, a *People* reporter who'd been on the Trump watch ever since Aspen, phoned Donald for a quote.

Donald called Sue back and, in a bizarre, rambling interview, pretended to be his own press agent ("John Miller"). Supposedly speaking for Trump, "John Miller" explained it was just too soon for Donald to commit to Marla. He also boasted that just about every gorgeous single woman in the country, including Madonna, was interested in Trump. And that the real estate business was doing "tremendously well." And what about Carla? She was, "John Miller" explained, the daughter of a wealthy Italian family. Trump, he said, had met her at a fashion show and was taken with her. He claimed she stopped seeing Eric Clapton to see Mick Jagger and stopped seeing Mick Jagger to see Donald Trump. Sue was justifiably skeptical and played the tape for columnist Cindy Adams, fellow staffers, and others, all of whom confirmed her weirdest suspicions. Then she played it back for Marla, who broke down and sobbed when she heard Donald's comments. Donald, she said, had already phoned Marla to assure her the *Post* piece was wrong.

This was just before the big four-day July Fourth weekend.

Donald called to invite Frank to play golf. I got on the phone and asked him about Marla. It was too soon to get married, he said. Donald had done nothing to dispel the rumors. Then he said, "I think she'd really appreciate hearing from you." He gave me a 609 area code, which was weird. If they were finished, I wondered why she was still in his Atlantic City apartment.

"How could he hurt me like that?" Marla asked. She sounded shell-shocked, and I felt an instinct to protect the poor girl. The real story as I heard it was that there *was* no affair with Carla Bruni.

Donald and Marla had mutually agreed to take a breather. The "John Miller" scam, Marla later said, was "one of Donald's cute little jokes."

"Well, if you want to exchange one zoo for another," I told her, "you're welcome to come here this weekend. We're having Frank's three kids and five grandchildren, and every room's taken. But Christine has the weekend off, so you can have her bed." I paused for a reaction, but all I heard was soft sobbing. "It might be good," I went on, "for you to be around children, get your head centered, see that another world exists. Do some healing, get in touch with who Marla is and what really counts. But I'm warning you," I added, "it won't be sexy and glamorous. Frank grills, we swim, play tennis. We'll take a boat ride on the Sound. At least no one will find you here. Think about it."

"I'd love that," she said, choking back tears.

A couple of hours later she was on her way, driven by a Trump bodyguard.

Many people—fans, family, friends—have criticized my offer, but there was no question at all in my heart. It was the Christian thing to do. My faith is based on hope and forgiveness, and Marla needed both. I did the kind, loving thing, which is not always the thing I end up doing. And then I sighed, thinking, Oh, boy, here we go. We were heading straight into the eye of Hurricane Donald-and-Marla.

Marla blossomed the moment she arrived. With no makeup and wearing some of my clothes, she was more radiant than ever. I left for the show, and she hung out and had her coffee, kibbitzed with Cody and the grandchildren, blended right in with the Gifford children, made small talk with our help, watched our show Friday morning, swam laps, played tennis.

Meanwhile, Frank did his Mickey Mouse waffle iron thing, serving up a side order of wisdom. "As much as I like Donald," he told her, "you've got to do what'll make you happy."

We hardly put on a show, but Marla saw plenty of the Golda and Moishe Having-It-All Revue: the laughter, caring, mutual support, the sharing of chores, the demanding yet joyous bonds of parenting, and the pleasures of a haven from the city's pressure.

Marla didn't take Donald's calls, and neither did we, but she got up early enough to check the morning papers before we could.

"I've got to get my life together," she said. "I'm going to be happy, and I'm going to get what you and Frank have."

For the first couple of nights she took Christine's bed in Cody's room and put herself to sleep playing his music. "It's like going back to the womb," she said, "with all the pillows and fluff all around. I peeked at Cody a few times and listened to his 'Jesus Loves Me' tapes."

Then she moved upstairs to our old master suite and read herself to sleep with the Bible Frank's mom had given him years ago. Marla knew her way through Corinthians and Psalms and found comfort in her little cocoon.

By Monday it was clear that Marla was staying on. She went sailing on a lake with friends, returning bouncy and bronzed. Her room-mate, Kim Knapp, arrived and Frank served us his famous grilled swordfish with baked potatoes and broccoli. We opened a bottle of wine and sat out on the deck under a beautiful summer night sky with candles flickering on the table.

The four of us began sharing our private thoughts on love and relationships. Frank was wonderful and offered his take on Donald. Then the woman-talk got so emotionally intimate, so intense and deeply spiritual, that he got up. Guess he couldn't stand the heat so he went back into the kitchen—after sweetly clearing the dishes. "I'll just leave you ladies alone," he said.

I'd seen how hurt Marla was, and I didn't want to see her get snared in Donald's world all over again. It turned into an incredible night of prayer and healing—each of us in our own way. I'm a Fundamentalist, and Kim is more broadly New Age–metaphysical, while Marla embraces the worlds of traditional Scripture and psychics. But we were all on the same wavelength that night. By midnight the candles had burned down, and we joined hands. I sent up a prayer that Marla would get her life together and discover God's plan for her. We cried and prayed for Donald's heart to open to the voice of the Lord and for his eyes to see that the pursuit of earthly kingdoms is inane. We prayed for God to break through Donald's ego and show him a peace he didn't think existed. We prayed for Him to reveal the real reason he'd been put here—to glorify our Creator and make the world better than it was when he got here. And I didn't mean net profit after taxes.

Marla prayed for guidance. Kim, the intermediary, told Marla that Donald had bought a second engagement ring and wanted to marry. Kim's reliable reading of the situation was that Donald "was coming from a beautiful place." Marla held out, though. She was frightened to see Donald again and didn't want to give up her newfound autonomy. "Lord, Please help me follow Your will," Marla prayed before sleep. "If it is meant for me not to see Donald, give me the strength not to. If I am meant to see him, please don't let me turn my back on him if he is really ready to be happy again and to trust in God. Give me something in my dreams so I'll know how to handle him tomorrow."

As I lay in bed I thought, How strange to be in the middle of one of New York's hottest, most inaccurately reported stories and not be able to tell anyone about it. Even my mother didn't know.

On Tuesday morning I was wiped out. I told Marla I didn't know how she could survive life under a microscope. But she had never looked better and you didn't need a pair of reading glasses, let alone a microscope, to see that I looked like death warmed over.

Frank and I were scheduled to take a 3:30 P.M. flight to Washington for a White House state dinner that night in honor of the president of South Korea, Roh Tae Woo. I was worked up and excited. Regis teased me about why I got picked to go and he didn't. "The only thing I can think of is I love their grocery stores," I said. *Such* a bizarre remark. "I really do," I went on. "The greatest produce in the whole world." The audience howled.

"Not good enough," he moaned.

Actually, the invitation was the Bushes' way of thanking me for helping Barbara Bush with some of her projects. She and I had in 1990 opened a Variety Club home in New York for babies born with AIDS; I also co-chaired her literacy campaign and sang at the second Reagan-Bush inaugural in 1985.

I rushed home in time to have lunch with Cody, when in walked Marla, who'd been swimming laps. From Thursday to Tuesday, the woman looked ten years younger and seemed happier than ever. She's got the tiny two-piece, the amazing bod, she's tossing her hair back and toweling off. I'm chowing down on chicken salad, Cody's slurping his baba and playing with his food and I'm going, What the heck is she doing IN MY HOUSE, this gorgeous creature? The fact that I could let this sexy knockout strut in a wet bikini with my husband around must say *something* about how safe and secure I am with him.

Marla told me she had agreed to let Donald come up that afternoon—if it was okay with me. "He says he's come to some insights, and I don't know if I even know him anymore, let alone love him." I said fine, if she was sure she wasn't running back into the relationship too soon. "And guard your heart," I warned her. She nodded. If our prayers had softened a spot in her heart for him, as she said, they certainly didn't have the same effect on her thighs. This woman had not one ounce of fat on her body, while I was, well, your basic healthy American girl.

An hour later Frank and I were off and running to the White House. I prayed for Marla to do the right thing. I wasn't sure she would.

This was classic. As Donald was getting ready to unload the famous Harry Winston ring, we were arriving in D.C. only to find out that the car sent to meet us never showed, that Frank had left home without his bow tie and cuff links, and that I'd left without deodorant and razor. Sound familiar, Reege?

The Trump Summit took place in our music room. Donald, acting like a giddy schoolboy, tried to hold Marla's hand, hug her, touch her. *Nothing doing.* Marla didn't want to hurt his feelings, but she told him to stand back and keep talking. Donald pulled the old carat-and-stick routine. He'd pry open the little box, then shut it, open and shut it, teasing her no end. "I don't want to see it," she shrugged.

Donald had the rock, but Marla was the one playing hardball. "I don't need you to make me happy," she said.

He didn't get it. "You have to be dependent on me," he argued.

"No," she said, "it's going to be a healthier love if you'll allow me that." But Marla finally said, "After four years I can't just walk away. I do love you. We're strong enough, we can work it out. I can't fight it, okay?"

No problem. But she couldn't fit it, either. The ring was too big. Donald slipped it back in the box, and off they went to celebrate over dinner at the Old Homestead, a charming and romantic Colonial-style restaurant. At dinner, Donald opened the box a couple times, his eyes twinkling in awe, as he slipped the ring back on Marla's finger each time. (That's why stories had them getting engaged there and not in our music room.)

Now, Marla had the rock but she wouldn't roll. She stood her ground and sent her frisky fiancé home around midnight. Though she "had the goods," as she later put it, she also had the good sense to assume we'd have been furious if she'd let him stay over while we were away. She got *that* right!

I knew none of this when we got up before sunrise the next day to leave our Washington hotel at 5:45 so we could catch a 6:30 shuttle.

We arrived at La Guardia, and Frank drove us into Manhattan. He will not ride when our driver, Zhi Lin, takes the wheel. So Z-100, as we call him, sat in the passenger seat and I was in the back.

I had this whole shtick planned for the show that morning. They had a tacky tiara ready for me, and I was going to make a big—and late—entrance down the stairs, thanking George Bush for dropping me from his helicopter on WABC's roof on his way to Mount Rushmore. I wanted to stick it to Reege about missing out on this great dinner. But I was a little nervous about host chat, and I was exhausted.

It had indeed been a grand and magical and memorable night. Cinderella wore a strapless emerald green satin ball gown. I was seated at Secretary of State James Baker's left. Frank was at Marilyn Quayle's table. It was the only time we allowed our hosts to separate us. I kept looking at Frank, like, Can you believe we're sitting here at the White House? If they could only see me now.

Or hear me. I was terrified I'd ask the secretary of state something like how Saddam and Madame were doing. The Velcro on my gown belt kept un-Velcroing all evening. Frank and I were pushed out on the dance floor with only the Bushes and the Quayles before 130 guests. I wanted to die. "How 'bout that Secretary Baker, huh?" I blurted out to the Bushes for no reason whatsoever—then buried my face in Frank's chest as they literally waltzed right by.

My kind of night.

But what a host chat it would make, if only I could pull it off!

I went over and over it as we went over the Triboro Bridge.

Suddenly Frank said, "The poop's gonna hit the fan any minute, Golda. You can't keep this Marla-and-Donald business a secret indefinitely."

At that very instant, the car phone rang. It was my assistant, Mickey, saying, "Marla wants to speak to you."

Marla was giggly when she broke the news: "Donald asked me to marry him last night and gave me this gorgeous Harry Winston diamond. Kim and I think it's about eight carats. I was happy but told her to make sure it's for real this time. Then she wanted *me* to make sure it's for real. Donald wants you to call him," she said, "so you can announce it on your show."

Did I need this? I freaked. "Honey, I'm gonna be in a ball gown with a fake tiara sliding off my head. You sure you want me to announce it?"

"Absolutely. Just call Donald."

I was flabbergasted. This was insane. I had no idea it would come to this. I couldn't get through to Donald as airtime approached. I was getting crazy. "What should I do?" I fretted to Frank, to whom I can always turn in crises.

"Go for it if it's what they want," he said.

I wasn't about to make a complete idiot of myself by playing along with another publicity stunt. Frank kept the redial going and gave Donald my dressing room number.

At 8:50 Donald confirmed Marla's account—and his request. "You've been a great friend to us and I want you to be the one to break the story." I was still leery: "I'll tell you what. I'll do it if you'll get on a phone hookup with Regis and me and confirm it yourself. Otherwise I won't. And be advised that I'm going to look like a complete dork, with this cockeyed tiara on my head."

He laughed. "Okay. But you call me. Otherwise it'll look like a setup."

I cracked up at this typical Donaldism. "It IS a setup!"

A minute before air, I called my parents and asked them to pray for me. I told my mother why. "Oh, good grief!" she gasped.

I knew my entrance could go either way—hysterical or suicidal. I needed just the right tacky effect. Now I was totally distracted. Regis opened the show sitting alone. "I knew she would do this," he crabbed, looking around bug-eyed.

Then I made my big entrance, sweeping down the stairs, waving to the imaginary commander in chief. "The President's on his way to Mount Rushmore and he just dropped me off."

"Did I *tell* you she'd make an entrance?" Reege asked.

"Is he a guy? What a night! What a party! What a country!"

"Looks to me like the President got a little frisky," Reege said, noticing my tired eyes and tiara.

It was a fabulous segment. Reege was brilliant. I told him all about the awesome White House evening, deodorant and all. "You don't want to turn South Korea against us, do you?" he asked. I told him how Frank whipped out pictures of Cody to show the First Lady and talked golf with the President Bush as people tried to nudge him along the receiving line.

"Frank *boring* Mrs. Bush again," Regis zinged, rolling his eyes.

Reege was dying to know if President Bush had sent his regards. I had read notes written to Regis by other luminaries who were at the dinner. One was from Famous Amos: "Aloha, Regis, sorry you could not make it. We had a great time. Wally Amos."

Regis's misery was hilarious. "Thanks, Wally. Not the President. But thanks."

I told of how when we were walking out—Secret Service guys were everywhere—one very elegant but very large Korean lady looked at me and shouted: "I know you. You nine o'clock," before lunging at me with her camera.

"Did SHE ask for me?" Regis wanted to know. He asked if the secretary of state had sent regards. I held up one last note. "Here it comes," Reege said proudly. "This is either the President or Secretary of State Baker."

I read the note: "Regis, sorry you couldn't make it. We missed you. Jim Baker." It was written on the secretary's official card.

"That's IT! Thanks, Jim!" The audience screamed for Regis.

I handed Reege some White House mints. "They look like the same mints I had at the Ramada Inn," I told him. "I don't want to say anything."

He rolled his eyes—"Now the gamey part"—when I said I had to go potty right before the cordials were served and met up with Jaclyn Smith—the two most beautiful women on TV, in the White House together.

"Jaclyn Smith goes to the *ladies' room?*" Reege barked incredulously.

"Only to brush her hair, Reege."

Reege nitpicked about a positive *USA Today* piece—Sally Jessy likened him to a crazy uncle in the family whom nobody really likes but who keeps getting invited to parties.

"Not the PRESIDENT'S party," I teased.

Regis then mentioned how nervous he was about a trip to Europe that night. As he spoke he popped a strip of plastic packing bubbles.

Then I had to make my move. I cut Regis short to say I had a "serious announcement." Panic swept his face. He never knows if I'm kidding or for real. He promptly started popping more of his worry bubbles.

I set it up by saying that Marla had been secretly hiding out with us and that the reporters had missed the story. "But the truth is, last night at our house, Donald Trump gave Marla Maples an eight-carat diamond ring from Harry Winston, and they *are* engaged, they *are* getting married, and they're very happy."

I thought Regis would drop his teeth. It got real crazy. I dialed Donald on the trivia question phone, only to hear, "I'm sorry but we cannot complete your call as dialed. Please try again later or ask your operator for assistance."

Reege was stunned. He kept popping bubbles. "This is a big story folks," he said. "And you heard it first on your uncle's show!" He got so flustered he gave away the trivia answer. "One of the more popular films shown on July Fourth," he read, "is the 1942 classic *Yankee Doodle Dandy* with Jimmy Cagney." Great. He was supposed to ask who starred in it. The audience screamed with delight.

We finally got Donald on the phone for the dramatic live TV world exclusive. "Hello," Reege said.

"Hello," Donald answered warily.

"Donald?" Reege said.

"Hello, who's this?" Donald asked.

" 'Who's *this?*' This is King FAROUK! Who's THIS?"

It had to be one of the wildest opening segments ever—a perfectly fitting climax to one of the craziest weeks since Frank and I got married.

But it wasn't over. After the show every camera crew in the world was lined up outside for interviews. I was ready to sneak out the back, but I called Donald first. He said it was okay to talk to them. I knew Donald had plans to fly off to Paris that evening with Marla. "By the way," he said, "I don't want to go to Paris now. I want to hang out with you guys. Let's play golf and have lunch at Winged Foot."

The sound bites took me an hour. I was shell-shocked. Living this way, I said to myself, would kill me in three days.

I was exhausted beyond eating. I was much closer to clubfoot than Winged Foot. I passed on Donald's golf and dinner invitation, but others went. Marla caused quite a stir when a Harry Winston rep showed up on the golf course to size the ring. That night we all celebrated the engagement at an Italian restaurant in Bedford, New York.

The next day, a Thursday, was July Fourth, and I had the day off. We had a bunch of friends over—including Donald and Marla, our new houseguests. The emperor, however, still had no tennis clothes. Frank had to drive into town to Woolworth's, the only store that was open, and buy Donald socks, underwear, a sweatshirt, and shorts. Donald wore Frank's tennis shoes again. I'd never seen him happier than in his five-dollar Woolworth shorts, knowing the press and paparazzi were hunting for him all over Paris.

That night we rushed out to catch *Dying Young*—Donald was dying to look at Julia Roberts. We quietly settled down in this mostly empty theater, and Donald, sitting in front of us, got cute. He turned around and said, "Hey, everybody, Frank Gifford! Can you believe it?

Right here. All-American! Hall of Famer!" Playful, boyish Donald. And we're going, "Donald, will you just shut up!"

We saw some fireworks and went for Mexican food at Tucson in Greenwich. Marla looked spectacular, but I mean to die—her hair tied back, her body poured into this form-fitting red body suit that left nothing to the imagination. As usual I was schlepping around in an outfit that left nothing to the unimaginable. I gave her a long blouse to drape over herself because I just think there are laws against walking around in bodysuits like that. I kept saying to myself, *It's okay, I had a baby, I had a baby. My breasts sag like this for a reason. It's okay.*

We got home and I gently directed Kim, Donald, and Marla to three rooms in the guest wing. I have no idea how many were used. My mother would have had a fit with anything fewer than three. I asked no questions.

It had become pretty clear to me why Marla envied us, and even clearer why she flourished and came to life during her stay. I doubted if Donald could ever give her what she really needed. Marla loves people, loves people to understand her heart. My feeling was that, for the sake of her mental and physical health, Marla should have just ended the relationship—divorce Donald before she ever married him.

On July 5, it was time for them to leave and for us to get back to normal. We were happy for them and wished them great happiness. I teased Donald. "I'll never let you build a helipad on our grounds or turn our ponds into skating rinks." But we were, in all honesty, relieved when they were gone. I told Frank, "Let's just get this over with and burn the sheets."

We certainly hadn't heard the last of their spats, though. Nor had the reaction to our July 3 show been unanimously supportive. Befriending them wasn't exactly a career move for me. Many fans harshly accused me, in so many words, of harboring a harlot, a slut, a home-wrecker. My mother, a loving Christian woman, also saw Marla that way. But when Mom met her in Atlantic City, she liked Marla. It's hard not to. So I wrote those people back, saying I was a friend to Marla in her time of struggle. Jesus, I noted, would have done the same. He took in Mary Magdalene, who was a prostitute.

Two months later, in early September, Marla was still struggling. She called me at 3:00 A.M. in my Atlantic City hotel room. I was awake, having hosted Miss America and just returned from the big post-pageant bash. I'd seen her, and she looked emaciated, haggard, ten years older. She looked like another human being.

"I broke up with Donald tonight," she said solemnly, without tears. "Every time I get around you and Frank I see what you have and it makes me so unhappy with the way Donald treats me."

"You'll never be his salvation," I said. "The Lord is. You can't be someone's salvation when you're sleeping with him. It only confuses the issues."

She said she understood me. "Well," I sighed, "your room is always ready, any time you want to come back and see us."

But a couple months later over a fall weekend, when Billy Graham came to town for his Crusade in Central Park, I had to draw the line. That Friday, I took Cody to visit his nanny, Christine, who'd had her tonsils out that week. She told me that Donald had gone golfing that day at Winged Foot and told his golf partner that he had "dumped her for the last time today," or words to that effect. The golf partner, Bobby Williams, happened to be Christine's brother-in-law.

I got on the phone, and Donald confirmed the remark. "Well, I guess I should make the bed upstairs. I know she'll be calling," I predicted.

The headlines hit the papers on Saturday; Donald had apparently told the press before he let Marla know.

Then, right on cue, Kim called. Marla was in Cape May and wanted to come up and go to Billy's Crusade with me. Yeah, right. Marla and me. The Restless Ones. Immediately, I think, this is a bad idea. Billy Graham does not need Marla Maples on that dais that day. He's there for deeply spiritual reasons, and Marla in a mini—I'm not sure even Billy Graham could deal with that. Plus, paparazzi and prayer wouldn't exactly mix well on the Great Lawn in Central Park.

"Tell Marla I kinda think that's the worst thing in the world she could do right now," I told Kim. "For her sake and the rally's sake, I don't think she should come."

I was relieved that their romance was over. My feeling was that if you're not blissfully happy when you're engaged, you don't have a whole lot of hope once you marry. As fiancés, they were a fiasco. But I did invite her to a dinner with my old pal Jantina from ORU. (She is married to Greg Flessing, whose company produces Billy Graham's television programs.)

What a strange time that was. I was so grateful for the one thing Frank and I clearly didn't have going for us—the life of tabloids, turmoil, paranoia, and paparazzi. As I told Donald, I'd last a week—and then I'd croak. I can't imagine living with all that.

I remember when Frank and Cody and I stood on our porch and waved good-bye as the Trump limo rolled away the morning after Independence Day. All I could think was, I swear, we've been in a David Lynch movie.

What the World Needs Now
Is Love, Sweet Love

☆

The doctor emerged from the examination room with words that only confirmed what I already knew.

"You've had a miscarriage, Kathie."

For months Frank and I had been hoping to conceive another child. We had made our decision on New Year's Day 1991, while Frank was covering the Sugar Bowl for ABC Sports in New Orleans.

Since Cody had been born, people had repeatedly asked us when we were going to have another child. Women, especially, floored me by saying, "Oh, just have one. What's Frank going to do, divorce you?"

I was shocked that some women thought it was perfectly okay to *deceive* a husband and *conceive* a baby even if he didn't want one.

I wanted another baby, but only if Frank wanted one, too. I decided to trust the Lord to change Frank's heart if it was His Will for us.

Then, out of the blue, on a beautiful balmy day while strolling in New Orleans, Frank surprised me and said, "You know, honey, I think Cody should have a little brother or sister. I think you should go off the pill right away." We immediately walked into a beautiful church and knelt and prayed together that the Lord would bless our decision.

Months passed as we waited for what had been so effortless three years before.

Finally, in early July 1992, my pregnancy test came back positive. I was even more ecstatic this time and Frank seemed genuinely overjoyed as well. We made plans to rearrange schedules and redecorate rooms in anticipation of the baby's April arrival. Cody was thrilled and was sure the baby was "a widdle gurl."

I told Regis and Joy and they were delighted.

"Oh, good grief," laughed Reege, "here we go again."

Then Frank and I left for a much-needed vacation in Colorado.

I was totally exhausted from taping our TV shows, finishing my book and album projects, performing our nightclub act, and fighting allergies. You can't take medications when you're pregnant, and so I felt like one huge throbbing mucous membrane.

I was also particularly upset by a tabloid cover story that was scheduled to appear within days on the newsstands, proclaiming in no uncertain terms that my first husband was gay. Sure enough, I was disgusted to find in the article statements from a so-called "longtime friend" quoting me as saying this was true. This was not true, but a flat-out lie, and I felt sick inside for Paul and his family. I left a message on Paul's answering machine, saying, "The only thing you're guilty of is having been married to me. You don't deserve this, and I want you to know that I ache inside for you and your family."

The whole tabloid episode left an emotional cloud over our vacation, though physically I still felt great, just as I had with Cody. No morning sickness or swelling or anything. I had no reason to expect that this wouldn't be an equally healthy pregnancy.

Then, on August 22, when I was seven weeks pregnant, I began to bleed and panic. I immediately called my dear friend Emily Beck, my Lamaze instructor, and she told me to stay in bed, drink plenty of fluids (I was suffering from a terrible cold as well), and call Dr. Langan with my progress. I finally reached him and he instructed me to retrieve any tissue I might pass and save it in hopes of discovering a reason for any sudden miscarriage.

I hung up the phone just as Frank came in the front door from fishing with Cody and Christine and I immediately lunged for the bathroom.

It happened that fast and I will never forget leaning over the toilet and crying, "Oh, my God! Oh, my God!" as I picked up the fetus—my baby—from the bottom of the bowl. Frank tenderly and silently kissed my head and brought me a paper cup. He took it into the kitchen and covered it.

Cody came into the bathroom and began hugging and kissing my leg, saying, "I make you feel bedduh, Mommy. See, I kiss you," while

I struggled to control my anguish. I wanted to mourn but I didn't want to frighten Cody.

Christine's eyes welled up with tears as she hugged me and softly told me how sorry she was. This dear friend who had been with me through so much since the birth of Cody now shared with me the loss of this child.

Frank was already on the phone seeking emergency medical care for me as I came into the kitchen, sobbing at the loss of what just moments before had felt safe inside me.

From the moment it happened, Frank tried to help me see that the baby was better off if it couldn't be healthy, that this was nature's and God's way of aborting a defective child. A child who was much better off in the arms of her Maker than in the womb of her caretaker. I knew Frank was right but still I had to scream and shake and sob and mourn what might have been.

Within moments the phone rang and a voice said, "Dr. Cohen . . . here."

It was an amazingly kind voice, and I answered, "Dr. Cohen, I think . . . I mean I'm sure that I've just had a miscarriage."

There was an audible sigh on the other end of the line and he gently said to me, "That's so sad . . . I'm so sorry."

He instructed Frank to drive me immediately to the hospital in Vail so he could examine me. We climbed into our jeep with the cup that held the fetal tissue. That broke my heart and I started to cry again as Frank stroked my hand and tenderly talked me through the ten-minute trip in the pouring Colorado rain.

Dr. Cohen met us in the parking lot and kindly led us through a maze of unlit corridors and offices until we reached his near the back. It was Saturday and he had avoided the emergency room to protect our privacy. Already we sensed this was a very special man.

Once in the examination room he suddenly asked me, "Are you the one who works with Regis?"

To this Frank laughed and answered, "Well, he's the one who works with *her!* The laughter relaxed us all and Dr. Cohen proceeded to examine me, perform a sonogram, and evaluate the fetal tissue.

Then he told us what I already knew. "You've had a miscarriage, Kathie. The baby could have been dead for two or three weeks and may never have had a chance to properly attach to the uterine wall."

That surprised me, as those same few weeks for me had been

painless, joyful, and full of life. I had never suspected for a moment that this baby was anything but perfect, just as Cody had been.

Dr. Cohen went on to explain that this didn't mean I couldn't get pregnant again or give birth to a perfectly healthy child. At that moment I was thinking about my friend at work, Kathleen, who had had two miscarriages in a row, and my friend Jacquie, who had been on fertility drugs and had just become pregnant, only to start bleeding immediately.

At least I have Cody, I thought, *at least I have one beautiful, healthy boy.* I felt so grateful suddenly, so blessed, and Frank told me later he was thinking the same thing.

As we prepared to leave, Frank asked Dr. Cohen about the forms we needed to fill out and how we should go about paying for his services.

At this question Dr. Cohen slowly looked at us and said, "Well, I've been thinking about that." He leaned forward and brought his hands to rest on his face. "I lost my mother a month ago"—he continued looking at me now—"and she was your biggest fan. You have no idea how much pleasure you brought her and I would just like to do this for her."

I was speechless and crying again so Frank answered for us both. "Well, Doctor, that is so very kind of you. But we want to do something, give to some charity, in your mother's name."

When Dr. Cohen answered he said something I have now written in my heart and will never, ever forget: "Just do something kind for someone," he said, "and tell them to pass it on."

Epilogue

In Our Hands,
There's a World in Our Care

I'm no saint. I've never taken vows of chastity or poverty. I like the things of this world. Being home in my farmhouse with my little boy and my husband is as close to heaven as any place I know on earth.

But it's nothing compared to what God has promised in the next life. Coming to grips with death as early on as possible makes it more imperative in life to find love and caring in your heart for others. We all begin dying the day we're born. That's the life cycle. I see death as a positive step toward a much better place. Meanwhile that means serving the will of God on this imperfect earth, striving as best I can to leave this a better world than I found it.

I've had euphoric glimpses of heaven in dreams, and it's not just strumming harps in white robes and singing hallelujah. It's where our creative limits are lifted off. It's where God has stored the 90 percent of our brains we never get to use in this life. I'll be painting in colors I never saw on earth, hitting notes I could never reach, decorating beautiful rooms with exquisite fabrics I never saw in the Designer and Decorator Building.

All that will be ours in heaven—a place with no angst, no conflict, no agents.

I know most people don't have much joy in the ordeal of this

286

lifetime. So many Christians sing hymns with titles like "In the Sweet By-and-By," a place where they hope to find everlasting peace and where, as another hymn boasts, "Jesus is building a mansion for me."

But in the bittersweet here and now, who's building homes and shelters for the poor? Who's buying toys, clothes, and food for the millions of poor children in this and every other country? Who's funding research for AIDS?

When I moved to New York, I was terrified not of losing my life but of losing my heart for people. I prayed: God, don't let me ever get so caught up in striving here that I lose my heart for people. It doesn't matter whether it's a quarter for a cup of coffee or $1,000 a plate for dinner. God doesn't judge based on whether you've aided a bum off the street or a benefit at the Plaza. He sees straight into the heart that led to the act, and it is God alone who will dispense perfect eternal justice on Judgment Day.

God didn't bless me with success so that I could eat caviar every day. Not a day goes by that the Lord doesn't etch in my heart the passages from Scripture I grew up with: "To whom much is given much is required. . . ." "What does it profit a man if he gains the whole world but loses his very soul?" "Don't store up your treasures on earth, for where your treasure is your heart can be found too."

I feel guilty that my plate is overflowing when millions of American workers and executives have lost their jobs and careers. It isn't fair. It breaks my heart that millions of children go to bed hungry and that others have parents who ignore or abuse them. Charity allows my conscience to coexist with my embarrassment of riches; being a light for the Lord allows me to help fill the void in us that only a spiritual bond can fill.

Not long ago my wonderful friend Neil Sedaka and his beautiful wife, Leba, invited Frank and me to a fashion industry dinner for AmFAR. This was a big event for a critical, politically "hot" charity. The featured attraction that evening was Harry Connick, Jr., whose thirty-five-piece big-band sound had revived the music I grew up hearing. I was eager to hear him.

A benefit gala is not Carnegie Hall. It's tables, waiters, silverware, and glasses. People chat. After his first number Connick said something outrageous like, "If you all don't shut up I'm not going to sing." Was he crazy? No one shuts up at benefits. You can't expect respect. People hadn't paid $1,000 to listen reverently to Harry Connick in concert.

I saw that he was perturbed as he sat at the piano and began his next number. Now, I've seen lewdness, I've seen rudeness (my own included), and I've seen performers walk offstage—but never at a charity event. Sure enough, Connick stopped and said, "It's obvious you people would rather talk than listen, so I'm outta here. Come on, guys." I'd never in my life witnessed such an arrogant move. The crowd was stunned—and outraged.

Frank took charge. "You and Neil've got to get up there and do something," he said. We were in a tough spot. The mood in the room was vitriolic. We walked around to a curtained off area and tried to get up to the makeshift stage, but a guard blocked Frank. "Well," Frank said angrily, "then you tell that little jerk to get his butt out there or I'll get him myself!"

Frank grabbed the mike. "Hey, everybody, I may not be Harry Connick, Jr., but I am Frank Gifford." The crowd went crazy. Then he said we'd be singing a couple of Neil's big hits with Neil at the piano. "You can talk, dance, eat, and laugh all you want. Just have a good time. You paid a lot of money to be here and you deserve better than that."

Neil and I did "Calendar Girl," "Laughter in the Rain," and "Breaking Up Is Hard to Do." Ugliness turned into a sweet moment. The La La Girl knew every word, and the guests danced, sang, and went nuts.

Maybe Harry Connick had his reasons for stalking off the stage, but his stunt left me shocked. Frank said that in forty years in New York he had never seen such rudeness. I hope Connick learned something that night that he'll never learn from a million standing ovations. I did.

My parents still watch closely to see if I've betrayed or abandoned the values they instilled. I know sometimes they think I have. They see our house, the city apartment, the vacation home; they hear the host chat stories of galas and opening nights and dinner at the White House.

But I've tried to show them there doesn't have to be a compromising, corrupting downside to success. They see my work with children's charities like the Police Athletic League, pediatric AIDS work, and the clothing line tied to the Variety Club Children's Charity.

The story of how the Variety Club was founded is a moving one. On Christmas Eve 1928, an infant girl was abandoned in a Pittsburgh movie theater with this note pinned to her little dress:

Please take care of my baby. Her name is Catherine. I can no longer take care of her. I have eight others. My husband is out of work. She was born on Thanksgiving Day. I have always heard of the goodness of show business people, and I pray to God that you will look out for her.

It was signed, "A Heartbroken Mother."

Police and local newspapers tried but failed to locate the parents. Coincidentally, a year earlier the theater's owner and a group of his "show business" colleagues had formed the Variety Social Club in the Pittsburgh area. When the baby was found, they agreed to support her. They named her Catherine Variety Sheridan— Sheridan was the name of the theater. Through the years, the organization has raised half a billion dollars for needy youngsters. It is to Variety—the Children's Charity, the New York chapter, that I have donated portions of the proceeds from my clothing line.

No charity is more rewarding to me than working with children. It was Jesus who said "Suffer the little children to come unto me, and forbid them not. For of such is the Kingdom of Heaven." Ministering to needy children is a way to directly serve the Heavenly Father. It's also investing in the future of this planet—the one Cody and his generation will inherit when we're gone. And it beats handing over all my money over to a wasteful, often corrupt government where an elected official can write hundreds of overdrafts with no penalty. When I donate or help raise money, I know where it's going and whom it's helping.

Yes, money brings a raw, acquisitive power, but it's not intrinsically evil. It's as good or bad as the way you choose to spend it. I love being able to send my parents on a trip, buy Mom a nice piece of jewelry, or send my sister-in-law to Israel to join Davy when he was leading a tour there. If my heart is moved, I love being able to help. There are few joys greater in life than making dreams come true for loved ones. Frank said his greatest accomplishment was buying his parents the only home they ever owned.

But beyond material things, I understand my parents' worry about ego and callousness. I know I've crossed the line and unwittingly hurt or embarrassed Mom by telling stories about her on TV. She sometimes feels that I'm not proud of her because I've taken my life to a different place from hers. The truth is, she is an extraordinary woman who did a spectacular job as a mom. She seems to feel insecure around my "stylish, slender" friends while she struggles with her weight and hasn't had a face-lift. Well, in her world, Mom is by far the most gorgeous woman her age and always has been. No contest. But she loves to cook and eat. I don't love her any less for being overweight. I just want to be able to love her longer. Mom thinks I live in this dream world where everybody's Ivana Trump. Her excuse has always been "Hey, I've had three babies," to which I always respond "Yes, and so has Jane Fonda."

I sure don't get star treatment anywhere around Bowie and Rehoboth. When I'm home, Daddy tells me I'm "just a spot on the wall." I tell Mom, who taught me to sew and cook, that in my heart of hearts I'm much closer to Betty Crocker than to Madonna. A part of me is still fourteen and running home to show her my A in home ec. It's just that this latter-day version is more like Betty "Boom Boom" Crocker, or is it Betty Crock?

One thing is certain: my success hasn't changed *them*. I can see their side, but I wish sometimes they were more open-minded about mine. I went from miserable, divorced, and struggling to a happily married mother and wife and the top share in my time slot—with major claims on my time and energy. To protect their families and their sanity, some performers build a wall around themselves, and before they know it, they start believing their yes-men, they storm off stages, they become the bullying, insulated "stars" they once vowed never to become. I know my parents would never let that happen to me without waging World War III.

Mom wonders if my high-wire act has me drinking too much wine. Of course, Mom has zero tolerance for wine, so when she sees me drink a glass at dinner she thinks I'm just a few steps from the gutter with the Bowery bums. Mom and Dad don't understand the pressure I'm under, and they worry about how I'm handling it. The reality is that when I get overwhelmed and crazed, I'm far more likely to *decorate* than to inebriate. Decorating can become an obsession, but it's therapeutic; it relaxes me. It might *cost* more than therapy, but, hey, no one's perfect. Someday, it's true, I could easily see myself in a twelve-step program at Decorators Anonymous.

Seriously, I don't deny that the potential danger for excess exists. Frank and I enjoy wine together, but I had two alcoholic grandparents. Who's to say that won't happen to me? It's true, though, that if I drank as much as I decorate, I'd probably spend a lot of time admiring the decor at the Betty Ford Center.

Mom, like me, tends to be controlling, and I get impatient and frustrated with her. (That's a bad trait of mine.) I want my parents' pride and approval but I don't wake up and ask myself how I can please them today. I gave up years ago trying to live within their bounds. So at times I'm sure I disappoint them.

For instance, they'll bring friends up from home to visit me backstage in Atlantic City. I shake hands, I'm gracious, I offer refreshments in my dressing room. And then I'm outta there to do a show. Mom wants me to hang out for hours. Her glaring eyes follow me out the door, like, You're *leaving?* I told them long ago that I need my voice and my rest. I don't owe my parents hours of socializing before my show. I owe them respect, gratitude, and boundless affection—which they get.

I make sure they get a beautiful hotel room, front row seats, great meals—the star treatment. But all that is meaningless to them unless they can have the last word before I go onstage and unless they feel they still have impact and, to some extent, control. "We're what matters," they're telling me. "We're here to keep your feet on the ground."

Daddy, at least, is a realist—more pragmatic. But Mom doesn't think twice about laying some heavy guilt trip on me a minute before showtime. Forget my need to focus energy on the show. As Frank says fondly, "Golda, her timing sucks."

Seconds before I walk onstage, she'll say, "Are you sure you should be wearing a dress that short tonight, dear?" Pressure? A full house at thirty dollars a pop? She just assumes her Teflon Tootsie can go on out there and just be brilliant and people will love her.

Then, when I come offstage an hour later, she's *waiting* for me. "Another thing," she'll point out, as if she'd been freeze-framed that whole time, "you really upset your brother when you didn't call on his birthday."

Maybe it *should* be like that. What's so important that it should intrude upon our sacred family bonds? As much as she irks me and makes me crazy in the moment, I love that quality in them. It anchors me to something bigger and better than self-importance. It shows me that, during more than forty years together, their lives have come to stand for something they cherish, something worth fighting to preserve. It would be the ultimate hypocrisy for me to criticize the decline of family values in our country—which I do feel is directly tied to our moral decline—and then not exult in the commitment to family my parents have made all their lives.

My mom's love and respect for me have come through loudest and clearest in something she's *never* said: "How dare you leave your son and go off and have a career? I never did that when you were kids!" She's been a real pillar for me, offering generous praise and keen insight: "You know, Kathie," she has said, "you always beat yourself up and praise me because I was *physically* in the house. But I was cooking, cleaning, laundering, sewing, chatting with girlfriends on the phone, and caring for two other children. None of you ever got the one-on-one love Cody gets when you, Frank, or Christine's with him."

At the heart of the matter is that for years they were able to control me, but they couldn't control David and Michie. And those two are now back in the bosom while I'm more or less the black sheep. The one they "molded" most has strayed farthest from the flock.

But I haven't, really. If anything, now that I am a parent in today's often difficult, depressing world, I feel more urgently than ever the need for a walk with God—not only to continue my own walk but to share Frank's and help Cody begin his. I'm not talking about ornaments and empty rituals, but a joyful, liberating and very personal attachment to a Divine Being. By allowing God's power to manifest itself in our lives, we find more forgiveness, patience, and love than we imagined possible.

I believe we need to turn as much of that power and love as possible toward the children in our world who need it the most—whether their need is food and shelter, education, emotional security, or moral grounding. As the song says, "in our hands, there's a world in our care." I am still haunted by the moment I came face to face with a child in desperate need of all of that.

Just before Thanksgiving 1981, a couple weeks after Paul left me, I was driving through Topanga Canyon to the store when I spotted a young father and mother with their little daughter on the shoulder of the road. Back then "homeless" wasn't a household word in America. They were just hitchhikers.

Seeing the girl's big blue eyes and blond curls, I thought, But for the grace of God she could be Shannie, my niece. I stopped. I had never picked up hitchers before. They wanted a lift to the Ventura Freeway ramp.

The father gave me the short version of their long hard-luck tale. The parents were married and in their mid-twenties. He was a logger from Maine who had lost his job. Eventually they lost their home, hitchhiked to Florida first, then all the way out to the Coast, obviously following the sun before winter. I took pity on them and offered to stop first at the grocery store.

They were a pathetic sight. The parents looked weather-beaten and twice their age. They were uneducated and could barely make sense in English. Their teeth were rotten, their hair was matted down and greased with dirt, and the smell from their bodies didn't leave my car for six months. The closest thing to a toy this little girl had was a foil gum wrapper, and in her obviously rich world of make-believe it had to serve as her baby doll.

My heart was breaking. I flashed on the stuffed animals and toys I stocked at home for Shannie and Davy's kids. The girl was so filthy I was almost ill. "Look," I said, "I have another idea. Let's get the food. Then you guys come back to my house and I'll put you up for the night. I'll wash your clothes and you can take showers."

Oral hygiene maniac that I am, I bought three toothbrushes and some toothpaste and gave them robes. I had two bathrooms. The mother went with her little girl. I started making dinner and loading their clothes in the washer. As I was dropping the man's grimy jacket in, a magazine slid out. I shuddered. It was a repulsive, explicit pornographic magazine. I felt nauseated.

Now I was scared and my mind was racing: I'm cooking dinner for these people, giving them robes and toothbrushes, doing their wash, they haven't slept in beds in months, the parents have no skills, no teeth, the guy's a sex pervert whose mind has been poisoned by a filthy magazine, he probably beats his wife, and this sad little girl, for all I know, has been sexually abused since the day she was born. I suddenly had an urge to take this girl away and keep her. My pity turned to anger. He had three or four dollars for a porno magazine, but his daughter had to play with a gum wrapper? He could have bought her a doll, a pair of shoes, a toy.

It was amazing the way that child's beautiful, innocent face lit up when she came out all sweet-smelling and I gave her Shannie's little books and dolls and tucked her in. I was almost in tears.

Then the phone rang. It was my close friend Michael Redman, who had been best man at Paul's and my wedding. I told him I couldn't talk and explained what happened. "You picked people up off the *street?*" he asked in bewilderment. "They're in your *home* right now? I'll be right over."

"No, please," I said. "That would be too obvious. I'll lock my bedroom door and if there's a problem I'll call immediately."

Then, of course, my mother called. She had a fit that I'd taken in a homeless family for the night.

That was the longest night of my life. I never slept. I lay there in the dark and stared at the door. The next day I called a friend who ran the People's Church in Ventura that had a program to help indigent families. I gave the young woman my number and their number and insisted she call me if she ever needed help.

She did call three times over the next six months, from all over the country, always after being beaten by her husband. I'd get so sad hearing about her and her little girl. These people seemed destined to drift among life's losers. To this day I still think of that poor child, one of God's creatures who never had a chance—an utterly lost human being.

But it's God's work, not ours, to understand the dark recesses of a human heart. Man is not supreme. That thought came to me, among many others, as I listened to the Clarence Thomas confirmation hearings. God's authority is the only perfect law. Our laws are only as good as the people who create and enforce them. True, this republic's Founding Fathers were visionaries and heroes; but they were also mortals with feet of clay. Now I'm raising a child in a world where so many "heroes" not only have feet of clay; they're sinking in moral quicksand. That's all the more reason to try to make the world a better place, not just to ensure our own place in eternity but to ensure our children's place in a safer, more decent, more loving society.

Our culture is in moral chaos. We exult in our First Amendment freedoms and then use them to pump a steady flow of decadent garbage into our kids' brains. On TV we celebrate freaks instead of honest, decent people. There seem to be endless numbers of transvestite orphans with a shoe fetish who married their cross-dressing cousins only to discover that in another lifetime they were aliens who were married to Shirley MacLaine. That's when I say, "Well, so much for wanting an Emmy!"

TV can educate, delight, and soothe. It can also offend, demean, and corrupt. I'm in TV, but I try not to be *of* TV. Our show won the Angel Award from a group called Excellence in Media—for having the highest standards of moral excellence on TV. I was honored but baffled. If we're the highest standard, I thought, let's get Lawrence Welk back here, quick.

Sensationalism and sex are pervasive in the cultural mainstream. We've got "Hard Copy" and soft-core. Where is this wallowing going to lead us? With CNN and satellite news technologies, the world has shrunk. But so has our capacity to comprehend and respond to human suffering. How much death and tragedy can our eyes take in before we're numbed or poisoned?

It's also easy for us to retreat into the sweet buy-and-buy, to place our faith in bank accounts, in the car we drive, the suits we wear, the figure we flaunt. Some people see me as just another part of the problem because I cheer people up and encourage them to take cruises and use skin moisturizers.

There's something wrong when virtues like loyalty, kindness, and integrity seem like liabilities and no longer apply to our heroes. Such virtues pass out of fashion in a society built on greed and ego. That's the kind of hero Frank was, though, and maybe that's why I love him so much.

But who are today's heroes? Pee Wee Herman—until the cops tracked him to an X-rated theater? Metallica? Mike Milken epitomized the 1980s as the top Wall Street "rainmaker"—and got sentenced to spend the 1990s in prison. Magic Johnson? He epitomized the modern sports legend until he tragically became infected with the AIDS virus.

Are we settling for any hero we can sell to the masses? Bart Simpson has more substance than many of our so-called heroes. But I'm sorry: as a mother, I hope Cody finds better role models than this.

How long will Cody be content to watch *Beauty and the Beast* and *The Little Mermaid?* And *then* what will he see or rent? *Basic Instinct VI: Return to Wayne's World?* What's he going to listen to? Much of our rock and rap music, despite MTV's veneer of hip political correctness, is as mysogynistic as ever and filled with messages—and video images—of sex, violence, and racial tension. Just because we can't censor something doesn't mean it's a positive force in society. The rockers and rappers are protected by the Constitution—and should be. But who's protecting our kids? That's every parent's duty—but it's getting harder every day.

Who can pretend this stuff doesn't affect the way our children will shape tomorrow's world? We've got a generation of aging yuppies and mid-lifers obsessed with staying young and thin—and a generation of kids turning into fat slugs and electronic-game junkies. They can't read, they're gorged with junk food, they stare at MTV and play with their joysticks, Game Boys, and computers. It's terrifying. I don't want to use my show as a pulpit, but as a citizen and a mother, I feel compelled to say that I regard a lot of what's going on as flat-out disgusting.

I don't pretend to have all the answers. I barely have a grasp on the complex questions facing us.

What I *do* still believe with greater clarity than ever is that, while human beings can leave the Lord through their actions, the grace of God is forever. Intellectually I've always accepted that we are frail, fallible creatures in need of help. We're made to feel we must live perfect lives or we have somehow failed. But the Bible says, even though we may blow it every day, God's mercy is fresh for us every morning.

We're imperfect people trapped in an imperfect world until we get to that place beyond. That's why it's so important for parents to instill reverence in a child. Our kids are looking to us for guidance and love.

There is a void in every human life that's tied, I feel, to our own awareness of mortality. Very few of us truly come to grips with the spirit part of our beings. We're obsessed with developing mind and body instead. We avoid, we negate the spirit.

Someone once said, "Religion is man's attempt to reach God and Christianity is God's attempt to reach man." It is faith, not religion, that empowers us to spread our wings and fly. The Scriptures tell us perfect love casts out all fear. If I believe God loves me perfectly, then I won't be afraid of life. I won't be afraid to try new things, to look silly or to fail. I always know that God loves me, regardless of the consequences of my actions.

Frank and I are trying to pass that faith on to Cody. We've started taking him to church. We make sure he says his prayers before meals and before he goes night-night. I'll never forget that the first full sentence out of his mouth was "Jesus loves me."

It has been the greatest wonder of my life to know the love of my own child—and to see the way a child develops a loving heart for people. When Cody was about eighteen months old we would pray before bedtime. Every night I'd go down the list—Jesus, bless Daddy, Mommy, Christine, Cousin Shannie, and on and on. I usually include my housekeeper Amanda, who calls Cody *"mi niño"*—"my little one." So I was about to say Amen when Cody shot me his little frown and said, out of nowhere, *"Mi niño."* I couldn't believe it. Cody knew the list so well he knew I'd left out Amanda—only he thought her name was Mi Niño.

It means the world to me that Frank has a happy home and that Cody is growing up in a safe and loving environment. We try to make every day count. Frank and I don't know how much time we'll have together. Frank will turn sixty-three the same day I turn forty. Cody will be three. I want Cody to have his dad for as long as possible. That's why our time is so special.

When we have talked about having another child, Frank muses. "When he's finishing high school I'll be eighty-two—either I'll be a good eighty-two or I'll be gumming everything to death and hobbling to the drugstore."

My time with Regis is also special because we don't know how long our show will last. The show may be hot for ten more years or ten more minutes. It won't last forever. Tastes change; ratings shift. With more success, people may not believe our "real connection" to people. They may resent what we've got and lose interest in our host chat stories. Will they still care, years from now, if a button pops into my soup at Le Cirque or if I spend an afternoon with Cody renting a tux for his senior prom?

However long it lasts, this whole trip I've been on still amazes me. I believe Regis and I caught on because we saw that what's mundane in life could, with humor, heart, and self-mockery, seem extraordinary. I hope I never wake up so jaded that I find the ordinary boring.

If the show bottomed out, could I handle it? I did before. If the label in my dress said Loehmann's instead of Kathie Lee for Plaza South, would that be the end of life as I know it? I've built my happiness on much more solid ground than material wealth. I don't equate wealth with peace and fulfillment. I never have.

What if Frank and I could no longer be sexual partners? Would that be the end of the marriage? Sex is an awfully sweet and rewarding part of the whole picture. It would be the end if we'd built everything on sex. But we haven't. And that's why the friendship we share has been such a precious and lasting treasure in our marriage.

Similarly, what if I discovered a tumor on my breast, or ovarian cancer, or if, God forbid, my worst nightmare in life came true and something happened to Cody? I know that our faith and friendship would pull us through.

I prefer not to spoil our treasured time together by worrying about what *could* be. But it does make me incredibly grateful for every day we've got. I agree with Mom. I'd rather have ten years of this than a lifetime of anything—or anyone—else.

But to tell the truth, I cannot imagine life without Frank, parenting without Frank, spring without him, or sleeping in our big canopy bed without him. I know it sounds goofy, but he is *so* special, *so* rare. I've shared my career, my home, my beautiful child with him. If I lost Frank, it would take me a long time to make another life for myself. I don't imagine I'd ever get married again, though that sounds so downbeat.

I hope that someday Cody will understand his parents' values and have a sense of his own spiritual journey on earth. I try hard not to "mold" him while instilling in him values like kindness, sharing, and love and compassion for others.

But what if my boy decides to go another way? There are two biblical teachings that will help me face whatever lies ahead. The first is: "All things work together for good to those who love God and are called according to His purpose" (Romans 8:28). The other is: "Train up a child in the way he should go and when he is old he will not depart from it" (Proverbs 22:6). I know there will be a natural rebellion, a turning away from all that is expected. But it's all in the plan that God has made for us. He promises that, when he is grown the child will return to everything he has been taught and come to appreciate its value. I know Frank and I both did. We had parents who prayed for us, who never gave up on us, and who took the same comfort in those Scriptures as we do now in the raising of our son.

We have heard so much in this election year about "family values," especially since Vice President Quayle stirred up a controversy by saying that single-mother Murphy Brown is a lousy role model. Perhaps he has a point. Sure, most kids would, in theory, be better off with two loving, caring parents under one roof. But that still leaves millions of kids. Would he rather Ms. Brown had had an abortion? I feel she showed courage in admitting her foolishness in not using birth control. She also accepted responsibility for her own actions, something too few of us are willing to do today.

We've become a nation of selfish, self-absorbed, and shallow people who seek immediate answers and instant fixes. I don't presume to know the cures for our domestic ills. But I do believe that healing begins with the individual. And the individual begins with the family, whether that family has one parent, two parents, a working mother, a welfare mother, or whatever.

This much is true: if a child is not taught by word and actions that he or she is precious and valuable and loved by God, that child has a major strike against him or her in a cold and impersonal world. From my earliest memory, I knew that God loved me, that my parents loved me, and that I had a purpose on this earth. That single truth formed every opinion, attitude, and decision I have ever made. A child who doesn't understand this, I believe, spends the rest of his or her life looking for it. I know in my heart that if we raise Cody right, he will not lose his way.

I know I'll ultimately find *my* way home as well. Everything I've seen in my own evolution bears that out. Until I learn differently, I'll continue to believe that no matter where life's journey takes me—as woman, wife, friend, mother, and daughter—I will never get lost so long as I trust my heart to guide me.

Have I been lucky? I don't think so. I feel I've been *blessed*. I've taken what I've been given and worked hard to make the most of all my opportunities. I believe all of us can do that, no matter what we start out with.

Both my parents were born with far less than I, but through love and dedication they created a new world for their family. Because of this great blessing I was able to prosper as a person and as a performer. I have come to believe it's not that God doesn't want us to have plenty; He just wants us to share plenty of it.

I believe that if Cody sees respect and affection between Frank and me as man and woman, husband and wife, I believe he will look for that in his own life in years to come. And Cody certainly knows we love him as perfectly as we know how. Children are such divine little creatures. When we had our first great spring thunderstorm this year, Cody was two, and I didn't want him to be frightened. So we turned off the lights to watch the spectacle in the sky. Suddenly there was a huge clap of thunder.

"What dat, Mommy?" he said.

"That's thunder," I answered.

"Who made dat tunder?" he said.

"Jesus makes the thunder, sweetheart."

"Jesus," he repeated, mulling it over. "Where Jesus?" he asked.

"Well, Jesus lives in the sky, making the thunder, and he's also in your heart."

Just then there was another huge crash of thunder and without missing a beat Cody said, "Jesus in airplane, too." I don't ever want that spirit crushed in him. His heroes right now are landscapers. He worships men who weed and seed. The list for night-night prayers always includes, "Lawn mowah men all over de world!" Earlier on, he developed an obsession with toothbrushes—or too-too's, as he calls them. He's got a collection of two hundred too-too's—not all of them acquired legitimately, I'm afraid.

My dentist gives me *boxes* of them—and they just flat out disappear. I know Cody's stashing them somewhere. Christine takes him over to her mom's, and he goes straight upstairs, marches right into her bathroom, and grabs her toothbrush. He steals them all the time. *My kid's a toothbrush klepto!* He'd go to the White House and steal the

President's too-too if he had a shot at it. I sure didn't teach him to do that, and neither did Frank. He probably stole Marla Maples's too-too, but he swears he never touched her shoes.

My guess right now is that we're raising a child who's going to be either a brilliant landscaper with perfect oral hygiene—or a brilliant dentist with a perfect lawn. Whichever it is, we *know* he'll be the star of the local volunteer fire department, too. And if we have truly succeeded as parents, he'll be secure in the knowledge that we love him no matter what path he has chosen.

☆

At this moment in time, the paths in *my* life have led me to this sweet and peaceful home of ours, which is as close to paradise as any place I've ever known. To me, paradise is the place where we reaffirm what is most precious to all of us in this world: the enduring joys of family.

I'm fortunate enough to be writing this in our backyard, surrounded by dense summer foliage and beautiful fragrant flowers. I can hear Beauregard the Bullfrog croaking in our pond, and the monitor at my side lets me know that Cody the Lawn Mowah Man is sleeping soundly. Frank has come home and is getting ready to work out.

In a little while Cody will wake up from his afternoon nap and start buzzing around again, proudly sporting one of his countless little hats. Frank will get the barbecue ready and go into the kitchen to prepare whatever he's decided to grill tonight. By the time we sit down for dinner, Cody, I'm sure, will have mowed a few lawns and put out any number of fires all over the house.

After dinner, Frank and I will play some more with Cody, and then I'll give him his bath and put him to bed. He'll scowl and he'll put up a fuss. And we'll strike some kind of deal as to how many books I'll read before it's time for prayers and night-night.

Finally he'll fall asleep listening to his Bible songs and clutching his fireman's hat and hose.

And as I leave his room I'll look at him and think: *The truest pleasures in life don't get any simpler than this.*

And I know they don't get any sweeter.

Thank you, Lord. It's so good to be home.

About the Collaborator

JIM JEROME is a freelance journalist who has written hundreds of celebrity profiles for national magazines. He is also the coauthor, with John Phillips, of *Papa John: A Music Legend's Shattering Journey Through Sex, Drugs, and Rock 'n' Roll;* and *How I Made a Hundred Movies in Hollywood and Never Lost a Dime,* with independent film mogul Roger Corman.